Afro-Latino Voices
Shorter Edition

*Translations of Early Modern
Ibero-Atlantic Narratives*

Afro-Latino Voices
Shorter Edition

Translations of Early Modern
Ibero-Atlantic Narratives

Edited by
Kathryn Joy McKnight
and
Leo J. Garofalo

Hackett Publishing Company, Inc.
Indianapolis/Cambridge

For further information, please address:
  Hackett Publishing Company, Inc.
  P.O. Box 44937
  Indianapolis, IN   46244-0937
  www.hackettpublishing.com

Interior design by Elizabeth L. Wilson
Composition by Aptara, Inc.

Maps 1–7, 9, 13, 15, and 16 by David E. Chandler. Map 8: From "Caught between Rivals: The Spanish-African Maroon Competition for Captive Labor in the Region of Esmeraldas during the Late Sixteenth and Early Seventeenth Centuries" by Charles Beatty-Medina in *The Americas* 63.1 (2006): 113–36. Courtesy of Charles Beatty-Medina. Map 10: Courtesy of the University of Texas Libraries, The University of Texas at Austin. Map 12: From María Elena Díaz, *The Virgin, the King, and the Royal Slaves of El Cobre: Negotiating Freedom in Colonial Cuba, 1670–1780.* Copyright © 2000 by the Board of Trustees of the Leland Stanford Jr. University. All rights reserved. Used with the permission of Stanford University Press, www.sup.org. Map 14: Reprinted with permission from *Planting Rice and Harvesting Slaves* by Walter Hawthorne. Copyright © 2003 by Walter Hawthorne. Published by Heinemann, Portsmouth, NH. All rights reserved.

Library of Congress Cataloging-in-Publication Data
Afro-Latino Voices, Shorter Edition : Translations of Early Modern Ibero-Atlantic Narratives / edited by Kathryn Joy McKnight and Leo J. Garofalo.
     pages cm
Abridgement, per publisher; chapter titles are the same as the 2009 version, Afro-Latino voices.
Includes bibliographical references and index.
ISBN 978-1-62466-400-7 (pbk.) — ISBN 978-1-62466-401-4 (cloth)
1. African diaspora—History—Sources. 2. Africans—Latin America—History—Sources. 3. Africans—Latin America—Social life and customs—Sources. 4. Spain—Colonies—America—History—Sources. 5. Portugal—Colonies—America—History—Sources. I. McKnight, Kathryn Joy, 1961– editor of compilation, author. II. Garofalo, Leo, editor of compilation, author. III. Afro-Latino voices. Abridgement of (work) :
DT16.5.A37 2015
980'.0049600903—dc23   2015004707

∞

To Lynn Mostoller, companion in life and love

—K.J.M.

To Natalia Sisa Garofalo-Iberico, my dear daughter

—L.J.G.

CONTENTS

List of Maps   *x*
Acknowledgments   *xi*
Introduction   *xiii*
Maps   *xxvii*

Part I: Politics and Wars

1. The Treason of Dom Pedro Nkanga a Mvemba against
   Dom Diogo, King of Kongo, 1550
   John K. Thornton and Linda Heywood   *2*
2. *Maroon* Chief Alonso de Illescas' Letter to the Crown, 1586
   Charles Beatty-Medina   *20*
3. Queen Njinga Mbandi Ana de Sousa of
   Ndongo/Matamba: African Leadership, Diplomacy,
   and Ideology, 1620s–1650s
   Linda Heywood; document translation by Luis Madureira   *26*
4. Afro-Iberian Subjects: Petitioning the Crown at Home,
   Serving the Crown Abroad, 1590s–1630s
   Leo J. Garofalo   *35*
5. Soldier, Slave, and Elder: *Maroon* Voices
   from the *Palenque* del Limón, 1634
   Kathryn Joy McKnight   *43*

Part II: Families and Communities

6. Juan Roque's Donation of a House to the
   Zape Confraternity, Mexico City, 1623
   Nicole von Germeten   *56*
7. Death, Gender, and Writing: Testaments of Women of
   African Origin in Seventeenth-Century Lima, 1651–1666
   José R. Jouve Martín   *68*
8. To Live as a *Pueblo*: A Contentious Endeavor,
   El Cobre, Cuba, 1670s–1790s
   María Elena Díaz   *81*
9. The Making of a Free *Lucumí* Household:
   Ana de la Calle's Will and Goods, Northern
   Peruvian Coast, 1719
   Rachel Sarah O'Toole   *93*

10. "El rey de los *congos*": The Clandestine Coronation
     of Pedro Duarte in Buenos Aires, 1787
     Patricia Fogelman and Marta Goldberg;
     document translation by Joseph P. Sánchez,
     Angelica Sánchez-Clark, and Larry D. Miller   101

Part III: Religious Beliefs and Practices

11. The Witchcraft Trials of Paula de Eguiluz,
     a Black Woman, in Cartagena de Indias, 1620–1636
     Sara Vicuña Guengerich   116
12. A Spanish Caribbean Captivity Narrative:
     African Sailors and Puritan Slavers, 1635
     David Wheat   126
13. The Saint's Life of Sister Chicaba, c. 1676–1748:
     An As-Told-To Slave Narrative
     Sue E. Houchins and Baltasar Fra-Molinero   137
14. The *Regent*, the Secretary, and the Widow:
     Power, Ethnicity, and Gender in the Confraternity
     of Saints Elesbão and Iphigenia, Rio de Janeiro,
     1784–1786
     Elizabeth W. Kiddy   153

Part IV: Claiming and Defending Rights

15. Confessing Sodomy, Accusing a Master:
     The Lisbon Trial of Pernambuco's Luiz da Costa, 1743
     Richard A. Gordon   170
16. Slavery, Writing, and Female Resistance:
     Black Women Litigants in Lima's Tribunals of the 1780s
     Maribel Arrelucea Barrantes; document translation
     by Joseph P. Sánchez, Angelica Sánchez-Clark,
     and Larry D. Miller   180
17. The Case of Javier, *Esclavo*, against His Master
     for Cruel Punishment, San Juan, Argentina, 1795
     Ana Teresa Fanchin; document translation by
     Joseph P. Sánchez, Angelica Sánchez-Clark,
     and Larry D. Miller   192

18. In the Royal Service of Spain: The *Milicianos Morenos* Manuel and
Antonio Pérez during the Napoleonic Invasion, 1808–1812
Jorge L. Chinea 200

Glossary 208
Bibliography 219
Notes on Contributors 247
Index 253

LIST OF MAPS

Map 1   The Ibero-Atlantic World   xxvii

Map 2   Central Africa: Kongo, Angola, and Ndongo   xxviii

Map 3   West Africa   xxix

Map 4   Europe and North Africa   xxx

Map 5   Caribbean and Central America   xxxi

Map 6   South America   xxxii

Map 7   Esmeraldas (Ecuador)   xxxiii

Map 8   Palenques (Maroon Settlements) in the Government of Cartagena   xxxiv

Map 9   Mexico City (1628)   xxxv

Map 10   Lima (Ciudad de los Reyes, 1685)   xxxvi

Map 11   Cuba: The Oriente Region   xxxvii

Map 12   Viceroyalty of Río de la Plata   xxxviii

Map 13   Guinea-Bissau Region and Its People   xxxix

Map 14   Mina Coast: Slave Ports   xl

Map 15   Spain, North Africa, and the Battle of Bailén   xli

ACKNOWLEDGMENTS

Many people contributed to this collaborative project. We express our thanks here knowing that we will forget someone. Most importantly, we thank the contributors whose names appear in the table of contents for their excitement and passion for this project, their words of encouragement, their dedication to carrying this through despite many individual setbacks and even tragedies, and their patience with our endless emails, multiple edits, and periods of silence as the sometimes sorrowful challenges of our own lives put the book on a back burner. We thank José P. Sánchez, Angelica Sánchez-Clark, Larry D. Miller, and Luis Madureira for their careful translations of some of the documents. And we recognize with great appreciation the ways in which our own many conversations have enriched our vision of the project and enhanced the final version of the book.

This project would not have gotten off the ground without the generous and inspiring guidance of Joseph C. Miller in his 2003 National Endowment for the Humanities (NEH) summer seminar at the University of Virginia, "Roots: African Dimensions of the History and Culture of the Americas (through the Transatlantic Slave Trade)." All the members of "Roots" 2003 led Kathryn McKnight to believe that this project was possible and that there were readers and, especially, teachers waiting for it.

Students at the University of New Mexico (UNM) test-drove some of the materials and helped shape their eventual presentation in this volume. Several colleagues read our proposal and made insightful recommendations, including Diana Rebolledo, James Sweet, and members of the Colonial Studies Working Group at UNM, especially Celia López-Chávez and Cynthia Radding. The enthusiasm and suggestions of the manuscript readers selected by Hackett also buoyed and guided us. The long hours of hard work that Andrés Sabogal put into the project in its final months were indispensable, especially in pulling together the glossary, maps, and suggestions for films and music to teach alongside the texts. It has been a pleasure working with everyone at Hackett, especially Rick Todhunter and Meera Dash, who was so helpful and flexible at every step of the process.

No book is written without financial support. We thank the NEH for the summer seminar stipend, UNM for sabbatical support, the Latin American and Iberian Institute at UNM for funding a graduate assistant who worked on the project, the UNM Research Allocation Committee, the Feminist Research Institute, and Connecticut College for grants that supported some of the translations in the volume.

Finally, we thank our families and friends who gave us support throughout, especially during those times when the book came before almost everything else. Thanks especially to Lynn Mostoller for her patience and for always seeing another possibility and to Yony for laughing when it mattered. Natalia Sisa brought joy and humor to both editing and parenting.

INTRODUCTION

Recovering Afro-Latino Voices from the Early Modern Ibero-Atlantic World

African and African-descent peoples played central roles in building Spanish and Portuguese empires and their American colonies from the 1500s through the 1800s. They sailed ships, built infrastructure, produced crops and material goods, provided services, shaped societies, and molded cultural attitudes, beliefs, and expressions; yet their voices have been largely barred from the published record. We know of their lives from recent historical scholarship and through historical and literary works of the period in which primarily European authors represent them, more often than not distorting their voices and experiences.

During the past twenty years, scholars made greater efforts to unearth and publish Afro-Latino voices as recorded more directly in documentary narratives, but the sources are still scattered and few.[1] *Afro-Latino Voices* offers for the first time a book-length collection of narratives of people of African descent in the early modern Ibero-Atlantic world.

Although some Afro-Latinos in the early modern world did read and write and many engaged with literate culture, almost none composed texts that were considered publishable at the time. Consequently, the written sources in which their voices survive are primarily juridical, ecclesiastical, and administrative documents located in the archives of Europe and Latin America. This collection includes judicial inquiries, letters, last wills and testaments, petitions, trial proceedings, written dialogue, and as-told-to biography. In these texts, people of African descent speak about war and politics; they define and support their families and communities; they reveal a broad gamut of spiritual beliefs and practices; and they claim and defend their rights against the cruelties of enslavement and the discrimination of a racialized society.

The Afro-Latino stories in this collection help break down assumptions, stereotypes, and overgeneralizations that continue to limit our understanding of the lives of people of African descent and how they themselves imagined their lives. These narratives counteract the still prevalent myth of Ibero-Atlantic blacks as primarily enslaved, working on plantations in Brazil and the Caribbean, and excluded from determining the course of their own lives.

These stories highlight the complexity of experiences and identities of a population that was enslaved, free, and slave owning, both urban and rural, and highly resourceful in its interactions with people of all ethnic, racial, and social types. They show that African-descent peoples were often divided by national origin, slave vs. free

---

1. The section Additional Publications of Afro-Latino Voices at the end of the Bibliography is indicative of the lack of such sources.

status, occupation, and political and familial relationships but that they also banded together for mutual support, for collective action, and to build communities.

The Afro-Latinos in this volume formed and exercised control within religious societies, autonomous communities, and states. They used the languages, institutions, and literate practices of the Ibero-colonial enterprise to improve their own situations. Their stories reveal how they transformed their lives as they moved between places, cultures, and historical moments. They help dispel that "absolute sense of ethnic difference" about which Paul Gilroy writes in *The Black Atlantic* (3) by showing how, in their daily lives, people of African descent participated in racially diverse social circles and often adopted and adapted European and indigenous American beliefs, practices, and elements of identity. Although these stories cannot represent the full range of black experiences and voices in the Ibero-Atlantic, they speak strongly to its diversity.

This book supports the reintegration of a black Ibero-Atlantic world broken apart by institutional structures that separate history, literatures, and cultures into distinct national frameworks and divide Africa from Europe and from the Americas. With Paul Gilroy, we see a black Atlantic as a space across which people moved back and forth, taking with them ideas, beliefs, practices, and artifacts in a rich international and transcultural exchange.

This volume brings together narratives from Kongo and Ndongo in Central Africa, Spain and Portugal in Europe, and Cuba, Puerto Rico, Brazil, Río de la Plata, Peru, Ecuador, Panama, the New Kingdom of Granada, and New Spain in the Ibero-American colonies. By gathering voices from around the Ibero-Atlantic, we ask readers to stretch beyond the national boundaries with which they are familiar to see cultural and historical connections that the academy's national divisions have dimmed or erased.

The list of places above shows, however, that the book does not achieve a full integration of the black Atlantic. The restriction of sources to the Ibero-Atlantic world is motivated by the uncomfortable tension we experience working and teaching within institutional parameters and the very real considerations of current academic curricula and readerships. We hope that by stretching readers past some traditional national and geographic boundaries, this book will invite them to take up texts from the Francophone Caribbean and Anglo-America, among others. The other limitation in the book's parameters that requires explanation is that of the time frame we have chosen: the mid-sixteenth to the early nineteenth centuries. These years roughly correspond to the Iberian colonial control of the Americas and to the historical period that suffers perhaps the greatest need for published source texts of Afro-Latino voices.[2]

We have envisioned this book for the needs of our own students, both undergraduate and graduate. Although the sources are valuable to scholars as an introduction to this area of study, our presentation is aimed at novice readers of early modern texts. We have edited the English translations for readers inexperienced with documents of this period.

---

2. In the Additional Publications section of the Bibliography, we provide a list of those late-eighteenth- and early-nineteenth-century sources available in published form.

We have designed the anthology as a coming together of two disciplinary perspectives—literary and historical studies—though the book fills a void in a much broader range of fields, including Latin American studies, African diaspora studies, black studies, cultural studies, ethnic and race studies, gender and women's studies, and anthropology. The editors and contributors teach and research in the fields of Latin American and African history, Spanish-American and *Luso-Brazilian* literature, African American studies, and gender studies. All these perspectives are evident in the introductions to the documents, where contributors contextualize the narratives and invite a variety of approaches to their reading.

The Book's Thematic Organization

The narratives are grouped thematically in four parts titled "Politics and War," "Families and Communities," "Religious Beliefs and Practices," and "Claiming and Defending Rights." Within each part, the narratives are in chronological order. These groupings express a sense of the different stages and aspects of the African experience in the Ibero-Atlantic world, even though they do not represent a strict chronological evolution.

Part I begins the volume with autonomous African political organizations and moves through Central African slave wars to the early armed conflicts between *Maroons* and European colonizers in the Americas. Parts II and III look at the rebuilding of social organizations and belief systems in the Americas by African-descent communities after the calamities of the *Middle Passage*. Part IV shows experiences of cultural integration in which Afro-Latino subjects draw on their knowledge of Iberian law to claim and defend their rights. These four themes are only a few of the many that enrich a consideration of both the common experiences and worldviews of these African diasporic groups and individuals and their great diversity. Other thematic groupings might include the following:

1) Afro-Latino responses to European expansion, imperialism, and colonization: Chapters 1, 2, 3, 5, 8, 12, 18

2) Gendered relationships and their representation: Chapters 3, 5, 6, 7, 9, 11, 13, 14, 16

3) Inheritance: Chapters 6, 7, 9, 14

4) *Maroon* communities: Chapters 2, 5

5) Racial, ethnic, and national identity: all chapters

6) Self-governance: Chapters 1, 2, 3, 5, 8, 10, 14

7) Slavery, slave ownership, *manumission*, and *coartación*: Chapters 3, 5, 7, 8, 9, 13, 15, 16, 17

8) Travel and movement: Chapters 4, 9, 11, 12, 13, 15, 18

9) Violence: Chapters 2, 3, 5, 8, 15, 16, 17

African Demographics in the Ibero-Atlantic World

The Atlantic slave trade began to take shape in the early fifteenth century with Portuguese traders and raiders seeking new trade routes and claiming territories for Portugal south along the West African coast. During this first century, the Portuguese merchants used their seafaring strength to establish sea routes along the coast and to insert themselves into land-based West African trade networks. They acted primarily as intermediaries and bought and sold kola nuts, cattle, salt, ivory, gold, and enslaved people, depending on African traders for goods and people.

The first European sales of enslaved people captured or purchased by Iberians in sub-Saharan Africa took place after a Portuguese raid in 1444 and established important precedents for all subsequent European participation in the Atlantic slave trade: traders operated with royal license; they paid a significant portion of the profit as a tax to the state (one fifth in Portugal and Spain); and they deployed a series of justifications for enslavement and sale, ranging from opportunity and economic need for commerce and labor to religious and moral motives such as eradicating paganism and winning converts to Christianity before people could be converted to Islam. In Iberia, peasants farmed the land; so people brought to Europe as slaves worked primarily in domestic and urban labor as they would initially in Spanish America.

In the sixteenth century, Portuguese, Italian, and Spanish merchants began to produce sugar on Madeira, the Canaries, Cape Verde, *São Tomé*, and Príncipe using enslaved islanders and then, increasingly, slaves from Africa, thus establishing the association of coerced labor and the production of sugar and other plantation crops that would be extended to the Americas. In this process and in the era of booming trade that it ushered in, Iberian merchants transported an estimated 5.7 million people to Europe and the Americas (mostly to the Americas) out of an estimated total of 12 million people forced into slavery in the African diaspora. These basic elements characterized the slave trade until the middle of the nineteenth century.

The African people sold as slaves in 1444 before the gates of the Portuguese port of Lagos were from many ethnic groups, some having already lived as slaves in Africa and others having been captured in Iberian raids and through trade. Edging out their Castilian competitors, the Portuguese built diplomatic and trading relationships with West and Central Africans, especially with the Kongo. Africans initially sold criminals and prisoners captured in war to the Europeans, but droughts in the 1570s created new demographic pressures and opportunities for Europeans to force more people into bondage.

Economic and political gain pushed this destructive dynamic of enslavement into Africa's interior. People were frequently sold and resold during the long and dangerous march to the sea, where African merchants organized them into warehouses for purchase and transportation overseas by the Europeans. Many perished before reaching European vessels waiting at ports arrayed along the coast. To buy and embark these slaves, the Portuguese built fortified bases at Arguim and *Elmina* (Ghana). The Dutch captured *Elmina* in the seventeenth century.

The Portuguese also established a trading center and holding pens in Central Africa at Luanda (Angola). In the nineteenth century, Brazilian traders developed a port farther south at *Benguela* (Angola). In these and many other coastal enclaves and trading centers, mixed Euro-African communities (complete with blended families, languages, and religions) developed from the late 1400s on, both as a product of the diaspora and to facilitate the expansion of the traffic in human beings.

The greatest motors driving the enslavement and sale of Africans were the demand for workers on tropical plantations and lowland gold and diamond mines in the Americas and the profits that could be made supplying coerced laborers. Small numbers of Africans and Afro-Iberians accompanied Spanish explorers and conquistadors to the Caribbean, Mexico, and Peru in the 1490s and early 1500s. Spanish and Italian entrepreneurs brought larger numbers when they introduced sugar plantations on the island of Hispaniola and then in Mexico, Venezuela, and Peru in the 1520s and 1530s.

Between this time and 1600, the Portuguese and Italians replicated in northeastern Brazil the Atlantic island sugar industry based on slave labor. In both the Caribbean and Brazil, planters depended on indigenous peoples as laborers until disease, abuse, and flight decimated this native workforce. Starting in the 1560s, the Portuguese began importing Africans to Bahia and Pernambuco. Brazil received half a million Africans during the 1600s and 1.7 million during the 1700s; in all, approximately 2.5 million Africans were imported by 1800.

Approximately one million Africans arrived in Spanish America during the same period. In both regions, enslaved Africans and their descendants grew sugar, coffee, tobacco, cacao, and cotton for export and extracted precious metals and stones from rainforest regions. Amerindians dominated the highland silver and gold mines of Mexico and Peru, but gold rushes in hot lowlands in the Pacific coastal regions of Colombia and Minas Gerais and Goiás in Brazil (where diamonds were also found) relied almost exclusively on African slave labor organized into work gangs (Klein, 1–46).

As Ibero-American economies developed, slaves and free blacks participated alongside other workers in a wide variety of economic activities. They worked in transportation as muleteers, porters, and stevedores. They labored in urban occupations such as construction and manufacturing, producing furniture, clothing, glass, iron, and ships. They also worked in artisans' workshops to make leather goods, shoes, clothing, metal items, and so forth. Some even rose through the ranks of apprentices and journeymen to become master artisans in the skilled trades and to exercise influence in guilds and even own slaves themselves. Bakeries also utilized many black slaves in the cities.

From the very beginning of the colonial period, and even before that in Europe, Portuguese and Spanish elites and even more middling sectors of artisans, professionals, and traders valued the domestic service of black slaves and the status owning slaves bestowed. In the Americas, slave servants became ubiquitous in major slave ports such as Bahia, Rio de Janeiro, Havana, Cartagena, and Buenos Aires and in major cities from Mexico in North America to Quito, Lima, and La Paz in South America. Black servants—enslaved and free—went to market, cooked and cleaned, nursed and raised children, and cared for horses and their masters in a thousand different ways.

Beyond the household, black men, women, and children in urban areas engaged extensively in street vending of all sorts as well as the production and public sale of food and drink. Their importance and successes in these urban occupations and in domestic service meant that slaves and their descendants often constituted a visible and significant presence in the cities and mining centers in regions of Mesoamerica and the Andes, which were populated primarily by indigenous peoples. Even in specific rural areas dedicated primarily to plantation agriculture or food production for local consumption in otherwise indigenous zones, black people could dominate the labor force, as in the subregions of Guerrero in Mexico and Ica in coastal Peru.

Mortality was high among slaves, and the importation of slaves declined in non-plantation regions after the mid-1700s, so it is easy to forget that more Africans than Europeans arrived to places like the Andes and created vibrant and diverse communities during the colonial era. In fact, cities such as Lima, the capital of the Peruvian viceroyalty, had an African and African-descent majority or near majority from at least 1614 until 1800. An export orientation and insufficient indigenous labor transformed Brazil, Venezuela, and—in the second half of the 1700s—Cuba and Puerto Rico into the most important centers of slavery and the heartlands of colonial Afro-Latin America.

The lack of indigenous workers and the inability of the enslaved population to reproduce itself guaranteed a steady flow of people from Africa. Harsh and brutal work and living conditions, malnourishment, and a sexual imbalance created by planters favoring the importation of men all militated against enslaved people bearing and raising children past infancy and childhood to adulthood. Despite considerable hardships, Africans and Afro-Latin Americans formed free and slave families; in some communities, they developed African-based cultures, and in others they became part of neighborhoods, guilds, religious brotherhoods, and the other institutions and activities that characterized life for all colonial subjects.

In some parishes and towns, blacks came to run their own artisan associations, confraternities, local town councils, and marketplaces. In others, blacks participated alongside others in the workplace, local governance, negotiation with authorities, and forms of worship. The appearance of free individuals and their growth into the majority of the black population in many areas was possible because Spanish and, to a lesser extent, Portuguese law permitted slaves to buy their own freedom or that of family members and to use the courts to secure freedom in the case of extreme abuse or notorious sexual impropriety by masters.

People saved from their earnings and worked on the side to purchase freedom. If owners resisted, they could sometimes be compelled in Spanish courts to accept a fair price for freedom. Likewise, especially abusive slave owners might be legally compelled to free a slave they had savaged or raped. More rarely, owners freed slaves as a gift, a negotiated reward, or in recognition of paternity. In short, despite the difficulties, Afro-Latino communities formed and included quite a few free members who built up their numbers over time.

Free communities in Afro-Latin America also appeared because slaves resisted slavery through flight and force of arms. Runaway or *cimarrón* communities were usually quite small, numbering a few dozens of escapees. Typically they replenished their numbers with other runaways or by seizing people to bring them to freedom. Hiding in inaccessible locations like marshes, mountainsides, or tropical forests, these groups usually found it hard to last for more than a few years or to form self-sustaining communities.

They usually survived by trading with and raiding the farms, haciendas (landed estates), Indian villages, and fishing communities nearby. In a few cases, larger and long-lasting *palenques* or *quilombos* formed, which brought together people from different ethnic groups who reconstituted aspects of African life and culture or invented new ones and subsisted through their own agricultural activities as well as trade with outsiders.

These larger *Maroon* communities tended to be located farther from colonial centers and excited considerable anxiety and hostility among colonial authorities, even though they proved impossible to completely eradicate and occasionally secured from the colonial state a right to exist as free towns. A few such communities endure to the present day in Mexico, Panama, Colombia, Suriname, Ecuador, and Brazil. Free and enslaved blacks also banded together in urban mutual aid societies, often within the structure of lay Catholic religious confraternities. These societies often organized along lines of ethnic identity, whether those bonds were formed in the African communities of origin or after enslavement.

Historical Protagonists and Questions of Identity

This book offers an opportunity to meet a few of the individual protagonists who participated in creating the history and the cultures of the diverse African communities in the Ibero-Atlantic world. The focus of the collection is on slave and free black agency understood as the actions people took against the structural and circumstantial forces arrayed against them. Actions ranged from flight and rebellion to more subtle forms of response such as negotiation with owners, altering the speed of work, or appealing to royal courts or Church authorities. At times the protagonists succeeded, at other times they failed. Most often, they created complicated and contradictory results that affected in small ways how slavery and colonial society functioned.

To capture some sense of the variety of these actions and their articulation by the protagonists themselves, this collection ranges over four continents—Africa, Europe, North America, and South America—highlighting the transatlantic nature of the legacy of the diaspora and its wide-ranging impact beyond the Americas. The documents also represent three standard historical periods that characterize the Iberian enterprise of colonialism: exploration and conquest, mid-colonial or mature colonial society, and the late colonial age of reform and revolution.

Happily, several monographs extensively treat some of the areas that fall outside this volume's selective sampling. Within the Americas, the range of documents offers an overview of the kinds of places Africans and Afro-Americans lived and worked. To this end, colonial societies in the Caribbean, Mexico, and South America are included, along with accounts from runaway (*Maroon*) communities and the views from both the rural and urban environments these protagonists inhabited. Likewise, both enslaved and free blacks find a place in the volume.

The interaction of these two legal statuses is particularly significant for Ibero-America and in many of the cases presented. Children appear infrequently in this collection, in part because of the difficulties youth adds to finding ways to articulate and record a voice. The collection draws together a broad sampling of young, middle-aged, and older adults and of men and women. A number of the occupations typical of Africans in the Iberian world can be viewed in these chapters; especially significant is the attention to religious, ritual, or spiritual expression and to economic activity. Again, the richness of African life in the Americas means that many occupations receive less attention, such as militiamen, surgeons/barbers, and midwives.

To understand the protagonists in this book, it is important to recognize and problematize the ethnic and racial naming and labeling employed inside and outside Africa in the diaspora. During the 1600s, enslaved Africans came primarily from the Atlantic coast of West Africa, Congo, and Angola. As demand intensified, trade routes reached farther into Central Africa but still remained closer to the coast in West Africa, with Biafra (Nigeria) leading the way in numbers. By 1800, Mozambique saw Portuguese and African slave traders linked to the Atlantic, where none had operated before. This regional scope of the trade created great diversity among Africans in the Americas. Although ethnic homogeneity was never achieved, some concentrations were discernable. For example, Rio de Janeiro connected to Congo and Angola held more speakers of Bantu languages than any other region; but West Africans and Mozambicans were also present. Bahia traded more with West Africa (three quarters of its slaves) than with Congo and Angola (one quarter). Between 1790 and 1806, Buenos Aires held 4,800 slaves from Mozambique, 4,000 from West Africa, and 2,700 from Congo and West Africa (Andrews, 20).

The point of embarkation proved notoriously unreliable for establishing accurate ethnic identification. In addition, many of the ethnic categories employed by traders and later scholars working with their records are in reality slave trade labels that provided a convenient, if inaccurate, shorthand for recording origin. These labels might suggest an affinity that did not exist, even if people were from the same region or the same linguistic group or boarded a ship in the same port.

African ethnicities did exist, however, as did complex histories of interaction and shifting organization among African polities. Both created bonds, but also divisions; and these divisions proved key to the success and longevity of the slave trade and explain many of the obstacles to creating African solidarity against the European slave trade and bondage in the Americas. In the Americas, people of African descent also divided themselves into *naciones* (nations). The word *nación* could refer to a place of birth or African origin, but it could also be a name imposed by European slave traders determined by the place of enslavement.

At times, an individual or a small group might adopt or choose to associate with a new ethnicity in order to fit in with a locally dominant group or create the links that allowed a person to survive the *Middle Passage* and life in the Americas. So, although a person's *nación* is a problematic marker of identity, *naciones* did function in important ways to organize black communities in Ibero-America and foster the preservation and re-creation of African cultural and social practices. Thus, all use of *ethnonyms* or names that apparently refer to ethnic identity must be interpreted with care.

Europeans used other important racial labels to categorize Afro-Latinos. One important distinction for both slaves and owners was that between *bozal*, or African-born, and *criollo*, or American-born. Generally speaking, *bozales* possessed little or no knowledge of European or local indigenous languages, often were not baptized, and had little understanding of Catholicism. Not surprisingly, they usually suffered lower colonial status, worse work assignments, and poorer treatment.

The term *ladino* could be used to highlight Christian status and a person's knowledge of Spanish and/or Portuguese even when that individual was not born in the Americas. Furthermore, in the Americas, individuals were identified as belonging to a certain *casta*, or caste.[3] Such identities were constructed partly through racial markers or phenotype such as facial features, skin color, and hair characteristics. But they also depended on perceptions of family history, language, economic success, occupation, religious practice, dress, cultural practices, residence, and marriage partnership to determine a person's legal status or local reputation.

The most common color terms used were *mulatto*, *zambo*, and *mestizo*, suggesting mixed African and European, indigenous and African, and European and indigenous parentage, respectively. In each case, these identity labels were combined with other markers and sometimes replaced with labels that suggested a finer distinction of the lineage. In other words, race and ethnicity operated as social constructions rooted in a particular place at a particular historical moment.

Voice and Mediation

This book claims to present "voices," but what is voice and how is it manifested in these narratives? The word "voice" appears to be deceptively straightforward, but the circumstances within which these narratives were produced make the voices they contain challenging to hear. Nevertheless, by using this term, we claim to offer the reader access to Afro-Latinos' words and thoughts. We even assert that these stories undo some of the inherent distortion of their representation in the chronicles and histories of European, *mestizo*, and Amerindian authors.

And yet, in almost all the narratives in this book, European scribes recorded the Afro-Latino voices, not with the word-for-word transcription enabled by modern recording devices, but as colonial officials intent on interpreting the speaker's words from within their own European ideological and discursive worldview. These are not stories that Afro-Latinos told within their own communities, not oral traditions that pass on cultural values and foster group identity. Such oral traditions have survived, but they, too, present complex issues of immediacy, as they have undergone the transformations of oral transmission across centuries (see, for example, Lienhard, "Padrões"). Rather, the voices in this anthology are mostly narratives told within the

3 José Ramón Jouve Martín contributed to the discussions of *nación* and *casta* in this Introduction.

bureaucratic systems of a European colonial world, recorded by European-educated scribes, often under circumstances of duress in which the recorded narrative contributed to life-changing decisions exercised against the speaker. That is, they are molded and transformed by layers of mediation and circumstance often outside the ordinary context of daily life.

How is it, then, that Afro-Latino voices speak in these texts? To hear these voices through the static of circumstance and mediation, we invite you to bear in mind two sets of issues. First, consider conceptions of voice, speech, and utterance that will help you identify those ways in which speakers have exercised control over their narratives, despite the molding of their exact words into bureaucratic formulas. Second, seek to understand the types of mediation that have affected the voice in these narratives, to better identify the lines between which you might read the voices. By giving attention to what constitutes voice and narrative perspective, and with a knowledge of the social relationships and circumstances in which each narrative was spoken, we argue that these highly mediated documents allow modern readers to approach the voices of these distant speakers and glimpse the ways in which Afro-Latinos saw, understood, and presented themselves and their worldviews in the early modern Ibero-Atlantic world.

We ask you to read these documents as rhetorical and symbolic texts rather than as straightforward sources of historical information. Some students of history or social sciences may find it uncomfortable to move from a search for what "really happened" and what people "really believed" to an examination of how historical actors presented that reality, but history as a discipline has already made that move with the New Philology (see Restall) and an appreciation for the "content of the form" (see White).

Some students of literature may feel at a loss as to where to begin and what tools to use to analyze such "nonliterary" texts, but as cultural studies' approaches have become more established in the literary corner of the academy, this discipline, too, has brought together literary texts with other cultural representations. For all readers, the introductions to each document provide some clues for how to proceed in reading these documents as rhetorical and symbolic texts.

The nineteenth-century Romantic understanding of voice as the individual's expression to the world of an inner vision still informs the way many readers understand voice in a text. But, although the narratives of this collection do express a vision or worldview, contemporary critical theory sees such a vision as informed by both individual and social experiences. By studying the experiences and symbolic worlds of the communities into which the speakers were born and in which they lived, as well as the symbolic worlds of those to whom they speak, you will be better able to sort out the worldviews they express.

In the black Atlantic, in the age of the slave trade and Iberian empire building, voice had a particular quality. Afro-Latinos spoke with a "double consciousness," that is, they saw themselves from within their own cultural worldview as well as from the perspective of the European colonizer and slave society (Gilroy, 1). So, you will find that even those perspectives that can be identified with the Afro-Latino speakers and their communities do not separate them absolutely or essentially from their European or Euro-American interlocutors. Here, several theoretical paradigms can be useful for understanding the relationship of these voices to their diverse contexts, including transculturation, hybridity, and cultural diglossia.[4]

Finally, it is important to understand that any voice and the identity it constructs are not essential or fixed qualities of a person or culture, but rather performances that are fluid and changing, as they respond to social structures, relationships, and circumstances (Butler, 177). Every voice that speaks in this book does so under particular circumstances among individuals whose relationships are molded by relative access to power and by specific interests and aims.[5] As you read the narratives, consider how the speakers mold their voices and stories in response to their audience and circumstances. You will find help in building this contextual understanding in both the introductions to each document and the bibliographies that correspond to each chapter.

So far, we have considered how the Afro-Latino speakers shaped their own words. These words have also been modified after they were spoken by at least three processes of writing. First, the European scribe transcribed the speaker's utterance into an early modern (often bureaucratic) genre. Second, the contributors to this volume copied the handwritten transcription, interpreting occasionally enigmatic script. Third, the contributors translated the transcription from Spanish or Portuguese to English. Just as the conventions of poetry, narrative, drama, or theater affect the meaning that a literary text produces, so too, the conventions of Ibero-Atlantic documentary genres shape the narratives in this volume. Understanding those genres will help you as a reader interpret their meanings and distinguish the speakers' voices from the forms and worldviews of these bureaucratic genres.

The genres in this volume include the following:

1) Official inquests in both criminal and civil causes: Chapters 1, 5, 6, 10, 12, 17

2) Petitions: Chapters 2, 8, 16, 18

3) Personal and official letters, including denunciations, negotiation, and diplomacy: Chapters 2, 3, 8

4) Last wills and testaments: Chapters 6, 7, 9

5) Records of inquisition trials: Chapters 11, 15

6) One as-told-to hagiographic biography: Chapter 13

7) One formal dialogue: Chapter 14

These genres were produced by scribes, notaries, and male religious personnel—men trained in the writing of bureaucratic or ecclesiastic forms and discourses. As they recorded the voices of the Afro-Latino speakers, they melded their words and narrative forms with bureaucratic conventions, which carry their own cultural and ideological content. In documents such as court and inquisition testimonies, the

---

4. See Ortiz (86), Rama, García Canclini, and Lienhard ("De mestizajes"), respectively.

5. Martin Lienhard sets out a framework for studying the forces that mold witness testimony by captured *Maroons* in "Una tierra sin amos."

scribes transformed the speaker's first-person testimony into a third-person—he said or she said—narrative. In wills and petitions, the dominant "I" represents a partial fiction as a scribe molds the testator or petitioner's wishes into conventional ecclesiastical or bureaucratic discourses. Some narratives underwent another layer of transformation as the speakers used an African language that was translated by a *ladino* translator. The chapter introductions offer clues to interpreting the ways in which each documentary genre mediates the speaker's voice.[6]

Finally, the contributors to these volumes have interpreted these documents as they have sought to make them more readable for you. In transcribing the documents, they interpreted them in ways that sometimes required fixing one interpretation in preference over another. They have often omitted repetitive bureaucratic language, particularly the "saids" and "aforesaids" (*dichos*). They have added explanatory headings and clarifications in brackets [ ]. In their translations, they have sought a conservative rather than fluid rendition of the original; yet no linguistic utterance in one language has an exact equivalent in another, and thus every translation is an interpretation.

Given these numerous layers of mediation, you may wonder whether these documents do provide access to Afro-Latino voices; yet we insist that they can. As you read, think of how the symbolic systems and genres of speaker and addressee shape the voice and narrative, and consider the ways in which worldview and agency might survive the mediation of the scribes and editors. Although original words are mostly lost, the speakers' choice of what they relate and in what order they present it often survives. At times speakers offer an "excess" of information, recounting something that is not required by interrogation or genre; these excesses give clues to voice and agency. Particular ways of naming and describing other people or specific uses of symbolic language stand out as more likely to be those of the speaker than of the scribe. When more than one witness speaks about the same event, the similarities and differences among their testimonies provide clues to what belongs to bureaucratic mediation and what belongs to a speaker's worldview. Occasionally, an abrupt shift from a formulaic quality of language to evident orality signals the eruption of the original voice. Although hearing the Afro-Latino voices in this text presents many challenges, and although as readers we must hold any interpretation as tentative, these challenges make the reading more exciting as we seek to move across time and space to hear voices so different from our own and so vital in their own time.

Reading and Teaching from This Book

When reading and teaching from this book, it is useful to understand its organization and the resources it contains. Following this Introduction, each of the book's

---

6. Pedro Luis Lorenzo Cadarso's study titled *La documentación judicial en la época de los Austrias* offers detailed help in understanding the documentary genres related to judicial cases, and, because other courts often modeled their documentary production on these, the study can be helpful for understanding a broader range of document genres.

four parts is introduced by a short description of the chapters it includes and how they relate to themes or trends in the field. The first part covers politics and wars and ranges from Africa to Europe to the Americas. The second part highlights how Afro-Latinos created families, communities, and relationships. The third part describes religious beliefs and practices. The fourth part presents cases of people defending themselves and claiming rights.

The chapters in each of these parts begin with a scholarly introduction to reading and interpreting the document or document excerpt(s). Following this introduction is the document in the English translation.

Footnotes throughout the book provide additional help to contextualize and interpret the texts. They define a specific meaning or term in the context of that narrative, place, or period. They give historical, biographical, and geographical information. They point out possible errors in the manuscript as well as difficulties in translation. They also point to other helpful resources.

A few unfamiliar words are italicized and defined in footnotes at their first appearance. Italicized words in general are defined and discussed in the book's Glossary. The Glossary brings out some of the regional and temporal variation in word use.

In the Bibliography, for each chapter you will find a list of sources that combines both the works cited in the text and recommended readings for further exploring the chapter's themes. Following the chapter bibliographies, you will find a separate listing of "Resources for Teaching Early Modern Afro-Latino Experiences and Their Legacies," which includes other published voices from the black Ibero-Atlantic, films that re-create or document both early modern Afro-Latino experiences and their legacies today, a sample of music that has developed within Afro-Latino communities in the regions represented, and sources for the study of African and Afro-Latino arts.

The Index offers a way to track themes, issues, and location throughout the volume and may help to reveal unexpected parallels and trends. Together the scholarly introductions, notes, Glossary, Bibliography, and Index are included as "readers' tools" in order to allow readers as much freedom as possible in deriving their own interpretations and insights from working with this new corpus of voices from the African diaspora.

Students in particular can apply their own critical reading skills when working with these chapters and the primary sources in English translation. We suggest the following specific strategies when reading the documents:

1) Define specific words by comparing their use within a document and between documents.

2) Consider the interaction between questions and answers in interrogatories:
   a. How do questions structure narrative?
   b. Where do speakers go beyond the question (agency)?

3) When there is more than one testimony regarding the same event,
   a. What can readers learn from the similarities?
   b. What can readers learn from the differences?

4)   What type of document is this? Who created this document, for whom, and for what purpose?

5)   What does this document tell readers? What questions does this document answer?

6)   Can one read "between the lines" of what is discussed to determine what issues motivated the participants in a document's creation and the events it recorded?

7)   What does the record leave silent?
     a.   What questions does it pose that one needs other sources to answer?
     b.   How can readers use other documents in this collection to address these silences?

8)   As you work through individual sources and through the book's parts, consider how these sources fit into or challenge a wider historical narrative or the established understanding of a period.

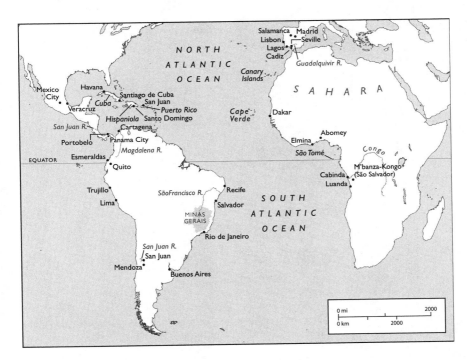

Map 1   The Ibero-Atlantic World

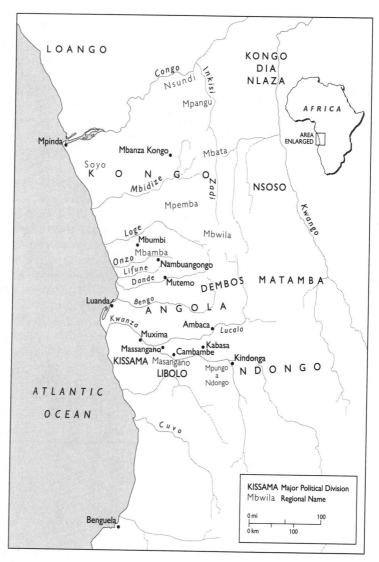

Map 2   Central Africa: Kongo, Angola, and Ndongo

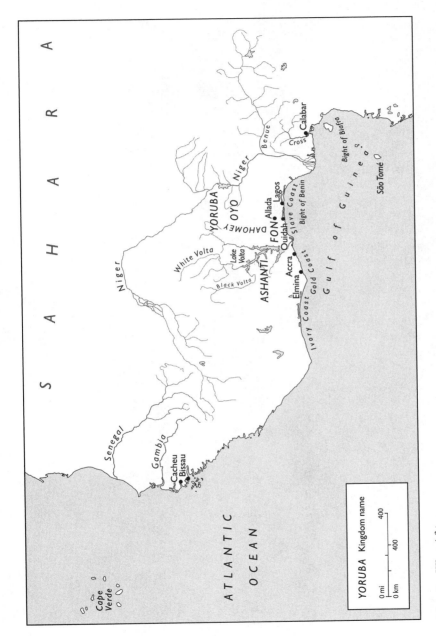

Map 3 West Africa

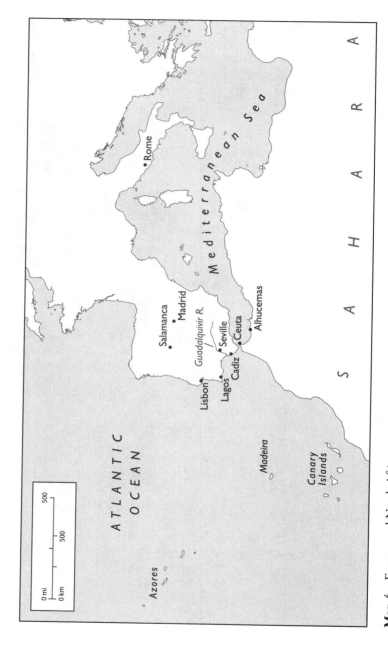

Map 4 Europe and North Africa

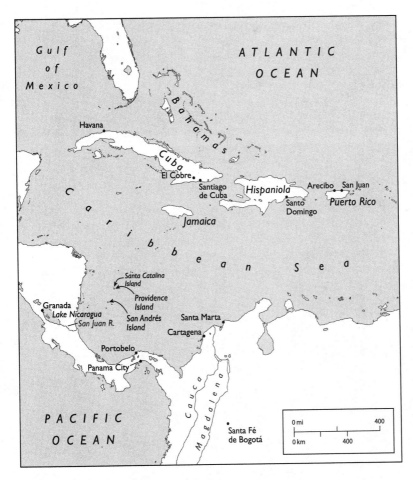

Map 5   Caribbean and Central America

Map 6   South America

Map 7   Esmeraldas (Ecuador)

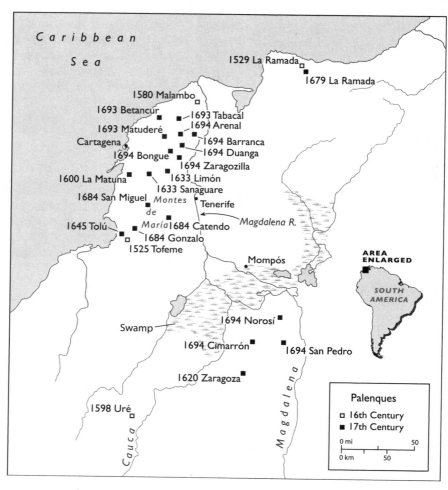

Map 8   Palenques (Maroon Settlements) in the Government of Cartagena

Map 9 Mexico City (1628)

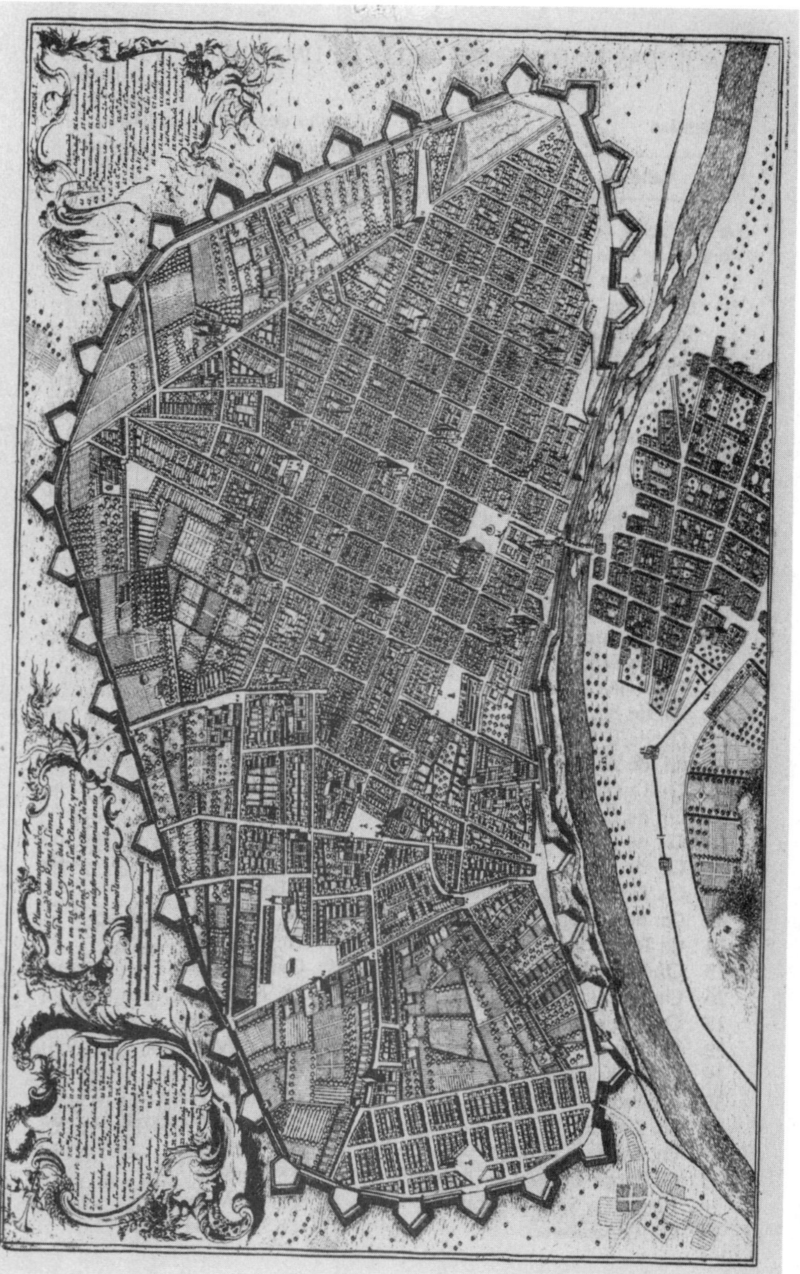

Map 10 Lima (Ciudad de los Reyes, 1685)

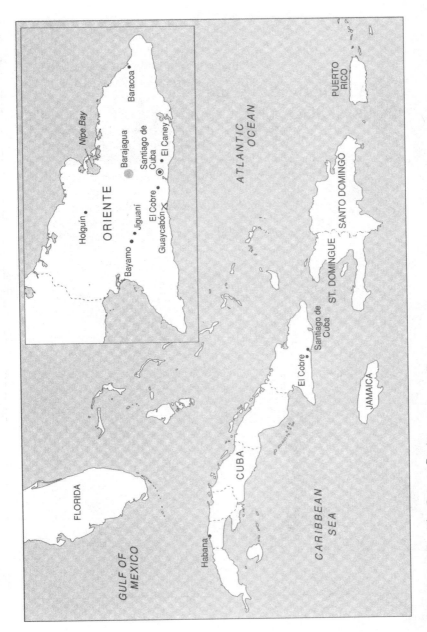

Map 11 Cuba: The Oriente Region

Map 12 Viceroyalty of Río de la Plata

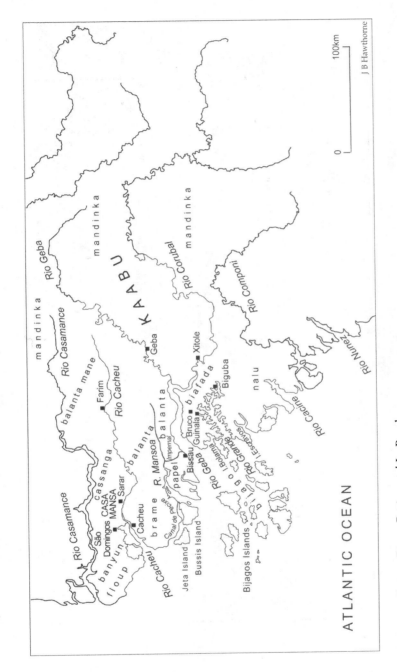

Map 13 Guinea-Bissau Region and Its People

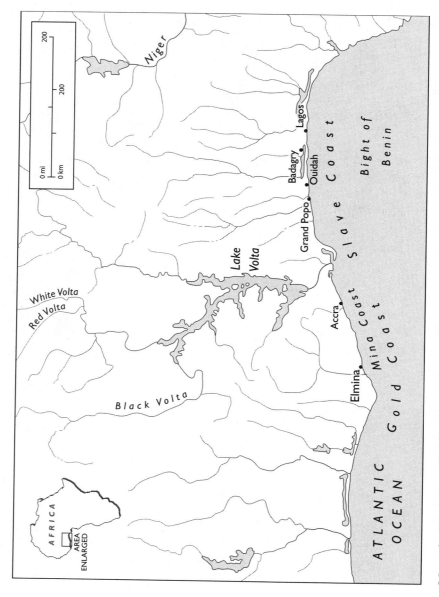

Map 14 Mina Coast: Slave Ports

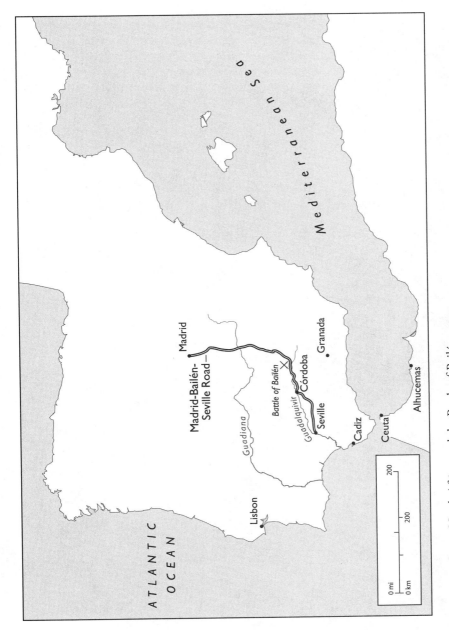

Map 15 Spain, North Africa, and the Battle of Bailén

PART I: POLITICS AND WARS

"Politics and Wars" highlights African communities and states in conflict with European or internal entities. This section represents an early stage in the struggles between African communities and European colonizing powers in Africa and Ibero-America. When the Portuguese first arrived in Central Africa in 1483, the Kingdom of Kongo controlled an area as large as Portugal itself. In the early sixteenth century, the kings of Kongo converted to Catholicism but remained politically independent. The 1550 inquest into a case of treason (Chapter 1) shows powerful Central African leaders engaging European modes of discourse and political action to work out internal divisions. The chapter informs a reading of Afro-Latinos in Ibero-America as often having had prior experience with complex political organizations and an Africanized Catholicism.

Brought forcibly to the Americas, many Africans escaped and formed clandestine communities called *palenques*. In numerous cases, leaders negotiated with Spanish authorities, promising loyalty to the Crown in exchange for a peaceful coexistence. Sometimes these negotiations were successful. Although Alonso de Illescas' 1586 petition was rejected (Chapter 2), the Spanish government granted his community its freedom less than two decades later. Illescas' community had settled in Ecuador before the first large boom in the Atlantic slave trade.

This boom occurred during the reign of Queen Njinga of Ndongo (*Angola*) in the early to mid-sixteenth century (Chapter 3). In letters spanning three decades, Njinga negotiated her relationship with Portuguese governors and showed her development of an African style of leadership while Portuguese slaving interests promoted local wars to feed the trade.

Although most Africans came to the Americas via the traumatic *Middle Passage*, some who shaped the Ibero-Atlantic world came from the Afro-Iberian communities in southern Spain and Portugal and crossed the Atlantic as soldiers and sailors in the service of the Crown. In the petitions excerpted in Chapter 4, their female relatives at home defended their rights before the Crown as loyal subjects, with corresponding social status.

Contemporary to Queen Njinga and near the slave port of Cartagena de Indias (Colombia), the autonomous *Palenque* del Limón thrived with about two hundred inhabitants, many of them Central Africans or their descendants. In 1633, Spanish soldiers captured many residents and took them to Cartagena. The testimony of three residents (Chapter 5) reveals the everyday functioning of this clandestine community and the varying attitudes residents held toward Spanish masters and the colonial government. It also reveals the role *palenques* played in the creative reconstruction and preservation of African spirituality and spiritually based military leadership in the New World.

1

The Treason of Dom Pedro Nkanga a Mvemba against Dom Diogo, King of Kongo, 1550[1]

John K. Thornton and Linda Heywood

A Document of Inquiry: Its Origins and Historical Value

On April 10, 1550, Dom Diogo I, King of Kongo, ordered his magistrate and pur-veyor, Jorge Afonso, to conduct an inquiry into a treasonous plot raised against him by Dom Pedro Nkanga a Mvemba, a former king of Kongo whom Diogo had recently unseated. A number of declarants were interrogated by the magistrate, and their comments were set in writing by the royal scribe, Belchior Dias. Some two years later, a copy of the inquest was sent to Portugal so that "in the Kingdom of Portugal, his brother the king will be informed of the truth" and to support the Kongolese throne's request that one of the culprits—a Kongolese noble named Dom Rodrigo who had fled to *São Tomé*—be extradited.[2]

The document found its way into the Portuguese archives, where it is today, the Kongolese original having been destroyed along with the Kongolese archives. It was first published in Portugal in 1877, and a revised edition was published by the Portuguese scholar-priest António Brásio in 1953.[3] The first was a somewhat defective transcription made by Paiva Manso and published in 1877. António Brásio published a better version in his magnificent collection of sources on Central African history in 1953.

The document, which gives a fascinating "insider's view" into the intrigues of the Kingdom of Kongo in the middle of the sixteenth century, has been used by several historians. Both Jan Vansina (Kingdoms) and Georges Balandier used it to illustrate points concerning Kongo's history. It is indeed a document of central importance for understanding Kongo's history and political structure in the mid-sixteenth century and is the earliest source to shed real light on these questions.

But (King) Diogo's inquiry has the added advantage of being, first, a com-pletely internal source, made by Kongolese witnesses for a matter of Kongolese domestic affairs and, second, a document not intended for public consumption in Europe. Although these two strengths make it an important source, they also make it a difficult one: it discusses Kongo from an insider's point of view, with

---

1. See Map 2.
2. Arquivo Nacional de Torre do Tombo, Corpo Cronologico, Lisbon, Parte II, maço 242, doc. no. 121. Henceforth citations to this document will be cited as, for example, "fol. 1." On its use to support the extradition of Dom Rodrigo, see Brásio (II:325), "Demands of D Diogo to King of Portugal," 1553.
3. The document is now in the Corpo Cronologico section of the Arquivo Nacional de Torre do Tombo in Lisbon (Brásio II:248–62).

vague references to structures and events known too well by the makers of the document to merit description but understood imperfectly by historians more than three centuries later.

The Kingdom of Kongo and Its Political Structure

The Kingdom of Kongo was probably founded toward the end of the fourteenth century and expanded from a nucleus just south of the Congo River to include its capital Mbanza Kongo in modern-day northern Angola and the Democratic Republic of Congo and then to the east to the Kwango River and south as far as modern-day Luanda (Thornton, "Origins"). When the Portuguese arrived in the area in 1483, the Kingdom of Kongo was probably larger than Portugal, though the population was smaller. Portuguese visitors regarded it as the most powerful kingdom south of the equator. Almost from the beginning of their interaction, Portugal and Kongo formed an alliance in which Portuguese soldiers assisted the kings of Kongo in their wars and obtained the captives taken in by them as slaves.

The kings of Kongo converted to Christianity, and a Kongo noble was named a bishop in 1518. Although Portuguese culture deeply influenced at least the elite's customs, from very early in the encounter, the Portuguese did not conquer or dominate in Kongo as the Spanish did in the Americas or as the Portuguese themselves eventually did in Kongo's southern neighbor Ndongo after they founded the colony of *Angola* in 1575.

As a Christian kingdom, Kongo built schools and started literacy in Portuguese. The kings of Kongo and Portugal corresponded regularly, and these letters are a vital source of information, not just about the relations between the two countries but also about the internal affairs of Kongo. The correspondence of King Afonso of Kongo (1509–1542) included more than twenty letters, some of them very long. These letters in fact are our most important source of information about Kongo. Written sources composed by Africans document the history of the Angolan kingdom for the first half of the sixteenth century—a unique situation for the lands that Europeans encountered along the Atlantic seaboard of Africa.

We learn from Afonso's correspondence that the relationship between Kongo and Portugal was not always smooth. Afonso complained that the Portuguese soldiers who helped him were cowardly and incompetent, that some of the priests were not paragons of Christian morality, and that Portuguese merchants sometimes promoted disobedience among his vassals, primarily in order to obtain slaves. In 1526, Afonso brought the situation under control by creating a board to supervise the slave trade.

Kongo's ruling class was often divided, and plots were common. These plots typically involved factions of the royal family maneuvering to determine succession, and, thus, they were particularly strong after the death of a king (Thornton, "Early Kongo-Portuguese Relations"). The document in question gives the fullest details we have for such a plot, in this case involving the relatively long crisis from the death of Afonso in 1542 to the final succession of Diogo I in 1545.

The Plot to Overthrow Dom Diogo, King of Kongo

It is clear from the testimony of witnesses that Dom Pedro "Cangua Mobemba" (Nkanga a Mvemba in modern Kikongo)[4] was deeply engaged (from his base in a church) in gathering a group of supporters to overthrow the king, but the document says little more about it. The comings and goings are quite mysterious, and it is difficult to place this plot in historical context by using contemporary or near contemporary documents. Dom Pedro Nkanga a Mvemba was, in fact, the son of King Afonso I (1509–1542) and handpicked by him to be his successor.

In a letter to the king of Portugal in 1549, Captain Francisco Barros da Paiva of the Portuguese island colony of *São Tomé* mentioned his problems with King Diogo of Kongo and then went on to refer to "King Dom Pedro who is in the church and Dom Rodrigo who is on this island."[5] From da Paiva's remarks, we can have no doubt that the Pedro who plotted in a church and involved a certain Dom Rodrigo on *São Tomé* in his plots was the main figure of the inquest and was a former king of Kongo.

This information allows us to establish a sequence of events with some certainty. When Afonso I died in 1543,[6] he was indeed succeeded by his son Pedro. But formal election as king of Kongo was never enough to ensure that the Crown would pass smoothly to anyone. The election was frequently followed by further jockeying as the newly crowned king rewarded his followers and supporters with offices, titles, and promotions and overcame the opposition of those whose futures were inevitably harmed by his actions. These latter would be the source, sometimes for many years, of friction, plots, and—as apparently happened in the case of Dom Diogo and his supporters—active attempts at usurpation of the Crown.

Pedro's rule lasted about two years, for it seems that Diogo ascended to the throne in 1545.[7] Pedro apparently sought asylum in a church, and from that safe, if constricted, location he fomented his plot. Five years later, Diogo was still dealing in delicate manipulations and still meeting opposition as he replaced Pedro's appointees with his own.

The real stake for most of the participants in the plot, and even those who wavered, was the granting or revocation of *rendas*, a Portuguese feudal term meaning, generally, any sort of income-bearing property. In Kongo, however, unlike in Portugal, the king closely controlled this rent-bearing property and no one held real property rights. During the inquest, Pedro reminded his nephew Dom Afonso that Diogo had

---

4. The writer spells this name "Camgua mo bemba" (or Cangua mo bemba), which probably is quite close to how it was pronounced in sixteenth-century Kikongo, which would be roughly Nkanga Mubemba. Since that time, Kikongo has changed, and words that once began with "mu" have become shortened to just "n," whereas the "b" of the older documents is often now a "v." Thus a modern spelling and one that is widely accepted by specialists is Nkanga a Mvemba.

5. Francisco Barros da Paiva to el-Rei Joao III, January 28, 1549 (Brásio II:236).

6. This date is established by the correspondence of his brother Manuel in Lisbon—Manuel to the Queen of Portugal, July 15, 1543 (Brásio II:124–25).

7. The date of Diogo's accession is established by testimony in an inquiry conducted by Diogo, November 21, 1548. A witness, Manuel Varela, indicated that Diogo had been king for three years, "more or less," at the time of the inquest.

not given him the *renda* of Nsundi, Kongo's northeastern province, which carried considerable income and prestige.

Likewise, when Pedro's close associate Dom Bastião visited *Mani* (governor) Mpemba (a large province south of the capital), he played on what must have been *Mani* Mpemba's real fears that Dom Diogo would eventually take his *renda* back. If the governor was able to retain his office, supporting the king would probably allow him to keep his *renda* or even move up to a better one. Opposing him would obviously mean deprivation of income, if not of life. On the other hand, simple support might not have been enough.

Apparently this is what Dom Pedro was banking on in his negotiations with *Mani* Mpemba, for Diogo, with friends, family, and supporters to reward, might easily take the *rendas* of those he judged less worthy and give them to his family or close friends. In his desperate letter to his cousin and ally Dom Rodrigo in *São Tomé* (which follows the document of inquest, below), Pedro makes this plight clear—Diogo had already taken his *renda* and was apparently taking those of Pedro's immediate family and giving them to his family and supporters—Pedro's own *renda* went to Diogo's son.

Family ties were obviously important, perhaps critical, in the delicate game of *renda* distribution. As indicated in his letter to Dom Rodrigo, Pedro clearly saw the threat of Diogo's rule not just as a personal one but also as one against his whole family and line—"*nossa geração de Quybala* [our lineage of Kibala]" (18).[8] That perception could scarcely have been a vain one if Diogo had indeed sent out letters to the provincial governors demanding that in case of Diogo's death they must not support anyone of Pedro's lineage (*geração*), "neither son nor daughter nor male nor female relative even if they are slaves" (18).[9]

The inquest clearly shows that the struggle for the throne of Kongo was never a personal one between rival kings but was, rather, a family one (often among rival branches of the same family), in which large groups of relatives, clients (like Dom Bastião, Pedro's frequent go-between), and even slaves stood in contention with each other. To the winning family group went prestigious and wealthy *rendas*, according to such criteria as loyalty, seniority, and degree of relationship; to the losers went imprisonment, poverty, or even death.

Diogo apparently moved rather slowly in consolidating his power. Five years after his accession to office, he was still allowing Pedro's followers considerable power; indeed, some of Pedro's group still held power in a variety of places. No doubt the king had to proceed slowly, first replacing a few top officials and then gradually working the others out. He needed to do this fast enough to satisfy his followers yet slowly

8. *Quybala* probably means the faction formed at court, as *mbala* means "court" in Kikongo (Thornton, "Elite Women," 445).

9. The Portuguese term *geração* is probably a translation of the Kikongo word *kanda* (plural *makanda*), which is often translated as "lineage" or "clan." In Kongo, however, *makanda* were complex sets of alliances including clients, allies, and slaves. It has a secondary meaning of "faction," so that brothers and their followers might form two separate *makanda* if they became rivals (Thornton, "Elite Women," 439–41).

enough to maintain the loyalty of those he had not yet forced out—and perhaps give the most loyal time to join his group.

Mani Mpemba was, it seems, one who hoped to gain Diogo's favor in spite of his position. The fact that Pedro's agents worked hard to convince *Mani* Mpemba that he would not be able to keep his position indicated that his position was a marginal one. On the other hand, *Mani* Mpangala (the lord of the market town that lay near the capital) was removed once the king was secure enough after five years in office to begin a general replacement of Pedro's group.[10] That all the lesser nobles of Vunda, Kondongo, and Lumbo were loyal to Pedro is an indication that Diogo had allowed them to stay in place for many years because he was afraid to move against them. Preserving the balance between removing potentially hostile but powerful people and continuing to keep the loyalty of one's closest supporters was no doubt the mark of a successful king in Kongo.

Essentially, Pedro was banking on the residual support left to him all over Kongo, both in the capital and in the provinces. His main striking action was to arrange the simultaneous murders of Diogo's top-level officials by lower ranking subordinates of Pedro's group. He had, in fact, even made some of these grants out; for example, *Mani* Mbampa (probably a subordinate of *Mani* Lumbo) was to cut off *Mani* Lumbo's head and get his *renda*. Pedro's nephew Dom Afonso and Dom Afonso's brother were to raise armies in Nsundi and Nkola (an unknown location), and after killing Diogo's appointments in Nsundi, they were to join Pedro in attacking the capital.

Pedro himself would leave the church where he had been closely watched for years and go to Mbata, probably to request the blessings of *Mani* Mbata, who held a traditionally neutral position controlled by its own line of hereditary nobility and attached to a *renda* that was not granted by the throne.[11] Although he did not say it, Pedro no doubt hoped to have both hereditary posts and *Mani* Vunda (apparently a nonhereditary post) as those holding these posts were the electors of Kongo.[12] The final acts needed to legitimize Pedro's reaccession to the throne were to obtain a papal bull recognizing Pedro's claim and to communicate this to all those who did not follow him—these tasks being left to Dom Rodrigo, who obviously had considerable international connections.[13]

Another point not made clear in the inquiry but visible in other documents of the era is the amount of support that Pedro could obtain outside of Africa. In addition to Dom Rodrigo, who apparently had land and influence in *São Tomé*, Pedro had

---

10. This interpretation rests on the reading of *tambuquado* as meaning "removed from office," as the term was defined by Lopes and Filippo Pigafetta (36), noting that if an appointed official failed to pay the tribute required of him he was said to be *tambocado* or "deprived of his revenue and government."

11. On the role of *Mani* Mbata, see the later tradition reported by Cavazzi da Montecuccolo (II:89); Cardoso (47–48); and João III to Afonso I, c. 1531 (Brásio I:535). Brásio dates the letter 1529; on the correct date, see Bontinck (166). Here Dom Jorge *Mani* Mbata is called the "first voice of Kongo and it is not possible to make a king without him, according to the custom of the land."

12. On the electoral system and its early history, see Thornton ("Origins," 113–14).

13. On Rodrigo's connections, see Thornton ("Early Kongo-Portuguese Relations," 192, 197).

connections in Portugal. Most significant was the Jesuit Order; for as late as 1552, Jesuit correspondence was still speaking of the overthrow of Diogo (who had thwarted the Jesuits' claims to authority) and the installation of a king who was "completely ours," that is, one who would favor the Jesuits.[14]

The Portuguese in Diogo's court were greatly favored, including those who were secular clergy and long-term residents of Kongo. However, those who had recently come from the *metropole* itself found it difficult to be established, even those who were high ranking and favored by the king of Portugal, including officials from *São Tomé*,[15] the bishop of *São Tomé*,[16] and those of the Jesuit Order.

All these groups met opposition from locally entrenched factions of Portuguese who were consistently favored by Diogo.[17] Not surprisingly, they entered into alliances with Pedro, who could promise them favors in Kongo once he was king. Pedro thought this alliance with high-status Portuguese in the metropole might work to his advantage. It is quite possible that it was they who succeeded in blocking Diogo's attempts to send a diplomatic mission to Rome (the first of which was sent in 1547; each failed).[18] In any case, Diogo succeeded in crushing the plot and began a long campaign to have Dom Pedro's ally Dom Rodrigo extradited from *São Tomé* to Kongo. A royal *alvara* was finally granted to this end in 1561, at the very end of Diogo's life,[19] but we do not know if Dom Rodrigo was ever delivered to his enemy. We have no information about Dom Pedro either, except that apparently he no longer threatened Diogo once his plot was discovered.

The Inquiry as a Source of Kongolese Political Culture

In addition to the light that it sheds on the political history of Kongo in the mid-sixteenth century, the inquiry gives us some interesting secondary information. The very existence of the document, for example, shows that in Kongo certain Portuguese legal forms were well established and in general use. We know of two other inquests similar to this one: one conducted by Afonso I in 1517 and the other by Diogo I in 1548.

---

14. Cornelio Gomes to Ignatius Loyola, July 18, 1552 (Brásio II:275).

15. Francisco Barros da Paiva to João III, February 18, 1549 (Brásio II:231–37).

16. Pigafetta (54–56); Cristovao Ribeiro to Francisco Barros da Paiva, January 25, 1549 (Brásio II:222); Diogo I to João III, August 15, 1546 (Brásio II:151–52).

17. Minutes on demands of Diogo I, c. 1553 (Brásio II:327–30). On the general interpretation of this correspondence, see Thornton, "Early Kongo-Portuguese Relations." It is obvious that neither Pedro nor Diogo could be considered either "pro-Portuguese" or "anti-Portuguese," as both used the services of the Portuguese extensively.

18. Diogo to Diogo Gomes, August 15, 1546 (Brásio II:147); Cornelio Gomes to a father of Portugal, October 29, 1553 (Brásio II:302). Also see fol. 11. Pedro's letter to Rodrigo that is cited in the text is undated, and the reference to a white man being sent by Diogo to Rome may refer to Gomes' mission of 1546, or more likely to Jacome da Fonseca's of 1552–1553.

19. Apontamentos sobre Paulo Dias de Novais, 1560–1561 (Brásio II). Also see minutes on dispatches of João III to Kongo, c. 1556 (Brásio II:396).

Both of these inquests, however, concerned Kongo's relations with Portugal and were conducted to inform the Portuguese king of matters relevant to that relationship.[20]

But only the Inquest of Diogo of 1550 concerned a purely internal affair and thus must indicate that the practice of a judicial inquest was established in Kongo, the copy that went to Portugal being only an "information copy" to support the request for extradition. It should be noted, however, that all the officials concerned were Portuguese. It would thus appear that Diogo had imported both the legal forms and the experts to conduct them. Because of a great lack of subsequent documentation, we cannot know if, in fact, the Kongolese later conducted the inquiries or even if the inquiry as a legal form survived the sixteenth century in Kongo.

In addition to the light it sheds on legal systems in Kongo, the inquest attests to the existence of archives in Kongo. That the document was created, filed, and then retrieved two years later for transmission to Portugal shows this as well as the fact that writing had obviously become an important system of information storage and transmission.

The writing of letters from one Kongolese actor to another is mentioned several times in the inquest. Dom Matias, when in Mpangu, wrote a letter to Dom Pedro that Dom Afonso testified to having seen. It was an intercepted letter from Pedro to Rodrigo that was attached to the inquest and gave the most damning evidence: that letter mentions five more letters sent from Dom Diogo to others in the kingdom.[21] The custom of writing was fixed enough that the custom of storing the correspondence must have been well established. A half century after the Luso-Kongolese contacts, Kongo was fully literate—at least, its upper classes were. In the sixteenth century, literacy was an upper-class phenomenon everywhere.

A final piece of incidental information concerns the presence of Christianity. Although it is sometimes believed that Christianity did not survive the reign of Afonso, an impression created in part by the slanderous correspondence of Jesuit missionaries and *São Tomé* officials written against Diogo,[22] in fact, all the actors appear as fairly solid Christians. For example, when he first broke the plan to Afonso, Dom Pedro asked him first to swear on a Holy Bible to keep it secret. Furthermore, Diogo apparently observed the right of Christian asylum in a church enough to allow Pedro to operate from a church for years after his deposition, even though officials from that same church were important witnesses in the trial and obviously played a significant part in revealing the plot. Both Pedro and Diogo respected the decisions of the Pope in the question of succession, and both sought to obtain the requisite bulls recognizing them as rulers of Kongo.[23]

---

20. Brásio published both (I:393–97 and II:197–206).

21. Fol. 3v, letter of Dom Matias, and fols. 10v–11v, other letters.

22. Cristovao Riberio to Captain of *São Tomé*, January 25, 1549 (Brásio II:222); Francisco Barres da Paiva to João III (Brásio II:231–36); Cornelio Gomes to Ignatius Loyola, July 18, 1552 (Brásio II:275); Jesuit Chronicle of Afonso Polanco, extract in Brásio II:227–28.

23. See note 18, above, fol. 11.

The Document

The text that follows is the complete inquest, made from a photocopy of the original found in the Arquivo Nacional de Torre do Tombo in Lisbon.[24] We have followed Paiva Manso's text, emending it from the original document. The text, like many from this period, uses little punctuation; therefore, the translation supplies enough to make sense of the text. We have also altered the reading of Kikongo words and titles in one or two places to change the division into words.

Lords Loyal to Dom Diogo	Lords Whose Loyalty Is in Flux	Lords Reportedly Loyal to Dom Pedro
Mani Kandongo	Mani Mpangala Dom	Dom Matias Mani Mitombe
Mani Kwanzila	Francisco	(appointed by Dom Diogo)
Mani Lumbo	(official of Dom Pedro's	Mani Mbampa
Mani Nsunda	rule, eventually replaced	(subordinate to Mani Lumbo)
Mani Vunda	by Dom Diogo)	Mani Wembo
	Mani Mpemba	Nsungo a Mala Mani Mpemba
	(official of Dom Pedro's	Tambuke Mpemba (ex-Mani
	rule, trying to gain Dom	Mpemba)[25]
	Diogo's favor, reportedly	Nsala a Kibela
	godson of Diogo)	
		Lords of Vunda, Left in Place by Dom Diogo, Reportedly Loyal to Dom Pedro
		Dom António Mani Nsimsa
		Dom Francisco Mani Mpangala
		Dom Francisco Mani Zalita
		Dom João Mani Katila
		Mani Tenga

Figure 1. Factions and loyalties as reported by witnesses in the "Judicial Inquiry Concerning the Treason Which Dom Pedro Nkanga a Mvemba Mounted against Dom Diogo, King of Kongo" (1550)

*****

---

24. We are grateful to D. Maria Teresa Geraldes Barbosa Acabado of the archive for transmitting the copy to us.
25. See note 31 in the document.

Copy of a Judicial Inquiry That His Royal Lordship [Dom Diogo] Ordered the Magistrate and Purveyor Jorge Afonso to Carry Out, Concerning the Treason That Dom Pedro Nkanga a Mvemba Mounted against Him[26]

May it be known by all those who see this public instrument, given by order and authority of justice, by the most powerful and Christian King Dom Diogo, by God through His Holy Grace: that in the year of Our Lord Jesus Christ 1552, on the tenth day of January of this same year, in the city of Kongo in the palaces of His Royal Lordship, this same lord ordered the magistrate and purveyor, Jorge Afonso, in the presence of me, the clerk, to complete the present instrument, with a copy of the inquest and inquiry which were gathered concerning the treason that Dom Pedro Nkanga a Mvemba raised against him. And as His Royal Lord [Dom Diogo] wishes that in the Kingdom of Portugal, his brother the king should be informed of the truth, he ordered the magistrate to have the present instrument completed for him with a copy of the inquest, which I, the clerk, copied before the above-named [*ouvidor* Jorge Afonso] completely word for word . . . which is what follows.

I, Belchior Dias, clerk and notary public of the Kingdom and Dominions of Kongo, transcribed it. And here it follows:

Act and Inquiry That His Royal Lordship Ordered the Magistrate and Purveyor Jorge Afonso to Gather, Concerning the Treason Raised against Him by Dom Pedro Nkanga a Mvemba.

In the year of Our Lord Jesus Christ 1550, on the tenth day of April of this same year, in this city of Kongo, in the palaces of His Royal Lordship [Dom Diogo, King of Kongo], after His Royal Lordship ordered the magistrate and purveyor, Jorge Afonso, in my presence—the clerk named below—to question certain witnesses and inquire into how Dom Pedro Nkanga a Mvemba had mounted treason against His Royal Lordship, so that he [illegible][27] the kingdom and take possession of it himself [illegible]. Thereupon the magistrate ordered me, the clerk, to make this act of inquiry and to question all the witnesses whom His Royal Lordship ordered to appear, all of which was completed.

I, Belchior Dias, notary public and clerk of the judiciary and orphans in this Kingdom and Dominions of Kongo, wrote this for the King [of Portugal], Our Lord, and for His Lordship [Dom Diogo, King of Kongo].

---

26. Arquivo Nacional de Torre do Tombo, Lisbon, Corpo Cronológico, parte II, maço 242, doc. no. 121. Also published by Brásio (II:248–62) and by Paiva Manso (101–10). All Portuguese names have been modernized, consistent with the rest of the volume. Kikongo names have been modernized according to current Kikongo usage.
27. Probably "so that he might usurp."

[Testimony by João Ane, Chapel Boy]

Item. João Ane, chapel boy,[28] a witness sworn on the Holy Gospels, on which he placed his right hand, which were given to him by the magistrate and purveyor, Jorge Afonso, and promised to tell the truth regarding all that was asked him. He, the witness,[29] said that it is true that on several occasions he saw Dom Bastião and Dom Pedro Nkanga a Mvemba speaking together, and he knew that they had conversed considerably and were friendly. And [João Ane] saw this because they were frequently both [at the church]. And that he knew nothing else. And [João Ane] further declared under oath that it was true that with his own eyes he saw Pedro Álvares enter the church many times and speak with Dom Pedro. And when [Pedro Álvares] was there, they [Dom Pedro and Pedro Álvares] entered the vestry and closed the doors, and they both spoke with each other. And nevertheless, [João Ane] did not know what they did and did not say.

And he said no more of this case. And to certify, he signed in the presence of the magistrate, and regarding the customary [questions], he said nothing.

[Bel]chior Dias, clerk, who set this down in writing.

[Testimony of Dom Afonso]

Item. Dom Afonso, witness sworn on the Holy Gospels, which were given to him by the magistrate and purveyor, Jorge Afonso, on which he placed his right hand and promised to tell the truth regarding all that was asked him. The witness [Dom Afonso] said that it was true that the said Dom Pedro Nkanga a Mvemba called him one day when [Dom Afonso] was in church, and that [Dom Pedro] said to [Dom Afonso] that he wanted to speak with him in secret, and that Dom Pedro told him to swear on the book of the Holy Gospels because he wanted to tell him a very important secret. And [Dom Afonso] contended that he would not swear, that [Dom Pedro] should tell him [the secret], that he would not tell anything that Dom Pedro told him. And Dom Pedro told him again to swear an oath, and [Dom Afonso] then swore to say nothing. Then Dom Pedro said to him that he had determined to leave [the church stronghold] and that he wanted [Dom Afonso] to go with him and so, too, [Dom Afonso's] brother, because if Dom Pedro Nkanga a Mvemba left and they remained, His Royal Lordship [Dom Diogo] would order them killed. And Dom Pedro Nkanga a Mvemba also told [Dom Afonso] that they should not be afraid to go with him, that they were not the only ones who would go with him, that a majority of the people of the kingdom would go with him. And [Dom Afonso] said that he did not respond to anything which Pedro Nkanga a Mvemba said to him.

And as Dom Pedro saw that [Dom Afonso] did not answer him at all, he sent him to his steward, named Dom Bastião, who gave him details on how he should proceed. And [Dom Afonso] left the church. And then on the morning of the next

---

28. Although "chapel boy" implies a youth, it is quite possible that in Kongo these chapel boys were adults, as we know that Diogo sent them on diplomatic missions and to evangelize foreign countries. They were in fact as much lay evangelists as simply youths who helped around the church.

29. This repetitive bureaucratic language is retained in the Portuguese, but hereafter it is replaced in the English translation with the names of the witnesses in brackets in order to facilitate comprehension.

day, Dom Bastião, confidante of Dom Pedro, who took care of his affairs, had [Dom Afonso] and his brother called. And [Dom Bastião] said that his lord, Dom Pedro, had ordered that the brother [of Dom Afonso] should go to Nsundi and Nkola and raise two armies. Then [Dom Bastião] would abandon the church where he was, and he would see if His Royal Lordship had enough power to stop the army of Nsundi or Dom Pedro.

And not long afterward, Dom Bastião, who looked after [Dom Pedro's] affairs, gave a message to [Dom Afonso]. And later that same day Dom Pedro called on [Dom Afonso] again. And then Dom Pedro asked him if Dom Bastião had given him his message; and [Dom Afonso] said yes. And [Dom Pedro] said again to [Dom Afonso] that he should be strong and have no fear, as there were many on his side, namely *Mani*[30] Mitombe, Dom Matias and Nsungo a Mala, *Mani* Mpemba, and also all the *fidalgos* of Vunda and *Mani* Wembo and Tambukwe Mpemba Nsala a Kibela.[31] And Dom Pedro told [Dom Afonso] on other occasions he should not fear anything, that Dom Matias would beg his forgiveness for things past.

And saying to him that His Royal Lordship [Dom Diogo] had promised him [Dom Afonso] the *renda* of Nsundi and that he had given him nothing, Dom Pedro said to [Dom Afonso] that when Dom Matias was in Mpangu there was a letter waiting for [Dom Pedro]; and it said that Dom Matias would go and kill *Mani* Nsunda and would rise up and revolt with the [people of the] land and that Dom Pedro should flee to Mbata; whereupon both would join their armies and attack Kongo, and Dom Pedro would be King of Kongo. And when he saw the letter from Dom Matias, he took counsel with his sisters as to whether he should abandon the church. And they told him no, [fleeing] was a mistake,[32] they had already killed his sons, and they wished to do the same to him. And now he sees that [Dom Matias' letter] is all true, because of excuses and compromises that Dom Matias had made to him. And with this [Dom Pedro] gave him, the witness [Dom Afonso], courage to do as he ordered him, [telling him] that Dom Pedro believes it to be true that all these above-named *fidalgos* are on his side and that they will follow him and that [Dom Afonso] said to [Dom Pedro] that he would not give him any response, that everything was in God's hands.

And [Dom Afonso] said no more of the case. And regarding the customary [questions], he said that he was a nephew of Dom Pedro.

Item. Dom Afonso said, and moreover declared under oath, that a *fidalgo* of Vunda by the name of *Mani* Zalita, and by the Christian name of Dom Francisco, spoke to him and gave him, the witness, an account of how Dom Pedro had decided not to leave this hill but to raise his army here, because he had more supporters than were with His Royal Lordship [Dom Diogo]; and that His Royal Lordship did not

---

30. *Mani* is a form that is frequently encountered in documents from Kongo meaning "lord of." Though its correct orthography in modern Kikongo is probably *mwene*, its use is sufficiently widespread in modern literature on Kongo that we will retain this spelling here.

31. This name is interesting; it suggests that Nsala a Kibela (a personal name) was a former *Mani* Mpemba who had been removed from power (*tambuquado*).

32. The wording *engano*, which has been translated as "mistake," is ambiguous, and the sentence may be saying that the letter was a trick.

have any followers other than *Mani* Kandongo and *Mani* Lumbo and *Mani* Vunda, who had no people[33] except for him alone; and that [Dom Diogo] had already given *Mani* Lumbo's *renda* to *Mani* Mbampa, who would behead *Mani* Lumbo without any other cause; and that *Mani* Vunda's people would behead *Mani* Vunda and *Mani* Kandongo.

And [Dom Afonso] said, moreover, that one day he went to the house of Dom Bastião and he, Dom Bastião, spoke to him about how [Dom Bastião] had spoken with Dom Pedro, about how they ought to conduct their war. And as he knew that *Mani* Mpemba was fleeing in this direction, [Dom Bastião] said to [Dom Afonso] that he was glad that he was coming, and that [his coming] was to support [Bastião's] army, and that with his coming, his negotiations would end, and there would be no more to be done. And [Dom Afonso] said that he made confession and that the father to whom he confessed ordered him to disclose all to His Royal Lordship [Dom Diogo], as this was a case of treason and concerned the Royal Person. Thus [Dom Afonso] disclosed [the matter] in the way he has declared. And [Dom Afonso] also said that since Dom Pedro knew that this was disclosed, he ordered that [Dom Afonso] and his brother be told that they should reveal nothing of what they knew to anyone, because what [Dom Pedro] was planning was only for their benefit.

And moreover [Dom Afonso] said that Dom Pedro told him that he was hoping for a [papal] bull, which would be sent to him by the Holy Father, so that they would return the kingdom to [Dom Pedro], and that for this reason he was thinking of leaving there [the church], because if he stayed, His Royal Lordship would order him killed when the bull arrived.[34]

And [Dom Afonso] said no more of this case. And regarding the customary [questions], he said that he was a nephew of Dom Pedro. And to certify, he signed in the presence of the magistrate. I, Belchior Dias, clerk, who set it down in writing.

Dom Afonso

Jorge Afonso

[Testimony of Pedro Afonso Milando, Chapel Boy]

Item. Pedro Afonso Milando, chapel boy, being from this city of Kongo, witness sworn on the Holy Gospels, on which he placed his right hand, which were given to him by the magistrate and purveyor, Jorge Afonso, that he was to tell the truth regarding what was asked him, and he promised to tell [the truth]. [Milando] said that it was true that he was interpreter at the confession of Dom Afonso, the witness previously questioned[35] and that the father ordered that as penance [Milando] should reveal to His Royal Lordship [Dom Diogo] everything that Dom Afonso had said, as

---

33. Supporters.

34. The plotters apparently believed that the law of sanctuary could be superseded by a papal bull, and Pedro could be seized by Diogo if he got a bull to that effect. For his own part, Pedro believed that a papal bull could declare him king.

35. The use of an interpreter suggests that the priest in question was Portuguese, as, presumably, a Kongo priest would not need an interpreter. However, the use of interpreters was also considered a part of confession in Kongo at later periods regardless of the linguistic skills of the priest.

it was treason and touched upon his royal state. This is what [Milando] has come to state. And [what he heard] is everything that has been written above.

And he said no more. And to certify, he signed in the presence of the magistrate. I, Belchior Dias, clerk, who set it down in writing.

> Pedro Afonso Milando
> Jorge Afonso

[Testimony of Dom Pedro Afonso]

Item. Dom Pedro Afonso, witness sworn on the Holy Gospels, on which he placed his right hand, which were given to him by the magistrate and purveyor, and promised to tell the truth regarding all that was asked him. [Dom Pedro Afonso] said that he was present when Dom Pedro Nkanga a Mvemba gave an account [of the plots] to Dom Afonso and that all that Dom Afonso testified and said in his sworn [testimony] was true.

And to certify, he signed in the presence of the magistrate. And regarding the customary [questions], he said nothing. I, Belchior Dias, clerk, who set it down in writing.

> Dom Pedro Afonso
> Jorge Afonso

[Testimony of Dom Bastião]

Item. Dom Bastião, *fidalgo* of His Royal Lordship, witness sworn on the Holy Gospels, on which he placed his right hand, which were given to him by the magistrate and purveyor, Jorge Afonso, who was imprisoned in a *lebamba*,[36] and he promised to tell the truth regarding all that was asked him. [Dom Bastião] said that it is true that before Dom Rodrigo left for the Island of *São Tomé*, [Dom Bastião] had no friendship or conversation with Dom Pedro Nkanga a Bemba, rather Dom Rodrigo told him [Dom Bastião] and encouraged him greatly and entreated him[37] to tell Dom Pedro to not leave the church until he had sent him his message that even if His Royal Lordship [Dom Diogo] ordered that he leave the church, he should not leave until he had seen his [Dom Rodrigo's] message. And [Dom Bastião said] that Dom Rodrigo told him that he was being run out of this kingdom, that he would look for a way whereby to obtain a dispensation from the Pope, which would mandate the return of the kingdom to Dom Pedro, and that if His Royal Lordship did not treat him with mercy and did not wish to pardon him, he would work to destroy this kingdom, not ordering a pardon for him and ordering that nothing be done according to his [Dom Diogo's] orders.

---

36. *Lebamba* or *libambo*, "a device," often a forked wooden object used to secure prisoners. Some included chains.

37. The Portuguese is unclear here, stating *e lhe encomendou muito que lhe rogava que dissesse*. If this meant that Dom Rodrigo begged Dom Bastião to entreat Dom Pedro, the verb *rogar* should be conjugated in the subjunctive *rogasse*.

And [Dom Bastião] said that Dom Rodrigo told Francisco de Almada to tell him [Dom Bastião] that he would send him word concerning everything that he did on the island, and that Francisco de Almada would bring him a report, and that he knew that Francisco de Almada was in Mpinda with the report from Dom Rodrigo for him.

And moreover [Dom Bastião] declared that it is true that Dom Rodrigo said that he trusted him more than any of his own relatives, even brothers, because when Dom Rodrigo said this to him, his mother was present and sisters and all his relatives. And [Dom Bastião] said that he could trust in him and in no one else.

And moreover [Dom Bastião] said that it is true that at the time that he entered the church and took up friendship with Dom Pedro, all the *fidalgos* of *Mani* Vunda were already in agreement with Dom Pedro that he should leave the church. And all of them would follow him, namely Dom António *Mani* Nsimsa and Dom Francisco *Mani* Mpangala and Dom João *Mani* Katila.

And [Dom Bastião] said that everything that Dom Afonso and his brother testified to is true, because he was present and knows it to be sure. And [Dom Bastião] declared moreover that Dom António *Mani* Nsimsa went in the church to say good-bye to Dom Pedro, that he went by order of His Royal Lordship [Dom Diogo] and of *Mani* Vunda. And although it was by order of His Royal Lordship, he would know about all the *fidalgos* of Vunda, whether they were ready and disposed to help him.

And [Dom Bastião] also declared that he went across the [River] Ambrize.[38] And before leaving, he went to say good-bye to Dom Pedro, and Dom Pedro told him that he should ask one of his clients, who was there with *Mani* Mpemba, if he had sold a sword which he sent there to be sold. And if it was sold, that he should bring the money back. And moreover Dom Pedro said to him [Dom Bastião] that he should go to Tenga to speak with *Mani* Tenga, a *fidalgo* of *Mani* Vunda, and tell him to send him something to eat.

And [Dom Bastião] said that he did all that Dom Pedro ordered him to do. And having met with *Mani* Tenga, he gave him the message from Dom Pedro. And *Mani* Tenga gave him five thousand *nzimbu*,[39] which he gave to Dom Pedro so that he could eat them or do whatever he wanted with them.

And moreover [Dom Bastião] declared that it is true that *Mani* Mpemba and Dom Pedro met together in the witness' house one night. And Dom Pedro asked *Mani* Mpemba to advise him how he should leave that church, where he had been for so long; and that *Mani* Mpemba responded that he had no solution, because there was still a *mocano*[40] taking place in his land where he was *tambuquado*,[41] and he was without supporters; and that those that he had were those of His Royal Lordship; and that he [*Mani* Mpemba] would do this if His Royal Lordship returned to him the

---

38. Kikongo speakers call the river "*Mbidizi.*"

39. *Nzimbu* is the Kikongo name for the seashells drawn from Luanda Island that were used in Kongo as money. Earlier documents suggest that several *lifuku* (a unit of ten thousand) would be the price of a single slave or wages for a mason for a long period. This would therefore be a relatively small amount of money.

40. A judicial process, *nkanu* in modern Kikongo.

41. See note 10 in the chapter introduction.

renda, and he would do and would know the will of his people. And Dom Pedro said to *Mani* Mpemba, "See how short a time it has been since His Royal Lord gave you the *renda*, and already he wants to take it back, and since he wishes to take it back, now is the time to help me."

And Dom Bastião said and declared, under the oath that he had sworn, that it is true that *Mani* Wembo, the brother of *Mani* Nkakate,[42] also went to the aid of Dom Pedro.

And he said no more of this case. And to certify, he signed here in the presence of the magistrate. And regarding the customary [questions], he said that he was the friend of Dom Pedro. And, I, Belchior Dias, clerk, who set this down in writing.

> Dom Bastião
> Jorge Afonso

[Testimony of Pedro Afonso]

Item. Pedro Afonso, being in this city of Kongo, witness sworn on the Holy Gospels on which he placed his right hand, which were given to him by the magistrate and purveyor, Jorge Afonso, and he promised to tell the truth regarding what he knew. [Pedro Afonso] said that he knew for certain, as *Mani* Mpemba had told him in confidence, that [*Mani* Mpemba] was invited by Dom Matias to rise up against His Royal Lordship. And *Mani* Mpemba told [Pedro Afonso] that he would not and was not going to do that, since His Royal Lordship was his godfather. And [Pedro Afonso] knew this because *Mani* Mpemba told him in confession, telling him to tell His Royal Lordship, but [Pedro Afonso] never did so, except on Maundy Thursday, when he went with *Mani* Mpemba to confess it to His Royal Lordship.

And he knows no more about this case. And to verify it, he signed with the magistrate. And regarding the customary [questions], he said nothing. I, Belchior Dias, clerk, who set it down in writing.

> Pedro Afonso
> Jorge Afonso

[Testimony of Francisco Fernandes]

Item. Francisco Fernandes, witness sworn on the Holy Gospels, on which he placed his right hand, which were given to him by the magistrate and purveyor, Jorge Afonso. And he promised to tell the truth regarding all that was asked and what he knew. [Fernandes] said that it is true that one day he was in the *casa dos Atabaques*.[43] And since he had just stopped playing, he went toward the *plaza* and there he met Dom Bastião. And [Fernandes] questioned him about the ships that were coming from the island, and he said that they had arrived; however, he did not know how many there were or anything.[44] And Dom Bastião said to [Fernandes] that Dom Pedro wanted

---

42. Modernization of *Manynoquaquate* is problematic. The position to which the title refers is unknown.

43. The "house of drums."

44. The original reads, *não sabia quantos nem quantos nem quantos não*, which either is a copyist's error or perhaps means "how many, how many, how many" or "how many were and were not there."

to speak with him, and [Fernandes] told him that he did not want to go there, and [Dom Bastião] argued with him, three times insisting that he go.

And seeing himself constantly pressed by Dom Bastião, [Fernandes] went to the church to speak with Dom Pedro. And as soon as he met with Dom Pedro, Dom Pedro begged him to go speak with *Mani* Mpemba and ask him to come to speak with him here in Kongo. [Fernandes] responded that he could not go there; that he was a well-known man; and that he was known to His Royal Lordship, and he could in no way go there, because His Royal Lordship had closed all the ports and roads, and he was afraid to go; and that they might capture him, and for that reason he would not go there.

And he said no more of the case. And to certify they signed, and regarding the customary [questions], he said nothing. And, I, Belchior Dias, clerk, who set it down in writing.

Francisco Fernandes
Jorge Afonso

[Testimony of Dom Pedro Afonso]

Item. Dom Pedro Afonso, witness sworn on the Holy Gospels, on which he placed his right hand, which were given to him by the magistrate. And he promised to tell the truth regarding what he knew. [Dom Pedro Afonso] said and declared that it was true that he had heard Dom Bastião say that he was frightened of the things that were to happen in this kingdom. And he named a man who was *Mani* Mpangala, *fidalgo* of His Royal Lordship, who was one of those who always went to war with His Royal Lordship, and that now, since he had been *tambuquado* [removed from office], he would see who would go with him [to war?]. And Dom Bastião told [Dom Pedro Afonso] that *Mani* Zalita told him that he and *Mani* Mpangala had related these things.[45]

And he did not know anything more of the case. And to certify he signed. And regarding the customary [questions], he said nothing. I, Belchior Dias, clerk, who set this down in writing.

Dom Pedro Afonso
Jorge Afonso

[Testimony of Dom João de Melo]

Item. Dom João de Melo, principal porter of His Royal Lordship, witness sworn on the Holy Gospels, on which he placed his right hand, which were given to him by the magistrate and purveyor, Jorge Afonso. And he promised to tell the truth regarding what he knew. [Dom João de Melo] said that it was true that Dom Pedro Nkanga a Mvemba told him that at the time when he was in prison, in a house where His Royal Lordship kept him and ordered him guarded by his people, Dom Pedro did not abandon the house where he was, except by the advice of Dom Rodrigo and after he,

---

45. The Portuguese is confusing and might also mean, "he and *Mani* Mpangala had overlooked these reasons."

Dom Pedro, had been in the church for some time. Sometime later, Dom Rodrigo encouraged him that they should flee to go to this kingdom. And Dom Pedro told him in response that he would not leave the church nor go anywhere, because above all else he wished to remain there.

And [Dom João de Melo] declared further that one day while he was in his house, His Royal Lordship ordered him called to the church where he was, and His Royal Lordship said to [Dom João de Melo], "Go there where Dom Pedro Nkanga a Mvemba is, who says he wants to speak with you about I don't know what." And [Dom João de Melo] went and said that he asked what he wanted. And Dom Pedro told him to tell His Royal Lord that Dom Rodrigo had proposed that he leave the church and that he did not want to.

And [Dom João de Melo] said that this is what he knew about the case and he said no more. And regarding the customary [questions], he said nothing. And to certify, they signed. I, Belchior Dias, clerk, who set this down in writing.

> Dom João de Melo
> Jorge Afonso

[The Clerk Made Copies of the Declarations]

And after this, on the thirteenth day of the month of April of this year 1550, the magistrate and purveyor, Jorge Afonso, ordered me, the below-named clerk, to make copies for His Royal Lordship, as many as he wanted and needed as an instrument that he requested, and all was done according to instructions. I, Belchior Dias, clerk, who set this down in writing.

[A Letter from Dom Pedro Nkanga a Mvemba to Dom Rodrigo]

And after this, on the eleventh day of January of the present year [1552], in this city of Kongo, a letter was given to me, the clerk, by His Royal Lordship, [and it was] signed by Dom Pedro Nkanga a Mvemba, which he sent to the island of *São Tomé* to Dom Rodrigo, and the letter is the following.

I, Belchior Dias, clerk, set this down in writing.

My dearly beloved brother,

I greet Your Lordship. I can hardly tell you the things that we have suffered with this traitor who still does not cease to take his revenge against our lineage. And he is always sitting in judgment at the *plaza* and will not rest until he has killed our whole lineage. And he says that he will kill me and that he will put his son in my *renda*, and that if he does not take vengeance on me, I will take it on him, and nothing but curses will come from his mouth concerning our lineage of Kibala. And he, *Mani* Vunda, has written five letters for his son to grant, namely one to *Mani* Nsunda, and another to *Mani* Lumbo, and another to *Mani* Kandongo, and another to *Mani* Vunda, and another to *Mani* Kwanzila, to show to his son and also to leave him in his will when he dies. And he said that he is not to associate with anyone of our lineage, neither son nor daughter nor male nor female relative, even if they are slaves. Praise to God for all time. And he said that if anyone reveals one who does not follow his son, nor will you Dom Rodrigo, neither should anyone plead to his son on your behalf, lest he be disgraced for all time.

Brother, I entreat you not to forget us. You have been there a long time, and all our help rests with you, for you to be such a bad person. Now we are not expecting the loss of our lineage, for you are still there, and we have no other hope except for you, because you are on the side of truth. We take care that you have now sent [word] to the king of Portugal [requesting that he] send to Rome to aid us with a Holy bull that will dismiss this traitor, because this traitor fears nothing but a bull, and if he hears news of the bull, he will not have any doubt.[46] The bull should come secretly, so that no one knows of it, because if anyone were to find out about it, he would carry out a general killing of everyone at once. And the bull should read in such a way that no one is condemned nor killed, nor rebel, but rather they should go back to their people, and also that he should obey his king, with a perpetual excommunication. Now he has sent a white man to Rome to seek a bull by which he will have us all generally killed. He is starting now; he has arrested your sister *Mani* Nambwa and sent her to be guarded in Nsundi with Dona Caterina, my sister, *Mani* Lukeni. There in Singa he has arrested your sister, the mother of Dom Bastião, who is with God. Do not be upset about this, because we have encircled this traitor in order to kill him, neither should you be upset, but rather work for the pardon of our souls or anything else, except that Our Lord in His Grace give you many more days of life.

This letter which I, the below-named clerk, certify is signed with a signature which says "Dom Pedro," and on the outside says, "To be given to the most esteemed Lord Dom Rodrigo, on the island of *São Tomé*, my brother."

This instrument of inquiry, I, Belchior Dias, clerk and notary public of this kingdom and Dominion of Kongo, for the King Our Lord and for His Royal Lordship, copied from the original, which is in my hand, well and faithfully, thus and in the manner in which it is found, letter for letter, without altering a line or anything which would create any doubt, and here I place my public seal, such as it is. [public seal] Approved by me, Jorge Afonso, magistrate of this Kingdom of Kongo.

    Jorge Afonso

---

46. The lack of punctuation creates ambiguity here. The sense may be that there should be no doubt that the bull must come secretly.

2

Maroon Chief Alonso de Illescas' Letter to the Crown, 1586[1]

Charles Beatty-Medina

The Esmeraldas *Maroons* in the Age of Spanish Conquest

In Spanish America, enslaved Africans employed strategies of escape, or marronage, in order to gain their freedom. Even while Amerindians suffered the convulsive shocks of European invasion, fugitive Africans carved out independent enclaves on the scarred landscape of the conquest. This happened in colonial Ecuador's northern coast region, Esmeraldas, during the second half of the sixteenth century. The letter presented here is the work of Alonso de Illescas, an African *Maroon* leader in Esmeraldas, and it reflects the roles that fugitive slaves acquired as Spain worked to subjugate and consolidate its empire.

Contrary to scholarship proposing that escaped slaves attempted to "resurrect an archaic social order," Illescas' letter suggests that African *Maroons* involved themselves in dynamic relationships with their environment, native societies, and colonial authorities and that their social order developed out of contingencies largely beyond their control (Genovese, 3). It illustrates some of the ways that escaped Africans became critical agents in the colonial process. In his missive, Illescas acknowledged Spain's power in the Americas. However, his purpose was to subvert colonial authorities' plans to establish Spanish settlements in the *Maroons'* homeland.

Not unlike the many native leaders who petitioned the Crown for redress from Spanish abuses, Illescas pled with authorities to reverse their policies. Far from archaic, the *Maroons'* project grew out of the interstitial spaces that fugitives claimed for themselves—spaces that they created and nurtured as they interacted with distinct cultures, peoples, and colonial practices.

The themes in Illescas' letter, in many ways, are shaped by the methods that marked the creation of Spain's colonial world. As Mathew Restall has shown, the "age of conquest" imagery, of well-armed Spaniards handily defeating indigenous armies, is a myth on many counts (*Seven Myths*). Indeed, Spanish success at subduing indigenous civilizations was limited to certain places, certain times, and certain conditions. In many areas of Ibero-America, where circumstances were less than ideal for European methods, the Spanish dominated the people they encountered only gradually and incorporated new territories piecemeal and over time (Elliot, 40, 41; Williams, 3). Such was the case in coastal Esmeraldas.

Between 1526 and 1603, the Spanish made more than fifty failed attempts—military, religious, and diplomatic—to subjugate the area (Alcina Franch, 80–99); their

---

1. See Maps 6 and 7.

repeated failed efforts demonstrated that Esmeraldas, along with much of the Pacific coast of northern South America, was a nearly impenetrable frontier to Spanish settlers (Calero, 50, 51; Williams, chapter 1). By contrast, Alonso de Illescas, and twenty-three fellow fugitives, succeeded in making Esmeraldas their home following a shipwreck in the early 1550s (Cabello Balboa, 18). Although they faced different challenges and arrived with different aims than the Spanish, Illescas and his small band of African renegades established a community that would thrive for generations; their survival resulted from factors that included the region's remote geography and its prolonged indigenous resistance to Spanish rule.

The Spanish named Esmeraldas for the precious green stones that they gained in trade during early encounters with the region's indigenous inhabitants. The dense forests and mangroves that covered the landscape added much to the region's mystery. Although the Bay of San Mateo became popular with ships plying the waters between Panama and Guayaquil (see Maps 1, 6, and 7), the area was of only marginal interest to Peru's viceroy and the Spanish Crown. In the highland city of Quito, however, merchants and Spanish authorities coveted Esmeraldas for its proximity and its potential as a port.

As John Leddy Phelan (5) notes, during the second half of the sixteenth century, Quiteños came to see securing Esmeraldas and San Mateo as critical to increasing trade with their neighboring colonies: Peru and Panama. After 1563 and the establishment of the Crown Court (the *Real Audiencia*) in Quito, creating a port in Esmeraldas became a priority of local government. In 1577 they sent an official mission to offer the rebel Alonso de Illescas authority over the region, in exchange for which he was to resettle his people near San Mateo. On the evening that the *Maroons* were to arrive, warfare broke out in Esmeraldas and the project was abandoned. Though a failure, the mission opened what would be a sporadic line of communication between authorities and the *Maroons* for decades to come.

By 1586 when Illescas wrote to crown authorities in Quito and Madrid, European pathogens and Spanish raids had destroyed much of Esmeraldas' precontact population (Newson, 68). However, the Spanish did not bring enslaved Africans in great numbers to replace the dwindling native population of Quito's coastal regions. During the sixteenth century, the small number of Africans taken to Quito, like those who traveled to Peru with the conquistadors, became servants.

After the conquest, Africans were employed and exploited in many urban occupations, such as bakers, ironsmiths, textile producers, marketplace peddlers, prostitutes, and muleteers. By the seventeenth century, as colonization expanded, Africans formed an important labor source for mining and sugar plantations (Bryant, 86; Lane, chapter 2). In addition, a population of free people of color came into existence, often competing for resources with native peoples and Spanish commoners. As a fringe territory, however, Esmeraldas remained less integrated into the patterns developing in and around highland cities like Quito, Ibarra, and Cuenca.

It was within this geographical and historical context that Alonso de Illescas and his companions rejected their status as slaves, risking their lives under dangerous circumstances to make Esmeraldas their new homeland. As rebels, they would learn to live side by side (and at times in conflictive relationships) with native societies. Some indigenous groups allied themselves with the *Maroons*, whereas others (like the

Campaces mentioned in Illescas' letter) remained the *Maroons'* bitter enemies. Two *Maroon* communities emerged in Esmeraldas and continually faced these competitive conditions. Each in turn gave birth to a first generation of mixed-race progeny, called *mulattoes* (and later *zambos*) by Spanish observers and authorities. By the 1590s, the children of these intermarriages were old enough to assume command of their communities.

Don Alonso de Illescas' Letter of Negotiation (1586)

The letter of Alonso de Illescas is an unusual document, primarily because it was produced by an unlikely author: an African slave with little formal education. The person most responsible for penning the missive was probably a young Trinitarian friar named Alonso de Espinosa, sent to aid in the colonization of the *Maroons* in 1583. At the time, Espinosa was supposed to serve on the military expedition of conquistador Diego López de Zúñiga. However, soon after arriving in the lowlands, the young friar became a vocal advocate for the *Maroons*. He roundly condemned López de Zúñiga's conquest and denounced the excesses of his soldiers, their greed, and their desire to find gold (Beatty-Medina, "Caught,"123–24).

Although Espinosa may have been the one to put pen to paper, much of the letter's content reflects the experience and knowledge gained by Illescas from years steeped in Hispanic culture. Unlike the Africans captured and brought directly from their homelands, called *bozales*, Illescas was repeatedly described as *muy ladino*; that is, he was well-versed in Spanish language, customs, and culture. He was raised on the Island of Tenerife, a Spanish possession since the 1400s, and later was taken to Seville, Spain's jumping-off point for the conquest and colonization of the Indies. His owners were members of Seville's merchant elite, and Spain trained Illescas in the Hispanic way of life (Cabello Balboa, 43). In his early twenties, he was uprooted once more, this time to travel to the Spanish Indies.

The time that Illescas spent in slavery influenced his actions as a *Maroon* leader. In captivity, he was a personal servant. Like many of the Africans who operated as agents for their Spanish masters, Illescas—would have experienced "considerable responsibility and relative freedom of movement" (Restall, "Black Conquistadors," 175). Illescas' letter reflects his years of exposure to the workings of Spanish authority. Rather than emitting raw defiance, the letter demonstrates a keen awareness of what was important to Spanish authorities and to the Crown. Instead of refusing to submit, Illescas supplicates the Crown and denounces its proposed conquest of Esmeraldas, calling it a disservice to the moral interests of Spain and the Catholic Faith.

Importantly, the letter was not a solitary interaction. It may be considered one piece of an ongoing dialogue between authorities in Quito and the *Maroon* leaders. That conversation began nine years earlier, in 1577, when the *Audiencia* offered Illescas the governorship of Esmeraldas in exchange for resettling his community near the Bay of San Mateo (Beatty-Medina, "Rebels," chapter 2). The failure of that project promoted Spanish attempts to have López de Zúñiga subjugate the *Maroons* militarily in 1583. By 1585, a wealthy merchant named Rodrigo de Ribadeneyra received full rights from the Crown to establish settlements in Esmeraldas. In response, Illescas petitioned the king to rescind Ribadeneyra's grant and allow the *Maroons* to pacify Esmeraldas' native inhabitants.

There are numerous ways in which this petition attempts to influence the court's policies, and Friar Espinosa may have proposed much of the rhetorical phrasing. First, there is a clear emphasis on religion and God—matters not taken lightly by the Spanish Crown as the defender of the Roman Catholic Church throughout Europe and the Americas. Second, Illescas carefully couches his defiance in the language of service. He states that the Crown's plan will only bring chaos, whereas his own solution will save souls. Finally, he presents his actions as being in the royal interest, when in fact they were more important to the *Maroons'* autonomy and independence.

Illescas' letter was a final attempt to stave off Ribadeneyra's and other Spanish attempts to colonize the region. But with Ribadeneyra's reputation, wealth, and connections at court working against them, the letter was received in Quito as little more than a bothersome attempt by Espinosa to manage events that Quito's *Audiencia* saw as within its purview. Upon receiving it, the *Audiencia* trumped up charges of murder against Espinosa and placed him in chains to be sent off to Spain. Ribadeneyra never gained the alliance of the *Maroons*, and his settlers failed to establish themselves in Esmeraldas: without the aid of the African rebels, neither could achieve their ends in Esmeraldas.

Fourteen years later, in 1600, the *Audiencia*, under new leadership, recognized the *Maroons'* dominance in the region, granted them their freedoms and liberties, and began a process of pacifying all of Esmeraldas' native societies (Lane, 48). Illescas did not survive long enough to witness this victory of *Maroon* diplomacy, but his sons and daughters lived to receive their legally recognized freedom from slavery.

*****

Letter from Don Alonso de Illescas, a Black Man in Esmeraldas [1586][2]

Most powerful sir,

Having the devout Fray Alonso de Espinosa of the Holy Order of Trinitarians, by me and on my behalf, in a letter that he carried from me to your *Real Audiencia*, requested that I desire to submit to God Our Father and to Your Royal Crown and that on your part I be sent a general pardon and remission, because I have not been in your service,[3] and that you send a priest to preach to us the Holy Gospel and teach our women and children. I will do everything in my power and I will try to pacify all the natives of this province.

And Your Highness having conceded what I have requested and entreated, I give thanks to God Our Father for the many mercies I have received from His most liberal hands and from Your Lordship.

And so Father Espinosa brought me news that Your Royal Highness in Spain has granted the government of this land to Rodrigo de Ribadeneyra, who will bring many people to pacify and populate this land. And so I ordered that we should all gather to discuss and communicate [to His Royal Highness] what will best serve your royal interest.

And if Your Royal Highness granted Rodrigo de Ribadeneyra this government, it was before, without our report expressing our desire and willingness to join in union with the Church and Your Royal Crown.

And so what can be conquered with the indoctrination of the Holy Gospel would only be of disservice to God and Your Majesty to conquer by force of arms and at the cost of many souls on the one hand, and on the other in order to dominate the Campaces and have them recognize and know of my God.

Therefore, because I have not been in your service, I will encourage the people under my command, and receiving your license to enter the territory of the Campaces and require them to surrender peacefully to your service. And I will settle them near the sea in the best place possible. And in time I will ask your *Real Audiencia* for aid in order to form two towns in another province for Your Royal Crown that will be in the service of Our Lord.

Thus I beseech and supplicate Your Highness: do not form another government of the areas I offer to settle. Likewise, I ask Your Highness to suspend the expedition of soldiers; it will only bring chaos to the peace the devoted father [Espinosa] has brought with the Holy Gospel.

If you must allow a [Spanish] settlement, let it be in the Valle Vicioso and Barbacoas,[4] as I am truly afraid because your captains have always broken their promises given in Your Majesty's name. The devoted father has gained our confidence, and we know it is from his heart that he comes to bring us into union with the Church and Your Royal Crown.

---

2. Ministerio de Cultura, Archivo General de Indias, Sevilla, Sección Escribanía 922b, fols. 192v–93v.

3. Here, Illescas refers to his recent illegitimate status as a *Maroon*, when he was not acting as an obedient subject of the Crown.

4. The Valle Vicioso and region of Barbacoas were both located to the north of Esmeraldas in modern-day Colombia. For more on the history of Spanish conquest in these regions, see Calero.

To prove and make credible what is contained herein, I am sending Juan Manga-cho with the said father [Espinosa] to the *Real Audiencia* [in Quito] to kiss the feet of Your Highness. And with the same trust as a most Christian king in all things, Your Highness will give us mercies, and [we desire] that Our Lord provide Your Highness with long life and the growth of many kingdoms and lands.

From the Province of Esmeraldas, the twenty-fourth of February [15]86, most powerful Lord, your humble vassal, Don Alonso de Illescas, kisses the feet of Your Highness.

And the letterhead of this letter says, "To the most powerful Lord, King Don Felipe, our Lord and his royal agreement in the *Real Audiencia* of Quito."

3

Queen Njinga Mbandi Ana de Sousa of Ndongo/Matamba: African Leadership, Diplomacy, and Ideology, 1620s–1650s[1]

Linda Heywood

Document translation by Luis Madureira

Portuguese *Angola* and Queen Njinga's Leadership in the Seventeenth Century

Queen Njinga of Ndongo/Matamba (1582–1663) lived during a tumultuous period in the history of Central Africa. Njinga's birth in 1582 occurred just two years after the unification of Spain and Portugal (1580–1640) and a mere seven years (1575) after the Portuguese had planted their first colony on the coast of modern-day Angola. Between 1575 and Njinga's death in 1663 the Portuguese made relentless attacks against the Kingdom of Ndongo and neighboring Central African kingdoms and had conquered large sections of Ndongo.[2]

Ndongo was a kingdom that measured about forty thousand square kilometers. Its population of about one hundred thousand people lived under local rulers called *sobas*. These *sobas* owed allegiance to the king who lived in the capital city of Kabasa. In their wars against Ndongo, the Portuguese had as allies *Imbangala* (*Jaga*) guerrillas, widely feared among non-*Imbangala* Central Africans because of their cannibalism, their disregard for settled life, their wanton destruction of settled communities, and their propensity for capturing and forcibly integrating young children into the *Imbangala* bands through horrific initiation rituals.

Njinga first came into direct contact with the Portuguese in 1622 when she traveled to Luanda, the capital of the Portuguese kingdom of Angola, to negotiate a peace treaty on behalf of her brother Ngola Mbandi, who was king of Ndongo. Njinga remained several months in Luanda, during which time she agreed to be baptized and received the baptismal name of Ana de Sousa. Before her baptism, Njinga followed the practices connected with Kimbundu religious beliefs, which included rituals connected to the ancestors (past kings) as well as others dealing with the seasons.

In Luanda, Njinga also succeeded in negotiating a treaty with the Portuguese. The treaty did not last long. With the death of Ngola Mbandi in 1624 and her election as queen by a faction of the eligible electors from Ngola's court, Njinga's rivals refused to regard her as the legitimate ruler of Ndongo, and they joined with the Portuguese in

---

1. See Map 2.
2. For an in-depth treatment of this period, see Heywood and Thornton (chapter 3).

an attempt to remove her from the throne. Njinga's efforts to be accepted as queen of Ndongo developed into a thirty-year struggle against the Portuguese and her Ndongo rivals. Like the Portuguese, Njinga sought *Imbangala* alliance and eventually became head of a band. Between 1626 and 1655, Njinga personally commanded her army in many of the wars that the Ndongos fought against the Portuguese.

Moreover, Njinga's life included the period when an armada sent by the Dutch West India Company attacked and conquered Luanda (1641) and thus brought the wars of the Protestant Revolution into Central Africa. Indeed, during the Dutch occupation (1641–1648), Njinga joined in an Afro-Dutch alliance that also included the neighboring Kingdom of Kongo and set up a siege of all the Portuguese forts in Angola. This action almost brought Portuguese rule in the region to an end.

The tide turned against Njinga and her Kongo and Dutch allies when an armada sent from Brazil under Salvador de Sá in 1648 rescued the embattled Portuguese, who had been pinned down at their fort in Massangano, some 160 kilometers from Luanda. Instead of continuing the alliance, the Dutch quickly capitulated, and Njinga retreated to Matamba, a state she had conquered in the early 1630s. Njinga continued her resistance against the Portuguese and their Ndongo allies until 1654.

In 1654, Njinga decided to give up the military life that had consumed so much of her time and turned again to diplomacy. Using *Capuchin* missionaries who arrived in her court as part of the negotiations to end the war between her and the Portuguese, she began a rapprochement with her former enemies and even wrote directly to the Vatican.

Between 1655 and 1663, Njinga signed a peace treaty with the Portuguese, welcomed the return of her sister Dona Barbara (Funji Mbandi) from Portuguese captivity, reconciled with the Church by giving up her many male consorts and marrying one according to Catholic rites, and built a chapel in Matamba. Moreover, Njinga set an example for the rest of the population who had followed her through her years of resistance: they, too, gave up their *Imbangala* ways, married according to Catholic rites, and began rearing children instead of following the *Imbangala* policy, which prohibited the birth of children in the camps.

The most important consequence of the Portuguese (and Dutch) presence in Central Africa during Njinga's lifetime was the expansion of the slave trade. Angola became a major center for slaves imported into the Spanish and Portuguese colonies in the Americas. In fact, during the period 1580–1640 when Portugal held the *Asiento*, the wars that the governors of Angola carried out against Ndongo were actually slave-raiding forays. Central Africa often annually accounted for more than 80 percent (and for some years 100 percent) of all the slaves transported to the plantations, mines, fisheries, and urban centers of Ibero-America.

Many of the slaves were also war refugees captured as Njinga and her supporters fled Portuguese advances. Others were purchased in the network of slave markets that developed throughout the region. Moreover, Njinga also engaged in slave trading, and some of the Africans exported through Luanda came from the regular slave trading that had developed between African rulers like Queen Njinga and the Europeans.

Njinga's Letters of Diplomacy

Njinga's letters are relevant to the history of Afro-Latin populations in Ibero-America, because the majority of the enslaved Africans whom the Portuguese (and Dutch) exported between the 1620s and 1663 came from Angola, Ndongo, and Kongo and went to Spanish America and Brazil. Many of these Central Africans came from communities that had long been integrated into the *Creole* culture, including the mixed Portuguese-Kimbundu vocabulary, and religious, dietary, and other cultural practices that had developed in Portuguese Angola.

In fact, some of the slaves would have been familiar with the Portuguese language, would have been baptized as a result of the religious activities of parish priests and missionaries of regular orders such as the *Capuchin* and Jesuits, and may even have adapted other elements of the *Creole* culture such as dress, food, and music. Notably, some of the African leaders in the *Maroon* communities in both Palmares in Brazil and Limón in Colombia conducted wars of resistance against the Portuguese, Dutch, and Spanish that resembled Njinga's wars against the Portuguese in Angola.

Njinga was the head of an independent African kingdom with its own army and the ability to engage in diplomacy, wage wars, or do business with Europeans. The states she ruled—Ndongo and later Matamba—had subjects loyal to her but also contained various groups of dependents, some of whom were slaves. Njinga was an independent monarch fighting to uphold her right to be the queen of Ndongo. Most of the peoples of African descent in the Ibero-Atlantic world never found ways to sustain years of wars against Europeans or live in autonomous communities.

In order to interpret Njinga's engagement with European writing as an instrument of negotiation, one needs familiarity with the history of European literacy in Central Africa. Exposure to Catholic Christianity and Portuguese customs made rulers like Njinga more familiar with European forms of governance and lifestyle than their counterparts in other areas of Atlantic Africa, whose states supplied slaves to the Portuguese or with whom they conducted diplomatic relations. The earliest European-style school for Kongos was established in 1491 by a literate member of the Kongo elite who had returned to the kingdom with the first Portuguese cultural mission.

From 1491 onward, the Kongo elite had access to European-style education. In 1625, for example, Jesuits in the capital of Kongo, São Salvador, had established a college for children of the Kongo nobility. Literate Kongos went as ambassadors to Portugal, the Vatican, the Portuguese in the Kingdom of Angola, and Njinga's court. Furthermore, some Kimbundus who had been integrated into Portuguese Angola were also educated by Jesuit missionaries in Luanda, and many joined Njinga's cause.

Njinga herself was not literate in Portuguese; in 1656, when she signed the peace treaty with the Portuguese, she placed her mark on the document. Nevertheless, she had Kimbundus and Kongos in her court who were. Njinga most likely dictated the 1626 letter to one of these individuals, although she might have dictated the letters of 1651, 1655, and 1660 to her secretary "Dom João" who she mentioned in a letter of 1657 (Njinga of Ndongo, Letter to Serafino, 131–32).

Starting in 1648, Njinga had a literate Kongo-born priest, Don Calisto Zelotes dos Reis Magros, who served as her confessor and secretary. Njinga had captured the priest in a war she made against the Kongo region of Wandu in 1648. When the *Capuchin* missionary Gaeta arrived in her court in 1656, Zelotes dos Reis Magros was turned over to the priest to serve as his translator. Zelotes informed Gaeta that he had been "a slave of the queen for many years" (Napoli, fol. 252).

The use of some Kimbundu terms (*muenho*, for example) suggests that the writers of the letters were Kimbundu or were familiar with Kimbundu, the language of Ndongo. The letters that Njinga wrote represented just one aspect of the strategies she adopted to deal with the Portuguese, because she also sent numerous emissaries to the Portuguese governors and other officials. These emissaries were famous for their skill in transmitting long complex messages from Njinga in the oral prose that the people valued and that astounded the Portuguese who heard them.

Njinga dictated a wide range of letters and sent them to various Portuguese governors and officials in Angola, *Capuchin* missionaries, Propaganda Fide (the Vatican agency responsible for overseas missionary work), and even the Pope. The letters that Njinga wrote in 1654 represent the period when she decided to pay less attention to the military life that had consumed so much of her time and to concentrate instead on diplomacy. Njinga's diplomatic skill and deep distrust of the Portuguese was based on more than thirty years of negotiating and having the Portuguese break the terms of the treaties they had signed. Her skill and skepticism are clear in her 1655 letter.

Although Njinga had agreed to make peace, she retained her voice as an independent African ruler, as is evident in her attempts to obtain the release of her sister Dona Barbara from the Portuguese. Despite several years of negotiations and large numbers of slaves sent as presents, the Portuguese continued to hold Njinga's sister prisoner. At the same time, the governor requested that Njinga turn over the *Jaga* Cabuco (an *Imbangala* leader), as the Portuguese wished to eliminate the *Jaga* influence in the region. Njinga insisted she would release Cabuco only after her sister arrived in her court.

These letters as well as others in the corpus that she wrote vividly illustrate Njinga's belief that she was fighting for a just cause and her skill at combining war, diplomacy, and religion to achieve her aims. Njinga employs the conventions of European diplomacy in her greetings to the various Portuguese governors and religions officials, but the African oral tradition stands out when she refers to her history of contact with the Portuguese, as she does in her long letter of 1655.

Perhaps the most intriguing aspect of these letters is that they also touch on Njinga's gender. In her letter of 1625, when she was forty-three years old, Njinga asked the governor to send her several items of personal adornment. Missionaries who knew Njinga personally all noted that she paid a lot of attention to her appearance. The way Njinga used her gender to achieve her goals is another intriguing dimension of this phenomenal African leader.

*****

[Letter from Queen Njinga of Ndongo to Bento Banha Cardoso, March 3, 1626][3]

It gladdens my soul that Your Honor has come to the Fortress of Ambaca[4] so that I may recount to you, as to my own father, how a war party led by Aires[5] attacked the men I sent [to escort] some slaves to the market of Bumba a Kissanzo and stole about thirty slaves from me. When I dispatched a party to seek redress, as I would against any vassal of mine, it happened that my army encountered about nine of the men who were stationed inland with Tigre.[6] Having decided to face my army outside the [Pungo Andongo] fortress, these nine men, by God's will, were defeated by my men, six of whom were brought to me alive. It caused me great grief that at Aires' fortress there were Portuguese forces that I have received with great kindness because they are vassals of the king of Spain,[7] to whom I recognize obeisance as a Christian. On Saturday, one of my *muenho* servants arrived here and told me that in Ambaca a large force had gathered, waiting for Your Honor to move against me to free the Portuguese held in captivity. Nothing is accomplished by force and to do so would bring both me and them harm because everything can be done peacefully and without force. And if some of the lords who have settled here have incurred heavy debts and have put it in the minds of Your Honor and the governor that you should wage war in order to get out of debt, they are welcome to do so, but I do not want to make war with the captain. No one else presents himself at this time. Our Lord, etc. On this, the third day of March in the year 1625.[8]

I ask that Your Honor send me a hammock, and four ells of red wool for a cover, a horse blanket, and good wine, and an *arroba*[9] of wax for candles, and half a dozen lengths of muslin, and two or three lace tablecloths, and some purple, wine-colored, and blue garnets, and a large broad-brim hat made of blue velvet, or the one Your Honor wears, and four measures of paper.

Ana Queen of the Ndongo

[Letter from Queen Ana Njinga to the Propaganda Fide (the Sacred Congregation for the Propagation of the Faith), August 15, 1651][10]

The holy zeal Your Eminences have shown concerning the salvation of my soul and that of my people, by sending us the *capuchin* friar Father Antonio Romano to preach

---

3. Heintze, *Fontes para a história de Angola do século XVII*, vol. 1, 244–45. Cardoso was military commander under Governor Fernão de Sousa (1624–1630) during the latter's campaign against Queen Njinga.

4. *Ambaca* was an Mbundu trading center located near the western edge of *Angola*'s eastern plateau region.

5. Hari a Kiluanji, or Aquiloange Aire, ruler imposed on Ndongo by the Portuguese after the death of Ngola Mbandi (Heywood and Thornton, 129).

6. Estêvão de Seixas Tigre, captain of forces sent by the Portuguese to reinforce Hari a Kiluanje against Njinga.

7. At this time, Portugal was under Spanish rule.

8. Should be 1626.

9. A measure of weight equivalent to about thirty-three pounds.

10. Brásio, *Monumenta missionaria africana. África Ocidental (1651–1655)*, 1971, XI:70–71.The

to us the Holy Gospel of Our Lord Jesus Christ, the one true God, has so filled me with good fortune that I must render my thanks to you. I confess I am very obliged to Your Lordships for this kindness, for now we have knowledge of the one true God that we did not have before. For this reason we had remained deceived by our idolatrous beliefs, possessed by the devil. God's compassion toward us is great, even though we are undeserving of his divine mercy on account of our grave sins. Nevertheless, mercy is what He is offering us through the arrival of the *capuchin* father, and now I live with my body and soul at peace. May Our Lord Jesus Christ be served by allowing us to reciprocate the benevolence you confer upon us, so that we may not deserve greater punishment for our sins. If Your Lordships send us other *capuchin* friars, we will welcome them with open arms, for there are many people in our kingdom ready to receive the Holy Baptism. May God grant Your [Eminences] many years of life for the good of our souls.

From our Kingdom of Matamba on the fifteenth of August 1651.

Ana

Queen Ana Njinga

[Letter from Queen Ana Njinga to the Governor General of *Angola*, December 13, 1655][11]

My Lord,

I received Your Lordship's letter, which was brought to me by Your Lordship's envoy Captain Manuel Frois Peixoto, where I read that Your Lordship is enjoying good health, which I hope Our Lord will increase for many long years, along with as much peace and tranquility as I desire for myself. I possess the health to serve Your Lordship in the name of His Majesty, may God preserve him, with all due authority. You stated your purposes with so much merit that I saw directly that you speak the truth in all you say. For I have many complaints about past governors, who always promised to return my sister to me. [To secure her return,] I have given an infinite number of slaves and created thousands of *banzos*, but they never returned her to me. Rather, they waged war against my person and harried me, and constantly forced me to live like a *Jaga* and resort to tyrannical edicts, such as prohibiting the raising of children and other ceremonies because this is what life in a *quilombo* entails. I give Your Lordship my royal word that I will give up these warlike [practices], as long as I have clergymen among us who will provide me and my grandees with good examples and teach them to live in the Holy Catholic Faith. I am therefore hoping Your Lordship will grant me the favor of sending forth Friar Serafim[12] and Friar João from the Carmelite Order, whom I wish to see because he belongs to a religious order and also because I am told that he is a good preacher and knows the language of Ndongo.

Propaganda Fide was the Vatican congregation responsible for missionary work. In 1982, Pope John Paul II changed its name to the Congregation for the Evangelization of the Peoples. Its basic mission has remained unchanged.

11. Brásio, *Monumenta missionaria africana. África Ocidental (1651–1655)*, 1971, XI:524–28. The letter is addressed to Governor Luís Mendes de Sousa Chicorro.

12. Frei Serafim de Cortona, Italian *Capuchin* missionary.

Your Lordship would do me a great favor to send my sister back to me along with these two clergymen, for with them she would come in good and accredited company. And if it please Your Lordship to allow someone else to come, let it be a soldier with knowledge in fireworks so I can celebrate my sister's arrival with them, God willing. A soldier can also come who may serve as sacristan to the reverend fathers. As soon as I get news that my sister has arrived in Ambaca, I will dispatch Captain Manuel Frois Peixoto from my court to get her. This task falls to him, since he made the effort of appeasing my grandees, who are quite suspicious of past treacheries. Your Lordship ought not to suppose that Captain Manuel Frois Peixoto is undeserving of high praise, for he succeeded in convincing them and me that this delegation was in good faith and not like the previous ones I mentioned. The one against whom I have the most grievances is Governor Salvador Correia [de Sá],[13] to whom I gave the slaves Your Lordship knows about and made two hundred *banzos* to get him to send someone like Commander Rui Pegado,[14] who arrived as an envoy of His Majesty, may God protect him, and assured me that my sister would be brought back to me and that there would be complete peace. I decided I could not break my royal word [and accepted his assurances]. Because of this and other treacheries, I roam the forests, far from my own lands, with no one to inform His Majesty, may God protect him, of my unease, when to be at peace with the said commander and His Majesty's governors is what I most desire. Yet all His Majesty's past [agents and governors] acted out of personal gain and not in the king's service, as I have been informed His Majesty bids them do, for this kingdom is of the utmost importance to his royal privilege. It would be worth even more if I were allowed to live in peace and quiet, bringing my markets closer [to the coast], so the *pombeiros* need not go through so much trouble to bring their wares so far, and I could enjoy them at a cheaper price. Finally, I trust with God that Your Lordship will be in His Majesty's good graces only if you leave me in peace and tranquility and conquer Quissama,[15] a thing that no governor has earned the glory of accomplishing.

I offer Your Lordship my assistance in the conquest of Quissama. If it refuses to pay obeisance to you, and if it pleases Your Lordship, I will dispatch one of my grandees with as large a force as can be mustered. This I will do as a sign of obeisance to His Majesty, may God protect him. I also give my word that as soon as the reverend fathers arrive with my sister, I will immediately endeavor to allow women to give birth to and raise their children, which I have not permitted until now because we have been living in the countryside, in *quilombos*. This would not happen if we had a firm and lasting peace. It would take only a few years for my lands to be repopulated as they once were, for up to now I have taken as servants only people from other provinces and nations that I have conquered, and they have obeyed me as if I were their native queen, some out of love and others out of fear.

---

13. He was the military officer who was sent from Brazil at the head of the Portuguese forces that recaptured Angola from the Dutch in 1648 and served as governor of Angola until 1651.

14. Rui Pegado was an ambassador sent by the Portuguese to Njinga.

15. Quissama (or Kissama) was the name of a region on the southern bank of the Cuanza (or Kwanza) River inhabited by various small independent states that were the traditional enemies of the Bakongo and the Ndongo. At the time the letter was written, some of these states had joined Njinga's coalition.

Your Lordship could not send me an envoy that would please me more than Captain Manuel Frois Peixoto, for he would well know how to convey everything to me in the language of this kingdom of mine [Kimbundu]. All my grandees are so happy that they say only he speaks the truth and reports everything that Your Lordship orders him to and in accordance with your instructions. I already consider myself in possession of the gift of peace and serenity that I desire for these few days I [have left] to live, for I am an old woman. I wish to bequeath my lands only to my sister, not to my slaves. Otherwise, great ruin will befall it, for they will not know how to obey His Majesty (may God protect him) and my sister, who has dwelled for so many years among the whites and is such a good Christian as they tell me. Your Lordship should not lend credence to what the settlers say; they have always tried to turn past governors into my enemies. As a relative of my godfather João Correia de Sousa,[16] who is in God's glory, [I know] Your Lordship will do me the kindness of attaining this peace, [and confirm it] in a letter signed by His Majesty's hand as greater assurance to me and my grandees, so they may rest at ease and turn to sowing their fields, as they once did.

Captain Manuel Frois Peixoto requested on His Majesty's behalf that I [hand over to him] the *Jaga* Cabuco.[17] [He asked me] with such fine manners that I could not refuse him, even though I have had many grievances against Cabuco for having devastated my lands. The satisfaction of so many losses as he caused me should be good enough reason for him to remain in my service a few years longer. Nevertheless, so great is my desire to see my sister again that as soon as Captain Manuel Frois Peixoto arrives in my court, I will give the said *Jaga* permission to leave with him and place himself at his orders. Of this Your Lordship can be certain, as well as of the aid I promised to give you in [subduing] Quissama, should Your Honor need it. This I will do and everything else you may instruct me to do. My friends' friends are my friends, and my enemies' enemies my own enemies.

With respect to the two hundred slaves Your Lordship requests as ransom for my sister Dona Barbara, that is a very exacting price, particularly since I have already given the slaves Your Honor must know of to past governors and envoys, to say nothing of my gifts to secretaries and servants from your noble house and to many settlers whose treachery I still endure to this day. What I am so bold as to offer Your Honor is one hundred and thirty slaves, a hundred of whom I will send as soon as my sister reaches Ambaca. I will keep your envoy hostage until I can see with my own eyes my sister arriving in my court to make sure that I will not be wrongly used again as I have been by past governors. Your Lordship should not regard it as strange that I want to take these precautions. Even though I understand that this delegation is a very honest one, I will avoid further grief, for, because they remember the deceits of the past, my grandees remain suspicious.

May Your Lordship forgive so long a letter as this, but it needed to be thus. The offering Your Lordship sent me, and for which I render you my thanks, was delivered to me by your envoy. I appreciated the mother-of-pearl goblet very much. Do not

---

16. The governor of Portuguese Angola in 1622 when Njinga was baptized.

17. *Imbangala* leader (see chapter introduction).

be weary of me, Your Lordship, but I want for nothing in my court. What I miss the most is my sister. Once she returns to me, Your Lordship will see that I will serve Your Lordship much to your liking. The bearer of this letter will relay to you by post what I have agreed upon with your envoy. Because he leaves in haste, he takes no more than twelve slaves. [Accept them as] my offering to mollify Your Lordship.

My Court at Matamba, on the thirteenth of December of the year 1655.

Queen Dona Ana de Sousa

[Letter from Queen Njinga to António de Oliveira de Cadornega, June 15, 1660][18]

Your Honor,

The letter Your Honor wrote me concerning your runaway slaves, claiming that my people abduct and sell them, must be based on charges made by those who wish me ill for being a Christian who lives in peace. Your Honor can make inquiries with all the *pombeiros* who work for the whites and travel to my court to trade their masters' wares. Your Honor ought to know that your black servants are such bold-faced [thieves] that when we sell slaves with them, we take caution to keep our slaves under close guard and in chains. Because they are such villains, the aforementioned [black servants] get their freed slaves to do their [dirty] work for them[19] and then inform Your Honor that many ladies who have resided for a long time at my *mbanza* have run away. It is all the more so with recent residents. Had these [courtiers] remained here, they would have been able to carry out official duties as the slave of the captain and of the Reverend Vigário [Vicar] did for so many years, and as the reverend fathers who bear the present letter will tell you. I will digress no more. May God keep you in power for many years, etc. The Court at Matamba, on this day, the fifteenth of June of the year 1660.

Queen D. Ana

---

18. Cadornega, *História geral das guerras angolanas. 1680*, 1972, 2:172–73. Cadornega was a Portuguese soldier and chronicler who participated in the wars against Njinga and wrote two volumes on the wars.
19. Though the passage is somewhat obscure, it appears to suggest that Portuguese agents and tradesmen were in the habit of abducting members of Njinga's royal court and selling them into slavery.

Afro-Iberian Subjects: Petitioning the Crown at Home, Serving the Crown Abroad, 1590s–1630s[1]

Leo J. Garofalo

History of Southern Iberia's Black Communities

Afro-Iberians made up a small, but well-integrated, segment of southern Castilian and Portuguese society. The men and women who traced their roots or part of their heritage to West and Central Africa settled or grew up in a European world oriented toward artisanal work, local and transatlantic commerce, and seafaring. Many people of African descent who arrived in the early Americas began their transatlantic journey from the black communities of Spain and Portugal, and not from the African continent. And not all of the people who became Afro-Latin Americans crossed the Atlantic Ocean as slaves. In fact, free Afro-Iberian individuals and families, such as the ones highlighted in this chapter, became part of a rapidly changing region within Europe and part of the European expansion abroad.

An examination of the records that constituted the Spanish Crown's attempt to regulate the flow of people to the Americas reveals hundreds of petitions to officials in Seville from, or on behalf of, people of African heritage living in southern Spain and Portugal. These Afro-Iberian petitioners were members of local communities, and some of their families had lived in Europe for generations by 1600. Others were newer arrivals to the Iberian Peninsula from Africa or the Americas or were the children of recent arrivals. In general, they were Christian, spoke European languages, and considered themselves subjects of the Spanish or Portuguese monarchies.[2]

The three cases in this chapter demonstrate how Afro-Iberians could resist marginalization and serve to strengthen the imperial system as soldiers and sailors and as adherents to an ethnic and religious ideology valuing European identity and Catholicism over others. The documents represent the voices of Afro-Iberian women in the form of petitions and testimonies directed to royal authorities. In Spain, these women and others like them wrote to the Crown or appeared in royal courts to request permission to travel, reunite families, recover property or inheritances, prove their eligibility to sail or serve the Spanish Empire, return to homelands in the Americas or Europe, and defend their status as free from slavery.

The narratives in this chapter describe individuals from Andalusia's black population involved in the transatlantic movement of Iberians. They also mention Afro-Iberians' involvement in defending the Spanish empire from attack or religious

---

1. See Maps 1, 4, 6, and 7.

2. Employing the Iberian term in use in the fifteenth and sixteenth centuries, scholars label this process of Christianization and the use of European languages "ladinoization."

heresy. In each case, the women addressed the judges of Seville's royal court that oversaw all trade, travel, and transactions with the Americas.

In the first case, the Afro-Iberian wife of a soldier stationed in New Spain asks to be allowed to join him as a way to remedy economic hardship. The second case shows an Afro-Iberian woman attempting to collect wages owed to a male family member who died while serving the Crown. The third case documents the successful efforts of an Afro-Iberian woman to follow her grown daughter to the Americas in order to escape poverty in Iberia while emphasizing her status as a Spanish subject and her family's freedom from the "taint" of other religions or investigation by the Spanish Inquisition.

The selections provide a view of key ways black Europeans in southern Iberia explained their position in society and their rights as subjects and militant servants of the Crown and Church. Afro-Iberians played a part in creating this early Spanish Atlantic world of networks, new kinds of people, and new cultures.

By the sixteenth and seventeenth centuries, Africans and Afro-Iberians were not necessarily newcomers to Europe or the Americas (Franco Silva, 73–84). Europe's first sales of slaves or people captured or purchased from African intermediaries in West Africa took place at Lagos in southern Portugal. Lisbon and the southern Portuguese Algarve region became home to numerous people of mixed African and European heritage. Many of them worked in shipping and all aspects of Atlantic commerce; they even took part in slave trading operations or relocated to European enclaves in Africa.

Overland routes, and eventually direct shipments, brought Portuguese slave traders to Spain. Castilian merchants and shipowners also engaged in raiding and slaving operations in West Africa, but they were soon eclipsed by the Portuguese. The Spanish Crown preferred to sell the rights to monopolize the trade in human beings to Portuguese merchants, leaving the Spanish sea captains and sailors to enlist with the Portuguese expeditions (see Stella, 23–37). Even without the monopoly, first southern Spain and then, after 1520, the Spanish colonies in the Americas constituted the principal markets for slaves until 1600, when Brazil's sugar plantations dwarfed all other enterprises in its insatiable demand for laborers.

In southern Spain, enslaved West and Central Africans labored in every economic sector, ranging from domestic service and small crafts shops to agricultural work and transportation on boats and mules (González Díaz, 23). African men and women entered southern Iberian society in roughly equal numbers, and they acquired freedom primarily by buying their freedom from their owners, although a few were freed by owners or as a legal remedy for abuse.

As both free and enslaved individuals, they intermarried and integrated into parishes, religious life (especially religious brotherhoods), artisanal professions, and petty commerce. Not surprisingly, Afro-Iberians became a permanent part of southern Iberian life (Pike, 345–60) and played a role in the enterprise to conquer and colonize the Americas (see Restall, 44–63).

The Afro-Iberian soldiers and sailors who perished while serving the Crown on ships and in garrisons and ports commonly left behind family members in the home communities of southern Iberia. More often than not, these relatives were Afro-Iberian women who petitioned to recover the deceased person's property and uncollected wages and rations.

Petitioning on Behalf of Servants to the Crown and the Faith

Witnesses, authorities, and members of local communities considered the black soldiers and sailors moving back and forth across the Atlantic to be servants of the Crown who served a royal purpose.[3] Black women living in the sailing and trading communities of Andalusia understood the implications and benefits of this service. They dictated the petitions excerpted in this chapter.

Felipa de Santiago, an Afro-Iberian woman[4] and former slave, appeared in Seville's royal court in 1594 to present a petition requesting permission to travel to New Spain with her children to be reunited with her husband, a soldier stationed there. She bolstered her request with affidavits from the priests who married the couple and baptized each of their children in Seville's San Vicente Parish and from neighbors who attested to their life together as a legitimately married couple with children. She also included sworn statements sent by her husband's commanders that he was indeed a soldier and stationed in New Spain. A month later she secured a royal order that allowed her and her *mulatto* children to travel to New Spain and also warned officials not to impede their passage because they were free from the restrictions placed upon slaves' movement.

The familial bonds and benefits of royal service extended beyond spouses to encompass other relatives, as shown in the second case. Clara Rodríguez, a free *morena* never subjected to enslavement, lost her young nephew Cristóbal López, described as a free *mulatto*, while he was serving in the fleet that sailed for New Spain in 1634 commanded by General Martín de Vallesilla. As was the custom at the time, the Spanish legal document offered a physical description of the nineteen-year-old Cristóbal taken from the ship's crew list: he was strong of body with a scar under his beard. The document noted that his birthplace was Ayamonte and his father's name was Antonio. Another sailor from his hometown, higher ranking and not an Afro-Iberian, testified that he knew the family well and that Clara Rodríguez and Juana López, *de color negras* and free of slavery, were his full sisters and born of married parents.

After his mother's death, Cristóbal enlisted in the fleet as a *grumete*, the lowest rank of sailor and just above cabin boy or *paje*. He appeared for muster (roll call) seven times during the voyage and the port calls in the Caribbean before failing to appear in the muster taken in Veracruz on June 21, 1635.[5] The older sailor, aged thirty-four and from Cristóbal's hometown, explained how he crossed the Atlantic on the same royal ship with the young man and took him to the hospital in Mexico where he died. After her initial petition offered here and the first round of witnesses that she called, Clara Rodríguez signed a power of attorney, allowing another to press her suit and act in her name. The royal judges in Seville eventually ordered that she be paid the nephew's uncollected wages.

---

3. See Garofalo, "The Case of Diego Suárez."

4. In the documents, she referred to herself as of *color negra*. Witnesses also used this label or called her *de color prieta*. In every case, they carefully emphasized her free status, and some mentioned the letter giving her freedom from Doña Beatriz de León, who owned de Santiago before she was married.

5. He still remained missing at the muster on September 11, 1635.

Felipa de Santiago's case mentioned above illustrates how an impoverished condition together with respectable Christian conduct and royal service could persuade officials in the *Casa de Contratación* to emit a royal license allowing legal travel to the Americas.[6] Some petitioners who did not have sailors or soldiers in their immediate families made successful arguments for their eligibility to travel based solely on economic need and good Christian standing. In fact, they even claimed old Christian status free from past or present association with Islam or Judaism. In theory, law prohibited *new Christians* from traveling to the Americas. If proven in court, violations led to the confiscation of property, which was given as a reward to the prosecuting judges and those who detected violators. Therefore, it is perfectly understandable why some Iberians with sub-Saharan heritage claimed old Christian status and piety in court and used it to legitimize emigration to the Americas.[7]

One of these successful claimants was Francisca de Figueroa. The documents from her case include her relatively short, almost terse petitions as well as more extensive testimony by several people she brought before the court or notaries to explain who she and her daughters were and to defend her *limpieza de sangre*. She played an important and active role in shaping her image in court and in pushing her case forward before the Crown.

At no point did she employ an attorney, and she apparently never authorized another person to speak for her. During the first stage of her case in 1600, she obtained a royal decree that allowed her and her daughter to travel to the Americas. In 1601, she returned to Seville's royal court to definitively establish her legal right to join her daughter in Cartagena de Indias. During this second stage, the court copied the royal decree into the records of the *Casa de Contratación*, and the judges agreed to give her the licenses and permissions she sought.

In each of these cases, the goal has been to select the portion of the larger documents in which the Afro-Iberian petitioner speaks most directly. In the case of Francisca de Figueroa, she both dictated portions of the document herself and directed others she knew well to provide exactly the kind of testimony she knew the judges needed to hear in order to approve her travel. Therefore, in the Figueroa case, this chapter includes both her own words and a representative example of the witnesses she coached.

The three cases selected are quite short (totaling fourteen to sixteen pages each). The number of documents for each case remained small because third parties did not intervene and royal authorities quickly approved each petition. The excerpts include all or almost all the words attributed to each woman in the respective document. Not included are additional witnesses' statements and notes from the notaries on the progress of the cases and the final decisions (except in the Figueroa case). These Afro-Iberian women's petitions speak both to how they constructed an identity as subjects and how their lives intersected with the imperial efforts to secure and hold territory and enforce a strict religious conformity as an equally important strategic goal.

*****

---

6. Certainly many traveled without such licenses and without the added protection they offered against bureaucratic hassles, bribes, jail, or being forced into slavery.

7. See Garofalo, "The Shape of a Diaspora."

Inquiries Regarding Felipa de Santiago, *Negra*, 1594[8]

I, Pedro de Barahona, Our Lord the King's notary, who serves in the capacity of scribe in the *Casa de Contratación* of the Indies in Seville.... I certify that Felipa de Santiago, of black color, appeared in the said house on the twenty-fifth of May of the present year of 1594, before the president and royal judges.... She presented a petition with three sworn testimonials, whose content and that of the decree she provided and of a certain account that she gave is as follows.

I, Felipa de Santiago, swarthy black, resident householder in the city of Seville, the legitimately married wife of Pedro Hernández de Rivera, a gunner who at present is serving in that occupation in the forts of the Island of San Juan de Ulúa,[9] declare that the said Pedro Hernández and I are legitimately married husband and wife. We celebrated our marriage in this city in the Church of Saint Vincent, as appears in the sworn certification that I present. We have lived as husband and wife in the said city until about three years ago, when my husband went to the Indies. He resides [there] serving Your Majesty in the forts of the Island of San Juan de Ulúa as appears in this certificate that I present. In our marriage we have had three children: one girl and two boys. I am a free woman not subject to any captivity, nor are my children. My husband wrote to send for me to live with him. It is to my advantage to go because I am poor and he is in the service of Your Majesty, just as it appears in the letter and missives that I have in my possession, and I want to appeal to Your Majesty for a license to travel [to the Indies] in order to live with my husband and to take my children with me.[10]

Suit over the Property of Cristóbal López, *Grumete*, Native of Ayamonte and Deceased in Veracruz without a Will, 1637[11]

In the town of Ayamonte on the ninth day of January 1637, Clara Rodríguez, *morena* and a resident householder in town, appeared before the lord Francisco Galves de Castro, magistrate and justice of the peace in this said town and its marquisate, and before me, Juan de Caliz, one of the Lord King's notaries in this town, and she presented the following petition.

Clara Rodríguez, *morena* of color, a free person of this town, as aunt and heiress ab intestate[12] of the *mulatto* Cristóbal López Riquel, my nephew and son of Juana González, my deceased sister, a free *mulatta* as was the said Cristóbal López, my nephew, whose property and inheritance I claim. It is advisable that an inventory be

---

8. Archivo General de Indias, Contratación, 5248, N. 1, R. 1, *Información de Felipa de Santiago, negra*, 1594, fols. 1r–7v.

9. Veracruz, New Spain.

10. The notary then entered the letters from Mexico attesting to Pedro Hernández de Rivera's employment as a gunner and his request for her to sail in the next fleet to join him with their children and the letters from Seville's clergymen certifying the petitioner's married status and the dates of her children's baptisms.

11. Archivo General de Indias, Contratación, 963, N. 2, R. 11, Proceso sobre bienes de Cristóbal López grumete natural de Ayamonte y difunto en Veracruz, 1637, fols. 1r–8r.

12. Died without making a will.

taken as soon as possible. I state that it is fitting to my rights that it be proven and shown that my said nephew was serving as a *grumete* in the fleet that sailed to New Spain in the Indies last year and of which Martín de Vallesilla was admiral. He served in that post, traveling to the port of San Juan de Ulúa of the Indies, until he died in the said Indies. My nephew died young and unmarried and he left no children or parents or other heir or closer relative than I, and as such the wage he earned in the voyage and whatever other belongings he left behind upon his death belong to me.

I beg and beseech Your Mercy to order that the information I will give be received, and the witnesses that I present be examined regarding this petition. And that you order that I be given an authorized copy of his declarations in a public form and manner so that I can present it before whom it suits me, placing in it Your Mercy's authority and judicial decree. I ask for justice et cetera.

Clara Rodríguez

Proceedings of the Inquiry and License for Francisca de Figueroa, *Mulatta*, to Sail for Cartagena, 1600[13]

Francisca de Figueroa, June 1600

Francisca de Figueroa, *mulatta* in color, declare that I have in the city of Cartagena a daughter named Juana de Figueroa. And she has written to call for me in order to help me. I will take with me in my company a daughter of mine, her sister, named María, of the said color. And for this I must write to Our Lord the King to petition that he favor me with a license so that I and my daughter can go and reside in the city of Cartagena. For this I will give an account of what is put down in this report. And of how I, Francisca de Figueroa, am a woman of sound body and *mulatta* in color.... And my daughter María is twenty years old and of the said color and of medium size. Once again, I attest to this.

I beg Your Lordship to approve and order it done. I ask for justice in this.

On the twenty-first day of the month of June 1600, Your Majesty's lords presidents and official judges of this house [*Casa de Contratación*] order that the account she offers be received and that testimony for the purpose she requests be given.

[Francisca de Figueroa Presented as a Witness Francisca de Mendoza, Forty-Four Years Old]

In the city of Seville in the *Casa de Contratación* of the Indies, on the twenty-ninth day of the month of August 1600, the said Francisca de Figueroa, for the account she has offered and that she is ordered to give, presented as a witness Francisca de Mendoza, wife of Sebastián de Sayavedra, mounted courier in this kingdom, resident householder in Seville, in the neighborhood of Magdalena. She was sworn in....

Questioned about the petition presented by [Francisca de Figueroa]. She said that she knows Francisca de Figueroa and her daughter María and Juana de Figueroa, another daughter of hers, who she has heard is in the city of Cartagena in the Indies.

---

13. Archivo General de Indias, Contratación, 5261, N. 2, R. 33, Expediente de información y licencia de Francisca de Figueroa, mulata, a Cartagena, Seville, 1600, fols. 1r–2v.

She knows that she sent to call for Francisca de Figueroa, her mother, to remedy her need, which she and her daughter María suffer in these realms because of their poverty. [Francisca de Mendoza] knows this because she has seen letters from Juana de Figueroa in which she wrote to say that [her mother] should go, offering money for the cost of the trip. And that she will help her as she has said in [Cartagena], where Juana de Figueroa lives. And she knows that [Francisca de Figueroa] is a woman, *mulatta* in color, of sound body, and forty-four years old. [María] is about twenty years old, medium sized and of the said color. All of this is publicly known and spoken of among all the people who know them as does this witness.... She did not sign because she does not know how to write.[14]...

Francisca de Figueroa, *Mulatta*, Petition for Cartagena, Seville, 1601[15]

On January 23, 1601, [I], Francisca de Figueroa, *mulatta* in color, do state that Our Lord the King conferred on me the favor of a license to sail to the Province of Cartagena and because I am a native of this city [Seville].

Before Your Lordship, I beg and implore you to order that the account of the *limpieza*[16] of my person be received and that the accountancy of this *Casa* dispatch my license....

[Francisca de Figueroa Presented as a Witness Elvira de Medina, Fifty Years Old]

In Seville in the *Casa de Contratación* of the Indies on the nineteenth of January 1601, [Francisca de Figueroa] for the inquiry, presented as a witness a woman who said she was named Elvira de Medina, widow of Pedro García Benítez, ropemaker,[17] resident householder in this city of Seville in the neighborhood of Magdalena.... She said that she has known Francisca Figueroa, who is present as a witness, for more than thirty-six years to date. And she knew her father Pedro de Figueroa and María de León his wife, a swarthy black. She knows that they were husband and wife legitimately married according to the laws of the Holy Mother Church of Rome.... She saw them live as a married couple together in the same house. And she saw that during their marriage they procreated as their legitimate daughter Francisca de Figueroa. This witness knows that she and her parents and her grandparents have been and are Old Christians and of unsullied caste and lineage. They are not of Moorish or Jewish caste or of those recently converted to Our Holy Catholic Faith. They have not been prisoners or penanced by the Holy Office of the Inquisition. Nor do they have other blemishes or defects that prevent them from going to the Indies, because this witness knew her parents to be Christians. And she has knowledge of her grandparents on both her father's and her mother's side from hearing them spoken of by her elders....

---

14. Two additional witnesses provide essentially the same information.

15. Archivo General de Indias, Contratación, 5268, N. 2, R. 68, Expediente de información y licencia de Francisca de Figueroa, mulata, a Cartagena, Seville, 1601, fols. 1r–4v. Dossier of the report and license granted to Francisca de Figueroa, *mulatta*, to travel to Cartagena, presented in Seville, 1601.

16. *Limpieza de sangre*, "purity of blood."

17. *Cordonero*.

This witness knows that [Francisca de Figueroa] is a native of this city and was born in it. She is single and unmarried and not subject to any religious orders. . . . This is the truth according to the oath she has [made]. She did not sign because she said that she cannot write. She is fifty years old.[18] . . .

Copy of a Decree from His Majesty Presented by Francisca de Figueroa, 1601

The King

My presidents and official judges of the *Casa de Contratación* of Seville. I order you to allow passage to the Province of Cartagena for Francisca de Figueroa, resident householder of that city, *mulatta* in color, of sound body, forty-five years old, who will be in the company of a daughter of hers. She can take with her the daughter María, *mulatta* in color, of medium stature, and twenty years old. Presenting before you accounts given in her jurisdiction before those justices, and with the approval of the same justices, that [the two women] are not married nor do they belong to those [groups] that are prohibited to travel to those lands. Dated in the Prado on the twenty-seventh of November 1600, I, the King. . . . The copy was corrected and certified with His Majesty's decree. Dated the twenty-third of January 1601.

---

18. Two additional witnesses testified in a similar fashion.

Soldier, Slave, and Elder: *Maroon* Voices from the *Palenque* del Limón, 1634[1]

Kathryn Joy McKnight

Historical Background

Early in 1634, Francisco *Angola*, Sebastián *Anchico*, and Juan de la Mar testified about the recent violence in which their community of Limón had engaged. They were prisoners called before Don Francisco de Llano Velasco, lieutenant general of the city of Cartagena de Indias, on the northwestern coast of what is now Colombia. In the documents to follow, the name Cartagena refers variously to the province and its principal port city. Limón was a *palenque*, a clandestine settlement of people of African descent who had escaped slavery, also known as *cimarrones* or *Maroons*. Africans founded the hidden village around 1580 in the Sierra de María, near Cartagena, in the early days of the city's boom as a slave port. In 1634, their *criollo* descendants—those born in the New World—dominated the community's population and leadership.

Palenque soldiers had recently attacked surrounding ranches and carried off indigenous people and slaves. They stole livestock, burned buildings, killed Spaniards, and attacked and killed many of the residents of the indigenous town of Chambacú. On December 9, 1633, Spanish soldiers responded with an assault on the *palenque* and eventually captured eighty or more community members, whom they put on trial and punished.

Under interrogation, Limón residents told fascinating stories of *palenque* life and colonial society as the Spaniards sought information from them about the violence. After testifying, thirteen men were publicly executed, their bodies quartered and displayed to instill terror in the thousands of enslaved people of African descent in Cartagena. The remaining residents were sentenced to be sold by their owners into exile from the province. In these punishments, Cartagena officials acted out of fear that more enslaved people would escape to *palenques*, attack colonial properties, or, worse, rise up en masse against the Spaniards. Francisco *Angola*, Sebastián *Anchico*, and Juan de la Mar were among the nineteen residents whose testimony was recorded in these trials.[2] All three men were executed.

---

1. See Maps 6 and 9. I wish to thank the helpful staff at the Archivo General de Indias, the University of New Mexico for a research grant to travel to Seville and Jan Ankerson and Anne Benscoter for their careful reading and insightful suggestions on the presentation of these documents.
2. To read the published testimony of three women residents, see McKnight, "Gendered Declarations."

Maroon communities like Limón persisted throughout the Americas for as long as colonials enslaved people of African descent.[3] Their soldiers raided ranches, attacked mule trains loaded with precious metals bound for Spain, and aided pirates who raided the Caribbean coasts. Their settlements attracted others who wanted to escape slavery. Some *Maroon* leaders became legendary, including Bayano in Panama, Yanga in New Spain (Mexico), Domingo Biohó in Cartagena, Ganga Zumba and Zumbi in Palmares, Brazil, and Nanny in Jamaica.

Colonial governments negotiated treaties with *Maroons* in Brazil, Cartagena, Cuba, Hispaniola, Jamaica, New Spain, Ecuador, and Surinam, establishing free black towns in exchange for promises of the cessation of anti-Spanish violence (Price, 3).[4] The letter from Alonso de Illescas in Chapter 2 of this volume represents an overture for such a negotiation. At least eight *palenques* existed in the seventeenth century in the province of Cartagena alone (Borrego Plá, 7, 26). Peace negotiations were underway between Governor Francisco de Murga of Cartagena and the *Palenque* del Limón in the months before the Spanish attack. However, it was not until 1714 that the province of Cartagena established the first free black town of San Basilio, which still exists today, as do black towns founded by *Maroons* throughout Latin America.

Palenques—elsewhere known as *quilombos, mocambos, cumbes, ladeiras,* and *mambises* (Price, 1)—provided important spaces where African-descent people preserved and created new cultural and social practices that had their roots in Africa. Such processes were dynamic and historically specific and varied from one *Maroon* settlement to another.[5] A *palenque*'s demographics, the birthplaces of its members, and the historical events through which these residents had lived all molded the community's social relationships and cultural expressions. *Palenques* did not exist in isolation, and thus these processes were also affected by the community's engagement with their European and Amerindian neighbors, the politics of nearby urban centers, and their interactions with free and enslaved Afro-Latinos outside the *palenque*. All these factors can be glimpsed in the Limón testimonies.

For years, Limón residents coexisted peacefully and exchanged labor and goods with neighboring Spanish ranchers and their slaves. Community members give conflicting explanations for the turn to violence. Some blame new arrivals for instigating attacks on ranches as revenge against cruel overseers, but others see the violence as part of a more global plan for the *palenque*'s future. A group of new residents brought to power the *criolla* woman Leonor as *palenque* queen and stirred in her a new and violent vision of antagonism against Spaniards.

---

3. See Price for an overview of *Maroon* societies.

4. See Navarrete, Rodríguez, and Ruiz Rivera for overviews of peace settlements in the Americas.

5. In "Identifying Enslaved Africans," Paul Lovejoy presents a framework for studying the historically specific dynamics of cultural preservation and change in the African diaspora. In *Central Africans, Atlantic Creoles, and the Foundation of the Americas, 1585–1660*, Linda Heywood and John Thornton provide an invaluable resource for such an analysis in a series of maps showing the areas in Central Africa from which people were taken for the Atlantic slave trade, organized in five-year periods from 1615 to 1660 (227–35).

In this explanation, the attacks are seen as a way to grow the *palenque*'s population by kidnapping slaves from surrounding ranches in an adaptation of an African form of slavery to a new American context. Before the advent of the European slave trade to Atlantic Africa, both West and Central African societies practiced forms of slavery in which social elites accumulated their wealth, not in land but in people. Such slaves could act as personal servants or as administrators or soldiers (Thornton, 101). In the new American context, Limón leaders sought to accumulate such slave wealth to increase the size of their fighting force and to provide Limón men with wives from outside the community.

As Spaniards planned their responses to the violence, *palenque* actions took on a more warlike character: for some the *palenque*'s attack on the indigenous town of Chambacú represented a preemptive strike. Chambacú's *encomendero*, Francisco Martín Garruchena, was planning to pay Chambacú residents to attack Limón. The violence itself also took on Central African forms. According to one resident, the *palenque*'s ritualized killing of a Spaniard "*era a uso de Guinea*" (was done in an African manner). He might have been referring to the practices of human sacrifice engaged in by the *Imbangalas*, mobile military groups that wreaked havoc on the Mbundu region in the early 1600s and provided slaves to the Portuguese in Angola (Heywood and Thornton, 93–95; Miller, 1976, 162–66). Another resident suggests that the attacks emulated the violence with which the legendary African Domingo Biohó pressured Spanish colonials in Cartagena thirty years earlier.

Juan de la Mar's testimony provides a glimpse into the dynamic creation and re-creation of Afro-Latino cultural beliefs and practices when he tells how *palenque*-born Leonor Criolla became queen and chief military leader. Queen Leonor's leadership style exemplifies the African models of monarchical leadership that dominated American *Maroon* life before a general shift to *criollo* leadership around 1700 (Price, 20).

Juan de la Mar speaks of newly arrived slaves putting "some devil into the black woman Leonor's head," after which everyone obeyed her. He identifies these men as *Malembas*, an *ethnonym* that suggests they were first-generation immigrants from east of the Portuguese colony of Angola. These men brought with them Central African beliefs about spiritual-military leadership, which they may have formed through knowledge or experience of the Angola-Ndongo wars and of the legendary Queen Njinga, whose letters are presented in Chapter 3 of this volume.[6]

Interpreting the Narratives

The Limón testimonies form part of a 990-page dossier sent to Felipe IV, the king of Spain. The dossier also includes petitions, *cabildo* minutes, decrees, the testimonies of Spanish officials, military men, and colonists, letters, and trial records.

---

6. There is no concrete evidence of when these men were enslaved and transported, but the spiritual-military rituals that Juan de la Mar described suggest this Angolan connection; see McKnight, "Confronted Rituals."

The trial declarations represent a kind of coproduction under fire, rather than stories that speakers shape within their own oral traditions. The residents respond to the questions of Spanish interrogators who seek information that will help them quell the rebellion. To sift out the narrative strategies and worldviews of Francisco *Angola*, Sebastián *Anchico*, and Juan de la Mar, readers must assess the effects on their stories of a context of interrogation in which they faced possible execution.

At some points, the interrogator exercises control through his questions; at others, Spaniards and Limón residents negotiate the presentation of information. The Spanish scribe imposes a bureaucratic language over the speaker's own expressions. An African-language interpreter filters the words of Sebastián *Anchico*, who speaks in a Central African language. Taking into account these thick layers of mediation, readers can hypothesize about those moments in which the *palenque* residents' voices break through and express their own perceptions and truths.[7]

To hypothesize about the speakers' own narratives and agency, readers can look for narrative "excesses," pay attention to ways in which speakers identify themselves and others, examine how speakers link these identities to their narration of violence, and seek out symbolic images.

1) "Narrative excesses" are those utterances that offer more information than is requested, such as when Francisco *Angola* is asked about his arrival and time in the *palenque*, and he responds by criticizing the whites' deceitful actions.

2) The ways in which speakers identify themselves and each other involve distinctions that both they and the interrogator make among community members. For the modern reader, thinking about identity can transform long lists of names with brief identifiers into challenging but vital sources of *palenque* thought. How does Juan de la Mar organize and describe Limón members in his list of names, and what does this list suggest about oral traditions or about his and his interrogators' perceptions of *palenque* social order and group identity?

3) Differences can also be seen between how older residents, such as Francisco *Angola*, do not discuss the violence, perhaps to protect their own kin, while newer arrivals, represented by Juan de la Mar, express abhorrence at the violence, painting themselves at times—perhaps deceptively—as helpless observers.

4) Finally, potent symbols emerge from the narratives, as when Francisco *Angola* recalls his homeland in the word "*Guinea*" and evokes the forest as a sacred burial place for a friend, when he places a cross on his grave.[8]

---

7. Martín Lienhard ("Una tierra sin amos") discusses methods of reading highly mediated *Maroon* texts such as these.

8. Lienhard (*O mar e o mato*, 20) analyzes the memory of the forest as a spiritual place in Afro-Brazilian and Afro-Caribbean oral traditions.

Readers of this anthology should keep in mind that the testimonies excerpted in this chapter comprise only a small portion of the Limón residents' testimonies and, therefore, only hint at their full content and complexity. Missing from the entire dossier are the voices of the top *palenque* leaders, who escaped capture. Although perceiving the *palenque* residents' *narrative agency* and voice is challenging and problematic, their stories offer rare and invaluable glimpses into *palenque* members' worldviews and the ways in which they molded their thoughts and expression out of African histories, ancestry, and cultures as well as their experience of the American world.

*****

Testimony of the Trials and Punishments Carried out by Field Marshall Francisco de Murga, Governor and Captain General of Cartagena, against the Rebel Black *Maroons* of the *Palenques* of Limón, Polín, and Zanaguare[9]

[Statement of African-Born Francisco *Angola*, Sixty Years Old, Long-Time *Palenque* Resident]

In the Manga Castle of the port of Cartagena de Indias, on the eighteenth day of January 1634, Señor *Licenciado* Don Francisco de Llano Velasco, *teniente general* of the said city and *auditor general* in this case, called before him one of the rebel black *Maroons* from the *Palenque* del Limón, of those whom they brought as prisoners yesterday from the *palenque*, who said his name was Francisco *Angola*, from whom an oath was taken as required by law. And having made the oath and promised to tell the truth, his statement was taken in the following manner: Asked if this declarant[10] has been in the *palenque* of the black *Maroons* of Limón, and how long he has been there, and what his activities have been, and if he is free or a slave, he said that he came as a small boy from Angola in the slave ship that Captain Antonio Cutiño brought to [Cartagena]. And while in this city, Juan *Angola*, Francisco *Angola's* friend, told him that the whites had them fooled. And pointing to the sun, he told Francisco that the sun came from *Guinea*. "There is the road. Let's go." And [Juan *Angola*] and Francisco *Angola* walked into the forest and were there for some time; he does not know how long, except that one moon passed. And later, as they were walking, they came on the *Palenque* del Limón, where, after three years Juan *Angola* died in the *palenque*. And they buried him in a hole in the forest, and they gave him a cross [on his grave]. And Francisco *Angola* was present in the *palenque* until the whites came and captured him. And he worked clearing and hoeing the blacks' fields and harvesting corn. And that is what he answered.[11] . . .

[Statement of Sebastián *Anchico*, Twenty-Two-Year-Old *Bozal*, Servant (or Slave) in the *Palenque* for the Past Two Years]

In the city of Cartagena, on the twenty-third day of January 1634, the said señor *teniente* and *auditor general* called before him one of the black *Maroons* whom they had brought [to Cartagena], who appeared to be a *bozal*, because of which his statement and confession were taken with the assistance of Andrés *Angola*, a black *ladino* slave—who belongs to the Jesuits—who was named as interpreter because he was *ladino* and understood the *Anchico* language. And under oath he promised to tell and state truthfully what the aforementioned black man responded. And the following questions were asked of him:

---

9. Ministerio de Cultura, Archivo General de Indias, Sevilla, Patronato 234, ramo 7, no. 2 (Digital images 283–84; 319–24; 533–42; 549–54; 556).

10. Some of the most repetitive language that is confusing for readers unfamiliar with colonial documents has been suppressed in the translation. For instance, from now on, the witness will be referred to as "Francisco Angola" or "Francisco" rather than the document's expression "this declarant" (*este declarante*). The same has been done in Juan de la Mar's testimony. This translation also omits the frequent repetition of the term "abovementioned" (*dicho*).

11. The Spanish reads, "And this he responds."

Asked what his name is and to what caste he belongs and who his master is, the interpreter stated that he says his name is Sebastián, he is *Anchico* by birth, and is the slave of Doña María de Viloria, resident of this city of Cartagena.

Asked how long it has been since he ran away, and with whom, and where, and in what *palenque*, and in whose company he has been, the interpreter said that the *Anchico* black man responded that, while he was fetching firewood along the big road, three black *Maroons*—Manuel *Quisama*, Simón *Angola*, and Sebastián *Congo*—came upon him and tied him up on the same day that they captured Domingo *Anchico*. And it has been almost two years since they caught him. And they took him to the Saragosilla ranch and were there two days. And they walked at night until they arrived in [the district of] María. And while walking, they stayed in the forest. And [the three *Maroons*] took them to the *palenque* of Polín, where Manuel *Malemba* was, as well as a *Bran* black man named Miguel. And a few days later Juan *Criollo* de la Margarita and Juan *Angola*—who belongs to Andrés Ortiz—arrived, both brought by Captain Sebastián and Manuel *Quisama*.[12] And there were also four black women whom [Sebastián *Anchico*] encountered when he arrived at the *palenque*.

And they waited there out of fear of the whites, and they ate plants and cassava that they had, and turtles, and game, and they did not leave the *palenque* to do harm to anyone. And while they were hiding there, the people from the *Palenque* del Limón arrived and caught them while they were sleeping in order to take them to their *palenque*. And because [those from Polín] did not want to go, [the people from Limón] took away their arrows, and wounded them, and tied them up and carried them off to Limón to make them work. In the *Palenque* de Polín, they killed Captain Sebastián *Congo*, asking him why he kept all the black women for himself and they did not have any [in Limón], and they killed him out of envy. And [the people from Polín] asked those from Limón why they were fighting, *Maroon* against *Maroon*. And they tied up all the black men and women that were in Polín and carried them off to work for them. And Sebastián *Anchico* served his master Juan *Angola Criollo*, and shelled corn, and carried water and firewood, and went to the fields to work....

And [Sebastián *Anchico*] did not sign [his statement] because he did not know how to, neither did he know his age. He appeared from his looks to be about twenty-two years old. Before me, Francisco López Nieto.

[Statement of Juan de la Mar, Black *Criollo*, Two-Year Resident of Limón, Identified by Some Residents as a Leader]

In the city of Cartagena, on the thirteenth day of February 1634, his mercy Señor *Licenciado* Don Francisco de Llano Velasco, *teniente* and *auditor general*, called before him to take his statement Juan de la Mar, black *criollo* of this city whom they brought from the *palenque* and who, by his own account,[13] is the slave of Captain Agustín de Barahona and, according to public knowledge, was with the black rebel *Maroons*

---

12. Many *palenque* residents are identified by adding to their names the name of their owner, as in "Juan Angola de Andrés Ortiz." Juan *Criollo* de la Margarita's name, however, might be a nickname he had acquired or might refer to a geographic origin, such as Isla Margarita, an island off the Venezuelan coast.

13. Or "who is reputed to be"; the syntax is ambiguous.

[of Limón]. And having sworn by God and on the cross, as required by law, he promised to tell the truth. And the following questions were asked of him:

[Juan de la Mar Tells How He Arrived in Limón]

Asked how long it has been since he ran away, and from where, and for what reason, and who took him to the *palenque*, and how long he was there, he said that it has been about two and a half years since he ran away from this city [Cartagena] and from the service of his master, whom he served as captain of his boat.[14] And because he was short some of the corn that the steward gave him and was unable to pay his master for it, he ran away. And he left this city with a black man, Francisco *Criollo* Corcovado[15]—slave of Don Juan de Sotomayor. After Juan de la Mar told him how he was hiding from his master because he was missing some of the corn he was to deliver to him for the port tax, [Francisco *Criollo*] told him to go with him to [the district of] María, that he knew where there was a *palenque*, and that the *Maroons* would come for him at his master's ranch.

And so Juan de la Mar determined to run away because he was afraid of his master, and he went with the black man Francisco *Criollo* to his master's ranch in María. And he was there seven months, during which time he was seen only by this black man Francisco and his other companions, and not by Don Juan. And he worked in Francisco *Criollo*'s fields. And at the end of the seven months, five blacks from the *Palenque* del Limón went to the ranch, including the *palenque criollos* Chale and Simón, and Juan *Angola*, and Nicolás, and the *criollo* Tumba—who belongs to the Trejos. And Francisco *Criollo* Corcovado handed [Juan] over to the blacks, telling them how he was a fugitive from his master. And they received him, and after two days of being [on Don Juan de Sotomayor's ranch], they took him to the *palenque*, where he was until [the whites] captured him.

Asked if Don Juan de Sotomayor or other people or blacks saw and communicated with the *Maroons* [from Limón] on the occasion that... they took him, and knew that Francisco *Criollo* handed him over [to them], he said that Don Juan was not at the ranch on that occasion and that only Francisco *Criollo* Corcovado, and his companions, and Alférez Piña's Indians saw the *Maroons* and spoke with them the two days that they were at Don Juan's ranch, and no other person did so. And that is what he answered.

[Juan de la Mar Names the Limón Residents and Tells How They Came to the *Palenque*]

Asked what blacks—*criollos* or outsiders—were in the *palenque* when he joined, and what black women and rabble,[16] he said that there were fifteen *palenque*-born black

---

14. The word *arráez*, translated here as "captain," might alternatively indicate the galley master or pilot.

15. *Corcovado* means "hunchback." This man is sometimes referred to in the testimonies as *el corcovado*.

16. Here, the interrogator divides up the *palenque* population in four groups. The terms he uses carry various meanings depending on who uses them and in what context. *Criollo* can refer to American-born vs. the foreign-born "*forastero*," but Juan de la Mar interprets the terms to mean those

criollos: Captain Francisco, and his father Domingo, Commander Simón, Nicolás, Juan *Angola*, another Juan, Manuel, another they called Roldán, Sebastián, another Manuel, another Juanillo *Criollo*, Luis, Pablo, Domingo Chale, and his brother Gonzalo Chale, and another—Gaspar Pemba—so there were sixteen adult male *criollos* and twelve black women: Leonor, who is the queen, Gracia, Chale's sister Andrea, whom they killed,[17] Madalena, Maquesu, Susaña, Antonia, Damiana, Vitoria, Juana, Inés, María, and the black woman Antonia *Criolla* was this witness's wife, and another black woman, María, who died at the Márquez ranch. And all these were *criollas* [born in] the *palenque*.

And there were many other *criollos*, male and female, children of these black women, and the ones he remembers are Leonor's two children named Marcos and Cristóbal; and Gracia had three children named Mateo, Felipa, and Antonico; and Madalena had two children named Francisco and Lázaro; and Lucrecia has a daughter named Beatriz and two small granddaughters named María and Blanca; Vitoria has four children named Pedro, and another Pedro, and Mariquita, and Francisco; and the black woman Antonia has a son named Diego and he is Juan de la Mar's son; and the black woman Damiana has a daughter named Juana; and Juana has five children: Esperanza and María and Colobi and Pedro and another daughter whose name he does not remember; and of these five children, [Juana] has three who are with her, and two are still in the forest; and the black woman Andrea has three children: Antonio and Jusepa and another son whose name he does not remember, and she has another son named Antonio who is in the forest; and another black woman, Marta, not mentioned above, who is Gonzalo Chale's wife, has three children: Guiomar and Madalena and Juan; and there was another black woman, Isabel *Criolla*, whom he forgot to name. And another six black Angolan women: an old woman they called Mohongo—Captain Francisco's mother—Ángela, Felipa, Lucrecia, Catalina, and another they call Gonga, who is small of body and old. And he does not remember any other black women being in the *palenque* when he entered. And that is what he answered.

And in addition to the aforementioned black men and women, he encountered another five—outsider black men—who are the *criollo* Tumba, Sebastián Cachorro—who belongs to Duarte de León—Manuel *Angola*, and Antón *Angola*, and another Manuel *Angola*, who they said was from the river.[18]

Asked what black *criollos* and blacks from *Guinea*[19] and black women came to the *palenque* after he arrived, and who brought them, he said that the black painter Francisco *Criollo*—who belongs to the Señor *Inquisidor Fiscal*—and three *Malemba*[20]

---

born in the *palenque* and those who have escaped their masters and joined later in life. The remaining categories the interrogator names are black women and masses; the word *chusma* has a negative connotation, meaning "galley slaves" or "rabble."

17. This appears to be a reference to a casualty of the Spanish attack.

18. Probably the Magdalena River, a vital artery for trade and travel, also referred to as *el río grande* and *el río grande de la Magdalena*.

19. Here the interrogator more clearly distinguishes between American-born and African-born (*de Guinea*).

20. The original reads *balembaes*, but the slaves who belong to Juan Ramos are repeatedly referred to as "*Malembas*."

black men who belong to Juan Ramos, one named Sebastián *Congo*, Cristóbal, and Antón, and another Francisco *Malemba* who arrived with them—and Juan de la Mar heard that he belonged to a potter who lives next to the Hospital of Espíritu Santo. And later a black man, Felipe *Angola*—who belongs to Captain Blanquesel—came, and then another two black *Angolan* men who belong to the *depositario*, one named Andrés, the other Antonio, a black man Juan *Carabalí*—who belongs to the *alférez* Márquez—another, Jacinto *Angola*, and Manuel *Angola*, and Manuel *Bran*—who belong to the same *alférez* Márquez. So all these black men who belong to the *depositario* and to Márquez went to the *palenque* on their own, and Juan de la Mar and the other *palenque* blacks found them as they were on their way there. And they told him how they were running away because they had cruel masters, and they wanted to be in the *palenque*. And so they took them there.

And in the Indian town [of Chambacú], the black hunchback [Corcovado] who belongs to Don Juan handed over to the people of the *palenque* the black man Francisco *Criollo* who belongs to the Señor *Inquisidor Fiscal* and [Juan de la Mar], who came with them. And after that he handed over Francisco El *Morisco*. And the black man Francisco *Bañón*—who belongs to Don Andrés Hortensio—also handed over another black man they said belonged to [Captain Alonso] Cuadrado. And the *criollo* Francisco Corcovado—who belongs to Don Juan—also delivered the black man Juan *Criollo*—who belongs to Francisco López Nieto. And another black man, García *Angola*—who belongs to Pedro Destrada—also went to the *palenque*, and the *Maroons* found him on Francisco Martín's savannas, and they took him from there. Lorenzo *Criollo*, and Gaspar *Angola*, and Gonga, and Juan *Angola*, and Lázaro, Alonso Martín's slave, also went to the savannas and with them went Jorge *Angola*— who belongs to Diego Márquez—and another young Angolan black man named Manuel, and Juan de la Mar does not know who his master is. And all of these went of their own volition to Francisco Martín's savannas, which are on the way to the lemon grove. And the blacks from the *palenque* took them from there, because they were running away from their owners. They also took an old black man with his wife, who said he came from Juan de Uriarte's ranch. And they found these two on their way to the *palenque* when the people went to Chambacú.

And [all] these were the blacks who came on their own [to the *palenque*]. And the others are the ones that [the *palenque* soldiers] carried off from the ranches. And another black man called Lázaro *Angola*, who belongs to Márquez, also went to the *palenque* without being taken there. And that is what he answered.[21]

[The *Palenque*'s Political and Military Organization]

Asked to state what arms the blacks from the *palenque* carried and what their activities were and who their captains and commanders were, Juan de la Mar said that El *Morisco* and the black man Francisco *Criollo* who belongs to the Señor *Inquisidor*

---

21. Juan de la Mar has been asked to name those who joined the *palenque* after he did and to divulge who took them there. The interrogators are seeking to identify those guilty of running away from their owners, facilitating such escape, or kidnapping others. Here, Juan de la Mar notes that there are two men still living as slaves on neighboring farms who have brought a number of the new residents to Limón; these men are Francisco Corcovado (the *Creole* hunchback) and Francisco *Bañón*.

Fiscal carried shotguns and had bullets and powder for them and the other blacks all carried bows and arrows. And the black man Francisco *Criollo* was captain, and the commander was Simón. And [he said] that when Juan de la Mar arrived at the *palenque*, there were no other commanders. And after the blacks who belong to Juan Ramos came, they put some devil into the black woman Leonor's head, because from then on she began to command. And everyone obeyed her, even the captain and commander, because something happened to her in her head that made her walk like a crazy woman, falling down and beating about her before she spoke, and when she came to, she uttered a great deal of nonsense. And in effect everyone feared her and obeyed her as queen. And this declarant lived with the *criollos* in the Chale band. And that is what he answered....

[The Attack on Diego Márquez's Farm and the Ensuing Human Sacrifice]

Asked who went to Diego Márquez's hog farm, which is a half league distant from the ranch, and carried off the steward and a boy who was his son and an Indian man and woman who were there, he said that he did not go to the hog farm but that he knows that Captain Francisco, and two *criollos*, Juan and Domingo, and Francisco El *Morisco*, and another four blacks from *Guinea* went under the orders of Queen Leonor: these are Gaspar—who belongs to Alonso Martín—*Camangala*, and Manuel *Quisama*, and Lázaro—the one who belongs to Márquez. And he does not remember that other blacks went.

And what they did was to bring to the *palenque* the steward and his son, and the Indian man and woman. And before they entered the *palenque*, they tied them up and brought them before the queen, and they put them in a hut. And that afternoon, the queen had them taken out of the hut and they took them to the banana grove in the *palenque*. And there Queen Leonor placed them on their side on the ground, and she cut their throats herself with a hatchet and she drank their blood, together with other black women named Susaña, Inés, Maquesu, and other black men, and Felipe, who belongs to Captain Banquesel, and the black men called Male[mba]—who belong to Juan Ramos—also drank.

And when they took them out of the hut to kill them, [the victims] walked along tied up with ropes. And the Spaniard asked that for the love of God they not kill him. And he said to Juan de la Mar that he thought he knew him, and asked him to plead with the other blacks on his behalf, and that he would serve them.[22] And Juan de la Mar said that there was nothing he could do, because they were more than twenty black men, and whoever opposed them, they would shoot and kill with arrows. And as he and the Indian walked along, tied up, the black man Tumba, slave of the Trejos, and Francisco *Criollo*, slave of the Señor *Inquisidor Fiscal*, and Juan de la Mar helped them in their dying and prayed with them.[23]

And after the black woman Leonor had wounded the Spaniard and Indian with the hatchet, a black man who belongs to a potter who lives next to the [Hospital of]

---

22. He offers to become their slave.
23. They helped him prepare his soul to face death with a Christian attitude and thus to "die well."

the Holy Spirit finished cutting off their heads and opening up their chests; and the black man is named Francisco *Malemba*, and the black men who belong to Juan Ramos helped him. And Juan de la Mar and other blacks wanted to bury them, and the Angolan blacks did not allow them to do so. And they left them on the ground and the buzzards ate them. And this is what happened there.

[The Whites Betray the Peace Negotiations]

Asked to state whether he went to Captain Francisco Julián de Piña's ranch and what they stole and looted and by whose order and for what reason they did so, Juan de la Mar said that he went to Francisco Julián de Piña's ranch by order of Queen Leonor, together with Francisco El *Morisco*, Francisco *Criollo*, who belongs to Señor Inquisidor, Captain Francisco, and Juan *Criollo*, Sebastián, Cristóbal, and Pablo, and Niculás, and Luis Manuel, another Juan *Criollo*, Rolán, Domingo, and Gonzalo Chale, and another Juan *Criollo*, and Commander Simón, and the queen, and all the people who belong to the *alférez* Márquez, and all the other black men that were in the *palenque*.

And when they left, they had resolved that Captain Francisco and the other *criollos* would come to Cartagena to negotiate a peace agreement with the Lord Governor and *maese de campo*, according to what had been decided with Captain Don Juan de Sotomayor. And while all the *criollos* were thus disposed, a black man named Francisco *Bañón*, who belongs to Don Andrés Hortensio Paravecino, gathered them and told them to examine what they were doing, because what was being planned for them was only an attempt to deceive them. And that [the Spaniards] were going to capture them, because in Cartagena people were being armed to be sent against them. And hearing this and also that Francisco Martín Garruchena had received royal monies to pay soldiers, and with many other explanations that Francisco *Bañón* gave them, the *criollos* changed their minds, and they resolved not to come to this city.

And the *criollos* talked among themselves, saying how well Francisco Martín Garruchena was repaying what they had done for him! Seeing that he was a poor man, they had made him rich, working on his properties and building his huts and clearing fields, sowing cassava and corn and harvesting them. And Francisco Martín Garruchena having offered to defend them and saying that he would warn them anytime an attack was being planned against them. Having thus considered what Francisco *Bañón* averred, they did not carry out their earlier plan, which was to come to this city; rather, they exploded in rage.

[Juan de la Mar tells that in their rage, the leaders decide to mount attacks on two neighboring ranches. Although the Spaniards ultimately win this battle, many of the Maroons *escape capture and continue creating their own lives in the forest.]*

PART II: FAMILIES AND COMMUNITIES

"Families and Communities" shows Afro-Latinos integrating into Ibero-American society in ways that supported their efforts to construct and defend families and communities and reshape African identities. Whether a reuniting of African groupings or the re-creation of "fictive kinship," family and community allowed Africans in the Americas to sustain and transform their systems of cultural beliefs and practices after the calamitous interruption of the *Middle Passage*.

Juan Roque's donation of a house in his will to the *Zape* Confraternity in Mexico City (1623) shows Africans using Catholic religious organizations for mutual support and to foster group identity (Chapter 6). In seventeenth-century Lima, women of African origin helped mold their social organization through their material legacies, by engaging the lettered culture of Spanish legal documentation and doing so more frequently than did black men (Chapter 7). Their wills reveal stratification among African-descent populations as they list possessions that include not only goods, but also slaves.

A unique case of community development occurred in El Cobre, Cuba, where the Crown confiscated the copper mines and transformed the mine's private slaves into *royal slaves*. These slaves founded a *pueblo* identity, speaking through a series of documents about their struggles to defend their *pueblo* against the former mine owners (Chapter 8). Another will and testament made by a black Peruvian woman allows a glimpse into the variety of attitudes toward identity construction among people of African descent (Chapter 9). The West African–born Ana de la Calle calls herself *Lucumí* to distinguish her superior status from that of other local blacks. A careful reading of her will shows how she uses this document of orthodox Catholicism to bequeath to her heirs the profits of a business based on African ritual specialization. Her will also speaks to the ways in which social identity changed from one generation to the next through marriage and colonial integration.

Finally, the judicial inquiry into events surrounding the coronation of Pedro Duarte as king of the *Congos* in Buenos Aires (1787; Chapter 10) shows the struggles African organizations had when they did preserve old-world practices that Catholic colonials saw as threatening. All these documents reveal individuals who gained vital knowledge of the Spanish colonial system in order to exercise a measure of self-determination over the vibrant lives of their communities.

6

Juan Roque's Donation of a House to the *Zape* Confraternity, Mexico City, 1623[1]

Nicole von Germeten

Zapes and Other Africans in New Spain

Africans living in colonial Mexico negotiated a place in their lives for an ongoing connection to their African ethnic identity, despite the desire to embrace some aspects of Catholicism and often the challenges of compromising to non-African spouses. From the time of the military conquest of Tenochtitlan, men and women of African descent inhabited the viceroyalty of New Spain. Some of these individuals were descended from Africans living in Spain for generations, but the majority, at least one hundred thousand Africans, arrived in New Spain on board Portuguese slave ships before 1640.

Although the descendants of indigenous peoples dominated population numbers for the entire colonial period, before 1640 more Africans than Spaniards came to New Spain. In urban areas, especially the viceregal capital of Mexico City, Africans and their descendants were a significant percentage of the population. Historians estimate that around sixty-two thousand people of African descent lived in and around Mexico City. Although many Africans in New Spain came from Central African regions under Portuguese influence, the participants in this case demonstrate that Mexico City inhabitants represented a much broader range of African ethnicities (Bristol, 4–5).

This reading is selected from a case disputing the rent of a house owned by the African Juan Roque, who died in Mexico City in 1623. Roque belonged to a religious brotherhood that, after the death of Roque's daughter Ana María, argued that they owned the property in question and its income. In 1634, the houses and their income had been under the control of a priest for the four years since Ana María's death. The first part of the document is Roque's last will and testament, dated 1623, and the second is testimony from several witnesses who gave evidence about what they knew about Roque's bequests. In these documents, Roque and his family and friends reveal fragments of their life stories, which subtly highlight the deep tensions Africans felt as they strove to incorporate into their lives the ideals of Spanish Catholicism, tried to maintain ties to the African community, and struggled to live up to familial duties.

Roque refers to himself as from the *Zape nation*. *Zape* is a word used in early modern Spanish and Portuguese to refer to Africans from coastal Sierra Leone.[2] The *Zapes* did not have a kingdom or empire but instead were organized in smaller political units. The term *Zape* was well known as a specific African ethnicity in the

---

1. See Maps 1 and 9.
2. *Zape* is also spelled *Çape* and *Sape*.

Iberian world of the 1500s—*Zape* slaves were characters in Spanish dramas from the 1500s—but this ethnicity was rarely mentioned in documents from colonial Mexico. *Zapes* became embroiled in the slave trade due to mid-sixteenth-century struggles with *Mande* speakers from the interior (Gomez, 89). The Portuguese took advantage of these hostilities and its prisoners of war to buy slaves in Sierra Leone before they had a consistent source of slaves from Central Africa.

Roque left the houses under dispute to his *cofradía* or Catholic brotherhood, founded by him and other *Zapes* living in Mexico City sometime in the late 1500s. The *Zape* brotherhood maintained an altar with an image of Our Lady of the Immaculate Conception in the Hospital of the Immaculate Conception. It is the only known brotherhood in New Spain based on an African ethnicity. Unlike in Cuba or Brazil, slaves were not shipped directly from Africa to New Spain after 1640. Therefore, New Spain did not see the same development of religious brotherhoods with membership from specific regions and language groups in Africa that other parts of the Ibero-American world did. By the 1700s, Afro-Mexicans formed brotherhoods based on their *mulatto* race label (von Germeten, *Black Blood Brothers*). The document excerpted here shows how difficult it was to maintain an African ethnic identity even in the 1630s.

During his lifetime Roque married a *Zape* woman with whom he had a daughter. His entire family was free by the time of his death, and his daughter married a non-African, a man named Juan Fraile, described as a *mulatto* tailor. If Ana María had borne children, they would have been members of the free working classes of Mexico City. Even if they had been poor, they would not have had to fear the abuses of slavery. However, they might have found it challenging to retain ties to their *Zape* identity, because by the 1630s, no *Zapes* were shipped to New Spain for at least a generation. Most Africans transported to New Spain as slaves in the 1600s were from Central Africa. Most *Zapes* already in Mexico City, including the ones who testify in this document, were relatively elderly, especially considering the shorter life spans experienced by the seventeenth-century poor.

Juan Roque's Bequest and the Dynamics of Maintaining the *Zape* Community

Roque's last will and testament is a unique document because few Africans in seventeenth-century New Spain left evidence of their final bequests. Although it seems likely that Juan Roque came to New Spain from Africa on a slave ship sometime during the late sixteenth century, he accumulated enough money and real estate to make a will and to make several pious bequests and arrange a moderately lavish baroque Catholic funeral. When he died in 1626, Juan's funeral cost fifty-four *pesos*.[3] Although his will emphasizes the Masses he wants to be said for the sake of his soul,

---

3. In colonial New Spain, a laborer's daily wage was often under four *reales*, with one *peso* worth eight *reales*. As can be noted in this document, Roque's house rented for six *pesos* a month. Although some funerals at this time cost hundreds of *pesos*, fifty-four *pesos* would be a significant sum for the average worker in colonial Mexico City.

it also shows how Roque valued community as he passed from this world to the next. The statements made by witnesses also reveal the strong *Zape* community that existed in seventeenth-century Mexico City, forged through lifelong friendships (possibly made onboard the slave ship) and surrogate family ties.

When Ana María's husband tried to force her to sell Roque's houses, she turned to *Zape* elders and brotherhood members for help. Although a close friend of her father advised her to submit to her husband's authority, the rest of the *Zape* brothers gathered together to strengthen their position and defend what they believed was their property. The *Zapes* living in Mexico City might have wanted to do more than protect the income of a Catholic brotherhood or guarantee that they had the funds to pay for Roque's pious bequests. Even though the *Zape* political organization in Sierra Leone was based on villages, societies or religious organizations of both men and women were a fundamental part of *Zape* life (Gomez, 94–100). According to European observers going back to the 1600s, these societies helped regulate diplomacy, culture, and education and even provided charity. Women were deeply involved in these societies and in some special cases could join the male societies.

Both the male and female societies functioned to "prepare each [person] for full participation in community affairs" (Gomez, 97). Rank was based on age grades. In the stressful situation of enslavement far from Sierra Leone, it is likely that the *Zapes* turned to these organizations to govern their lives according to their traditional values. Europeans highlighted the secrecy of these societies, perhaps to make them seem more exotic and strange. However, the fact that the societies were known to be exclusive and secretive, especially to Europeans, lends weight to the conclusion that Juan Roque and the several other *Zape* men who testified in this case were protecting a brotherhood. That brotherhood was probably tied as strongly to their African identity as to their immersion in New Spain's Catholicism.

Later documents relating to this case reveal the *Zapes'* desire to retain the exclusivity of their organization and the ultimate futility of these efforts. In 1644, a free black man called Juan *Jolofo*[4] had taken over the brotherhood and the houses' income for ten years. Other *Zapes* determined that the houses had earned over a thousand *pesos* of rent in this period. Although other members had allowed this non-*Zape* takeover, in 1644 they wanted to revoke it, demanding that only *Zapes* enjoy membership in the brotherhood. In response, the defendant proclaimed that not only were many of the other leaders of the brotherhood not *Zapes*, but one had even had his ears clipped for being a thief![5]

Two decades later, this brotherhood continued to experience conflicts within its leadership. In 1668, a petitioner mentioned that only three Africans remained among the original founders of the Immaculate Conception confraternity. He did not specify that they were *Zapes*.[6]

*****

---

4. Or *Xolofo*.

5. The source for this document is the same file as the testament: Archivo General de la Nación, Mexico City, Bienes Nacionales, vol. 1175, exp. 11. These statements are made on fol. 71r.

6. Archivo General de la Nación, Mexico City, Cofradías y Archicofradías, vol. 6407, exp. 51, fol. 2r.

Last Will and Testament of Juan Roque, Free Black[7]

In the name of God, amen. This document testifies that I, Juan Roque, free black from the *Zape* land, fluent in the Castilian language, and Christian by the grace of God, believe in the mystery of the Most Holy Trinity, Father, Son, and Holy Spirit, three persons and only one true God, and in all the rest that the Holy Mother Roman Catholic Church preaches and teaches, in whose faith and belief I have lived and continue to live and will die. I take as my advocate the forever glorious Virgin, Mother of God and Our Lady, with all the other male and female saints of the celestial court so that they intercede with Our Lord Jesus Christ and that he might pardon my sins. Being sick in bed with the sickness given to me, but being myself and having my natural understanding, I offer this last will and testament.

First, I entrust my soul to God, Our Lord, who cared for it and redeemed it with his precious blood, and my body I return to the earth from which it was formed.

Item. I order that if God wishes to take me with this illness, my body be buried in the church of the Hospital of Our Lady of the Immaculate Conception of this city, administered by the Marquis of the Valley. If this is not convenient, I wish to be buried in the Santísima Veracruz Church in this city, where I am a parishioner. I order that twelve people accompany my body, along with the brotherhoods that I belong to, to be paid for by my property.

Item. I order that on the day of my burial, if time allows and, if not, on the following day, a sung Mass be said for me in the presence of my body with a deacon, subdeacon, and offering, to be paid for by my property.

Item. I order that ten spoken Masses be said for my soul in the Veracruz Church, at the altars of indulgence, paid for with the customary donation.

Item. I order that twenty spoken Masses be said for my soul in the Convent of Our Lady of Mt. Carmel, to be paid for by my property.

Item. I order that ten spoken Masses be said for my soul in the Hospital of Our Lady of the Immaculate Conception in this city, to be paid for by my property.

Item. I order that four Masses be said for my soul at the Hospital of the Holy Spirit in this city, to be paid for by my property.

Item. I order that ten Masses be said for my soul at the Royal Indian Hospital, to be paid for by my property.

Item. I order that twenty Masses be said for the soul of my deceased wife Isabel de Herrera, free black woman, and for others I may be indebted to and for the souls in purgatory, to be paid for by my property.

Item. I order that the Brotherhood of the Most Holy Sacrament, founded in the Veracruz Church in this city, accompany my body to its burial, carrying candles. Twenty gold *pesos* from my property will be donated to them.

Item. I order that three *pesos* be given from my property for two bulls of composition[8] for that which I may have forgotten I owed or with whose care I was charged.

---

7. Testamento de Juan Roque, *negro* libre, Archivo General de la Nación, Mexico City, Bienes Nacionales, vol. 1175, exp. 11, fols. 6r–7r and 17r–29r.

8. A bull that gave permission to someone to keep property belonging to another.

Item. I order that a *real* from my property be paid to each of the obligatory donations.

Item. I declare that I do not remember that I owe any person anything, and I declare this to relieve my conscience.

I declare that the *licentiate* Benavides, cleric from the Veracruz Church, owes me 100 *pesos* of gold, which is the remainder of the 180 that I gave him in *reales* with other goods held. The said goods were returned to me, and 100 *pesos* are still owed to me. I order that they be collected as my property.

I declare that the Spanish woman María de Sosa who lives near the Alameda owes me twenty-eight *pesos* that I loaned her in *reales*. I order that they be collected as my property.

Item. Pedro *Indio*, tailor, owes me a quantity of gold *pesos* for the rent of my house, where he lived, for which I have proof in a written document, which records the amount. I order that this be collected as my property.

Item. I declare that I was married according to the Most Holy Church to Isabel de Herrera, a free black woman from the *Zape* land, and during our marriage she gave birth to my legitimate daughter, Ana María, free black woman. I declare that she is my legitimate daughter, and she is married to Juan Fraile, a free *mulatto* tailor.

I declare that I own the houses where I dwell in the neighborhood of San Hipólito in the lane next to the College of San Juan where it meets the open air market of San Hipólito, bordering the houses of the marshal and those of Don Ángel de Villasaña, along with everything inside them, and I include their titles here.

Item. I declare that I have other possessions of slight value that will be inventoried.

I name for the executors of my testament Francisco de León, *alguacil* for vagabonds in this city, and Ana María, my daughter. To each one separately and jointly, I give legal power sufficient to take from my property what is necessary and to carry out and pay for this, my testament, its orders, and inheritance, for as long as is necessary even if it exceeds the year of executorship.

Once my legacies and wishes as stated in my testament are carried out and paid, I leave everything to my heir Ana María, my legitimate daughter, a free black woman and wife of Juan Fraile, *mulatto*. I wish her to be my heir with God's blessing and my own.

I revoke, annul, and declare null any other testaments, bequests, or codicils that I have made in writing or have spoken, such that they are worthless; and only this testament that I currently make and grant, do I wish to be valid, in the best way and form allowed by the law. I make this statement on July 26, 1623.

And the grantor, whom I give my word that I know, did not sign, saying he does not know how to write. A witness signed for him, with the following witnesses: Felipe de Herrera Ibáñez, Juan Fernández, Gregorio de Loayza, Juan Giles, Jacinto González, and Antonio Márquez, citizen and [illegible]. Done in my presence, Juan de León Figueroa, Notary of His Majesty.

Certified as authentic testimony,
Juan de León Figueroa, Notary of His Majesty
I give faith. . . .

[Interrogatory in the Litigation of the Houses That Belonged to the Black Man Juan Roque, of the *Zape Nation*]

July 11, 1634

[illegible]

The following questions are to be used to examine the witnesses presented by the foreman and deputies of the black brotherhood of the *Zape nation*, founded in the Hospital of Our Lady of the Immaculate Conception of this city, in the suit against the *licentiate* José de Peñafiel, presbyter, who has in his possession some houses that belonged to the black *Zape* man Juan Roque and his daughter Ana María, a black *Creole* woman, regarding which it is declared that they belong to the said confraternity together with the income from their lease.

1. First, if they know the litigants and if they knew the black man Juan Roque and his daughter, the black woman Ana María, and if they know about this case and the disputed houses, they should state what they know, etc.

2. If they know and saw whether the black man Juan Roque gave to his daughter Ana María, wife of Juan Fraile, *mulatto*, houses in this city in the lane behind the College of San Juan de Letrán, that remained on his death, and if they know that Ana María died and passed from this life without legitimate or illegitimate children or any other heirs and that she passed away childless and intestate, they should state what they know, etc.

3. If they know and saw that Ana María publicly demonstrated and said that her father had ordered that if she died without children or heirs, that his will was that the houses would be left to the aforementioned brotherhood to use their rent for pious works. And Ana María, during her life and just before she died, and at the time of her death, when she was ill but of clear mind, said publicly so that many people heard that her final and deathbed wish was to leave to the brotherhood the aforementioned houses, in conformity with the will and disposition of her father, and for the same purpose of pious works, whereby they know that the houses belong to the confraternity, they should state what they know, etc.

4. If they know or saw that the said houses have been rented for six *pesos* a month, which is the rent they have always earned, under the control of the *licentiate* José de Peñafiel since Ana María died four and a half years previously, and that he has not notified the brotherhood of these earnings, they should state what they know, etc.

5. Item. Let them state whether this is publicly known by all.
   Don Agustín Guerrero

In Mexico City, July 11, 1634, in the presence of the *Señor* Doctor Andrés Fernández, judge for testaments, chaplaincies, and pious works in this city and archdiocese, the following interrogatory and its questions were presented.

His Mercy recognized the interrogatory as presented and ordered that the witnesses presented be examined accordingly and the pertinent facts be presented and examined.

Before me,

Pedro de Becerro, Notary

Examination by the Blacks of the Brotherhood of Our Lady of the Immaculate Conception

[Testimony of the Black Man Juan, of the *Zape Nation*, Slave, an Acquaintance of Ana María]

Witness In Mexico City on July 13, 1634, Andrés de Galvez, procurator of the archdiocese court, in the name of the foreman and other officers of the *Zape nation* of the Brotherhood of Our Lady of the Immaculate Conception of this city, in the case to determine if they own some houses in this city that were owned by Juan Roque, free black, and later by his daughter, the black woman Ana María, both now deceased, and the other aspects of the case, presented as a witness a black man, *ladino* in the Castilian language, who says his name is Juan and that he comes from the *Zape* land and *nation* and that he is a slave of Juan Días, *alguacil*, resident of this city. I, the notary, received his oath. And he swore by the Lord Our God and made the sign of the cross, as required. And having sworn, he promised to tell the truth. And being asked these questions presented by Andrés de Gálvez in this case, he said the following:

1. To the first question he said that he knows the litigants and he knew Juan Roque and Ana María his daughter, deceased black residents of this city. And this is his response.[9]

General questions: Regarding the general questions of law,[10] he stated that he is forty-six years old and that they do not apply to him.

2. For the second question, he said that he knows that the houses in this suit are on the street by the College of San Juan del Letrán and that Juan Roque, free black, being deceased, left the houses to the black woman Ana María, his daughter, also deceased. This witness saw her enjoy the houses in her possession for many years. And this witness, communicating familiarly with Ana María, knew that no children came from her marriage with the *mulatto* Juan Fraile, now deceased, and that before her marriage Ana María had no children, nor did she have any children after her husband died, nor did she have any other heirs. She did not make a testament because she died quickly of a *cocoliste* [typhoid] in the Hospital de los *Desamparados*. This witness saw her die and saw her burial in the church of this hospital, so he knows that she did not make a last will and testament.

---

9. The answer of every witness to every question contains this repetitive phrase, *Y esto responde* [And this he responds], and occasionally, *Es lo que sabe y responde* [This is what he knows and responds], both of which are omitted from here on. The initial instance in each testimony is maintained to communicate some of the feel of the bureaucratic language.

10. These are questions asked to ascertain the relationship of the witness to the parties and thus to assess the witness' partiality.

3. To the third question, he responded that he knows that fifteen days before she died, the black woman Ana María called on the foreman and officers of the Brotherhood of the Immaculate Conception of Our Lady, founded in the hospital of the Marquis de Valle by the blacks of the *Zape nation*, and she took them to the house about which these claims are made, and this witness being present there, as a person of the aforementioned *nation*, Ana María declared that the black man Juan Roque, her father, had urged her strongly when he died that if she did not have children, she was to leave the house to the brotherhood, so that the blacks of the *Zape nation*, of which Juan Roque himself was, would administer the houses and use their income to do good for his soul and the soul of Ana María. In conformity with this, she called together the members to inform them and, given that she was the widow of Juan Fraile her husband and that she did not have children or heirs, it was her express will to carry out the wishes of her father, and that they should take possession of the houses for this purpose. The foreman and officials discussed the case, and they resolved to accept this decision. And that as long as the black woman Ana María was alive, she was to own and enjoy the house. After her death, they would administer it and its rental income in order to do good for her soul and the soul of her father. It was thus that this witness knows that this house belongs to the brotherhood according to the last will of Ana María.

4. To the fourth question, he also said that all of this information has been discussed publicly by many different people whose names he cannot remember.

5. To the fifth question, he said that what he has said is known publicly and he swears on his oath it is true, and he affirmed and ratified it. He does not sign because he says he does not know how to write.

Before me,

Pedro de Becerro, Notary

[Testimony of Diego, of the *Zape Nation*, Slave, Friend of the Roque Family]

Witness   In Mexico City on July 13, 1634, Andrés de Gálvez, procurator of the archdiocesan court, presented for the purpose of giving evidence on behalf of his parties, as a witness, a black man, fluent in the Castilian language, who said his name is Diego, of the *Zape nation*. He is a slave of Juan de Santillán, resident of this city. I, the notary, receive his oath by God and the sign of the cross, made in the correct form. And having sworn, he promised to tell the truth. And being asked the questions of interrogation in this case, he answered with the following:

1. To the first question, he said that he knows the litigants and he knows about the case, and he knew Juan Roque and Ana María, the black woman, his daughter, both of them free from captivity and now deceased. This is his response.

General questions: To the general questions, he said that he is more or less sixty years old and that they do not apply to him.

2. To the second question, he said that the houses involved in this case are in the lane behind the College of San Juan de Letrán, and they belonged to Juan Roque, a free black man, and Ana María, a black woman, his daughter, both now deceased. This witness saw Juan Roque enjoy and possess them as his own for many years until he died. And by his death, his daughter Ana María inherited them. She was the wife

of Juan Fraile, *mulatto*, now deceased. And their marriage did not produce any children nor did she give birth before marrying nor after she became a widow, and she died without heirs. This witness knows this as one who dealt with and communicated with Ana María from her girlhood to her death.

3. To the third question, he said that after the black man Juan Roque died, Ana María took on this witness in place of her father and treated him as such, discussing her concerns and business with him and asking his advice. She told him how Juan Fraile *mulatto*, her husband, wanted to sell the houses and because of this he asked her for her father's testament. And that she could not allow this sale, because her father said that if she did not have children she must leave the house to the Brotherhood of Our Lady of the Immaculate Conception, so that the blacks of the *Zape nation* would administer it and its income, to do good for her father's and her soul. This witness advised her to call the foreman and the officials of the aforementioned brotherhood to tell them what she had told him. And he does not know whether she did so then. Within a few days, the aforementioned Juan Fraile died. And around fifteen days before she died, according to his memory, and while she was still entirely healthy, Ana María called the foreman and brothers to her house, which is the same one referred to in this case. This witness was there, and she declared what she had told this witness. And that she had already defended [the houses] from her husband, and so she wished and desired that the foreman and officials take possession of the houses. They conferred and resolved to accept the administration of the houses, but only after Ana María's lifetime, because while she lived it was not right for her to cease living in them. They made this arrangement. And after this happened, Ana María suffered a *cocoliste* that killed her within three days, leaving her with no time to make a testament, by which evidence this witness knows that the houses belong to the aforementioned brotherhood in conformity with Ana María's last will.

4. To the fourth question, he responded that he does not know.

5. To the fifth question, he said that what he said is publicly known to be true, by the oath he has taken, which he signed and ratified. He did not sign because he said he does not know how to write.

Before me,
Pedro de Becerro, Notary

[Testimony of Simón, of the *Zape Nation*, Slave]

Witness   In Mexico City on July 14, 1634, the aforementioned Andrés de Gálvez presented as a witness in his case on behalf of his party a black man fluent in the Castilian language, who said his name is Simón, of the *Zape nation* and a slave of Captain Rodolfo, from whom I, the notary, received his oath, made by God, Our Lord and the sign of the cross. And having sworn to tell the truth, being asked the questions of the interrogation, he said the following:

1. To the first question, he said that he knows the litigants and he knew Juan Roque and Ana María his daughter, both blacks, and that he knows about this case and the houses in question. And this is his response.

General questions: In response to the general questions he said that he is over fifty years old.

2. To the second question this witness said that he knew for certain that Juan Roque, free black man, when he died left some houses that he had in the lane behind the College of San Juan de Letrán to his daughter Ana María, a free black woman, who was the wife of a *mulatto* tailor named Juan Fraile, who is now dead. This witness saw the aforementioned Ana María die a natural death about four years ago. And he was present at her funeral, which was in the Hospital de los *Desamparados*. She left no children or heirs and, without making a testament, she died of the *cocoliste* disease that did not last three days. He knows this because he knew her and visited her when she was sick, until she died. And her father was of the same *nation* to which this witness belongs.

3. To the third question, he says that he knows and can testify that when Ana María was widowed by the death of Juan Fraile her husband, fifteen days before she herself died, being in good health, she called the foreman of the Brotherhood of Our Lady of the Immaculate Conception of this city, founded by the blacks of the *Zape nation*. The officials went to the houses where she lived, the ones mentioned in this question. This witness was an official of the aforementioned brotherhood and he joined this meeting because they notified him. In her house, Ana María said that when her husband was alive, he pressured her because he wanted to sell the houses, and she defended what her father Juan Roque had entrusted to her: that if she died without children she must leave the houses to the brotherhood, so that the blacks of the *Zape nation* would administer them and care for them, and what they earned would be used for the good of his soul and that of Ana María. Ana María said that she wanted the foreman and the officials to be entrusted with the houses, which she conveyed to them. And the foreman and the black elders and officials accepted and conferred regarding this business, resolving that Ana María would remain in the houses, but after she died they would administer them and do what she asked. This was the agreement. Thus this witness knows for certain that the houses belong to the brotherhood, because she died without heirs and without making a testament the year that Mexico City flooded.

4. To the fourth question, he said that he does not know.

5. To the fifth question, he said that what he said is publicly known to be true, under the obligation of his oath, which he ratified. He did not sign because he says he does not know how.

Before me,
Pedro de Becerro, Notary

[Testimony of Juan, of the *Zape Nation*, Free Man, Acquaintance of the Roque Family]

Witness   In Mexico City on July 13, 1634, Andrés de Gálvez, procurator, presented on behalf of his party for his case as witness a black man fluent in the Castilian language, who said his name is Juan and that he is of the *Zape nation* and is free from captivity and lives in the Santo Domingo neighborhood. I, the notary, received his oath by God, Our Lord and the sign of the cross. And having made his oath, he swore to tell the truth. And he said the following in response to the questions of the interrogation:

1. To the first question, he said that he knows the litigants and he knew the black man Juan Roque and the black woman Ana María, his daughter, and he knows about this case and the houses under litigation.

General questions: Regarding the general questions of law, he said that none of them applies to him and that he is around seventy years old. And this is his response.

2. To the second question, this witness said that he was a good friend to Juan Roque because they were together almost every day until the day that Juan Roque died and that he left Ana María, his only daughter, the houses she lived in, in the Alameda neighborhood in a lane behind the College of San Juan. She inherited and enjoyed these houses in the company of Juan Fraile, *mulatto*, her husband until he died and then until her own death. Ana María did not have children nor did she give birth. And she did not make a testament, because she died only three days after falling sick with a terrible *cocoliste*. She did not have any heirs, and this witness knows this because he interacted and communicated with Ana María from her birth until the day she died, entering and leaving her parents' house and the house belonging to her and her husband after her parents died.

3. To the third question, he said that he knows that before he died, Juan Fraile tried to sell the houses that she had inherited from her father and that Ana María did not want to consent to this. This led to some arguments between them. This witness wanted peace and the best for Ana María, whom he thought of as a daughter. One day she complained of her husband's aspersions regarding the sale of the houses, and this witness advised her to do what her husband asked in order to conserve the peace, to which Ana María replied that she could not do that because although the houses were hers, her father, from whom she had inherited them, had entrusted them to her and charged her that if she did not have children she should not dispose of the houses but give them to the Brotherhood of the Immaculate Conception, of which he was a brother and founder, so that the blacks of the *Zape nation* would administer them and take care of their earnings for the benefit of his soul and that of Ana María. And that thus she was firm in her intention to comply with her father's will. This witness told this to the foreman and the other members of the brotherhood so they would take care of it. Time passed, and Juan Fraile died, and when he died this witness was the majordomo of the brotherhood. And they notified this witness that the foreman, who was then Antón de Medina, and the other officials were meeting in Ana María's house. This witness attended the meeting, where Ana María told the foreman that the will of her father Juan Roque had been that these houses go to the brotherhood. She said that she had defended the houses against her husband many times because he had wanted to sell them. As she was a widow without heirs, debts, or relatives, she wanted to do what her father wished. And she entrusted the houses to the foreman and the other officials, who received them. This business was discussed and confirmed, and they came to resolve that Ana María should continue to enjoy the houses as she had up to that point and that after her death, the foreman and the officials of the brotherhood would take possession of them and administer them, in compliance with Ana María's will, to which she agreed. She died fifteen days after this meeting, passing from this life from a *cocoliste* that lasted less than three days. This witness saw her dead and buried in the church

of the Hospital de los *Desamparados*, and therefore he knows that the houses now belong to the brotherhood.

4. To the fourth question, he said that it had been around four years since Ana María died. He does not know with certainty who possesses the houses nor who rents them or enjoys their rent.

5. To the fifth question, he said that what he said is known to be true, public, and notorious, and according to his oath, which he ratified. And he did not sign, because he says he does not know how to write.

> Before me,
> Pedro de Becerro, Notary
> For this examination, two and a half *pesos*, I certify.

7

Death, Gender, and Writing: Testaments of Women of African Origin in Seventeenth-Century Lima, 1651–1666[1]

José R. Jouve Martín

In 1651, Juana Barba, a free black woman, went to the office of Marcelo Antonio de Figueroa, a public notary in the city of Lima, in order to have him write her last will and testament. She was ill, feared that her death was imminent, and wanted to put her soul on the path to salvation. She also wanted to leave a detailed account of her belongings, which included clothes, money, jewelry, and no fewer than four slaves. She dictated clear instructions for how her property should be divided and used after her death.

In 1666, María de Huancavelica, another free black woman, carried out the very same ritual. Believing her end to be near, she went to a public notary to draw up a written document to guarantee that her religious obligations would be met and that she would have the final say over distributing the property she had accumulated in her lifetime. Her property included clothes, jewelry, money, and five slaves.

During most of the seventeenth century, a great number of women of African descent, some poor, others relatively rich, ordered their testaments to be written by colonial officials in a proportion that greatly surpassed that of men. These women testators left us with extremely rich documentation about their lives and deaths in colonial Lima. Their actions underline the important role that writing and gender played in the structure of this urban slave society.

The Racial Demographics of Seventeenth-Century Lima

When Juana Barba approached Marcelo Antonio de Figueroa in 1651, Lima had become a predominantly black city, a feature accentuated by the forced relocation of most of its indigenous population to the nearby parish of Santiago del Cercado in 1590. The black population peaked as a proportion of the total probably around 1636, when a census ordered by the Marquis of Chichón showed that the capital of the Viceroyalty of Peru had a total of 10,758 Spaniards compared to 13,620 individuals classified as *negros* and 861 as *mulattoes* (Bowser, 341).[2]

In the second half of the seventeenth century, the city's black population began a slow decline in both absolute and relative terms. This decline was due partially to

---

1. See Maps 6 and 10.
2. For the usage of *negro, mulatto,* and other terms associated with individuals of African origin, see the Glossary.

the emergence of new and more profitable markets for slaves in the Atlantic and the Caribbean and partially to the problems that the Spanish slave trade experienced after the collapse of the dynastic union with Portugal in 1640, when the colonies were left without access to their main supplier of slaves (Vila Vilar, 557–64; Torres, 117–18).

The reintegration of the Indian town of Santiago del Cercado into the city of Lima in the 1680s further modified the numeric and racial composition of the city. Although in 1700 peoples of African descent still constituted an important part of Lima's population, their numbers were only slightly more than 10,000 of a total population of 37,234, according to the *Numeración general* (General Enumeration) commissioned by Viceroy Melchor Antonio Portocarrero Lazo de la Vega and completed by the Conde de la Monclova in 1700.

Gender and *Manumission* in Lima

Colonial censuses also show that, unlike the situation in the plantation setting, slightly more women of African descent than men of African descent lived in Lima. Of the 14,481 individuals classified as either black or *mulatto* in the 1636 census, 6,820 were listed as men and 7,661 as women. Similarly, in the *Numeración general* completed by the Conde de la Monclova in 1700, 4,012 were men and 5,323 were women. However, the gender imbalance reflected by these documents was much more marked when it came to freedom.

According to this latter census, 3,120 individuals of African descent were considered free, 1,762 of them women and only 553 of them men. The rest were children for whom no gender information is provided. This imbalance is also widely reflected in the *Protocolos notariales* stored in the Archivo General de la Nación in Lima, in which women appear as the main beneficiaries of *cartas de libertad* (deeds of *manumission*). Women were much more likely than men to be manumitted, partially due to their role as house servants. Working as servants allowed women to have a closer relationship with their masters and even to participate in the household economy by freely selling and buying in the market. Men were allowed into the house less frequently and were usually employed in more strenuous physical tasks or were "hired out" to others (Aguirre, 65). The decision to free slaves often took place at the end of their owner's life, and women slaves proved more likely than men to be granted their freedom in these testaments or to receive conditions that better enabled them to purchase it themselves. In addition to this, Spanish legislation established that bondage was transmitted matrilineally. Women were the child bearers; therefore, it made more economic sense for the families of African descent to try to put together their scant resources to free women first to ensure the freedom of their children (Hünefeldt, 32–36).

The fact that women were manumitted more often than men had a major effect on the position of women of African descent in colonial society vis-à-vis their male counterparts and members of other *castas*. Freedom allowed them to participate more fully in the social and economic life of the cities. Many remained in a position of servitude, barely making a living doing small household jobs such as cleaning, sewing, or cooking; others were able to buy land and trade in the city markets or set up small food shops, known as *chicherías*, or other businesses.

The most resourceful of these women, such as Juana Barba and María de Huan-cavelica, ended up amassing a small fortune. As their testaments indicate, they were able to participate in the informal, but more lucrative trade of lending money to others. This lending sometimes had freedom as the object of negotiation. Given the difficulty slaves had raising the large sums needed to free themselves or their families (at the same time keeping their masters away from their earnings), borrowing money from other members of the black community was important for buying their own freedom.

Gender and money also allowed free women of African descent to interact with members of other *castas*, particularly other women, in a way that men could only dream of. In fact, most communication with women classified as Spaniards was all but closed to black and *mulatto* men but remained mostly open to black and *mulatta* women. Their testaments show that this communication took place and that it frequently involved social and economic exchanges. Freedom and trade also allowed women to establish extensive interactions with colonial lettered culture; and although many did not even know how to write their name, they knew full well the power of the written word and carefully guarded notarized documents in their possession.

Literacy, Orality, and the Preparation of a Last Will and Testament

Not surprisingly, the combination of social, economic, and spiritual concerns led many women of African descent to interact with colonial officials and write their testaments. Perhaps more than any other document in the life of an individual, a testament was a compendium of material and religious negotiations. Testaments were used to decide who inherited the possessions of the deceased, what moral and economic obligations needed to be satisfied, where the corpse was to be buried, which confraternities, if any, should be present at the funeral, how many Masses would be celebrated for the salvation of the soul, and so on.

The Church strongly recommended that the faithful, rich or poor, write their testament before leaving this world for the next; the Church also benefited from this practice—both spiritually and economically (Le Goff, 289–333; Van Deusen, 32–37). Even though colonial notaries kept testaments within the boundaries of orthodoxy, testaments offer a wealth of information about the religious beliefs and concerns of peoples of African descent in colonial times.

They are also key documents in our effort to reconstruct the material culture of the members of this community and the myriad social interactions built upon it; they allow us to observe the processes of social stratification and racial negotiation that took place within this population. In fact, testaments are one of the few large bodies of documentation that permit us to analyze in depth the social and cultural life of this group from the perspective of both gender and literacy.

The writing of a testament was one of the most important occasions in which men and women of African descent had the opportunity to interact with colonial lettered culture. Even if the colonial legislation permitted the testator to write his or her own testament, it still favored mediation by those who had the capacity for legal representation: the *escribanos*, or notaries (Eire, 34). Of course, most people of

African descent were illiterate, and, even though a few were able to write and read, a testament was a complex and important enough document that it required the mediation of colonial officials.

The place where a testament was written could vary according to necessity and the moment in which it was written. Usually it was redacted in the *escribanías*, but, in more exceptional cases, and in particular if the person was gravely ill and unable to stand up, the notary could write the testament at the bedside. Other people were present with the individual making the will and the notary; these were either companions of the testator or other individuals from the notary's office, who served as witnesses and helped to ratify the validity of the document (Jouve Martín, 78–82). Access to the services of the *escribanos* was facilitated by the fact that most *escribanías* were located in Lima's central square or close to it, which made them highly visible to all members of colonial society, including blacks.

The language in which a testament was written was highly formulaic, particularly in the initial and concluding parts of the document. These formulas could change from one notary to another, but in general terms they were fairly standard (Herzog, 33). This standardization was a response to the fact that, since the thirteenth century, Spanish law had produced models on which these documents were based. From a linguistic point of view, they were texts written in the first-person singular, which created the autobiographical fiction that the person named in the document was also its author.

Only at the end of the testament is the identity of the colonial notary and his role in the creation of the document established. His signature, along with the signatures of the testator and witnesses, gave the document legal validity. In case the testator did not know how to write his or her name, a witness was called to do it in the *testador*'s place. Despite the decisive role of the notary in the writing of the testament, its creation frequently bridged the oral/written divide in several ways. Apart from the clearly formulaic sections and the beginning and end of the document, the testator basically dictated to the notary his or her final dispositions concerning the funeral and possessions.

This fact frequently allows us to find elements of orality in the document. Once finished, the document was read aloud before being signed. Translating silent signs into oral ones, reading aloud was of fundamental importance for the effective participation of illiterate people in the colonial legal culture. Perhaps more importantly, black women might not have been able to read these documents by themselves, but they were acutely aware of documents' role in colonial society and usually knew how to use them. They might not have known how to write or read them, but they were familiar with the language of the law. The existing documentation demonstrates that the writing of a testament was not exclusive to women of a determined *casta* (*negro*, *mulatto*, *zambo*, *pardo*, *cuarterón*, etc.) or a specific *nación* or ethnic group (*Folupa*, *Caboverde*, *Terranova*, *Bran*, etc.). Not even the condition of being an *horro* or *horra* (a freeman or free woman) was necessarily fundamental to be able to commission a will or a testament, and there are examples of slaves who gave their last wills under the supervision of their masters. Furthermore, although those with more material possessions were more likely to write a testament, there is also ample evidence in the Archivo Arzobispal de Lima of women of African descent who lived and died in poverty but still wanted to make sure that their scant resources were sent to close relatives or used for the salvation of their souls (Jouve Martín, 155–79).

The testaments of Juana Barba and María de Huancavelica, which follow, are remarkable as examples of economically successful black women. It is not remarkable, however, that black women made testaments. Both women were categorized as *negras*, which means that their socioeconomic position was not due to any genealogical relation with a Spaniard. In fact, María de Huancavelica was born in Africa and was probably brought to Peru as a slave. At the end of her life, like Juana Barba before her, she had become a slave owner herself. Both were relatively affluent and, although Juana Barba's list of possessions is longer and reveals her involvement in the cloth trade, María de Huancavelica did not lag behind and had the means necessary to establish a *capellanía* (chaplaincy) for her confessor.

Their testaments have left us with a testimony of power, stratification, and spirituality in colonial Lima and of the important role played by gender in its black community. Both documents come from the Archivo Arzobispal de Lima (Archiepiscopal Archive of Lima), which houses the ecclesiastical records for Lima, including court cases, divorces and separations, charges against priests, and many wills. They arrived at this repository through the *Tribunal de bienes de difuntos* (Colonial Tribunal of Property of the Deceased), which had authority over all mortuary dispositions registered in the testaments.

Due to the importance given to the testament in canon law (Church law), they were supervised by the ecclesiastical authorities even though they were written by civil officials. The wills themselves are a small but fundamental portion of the documents that make up each testator's full legal dossier. As is true with most testaments, they are accompanied by subsequent judicial proceedings and decrees (inventories, records of sale, provisions and reprimands to the executors, challenges, etc.).

In some cases, these *autos* (deeds) number twenty, thirty, or forty pages and, therefore, exceed the limitations of this anthology. A complete evaluation of the role of testaments in the life of this community would require taking into account the other documents and accompanying litigation. Although heavily mediated, wills constitute an important way through which people of African heritage expressed themselves and found a voice that endures to our day. They occupy a privileged position in the historical record for those interested in exploring not only the changing nature of religious beliefs, but also the role of gender, literacy, and freedom in shaping the life of a black community in colonial times.

*****

Last Will and Testament of Juana Barba,
Free Black Woman [Lima, 1651][3]

In the name of God, Our Lord, and of the glorious Virgin Mary His precious mother, Our Lady, who was born free of original sin, know those who read this last will and testament that my name is Juana Barba, a free black woman, born and resident in this city of Lima, daughter of Domingo Hernández and Simona Barba, both deceased; and that I am ill, although able to stand and in possession of all the judgment and natural understanding that God, Our Lord, has seen fit to give me; and believing as I firmly believe in the mystery of the Holy Trinity of the Father, the Son, and the Holy Spirit, three persons in one true God, as well as in all that our Holy Roman Catholic Church believes, confesses, and teaches, as a faithful Roman Catholic and as a Christian; and fearful of death, which is consubstantial to all human creatures, and wishing to set my soul on the path to salvation, I hereby declare that I give and arrange my last will and testament in the following way:

First of all, I entrust my soul to God, Our Lord, who created it and redeemed it through his precious blood, death, and passion; and my body shall return to the dust from which it was formed.

Item. I order that, when God, our Lord, wishes to take me from this present life, my body be buried in the Chapel of Saint John of Letrán in the Convent of Saint Dominic in the place that my executors deem most appropriate and that my body be shrouded with the habit of Saint Francis.

Item. I order that on the day of my burial my body be accompanied by a presiding cross [a "+" above the word "cross"], a priest and a sacristan from my parish, which is the Holy Cathedral of this city, and that the rest of the retinue be decided on by my executors to whom I leave all other details of my funeral and burial.

Item. I order that at some time during the day of my funeral or the next one, a Mass be sung for the salvation of my soul, with my body present, followed by a vigil and a pious offering, and that another Mass be celebrated on the day of my commemoration in the same way and the customary alms be paid from my estate.

Item. I order that as soon as possible after I die my executors pay and arrange fifty Masses for the salvation of my soul, and they shall be celebrated in the church and by the priest of their choosing.

Item. I declare that, by God's Mercy, I do not owe anything to anyone.

Item. I declare that I have in my power some stirrups of solid silver pawned at fifty *pesos* by Don Fernando de Castañeda. I order that, if Don Fernando or Don Francisco Barba pay the said fifty *pesos*, the said stirrups be returned to him.

Item. I order that ten *pesos* of eight *reales* be sent as alms to the Holy Sites in Jerusalem.

Item. I order that one hundred *pesos* of eight *reales* be used to make a cloak for the figure of the Virgin, Our Lady, found in the main altar of the Cathedral Church of this city as an expression of my devotion to Her.

---

3. Testamento de Juana Barba, morena libre, Archivo Arzobispal de Lima, Tribunal de Bienes de Difuntos 31:39, 1651, 57 folios.

Item. I set aside eight *pesos* to pay for the customary and obligatory alms.

Item. I bequeath to my sister, Agustina de Ampuero y Barba, five hundred *pesos* of eight *reales* so that she may do as she sees fit with the money after I die.

Item. I also bequeath to my sister two pearl necklaces weighing around six ounces, a pair of gold earrings with green stones, and two petticoats, one with its [illegible] of gold and silk and the other green and purple, and two white bodices. I also order that [my sister] be given all the chinaware and glass found in the top part of my glass cabinet.

Item. I bequeath to my sister, Agustina de Ampuero y Barba, a young black girl, my slave, who was born in my house and is named María de la Cruz, and who is more or less about ten years of age, so that she may serve my sister until she dies, and after that, I order that she be free of all subjection and captivity, and that this clause act as her deed of *manumission*.

Item. I bequeath to my friend, Juana Barrezo, thirty *pesos* of eight *reales* to alleviate her poverty.

Item. I bequeath to *Doña* Bernarda de Morales and to her two daughters fifty *pesos* of eight *reales* that are to be taken from the money collected once the silver stirrups are redeemed, and I do so out of the love I have for them.

Item. I bequeath to María Santoja, lay sister in the Convent of the Immaculate Conception of this city, fifty *pesos* of eight *reales* to alleviate her poverty.

Item. I bequeath ten *pesos* of eight *reales* as alms to the Brotherhood of Our Lady of the Presentation founded in the monastery of Saint Dominic of this city. I order that they be given to the prioress of the said brotherhood, of which I am a slave.[4]

Item. I bequeath ten *pesos* of eight *reales* as alms to help raise orphan children.

Item. I order that a thousand *pesos* of eight *reales* be given from my estate to the licenciate Diego de Ocampo, priest, so that, in consultation with Father Francisco de Soria, my confessor, they be distributed in the way that I have communicated to them for the unburdening of my conscience and my soul, and I exempt the ecclesiastical and secular justice of their obligation to oversee them based on the high esteem in which I hold them.

Item. It is my will that Laura *Carabalí*, my slave, who is married to Alejandro *Carabalí*, be freed from all subjection and captivity upon paying fifty *pesos* of eight *reales* and that my executors grant her the deed of *manumission*. She will give to my executors these fifty *pesos* at a rate of eight *pesos* each month, from the day of my death forward, until she pays the total amount.

Item. I declare that I own as my slave a married black woman named Clara, of the *Bran nation*, and it is my will that she be allowed to pay a hundred *pesos* of eight *reales* to be freed of all subjection and captivity, and once she does so, I order my executors to give her the deed of *manumission*.

Item. I declare that I own as my slave a black woman named Juana, of the *Bran nation*, thirty years of age. It is my will that she serve my sister Agustina de Ampuero for four years after my death, after which I order that she be freed from all subjection and captivity and that this clause act as her deed of *manumission*. If the said black

---

4. Members of certain brotherhoods, particularly those devoted to the Virgin Mary or to the Sacred Heart of Jesus Christ, are frequently referred to as "slaves" (devotees of the Virgin or of Jesus), but they are not slaves in the usual sense of being the possession of another individual.

woman would like to enter in the Convent of the Immaculate Conception in which my sister will take vows, then so be it. If not, then she may serve her from the outside.

Item. I declare the following as part of my estate:

First, two thousand two hundred *pesos* of eight *reales* that Mateo de Samacola and Martin de Larrinbe owe me according to a deed given before Sebastián Ortiz, public notary of this city, and that I lent them for the term of one year starting in 1650. Since the term is passed, I order that they be collected.

Item. A necklace of bits of pearls that has thirteen strings and is decorated with an image of the Immaculate Conception and beads of gold

Item. A bracelet of small pearls

Item. A pair of earrings of pearls and gold

Item. A ring of gold with a purple sapphire

Item. A bracelet of blue garnets with beads of gold

Item. A choker of gold beads

Item. Two medium-sized, double-handled bowls [or cups] of silver, and seven ordinary silver spoons, a silver fork, three knives of silver, and four silver thimbles

Item. The four slaves that I have declared in this testament

Item. A pair of earrings of green stones, and six ounces of pearls in another bracelet, and a necklace that I have already declared in this testament, which is the one that I ordered to be given to my sister

Item. A large glass-fronted cabinet and the chinaware and earthenware in it

Item. A large trunk from Panama

Item. A medium trunk from Panama

Item. Another small one for sewing items

Item. Eleven new shirts for women, some already made and others to be made

Item. Four new embroidered petticoats

Item. Three new ruffs with needlepoint stitching

Item. Three new chambray head kerchiefs and fine needlework

Item. Three new handkerchiefs of chambray with fine needlework

Item. A pair of green silk stockings, never worn

Item. Two or three pairs of new stockings and their slippers

Item. Six new white pillows of fine Rouen cloth,[5] four of which have their loops and buttons, and another four pillows [that] have their cases of blue taffeta

Item. Eight new sheets of fine flowered Rouen cloth, never used

Item. A pair of embroidered pillows made of fine Rouen cloth with crimson silk and others of the same form, and two of these pillows I bequeath to my sister Agustina de Ampuero y Barba

Item. Seven handkerchiefs of fine Rouen cloth and homespun linen, some of [illegible] and others embroidered and others plain

Item. Three tablecloths, two new and another used

Item. Twelve used napkins

Item. A fine crimson and green [illegible]

Item. Two blue woolen bedspreads from Quito and a blue blanket

---

5. Probably fine linen.

Item. Two good canopies, one that is on my bed and the other that is in the box, and I bequeath the latter to my sister, Agustina de Ampuero y Barba

Item. Two white bedspreads, one new and the other used

Item. Another used blanket embroidered with [illegible] thread

Item. An ordinary wooden bed frame

Item. A wooden stand from in front of the bed

Item. And another large platform in two parts

Item. A large chest of drawers and another small, both used, and another new small one

Item. A used wall cushion

Item. Four ordinary new mats

Item. Four tables, two large and two small, and a screen, and two benches and nine or ten large ordinary chairs and one small one for sitting

Item. I bequeath to my sister Agustina de Ampuero y Barba one of the small tables I have just mentioned

Item. A wooden stand for earthenware jars with its cabinet and many plates, large and small

Item. A round whetstone with its mechanism

Item. A trough for kneading, and a large door, and some wooden boards

Item. Five skirts of different colors

Item. Two black shawls, the new one with five trimmings of velvet and the other used

Item. One new blue shawl with three bands of gold sevillaneta cloth, and three cloth bodices, one green, one purple, and the other blue; two from the last period of mourning and the other one of double black taffeta, and a skirt of green cloth, and one of Mandarin damask, and another of blue [illegible]

Item. Three basins, two large, the other medium, and the other smaller

Item. As to the rest of my household furniture and wares found to be part of my estate after my death, I order my trustee to make an inventory.

Item. I order that a medium-sized box and the medium-sized basin be given to my sister Agustina de Ampuero, and so it is my will.

Item. I order that all of my slaves [the word "sisters" has been crossed out] receive thick flannel for their mourning clothes, and my sister receive flannel from Castile, of the blue kind, and a veil.

Item. A used chair

Item. Two small tables and two benches for sitting

Item. A large mortar and a skillet, and a new pot, and another used one, two grills, a large, shallow pan for watering, and three brass candlesticks

And, in order to carry out this testament and its contents and pay for its dispositions, I name as my executors the *licentiate* Diego de Ocampo, priest, and my sister Agustina de Ampuero y Barba, and as trustee of my estate, I name the above-mentioned *licentiate* Diego de Ocampo. I give them complete power *in solidum* for the use and exercise of the said execution. I authorize them to appear in court and claim what they may deem necessary, and I allow them to issue deeds of payment and to cover all expenses that may arise and make all the decisions that may be required in the execution of this will, in all ways and cases, for as long as they may need even if it exceeds the period of one year and one day established by law to carry out this execution.

Once this testament and its dispositions have been carried out and paid, I leave and name my soul as the universal heir of whatever might remain of my estate, debts, rights, and actions. My executors together with the Jesuit Father Francisco de Soria will ensure that this is done in the way and form that I have expressed and communicated with them, and they will not be held accountable by any ecclesiastical or secular justice, because I relieve them of such, due to the high esteem in which I hold these persons and to the fact that I do not have any heirs, and this is my last will.

And through this document, I hereby revoke all former wills, codicils, powers to make a will, and testamentary dispositions of every nature and kind heretofore made by me in word or writing or in any other way, and I do not want them to be valid nor can they be used in or outside court, except for this one that I now declare as my testament, and I want it to be carried out and executed as my last will in the way that follows best what is prescribed by law, in faith of which I granted this testament in the City of Kings [Lima] on the twenty-eighth of February of 1651. And the said testator, whom I, the notary, testify that I know, did not sign it because she stated that she did not know how to, and at her request, a witness signed on her behalf, being called and requested as witnesses Gregorio de Herrera, royal notary, José Lozano de Esquivel, Bartolomé Canelas, Don Álvaro de Lereceda, Agustín de Barragán, all of whom were present at the request of the testator, and Gregorio de Herrera served as witness. In witness thereof, I, Marcelo Antonio de Figueroa, public notary.

[Signatures]

[Last Will and Testament of María de Huancavelica, Free Black Woman of the *Folupa Nation*, Lima, 1666][6]

In the name of God, amen, in whose beginning all things have their just, praiseworthy, and fortunate end: Know, those who read this last will and testament, that I, María de Huancavelica, a free black woman of the *Folupa nation*, native of Ethiopia in *Guinea*, resident of the City of Kings [Lima] in Peru, daughter of unknown parents, being sick in bed of an illness that Our Lord God has seen fit to give me and believing as I firmly and truly believe in the mystery of the most Holy Trinity, the Father, the Son, and the Holy Spirit, three distinct persons in one true God, and in all the rest that the Holy Mother Roman Catholic Church believes, confesses, and teaches, under whose faith and belief I have lived and I profess to live and die as a Catholic Christian, and fearful of death, which is consubstantial to all human creatures, I hereby make and declare my last will and testament in the following way and form:

First of all, I entrust my soul to Our Lord God, who created it and redeemed it with the infinite price of his blood, and my body shall return to the dust from which it was formed.

---

6. Testamento e inventario de bienes de María de Huancavelica, morena libre, de casta folupa, Albacea: Gracia de la Paz, *negra folupa* libre, Archivo Arzobispal de Lima, Tribunal de Bienes de Difuntos 69:6, 1666,70 folios.

Item. I want and it is my will that, once Our Lord sees fit to take me from this present life, my body be buried in the Convent of Saint Francis in this city or in the place that my executors deem most appropriate, and that my body be shrouded with the habit of Saint Francis to earn the graces and indulgences that it brings, and a presiding cross, priest, and sacristan from my parish accompany my burial. And with regard to the rest of the retinue and details of my burial, I leave them to the discretion of my executors, and I order that the day of my burial, or if not, the day deemed appropriate by my executors, a funeral Mass be celebrated with my body present that includes offerings of bread and wine, and it must be done as is customary and paid for from my estate.

Item. I set aside from my estate two *pesos* to pay for the customary and obligatory alms.

Item. I order ten *pesos* of eight *reales* to pay the ransom of captive children in Moorish lands, and it must come from a legitimate part of my estate.

Item. I order another ten *pesos* to be sent to the Holy Sites of Jerusalem where our Holy Redemption took place and to be given to the priest who asks for these alms.

Item. I declare that I do not owe anything. I declare it so that there is no doubt.

Item. I declare as my assets the following:

Item. I declare that the laborer Juan de Villegas Álvarez owes me two thousand *pesos* of eight *reales* according to a notarized document that I have among my papers. I declare it so that there may be no doubt.

Item. I declare that Antonio *Carabalí* owes me 350 *pesos* of eight *reales* that I lent him for his *manumission*. I pardon and forgive what I lent him for his freedom so that nothing more is asked of him, and in the same way, I implore my executors not to ask anything more of him because such is my will.

Item. I declare that Jacinta of the *Folupa nation* owes me four hundred *pesos* of eight *reales* of the eight hundred *pesos* that I lent her for her *manumission*. I order that the four hundred still owed be collected and nothing additional.

Item. I declare as my slave María, of the *Folupa nation*, and I order and it is my will that after my death she be manumitted, and she needs only this clause and my death to obtain her freedom, without collection of any payment nor the writing of any other document, and this is my will because of how well she has served me.

[I declare as my slave] María, of the Mandinga *nation*, and I order and it is my will that she be freed and my executors give her the deed of *manumission* upon payment by her or by any other person of three hundred *pesos* of eight *reales*, and that she must not be sold for more than the said amount and, in the meantime until she can pay the full amount of three hundred *pesos* for her freedom, I want her to pay only four *pesos* of eight *reales* of wages each month to my executors, and this I order.

[I declare as my slave] Ambrosio *Folupo*, and I order and it is my will that upon his payment of three hundred *pesos* of eight *reales*, he be freed and my executors give him the deed of *manumission* and that he must not be sold for more than the said amount, and, in the meantime, until he can pay the full amount, he will be obligated to pay to my executors four *pesos* of eight *reales* of wages each month.

[I declare as my slave] Antón *Folupo*, and I order and it is my will that upon his payment of two hundred fifty *pesos* of eight *reales*, he be freed and my executors give him the deed of *manumission*, and he cannot be sold for an amount above the stated two hundred fifty *pesos*, and, in the meantime until he can pay the full amount, he will be obligated to pay four *pesos* of eight *reales* of wages each month.

[I declare as my slave] Susana *Folupa*, and I order and it is my will that upon her payment of two hundred *pesos* of eight *reales* for my burial she be freed and that my executors give her the deed of *manumission* and that she should not be sold for more.

Item. I declare two small double-handled bowls [or cups] of silver, a box from Panamá, a trunk, and the clothing that will be made clear in the inventory.

Item. I declare that [I have] a skirt and a shawl of black flannel, a skirt of silk, and a bodice of [illegible] that belongs to Rafaela Zapata and one hundred and five *pesos* of eight *reales* that also belong to her. I want my executors to return all these things to her and that she give them either a written receipt or that the transaction be done in front of a notary.

Item. I declare that María of the Congo *nation* is indebted to me in a certain amount of *pesos*. I order that only fifty *pesos* of eight *reales* be collected from her, and I forgive her the rest on the condition that she pray for me to God.

Item. I declare that I owe Manuel Espadero, a black man, a total of thirty-five *pesos* of eight *reales*, the remainder of some *reales* that his deceased wife, María *Folupa*, gave to me. I order that he be paid this amount and also that he be given some bracelets made of coral and a small box, and he must give a receipt for it.

And to fulfill and pay for this testament and the bequests and legacies in it, I leave and name as my executors my confessor, the *licentiate* Juan [Zapata de Henao?], presbyter, and Gracia de la Paz, of the *Folupa nation*, [and] as the trustee, the said Gracia *Folupa*. And I grant them power as executors to organize, sell, and resolve my estate at public auction or otherwise, in order to fulfill and pay for this last will and testament and its bequests, and I also grant them all the time they may require to do so even if it exceeds the year that the law concedes.

Item. I declare that Miguel *Folupo* gave to me thirty-three *pesos* to safeguard. I order that it be paid back to him from my assets.

Item. I declare that Simón *Folupa* gave me twenty *pesos* to safeguard, and I order that it be paid back to him from my assets.

Item. I declare that I bought a black woman, María *Folupa*, at a price of 350 *pesos* as certified in writing by Francisco de Acuña, royal notary, from a *parda* woman named María de Bilbao who assists at the hospital of Saint Bartholomew, and I declare that the said slave belongs to Juliana *Folupa*, who gave me the money for this transaction, and I declare it for the unburdening of my conscience.

Item. I declare that I have in my possession a double-handled bowl [or cup] and a silver spoon belonging to Susana *Folupa* that she gave me to safeguard. I order that it be returned to her.

And I leave and name my soul as heir of whatever assets, debts, rights, and actions might remain from the liquidation of my estate, and it is my wish that this money be used to establish a chaplaincy, which should be founded by the *licentiate* Juan [Zapata de Henao?], my executor and confessor, whom I leave as its patron and chaplain. And he is allowed to name his successor after he dies, and he can establish the alms to be given for each Mass according to what I have communicated to him, and this chaplaincy must be established after I die, and no judge should interfere because this is my will, and he can establish all the necessary clauses according to his judgment because I do not have any heirs who can inherit my estate.

Item. I order that twelve *pesos* of eight *reales* be sent to the Hospital of Saint Bartholomew.

Item. I order that six *pesos* of eight *reales* be sent to the Sweet Name of Jesus against Blasphemies.

Item. I order that twelve *pesos* of eight *reales* be sent for the rearing of the orphan children on the condition that they accompany my body the day of my burial.

Item. I declare that I have in *reales* a total of nine hundred *pesos* of eight *reales*, more or less, and the exact amount will be determined in the inventory.

I hereby revoke all former wills and testamentary dispositions of every nature and kind heretofore made by me in word or in writing or in any other way and I do not want them to be valid nor can they be used in or outside court, except for this one that I now declare as my testament, and I want it to be carried out and executed as my last will in the way that best follows the law. And I testify that this testament is done in the City of Kings [Lima] of Peru, the sixth day of the month of January of the year 1666. And the testator, whom, I, the notary, certify that I know, seemed to be in complete possession of her judgment and natural memory, judging from her answer to the questions that I asked her, and this is what she ordered, and she did not sign it because she said that she did not know how to write, and at her request a witness signed it. . . .

To Live as a *Pueblo*: A Contentious Endeavor, El Cobre, Cuba, 1670s–1790s[1]

María Elena Díaz

A *Pueblo* Founded by *Royal Slaves*

Spanning a long period of some 120 years, the four document excerpts in this chapter provide a rare composite view through time of an "unusual" community of people of African ancestry in colonial Latin America. The community was founded by "*royal slaves*," that is, slaves belonging to the king of Spain. After the Spanish Crown confiscated the copper mines of Santiago del Prado (also known as El Cobre) in the 1670s, the slaves who had worked in the previously private mining settlement became the king's slaves. The transformation from "private" mining slaves to *royal slaves* produced a number of significant—even radical—changes in these enslaved subjects' identity and in their living and working arrangements. Foremost among these was the opportunity to found a *pueblo* in the newly deprivatized mining jurisdiction.[2]

The various direct and mediated voices represented in these documents evoke the difficulties that this controversial community faced after its inception in the 1670s. The texts also reflect the range of social categories, self-representations, and identities that these bonded subjects deployed in their lives and dealings with the state throughout the period in question. Of particular interest is the way they initially negotiated the discursive and practical meaning of the abstract category of *royal slavery* and combined it with a *pueblo* affiliation. In fact, one of the most fascinating aspects of the present case is precisely the communal identification as a *pueblo* that these subjects conjured and endeavored to make good despite their racial and ambiguous enslaved status.

Communities can take many formal and informal shapes, and not all communities can be considered *pueblos*. In the Spanish empire, *pueblos* were communal corporations with some land rights and limited self-governance, and they constituted political units within the broader imperial polity. Various legal, political, social, and cultural presuppositions underwrote these entities. For instance, only free people could constitute a corporate *pueblo* (enslaved subjects could not). Free family households were the basic building blocks of such communities. Local citizenship (*vecindad*) entailed rights to land and to local self-government by way of a municipal council (*cabildo*). In many localities local citizenship may have been constrained by "purity of blood" (that is, racial) considerations. In the New World, however, *indios* constituted

---

1. See Maps 5 and 11.
2. For a quasi-ethnographic study of the transformations that took place in various spheres of life and work, see Díaz, *The Virgin*. For an examination of changes in specific areas, see Díaz, "Conjuring Identities" and "Mining Women."

autonomous corporate *pueblos* of their own based on a separate jurisdiction known as the Republics of Indians (Díaz, "Conjuring Identities"). Given some of these legal and political criteria, a *pueblo* of *royal slaves* represented an anomalous formation in the Spanish colonial world.

Other criteria of affiliation to *pueblos* included territorial origin by birth (although marriage and long-term residence could also serve as bases of inclusion). Christian identification was paramount for membership, and at the center of every duly constituted *pueblo* there was a parish church. *Pueblo* identities were linked to the performance of local traditions and festivities, most of which had a religious character at the time (for example, celebrations of local patron saints). In the case of El Cobre, there was even a Marian shrine that may have helped legitimize this unusual community of *royal slaves* as a *pueblo*. Although *Maroon* communities of escaped slaves emerged on the margins of the colonial world (see Chapters 2 and 5), black corporate *pueblos* within the colonial body polity seem to have been rarer, even in the case of free people of African ancestry. Historians are beginning to find them scattered throughout the vast peripheries and frontiers of empire partly incorporated into the Crown's broader defense projects (see, for example, Granda; Landers; Taylor).

More generally, however, free and enslaved subjects of African descent lived in Spanish towns and cities or on plantations and other production locations and did not tend to constitute autonomous corporate *pueblos* of their own, particularly if they were bonded subjects.[3]

Enslaved status in the colonial context constituted virtual "social death" and exclusion from the body polity (Patterson, 1–14). Although no longer private slaves, most of the former mining slaves of El Cobre remained juridically enslaved to the king (or the state) and, in principle, they remained "socially dead" subjects with few, if any, rights and a legal condition in many ways analogous to that of chattel. Notwithstanding their bonded status, the *royal slaves* of El Cobre were able to capitalize on what they deemed to be their special status and relation to the king, linking it, with some success, to a number of prerogatives, including the option to live as a *pueblo*. Part of this case's interest lies in how the collective identity and the prerogatives of this anomalous community of enslaved people were negotiated and justified.

To be sure, *royal slaves* did not abound in the Spanish empire. Most bonded subjects throughout the Americas were private slaves subject to private masters. But the state did have some slaves at its disposal who were employed in public works and fortification projects. The strategic frontier location of this mining jurisdiction in a multinational Caribbean contributed to the concessions the community was able to obtain as the *royal slaves* took on an important role in the Crown's defense system.[4]

No less surprising is how far these *royal slaves* mobilized to defend their right to live as a *pueblo* against the attacks of various sectors of colonial society, including

---

3. The most recent overview of African slavery in colonial Latin America can be found in chapter 1 of Andrews, *Afro-Latin America*.

4. For the role of blacks in the Spanish Crown's imperial defense system, see Deschamps Chapeaux; Klein; and Vinson. For the Caribbean as a frontier region, see Pérez (39–45). See also the map section in Díaz, *El Cobre*.

some governors, royal officials, and, especially, the heirs of the former private owners of the mines. By the end of the eighteenth century the community had taken the extraordinary step of sending one of their own local leaders to Madrid to directly oversee a litigation process that dragged on for fifteen years over the community's collective freedom and the legality of the heirs' rights to the mining jurisdiction.

There are no cases on record to date of enslaved people in colonial Latin America, or for that matter of free people of African ancestry, who have litigated collectively so far up in the judicial system.[5]

This community's strong engagement with the colonial state throughout the years resulted in the production of abundant documentation. Moreover, as a result of the above-mentioned litigation in Madrid, documentary material that would have normally been scattered throughout different local and state archives (if not altogether lost) was carefully compiled into a legal dossier and subsequently conserved as a unified record in the Archive of the Indies. That opportune intervention has led to a particularly strong preservation of Afro-Latino voices in the record for this case.

Although some of these voices were mediated by the hand of an amanuensis—or perhaps a scribe—and by the conventions of the various genres to which their texts subscribed, at least two documents were allegedly written directly by literate subjects in this community. The selections in this chapter include a petition to authorities and three letters with varying purposes. All four constitute rich and unusual documents for the narratives they display, the representations of collective self they invoke, the remarkable claims they put forth, the events and details of life they portray, and the uses of writing among free and enslaved subjects mostly associated with oral culture. All things considered, many factors conspire to make of El Cobre a truly remarkable case study, one that opens up unexpected vistas of the Afro-Latin experience in the Iberian black Atlantic world.

Historical Background

When the Spanish Crown deprivatized the copper mining jurisdiction of El Cobre (from the Spanish for "copper"), some 270 former private mining slaves then became the king's slaves. By 1773, the community had flourished into a hybrid *pueblo* of some 1,200 inhabitants, of which 65 percent were *royal slaves*, 33 percent were free people of color, mostly relatives of the *royal slaves*, and 2 percent were private slaves (belonging to the clergy and to other members of the community, both free and *royal slaves*).[6] The transformation into a *pueblo* came to entail, among other things, a collective land grant, four militia battalions, and even a local *cabildo* (or municipal

---

5. Although it was not uncommon for slaves in Iberian colonial societies to access local courts to seek redress regarding a series of issues including individual *manumission*, ill treatment, and other matters, few, if any, are known to have made it to the highest court of appeal in Madrid. For slaves' use of the courts, see Aguirre (181–210); Chaves (108–26); Díaz, *The Virgin* (285–313).
6. For an account of these personal or private slaves and of slaveholding in El Cobre, see Díaz, *The Virgin* (179–98).

self-government) of *royal slaves*. Other transformations included *royal slaves'* appropriation of some mining resources and their creation of a small, informal, and mostly female mining industry in the village.

An important shrine to the Virgin of Charity also flourished in this black *pueblo* after 1670. That local Marian tradition became so important that more than two and a half centuries later Our Lady of Charity of El Cobre became the symbol of the Cuban nation, although by then her memory as the local patroness of a black *pueblo* had faded away.[7]

Yet the juridical and political status of this community remained tenuous throughout subsequent years. In the 1770s, the Crown decided to reprivatize the mines and return them to the heirs of the private contractor Don Juan de Eguiluz. That decision resulted in the most serious challenge to the *royal slaves'* collective existence as a *pueblo* in a whole century. After the new generation of owners repossessed the mining jurisdiction, they removed, "re-enslaved," and even sold away the *royal slaves*—whom they considered their private slaves—and demanded rents for land from those who had become freemen and freewomen and could not be captured as repossessed slaves.

In the face of such an attack, the besieged community sent Gregorio Cosme Osorio, a literate freedman from El Cobre, to Spain to contest the Crown's decision and to litigate their claims. Sponsored by the free *cobreros* (natives of El Cobre) remaining in the *pueblo*, Osorio represented his compatriots in the metropolitan tribunals and corresponded with them over different aspects of the case.

In 1800, the community's long endeavor culminated in a royal edict granting collective emancipation to all the *cobreros*, formal recognition as a corporate community, and land rights.[8] The community's legal victory, however, opened up a new period of local struggle to bring about the local implementation of some of the concessions obtained in Madrid. Yet, freedom and the right to live as local citizens of a corporate community had been legally secured—at least for the first three or four decades of the nineteenth century.

A Letter from a Slave to His Owner, 1672

The first two documents belong to the initial transitional decade of the 1670s and point to the transformations that took place as the former private mining slaves became a community of *royal slaves*. The first document, a letter allegedly written by a literate slave to his owner in Havana, is of enormous interest in all its apparent simplicity. It not only chronicles the transformations taking place in the mining settlement barely two years after the Crown's confiscation of the mines but exposes as well a web of conflictive voices, stances, claims, and understandings colliding over what

---

7. See Díaz, *The Virgin*, for the emergence and development of this local Marian shrine (95–145) and the local mining industry (199–223). For the present significance of the cult to the Virgin of Charity and other related Afro-Cuban traditions, see Díaz, *El Cobre*.
8. The status of the community was also upgraded from *pueblo* (village) to *villa* (town). See Diaz, *The Virgin* (325–27).

royal slavery entailed at that early crucial moment. Note in particular the oblique association made by these former private slaves between the practical meaning of royal slavery and having become *horros*, or free.

Nicolás de Montenegro's own critical voice betrays his alliance with the interests of the Eguiluz family, which until recently had owned the rights to the mines and their slaves. It is the voice of a privileged family slave betraying a conventional understanding of slavery and pining for a previous order of things now rapidly falling apart before his very own eyes. There is, however, a hidden history further layering Montenegro's stance in this document. Although not evident from the text, we know that he was related by blood to his owner, Doña Paula, and, in this sense, their bond also embodied the disavowed hidden genealogies that often linked master and slave classes in colonial slave regimes.

Whether aware of it or not, Nicolás de Montenegro was the slave son of the long-deceased private contractor of the mines, Don Juan de Eguiluz, and the contractor's slave Paula de Eguiluz, who was prosecuted for witchcraft by the Inquisition of Cartagena de Indias when Nicolás was only an infant (see Chapter 11). To complicate identities and genealogies even further (and to note a slight Freudian twist), Eguiluz's own daughter was, like his slave mistress, named Paula de Eguiluz. In short, Doña Paula, who shared a name with Nicolás' mother, was also his stepsister and owner and may have raised him as a house slave after his mother's banishment from El Cobre in 1622. Nicolás could have identified with his paternal family's house and property—even regarding it partly as his own—in an analogous move to that of the *royal slaves'* identification with the king and his property (Díaz, *The Virgin*, 54–73).

Reading this letter today, we might consider the following questions: What were the conventional understandings of slavery to which Montenegro seems to subscribe? What kind of arrangements and prerogatives did these slaves associate with their new status as *royal slaves*? Did Montenegro identify himself as one of them? In what ways was the old social order collapsing and a new one emerging as Montenegro writes?

Petition from Captain Juan to Judge Don Antonio Matienzo, Mines of Santiago del Prado, 1677

The second document constitutes a "foundational" text insofar as in it enslaved subjects, in this case *Creole royal slaves*, display for the first time claims related to a *patria* and *pueblo* identity. The context for this petition was a royal order that came down in 1677, once the Crown decided how to dispose of its confiscated property in the recently deprivatized jurisdiction. The edict ordered the transfer of part of the male slave population to work in the fortification projects of Havana and others could be allowed to purchase their own freedom.

This order would have meant the dispersal of the enslaved population and in effect the breakup of the community. The *royal slaves* responded with a political act of flight to the mountains and from there negotiated their stay in El Cobre as a community, thereby demonstrating that petitions and discursive negotiations of identity had to be backed up with political action to be effective. The document is the first on record in which these enslaved subjects make collective claims.

Many other petitions would follow in the following century. In this one, the petitioning subjects portrayed themselves in various ways, including as soldiers.[9] Given the frontier character of this location in eastern Cuba (see Map 11), military service had special significance (Pérez, 39–45).

The title of captain that Juan Moreno held, however, did not at this time refer as much to a military rank as to authority in the enslaved community, perhaps along the lines of a *mandador*, as in the case of Nicolás de Montenegro. Captain Juan Moreno coauthored another foundational text ten years later: a deposition of the "apparition" of the Virgin of Charity that he had witnessed when he was a boy.[10] Perhaps his authority was partly related to his participation in that holy event of the past and the Christian identification it evoked.

Note that Moreno offered to allow the slaves to pay for their own freedom at some point in the future, a well-established practice in Cuba and many locations of Spanish colonial society that was known as *coartación* (self-purchase). Although a few members of the community eventually purchased their freedom, most never did. It was unlikely that they could come up with the sums required to purchase the freedom of 270 slaves; therefore, the allusion to *coartación* may have been a formality to strengthen their case for the main requested concession.

Moreno was not literate, so an ally or protector in the nearby city of Santiago de Cuba may have redacted the coarse petition. Despite the formulaic opening and closing, the text invokes a wide range of affiliations that the slaves claimed—as soldiers, family heads, and members of a *pueblo* and a local homeland. These affiliations could presumably trump the sheer property-like or "socially dead" status of enslaved subjects and their absolute subservience to a master's will. Questions we might consider include the following: What loyalties and claims were implicitly associated with these identities? How would they override conventional understandings of slaves as chattel? What concessions did the petition request? How did it make its case? What practices among these enslaved people seem more striking to you? How do Moreno's voice and account compare with those of Montenegro?

A 1792 Letter from Martín de Salazar Denouncing Abuses

The third and fourth documents are set more than a century later, in the 1790s. They were produced in the context of fighting back the threat of reprivatization of the mining jurisdiction and the brutal dismantling of the community as it had existed for more than a century. The identities laid out in the first two documents were tested and even reworked at this point as the *cobreros* now claimed full freedom.

This set of documents provides a window into the development of the *pueblo* during the previous century and the identities that were currently deployed. They

---

9. For a detailed analysis of this petition and its implications, see Díaz, *The Virgin* (74–94).
10. See period maps and Moreno's "apparition" document in Díaz, *El Cobre*.

also show events unfolding locally and in Madrid, as Gregorio Cosme Osorio represented the community in the Council of Indies and the Supreme Council of Justice denouncing the heirs' attacks and violent repossession of the jurisdiction and claiming collective freedom. The communication network established through metropolitan and local correspondence shows how the community's transatlantic litigation efforts were coordinated.

Specifically, the third document constitutes a chronicle of the atrocities and violence perpetrated by the heirs of the Eguiluz family against the *cobreros*, and more specifically against free members of the *pueblo*. The heirs had staged a private expedition akin to those of slave hunters to reclaim "their" escaped slaves who had taken refuge with their families in El Cobre and to collect rents for the use of land and wages for the labor of enslaved *cobreros* living on their own in the *pueblo*. Note the author's portrayal of all the subjects as *cobreros* to highlight their status as native members of the *pueblo* of El Cobre and as "captives" to refer to (illegally) enslaved *cobreros*. Why is the choice of language important?

The document also provides a glimpse into the internal orderings of the community: living arrangements; kinds of property holding; internal class, race, and gender distinctions; honor-related criteria and claims; and the mix of free and enslaved individuals within families.[11] Through this document, the *cobreros* not only communicated local news to their man in Madrid, but also filed a formal grievance that Cosme Osorio would incorporate into the community's dossier.

Although there were some literate *cobreros* in El Cobre, the redaction and writing of this text may have been in the hands of an attorney or *letrado*. In this sense it may be a mediated or coauthored text that also reveals the local networks, resources, and alliances of the *cobreros* in Cuba. A *cobrero* familiar with the narrated events would have had to describe them to the scribe.

How might a present-day reader construct a profile of the community from the bits and pieces of information provided in this text? For example, what kind of property did people in this community own? How may they have made a living? How significant do racial and color classifications seem to be? What other considerations seem important? Is gender significant in this narrative? What seem to be the assumptions on each side that feed the conflict between them?

Gregorio Cosme Osorio's 1795 Letter from Madrid

The fourth document was written directly by Gregorio Cosme Osorio and describes his role and travails as the community's *apoderado*, or legal representative, in Madrid. Although Cosme was a free *cobrero*, his wife and children had been among the *royal slaves* repossessed by the heirs. This letter reflects the kind of communication he maintained with his community back home during the more than twelve years he spent in the court of Madrid. Also important here is the significance attributed to litigation, particularly given the enormous material and human resources required by such a community to pull off such a feat.

---

11. For a study of some of these arrangements, see Díaz, "Of Life and Freedom."

Readers may speculate on the significance of skills such as literacy in this community to sustain such an enterprise. Note Cosme's reference to El Cobre as a *villa* rather than as a *pueblo*. Of special interest here as well is Osorio's claim to have spoken to the king himself, a vague and uncompromising encounter that may well have happened but that was also directed at enhancing his status in the community that sustained him.

What does this letter reveal about the work Osorio performed as the community's *apoderado* in the court of Madrid? What does the ability to send a representative to litigate in Madrid say about this community? How did Cosme portray himself and his work? How indispensable was literacy in this whole endeavor? Overall, what do these documents suggest about subordinate subjects' views and uses of legal venues for redress in the Spanish empire?

*****

[Letter from Nicolás de Montenegro to Doña Paula de Eguiluz, El Cobre, 1672][12]

Transcription of a chapter of the letter of Nicolás de Montenegro, *mulatto* slave son of a [female] slave of the accountant Juan de Eguiluz, who is one of the *mandadores* in the copper mines appointed by the governor of [Santiago de] Cuba, Don Andrés Magaña, where he deals with matters regarding the mines and written in his own hand and signature to Doña Paula de Eguiluz y Montenegro, who resides in the city of Havana. Dated in the said mines on July 7, 1672.

I have written two, and with this three, letters where I have given notice to my Lady of what has been happening since she left these mines and now I will again [write] in this one about the many new things that are taking place hour by hour.... My Lady, regarding the copper from the river, it has been [obtained] without [due] regulation [*ajuste*].... Copper is the currency that nowadays moves around in the mines because men, women, and children occupy themselves in nothing else from sunrise to sunset.... And as I tried to stop him [from taking copper] Pedro Viojo said to me that he did not recognize these mines as belonging to my Lady Doña Paula but that they are the king's. All the others said the same.... Before there used to be much arrogance among these men and women, as my Lady well knows, but today it is too much, for they say publicly that they are free [*horros*].... Father Ramos rented the cattle ranch lands [*hato*] of Barajagua for two hundred *pesos*, but only the grass, leaving free the hunting grounds [*monterías*] for the people of these mines. And they did not like it because they say that Barajagua and the *monterías* are all theirs, that the king gave it to them.... Since my Lady left these mines, Miguel Congolo has set himself up in the shanty [*covacha*] and has taken advantage of all the cacao produced in both harvests this last year. And when I asked him how he could do that, that those cacao trees belonged to my Lady Doña Paula, he answered me that they belonged to the king and so did he. Manuel del Río, after idling there on his own, came back only to help cause trouble in these copper mines.

[Juan Moreno's Petition to Judge Don Antonio Matienzo, Mines of Santiago del Prado, July 13, 1677][13]

Captain Juan Moreno, a *Creole* black/slave and native of the mines of Santiago del Prado of El Cobre in this city of [Santiago de] Cuba, in my name and on behalf of all the other *Creole* black/slave natives of these mines, slaves that we are of His Majesty, may God bless him, and especially those who were named in the division and settlement ... we approach [*Vuestra Merced*, Judge Matienzo] by way of the best means available by right and say that most of the *Creole* black and *mulatto* slaves of

---

12. Copia con carta de don Antonio de Matta y Haro, 15 diciembre 1672, Ministerio de Cultura, Archivo General de Indias, Seville, Santo Domingo 104 [no folio numbering]. Doña Paula de Eguiluz is the daughter of Juan de Eguiluz, who is the owner of the black slave woman of the same name (Paula de Eguiluz), protagonist of the documents in Chapter 11 of this volume.

13. Minas de Santiago del Prado, trece de julio de 1677, Ministerio de Cultura, Archivo General de Indias, Seville, Santo Domingo 1631, fols. 424–52v.

these mines are married, and we have our families, which we have always sustained in a calm and peaceful way, [that] we have been occupied in the mining works when needed, [in] the construction of the Holy Church, and other [tasks] in which we have been employed when there have been attacks, and we have responded promptly as loyal vassals of His Majesty at our own cost and expense, [always] complying with and obeying all the laws of our superiors and of other justices in the City of [Santiago de] Cuba, who have employed us in all this as well as in [the hunt for] hamlets and *Maroon* communities of fugitive black slaves of the citizens [*vecinos*] of all of this island whom we have captured. We have always desired greater opportunities to do royal service and to be employed in important [military] actions; even if they are not rewarded, we will merely be content to have performed them. All this is so true, and our readiness for the occasion and defense of the fortress of [Santiago de] Cuba[14] or any other place is so real, even if it is [also] true that all of its citizens are ready as well to engage in any action, that the lord governors have called on us whenever there has been an occasion of any novelty remembering us even though we are [only] humble slaves of our king and lord, acknowledging perhaps our strong desire [to carry out military actions].

And it has come to our attention that those of us who will remain in the settlement that they say our king and lord will make with our master Don Francisco, giving him many slaves, [we] will be removed by *Vuestra Merced* [Judge Matienzo] to send us to the city of Havana. And the love for our *patria* and our work move us to beg *Vuestra Merced*, if it is possible, to grant us the mercy that we stay in our *pueblo*, paying tribute in whatever manner it is decided, while we find [the means] to [purchase] our freedom, or whatever is disposed so that in equity and piety *Vuestra Merced* can protect us in the name of our king and lord in whatever lawful way it may be possible.

Therefore, we ask and plead of *Vuestra Merced* that you consider us presented and order that we be given license [to stay], for this is the justice and mercy that we ask for and the most [necessary? illegible].

Juan Moreno

[Letter from Martín de Salazar][15]

El Cobre, August 21, 1792

We call attention to the violent despoliation, atrocities, and mischief that all of us free people of El Cobre have suffered for the last eleven years and months and are currently suffering and enduring in this captivity with Don Fernando Mancebo, one of the heirs of the said *pueblo*. First he convened men there in [Santiago de] Cuba and prepared them to form an armed band, and he obtained a license to come by and collect the wages of the *cobreros* who worked in the population settlement of the territory of El Cobre. Because [the heirs] had received the [illegally enslaved] captives and all the land [comprised in the jurisdiction of El Cobre], he [Mancebo] came to El Cobre

---

14. See maps of the fortress and its location in Díaz, *El Cobre.*
15. Ministerio de Cultura, Archivo General de Indias, Seville, Santo Domingo 1627, Havana y Cuba, Año de 1792, cuaderno no. 1, fols. 209r–10v.

on that pretense with the greatest authority and violence. He went to the house of the widow Ignacia de los Reyes and collected what the woman owed him, settling the debt for fifteen *pesos*. He went inside and got them from her. After receiving the [fifteen *pesos*], he went out to the patio and called a man from his band and ordered him to untie a cow with whose milk she supported herself and on his own authority sent it to his house in [Santiago de] Cuba. From there he moved on to the farm [*estancia*] and residence of Angolosongo, where he found one of the captives, named Diego Ortiz. And this young man fled, and he shot and felled him to the ground and went up to him and taking out his saber struck him, cutting away one half of a side of his buttocks, and left him for dead. He came to the *pueblo* boasting of his act and then the Lord priest left, running to see if he could find him alive to administer him [the last sacrament].... From there, the mentioned Don Fernando left for the tobacco farm [*vega*] and house of Jacinto González, [who is] also white-brown [*blanco pardo*]. But Don Fernando did not find him at home; only his wife and children were there. He ordered the men of his band to tie her up for him, making her take her clothes off and fully bare herself. [She was] thrown on the ground, [and] he put a stick between her knees. They tied her hands and had her flogged so harshly that her screams could be heard in Heaven. They gave her more than one hundred lashes with a whip; and after having punished her, he began thrusting the tip of his shoe inside her parts so that her husband could not copulate with her. Everything that I have related and what I now turn to describe has happened to free people.... He then moved on to the house and residence of the corporal of the urban militias Buenaventura Cosme. He also had him tied up, [but] did not flog him. Then he moved on to the house and tobacco farm of Buenaventura Quiala, and because he has two captive sons he gave the two sons a heavy flogging. From there he came to the *pueblo*, arriving at the farm named Las Animas that is Priest Caraballo's farm. He tied up those he found there, and took with him two hogs that were there that belonged to the Señor priest. He then moved on to the farm of the widow Marcela Sánchez, who had gone out to look for food. He found there two maiden daughters, free women, mistresses of their home, who were sleeping. He took off the bed sheet that covered them and went on to take all the trinkets that he found, including their earrings, hair ribbons, gold rings, locks, scarves, shoe buckles, and clothing and all that he wanted. He went to the patio, asked for the keys, and took the chickens and turkeys, loading up a horse with them, and left. He went to the house of Sale Cuzata asking for a captive son of his but did not find him. He ordered the father, who is brown of white color and free, be tied up and gave him more than a hundred lashes. Afterward he left with the whole load that he had unduly taken for his home in [Santiago de] Cuba....

Friend, all these events have happened to free people, men and women of honor, assuring *Vuestra Merced* that this is an instance of what we are currently enduring because the insults have been outright so enormous and boundless that a whole ream of paper would be needed to explain them. In sum, friend, God will that we be freed from all this persecution and may He grant much health and life to *Vuestra Merced* so that you may do everything that can be done on your part, insisting to the gentlemen who favor us that the man who will restore the above-mentioned slaves to their *pueblo* be sent promptly, before they destroy all the *cobreros* [because] so many enemies are persecuting us, and in this city [Santiago de Cuba] no one heeds orders or dispositions of superior mandates. May Our Lord praise and guard your life for many years, as your most humble compatriots wish you and on behalf of all.

>   Martín de Salazar
>   Our Friend Gregorio Cosme Osorio

[Letter from Gregorio Cosme Osorio]¹⁶

>   Madrid, March 16, 1795

My Dearest Owners,

Francisco Sales Cruzata, I inform you that in this mail are going out orders from the king in person to put the *cobreros* in possession of their freedom, and the orders are remitted to the governor of Havana and of [Santiago de] Cuba to see if they will heed his orders recommending a speedy resolution of the matter. . . . I am announcing to all of you that you are free and that it has cost me great amounts, but it is really nothing because I would gladly give my life just so that they [the heirs] do not get away with their wishes. You will see how much I have worked by myself with only the help of the lawyer, attorney, and moneylender Señor Don Pedro Sedano. Friend Sales Cruzata, if you saw me you would not recognize me because I have become very thin with these paper battles and with the illnesses even more, and with the distress and troubles. Because I have had to appeal everything five times and therefore it has been necessary to find a way to speak to the king himself in person through a great friend [who] placed me where I would not have thought [possible]. And I talked to him [the king] and presented to him the report that you sent me, along with the Church testimonial, where all the generations [baptism records] of slaves were [recorded], whereby he came to know all that was untrue. And the king offered that if everything I said on their behalf was true, he would have me and all of them [the *cobreros*] present. And he has carried [everything] out exactly as he offered to me, but it has been so hard for us. I let you know that I write to all in this same mail: to Ventura Cosme [and seven other names], to all in that town [*villa*] I am sending soon two provisions that I have won for you. . . . And finally, I cannot go on any further in this letter, because I am busy. Do not do anything in those tribunals [on the island]; only send me everything that comes up, and otherwise do not do anything because it has been very hard to annul all the writs [*autos*] that you told me had been issued in those tribunals, which are null. And enough; I am in a hurry in the council. This, your true servant, who kisses your hand, is at your command.

>   Gregorio Cosme Osorio

---

16. Ministerio de Cultura, Archivo General de Indias, Seville, Santo Domingo 1631, fols. 11v–14r.

The Making of a Free *Lucumí* Household: Ana de la Calle's Will and Goods, Northern Peruvian Coast, 1719[1]

Rachel Sarah O'Toole

Who was Ana de la Calle? At first the question appears to be easily answered from the historical sources that survive in the provincial archive of Trujillo, a small city on the northern Peruvian coast: she was a freewoman of color, as indicated by her claim to be a *morena*. When she died (in or around 1719), she had a small, but close-knit family consisting of a daughter and a granddaughter and both of their husbands. Her household also included an enslaved woman with her young daughter.

Among Ana de la Calle's goods were trays she used to sell bread; selling bread was a common business for women of color. The name she called herself in public documents—de la Calle, "of the Street"—also explained that she sold her goods in the public thoroughfares and *plazas* of Trujillo, the center of a bustling regional economy. Merchants from the city purchased woolen cloth from the highlands, along with the locally produced sugar, molasses, alcohol, soap, and wheat, to sell along the Pacific coast stretching from Lima to Panama. Together with other free people of African descent, Ana de la Calle would have joined indigenous vendors, muleteers, and artisans who all sold their goods and labor to maintain their families.

Ana de la Calle: *Lucumí*

Yet, the will and the estate that Ana de la Calle left to her family present a more complicated picture of her identity. She also called herself *de casta lucumí* ("of the *Lucumí* caste") in the will that she paid a notary to record in his bound volumes of public documents. By calling herself *Lucumí*, Ana de la Calle employed a term used by transatlantic slave traders to identify men, women, and children who were sold by Yoruba states to Atlantic merchants (Law, *Kingdom*, 18).

Slave traders and slaveholders in Cartagena and Panama, along the Pacific coast, and in the Andean highlands also employed the term *Lucumí* to distinguish certain enslaved people from others they called *Angola* (those sold through the West Central African port of Luanda) or *Mina* (captives from the *Gold Coast*). Slave traders employed these terms to indicate the port or region of origin for African captives, but slaveholders used the labels to suggest characteristics that they projected onto enslaved men and women.

---

1. See Maps 3 and 6. I thank Juan Castañeda Murga for his assistance with the transcription of the document.

In seventeenth-century colonial Trujillo, slaveholders imagined that *Mina* slaves were more "haughty" than those of other *nations* ("Demanda," fol. 58v). Yet, the constructed nature of the qualities attributed to these terms can be seen in the fact that, in contrast to their Spanish counterparts, eighteenth-century British colonists in South Carolina preferred enslaved men and women from the *Gold Coast*, or *Mina*, because they thought these African women and men were from a barren place and therefore more "hardy" (Littlefield, 18). In both cases, slaveholders created meanings that assisted them in assigning value to their property, enslaved men and women.

Even though Ana de la Calle was also a slaveholder, she employed the term *Lucumí* to describe herself, suggesting that she was laying public claim to an African diaspora identity. She may have employed the term to underline that she was a Yoruba speaker. This West African language was associated with nobility and elites among the people who lived close to the rising states of *Dahomey* and *Oyo*, in the interior of the Atlantic coast stretching from southeast Ghana to southwestern Nigeria.

By the seventeenth century, coastal people had begun to adopt the hinterland Yoruba (of the *Lucumí*) deities, providing evidence of the prestige associated with *Lucumí* (Anguiano, 238–40). As historian Robin Law explains, *lukumi* also became synonymous with valuable trade goods such as salt, cotton cloth, and other exports of the Yoruba kingdoms.[2] Whether Ana de la Calle originated within these interior West African states or survived the horrifying transatlantic passage by naming herself a *Lucumí*, she claimed a superior status to that of the majority of Africans in colonial Trujillo, who, in the early eighteenth century, were people from the Slave Coast on West Africa's Bight of Benin (see Map 3).

In doing so, she marked herself off from the majority of enslaved men and women who called themselves or were called *Arará* and *Popo*, or *Chala*.[3] Her claim to be a *Lucumí* woman, in addition to a free woman of color, may explain how she supported her family by selling bread on the streets of Trujillo.

A Diverse Family and Household

Even though Ana de la Calle identified herself as a *Lucumí* free woman of color, she did not pass on this identifier to her daughter or granddaughter. Instead, she recorded each of her female descendants with surnames that reflected their distinct positions in colonial society. She called her daughter by the full name of Doña María de la Cruz Cavero to suggest that unlike herself, her offspring had achieved a title of honor and respect in the provincial town. De la Cruz was a common surname that lower-status people chose, including those who had been slaves. Lacking a Spanish family name, de la Cruz expressed their piety. Yet, María had gained the additional surname Cavero, that of a powerful family that owned sugar haciendas on Peru's northern coast; therefore, this household of free people of African descent was connected through patronage or kinship with these Spanish, slaveholding elites.

---

2. *Slave Coast*, 46–47. Law uses a different historical spelling of *Lucumí*.

3. *Chala* was an identity also associated with Yoruba kingdoms, but *Chala* did not imply the same superior social status of *Lucumí*.

In the legal document that Ana created, her last will and testament, she named her daughter a *parda*, or a woman of color who had been born free, rather than a *morena*, a term that was more often associated with enslaved or freedwomen. By naming her daughter in this way, Ana de la Calle established a public record that created honor for herself and her family. Lastly, Ana de la Calle reserved a special place for her granddaughter to whom she gave no Spanish colonial or African diasporic identifier at all, naming her simply "Juana de Silva." Indeed, one possibility is that the *Lucumí* free woman passed her family out of any public categorization associated with enslavement or the transatlantic slave trade.

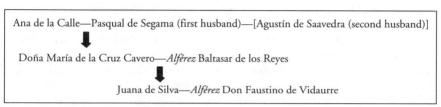

Figure 2. Ana de la Calle's family

The goods that Ana de la Calle left to her daughter and granddaughter, in addition to the roles each played within the family, raise questions about how she sought to construct public identities for her family, including her own. Ana de la Calle did not ascribe the *casta Lucumí* to either her daughter or her granddaughter, although she did apply this elite Yoruba identifier to Isabel, the enslaved woman who served the household. Perhaps, although she clearly chose an enslaved *Lucumí* woman to serve her, she understood that the term signified a slave in colonial Peru—an identity she wished to shed for her descendants.

More interestingly, Isabel's young enslaved daughter, who had been born in Ana de la Calle's house, carried the unusual name of Eduvigia—perhaps the notary heard Eduvigis or Saint Hedwig (a thirteenth-century Bavarian convent reformer). Still, provincial scribes were notoriously creative orthographers, especially of unfamiliar names and words. Ana de la Calle could have also been suggesting Saint Efigenia, an African martyr associated with Saint John and worshipped in African-descent communities in Peru, Brazil, and Mexico (Karasch, 85; Obregón, 31–32; von Germeten, 18–19).

The free *Lucumí* woman then passed on this infant to another member of her household, suggesting on one level how a slaveholder controlled the lives of enslaved people and how she determined who would raise the saint's namesake. Could this stipulation in the will have been a way to keep the child with the unusual (and possibly spiritual) name within Ana de la Calle's household? Finally, Ana de la Calle may have guarded her own identity by entrusting certain members of her family with the separate accounts that she kept for what appear to be two businesses, one selling bread "in the street" and another that operated within a community of people who "commonly called her" Mama Anica.

Her name suggests that she may have been a ritual specialist, as "Mother" was a title of respect in Brazilian houses of *Candomblé*, an African diasporic religion, and may have been used in the same way among Afro-Peruvians. Given the clerical supervision of Catholic orthodoxy, Ana de la Calle would have been wise to keep her second occupation discreet, just as *Candomblé* followers celebrated public Catholic rites that paralleled private or near-secret African rituals (Reis, 145).

She owned a number of Catholic religious images as well as a silver-covered gourd, suggesting that within the walls of her house, Ana de la Calle may have served as a spiritual leader who healed, divined, or conducted religious services as did other Yoruba women in African diasporic religions of the Americas. Ana de la Calle's intentions are difficult to discern, but clearly she carried more identities than that of a mere bread seller.

Ana de la Calle molded her identity and fit her wishes into the dry and formulaic language of a last will and testament. But her last will and testament is also a document that can reveal a rich world of relationships and identities. A common record throughout colonial Spanish America and most regions of the early modern Christian world, a will was understood as both privately confessional and publicly declarative. When people dictated these documents, either alone with the notary or surrounded by their families, they revealed deep secrets, forgotten sins, and intimate surprises.

At the same time, in these handwritten entries, later bound in large notarial ledgers, colonial Spanish-American people who could afford to pay for the privilege explained who their legitimate children were, who would inherit their possessions, and who their debtors and creditors were. Wills were serious legal texts that formed the basis for the distribution of goods, recognition of kin, and protracted judicial disputes. In fact, Ana de la Calle's children and grandchildren employed her will in a protracted legal dispute over the ownership of her house.

Thus the language attributed to Ana de la Calle in the document is correspondingly formal and formulaic. The notary she employed, like others, followed the standard conventions for the drawing up of a will and its accompanying documents. These papers exhibit the required language and convoluted terms that were necessary to proclaim oneself a practicing Catholic, including the order in which the declarations are made and the stipulations regarding who could sign as witnesses.

People counted on the information in the document to be taken as factual and its provisions to become reality. They intended the orders and the relationships that they recorded in their wills to become truth as much as they recorded what they knew to be true (Burns, 352–53). Even though a will, like any legal document, could be disputed with regard to these provisions, these written sources of a testator's wishes were powerful in a predominately oral culture where the literate and illiterate alike counted on recorded language to "fix" realities—for better or for worse. The documents that Ana de la Calle caused to be created in her name invite interrelated questions and explorations. First, how can we use the will and list of possessions, mediated by the Spanish judicial official's act of writing, to understand Ana de la Calle's intentions? Second, what do her wishes tell us about her family, her livelihoods, and her understanding of slavery? And third, how well does the colonial document capture her reality and what still remains unsaid in this verbal legacy of a free *Lucumí* woman who lived her life in a provincial Peruvian town?

*****

[The Will of Ana de la Calle]⁴

In God's name and with His Most Holy Grace, amen: Let it be known to all those who see this letter of testament that I, Ana de la Calle, free *morena* of *casta lucumí*, *vecina* that I am of this city of Trujillo of Peru, being sick in bed of an illness that God Our Lord has seen fit to give me, believing as I firmly believe in the mystery of the Holy Trinity, Father and Son and Holy Spirit, three distinct persons and one single, true God, in whose faith and belief I have lived, and I proclaim to live and to die as a Catholic and true Christian and in all the rest that Our Holy Mother Catholic Church in Rome holds, believes, confesses, and preaches. And fearing death, which is a natural thing for all living creatures and so that this [death] may not take me until I have arranged matters for the sake of my conscience, I make and order this my last will and testament. And to do so with the prudence [good judgment/wisdom] that I desire, I elect and choose for my petitioners and intercessors the eternally Virgin Mother of God and Our Lady and the Holy Apostles, Saint Peter and Saint Paul, and my Holy Guardian Angel, with whose protection and favor I make and order this my last will and testament in the following form and manner:

First, I offer and entrust my soul to Our Lord God. When he is served to take me from this present life, may I be buried in the Church and Monastery of Our Father Saint Francis of this city where Pasqual de Segama, my husband, is buried, or in any other church or monastery of the Church that my executors choose. And [that my body] be accompanied on the day of my burial by the high cross, priest, and sacristan of my parish. And the donation for my funeral and burial will be paid from my estate.

Item. I order that a charitable donation of four *reales* be given from my estate to the holy places of Jerusalem where Christ Our Redeemer performed the redemption of humankind.

Item. I order for the aid in the re-edification of the monastery of Saint Francis of Assisi that is in Italy four *reales* that will be paid from my estate.

And I declare that I was married and veiled according to the order of the Holy Mother Church with Pasqual de Segama, free *moreno* who is deceased, and during our matrimony we did not have any children. Thus, I declare it so that it is known.

Item. I declare that at present I was married and veiled according to the order of Our Holy Mother Church with Agustín de Saavedra, free *moreno*, of which [matrimony], we also do not have any children. Thus, I declare it so that it is known.

Item. I declare that before I contracted my first marriage with the said Pasqual de Segama, as a weak woman I bore a daughter who is alive today named María de la Cruz, *parda*. I declare her, as such, to be my daughter.

Item. I declare as my property this house in which I live at the moment, which I had and purchased from Claudio Juárez, son and heir of María de Lorito, by public

---

4. Expediente seguido por don Ambrosio Girón de Estrada promotor fiscal del obispado de Trujillo, albacea de Ana de la Calle, morena libre difunta, contra don Faustino de Vidaurre albacea y tenedor de bienes de doña María de la Cruz Cavero, difunta, sobre pago de los corridos que estuviere debiendo del censo impuesto acerca de la casa que hubo y heredó de la dicha Ana de la Calle. Archivo Departamental de La Libertad, Cabildo, Causas Ordinarias, legajo 41, exp. 753 (1727), fols. 8v–14v.

deed sworn before Miguel Cortijo Quero, public notary and who was of the municipal council of this city on the eleventh of the month of August of the past year of 1692. We took possession of it before the royal justice who delivered it to me and the said Pasqual de Segama. I declare it as my property.

Item. I also declare as my property a little black *criolla* girl named Eduvigia, who is a little more than a year old. I declare her as my property.

Item. I declare that I have given, in different allotments, to my said daughter María de la Cruz and her creditors, 461 *pesos* of 8 *reales*. I declare it thus so that it is on record and it is taken charge of.

Item. I wish and it is my will that to the said Agustín de Saavedra, second husband, be given from my property 25 *pesos* of 8 *reales* for his burial. That he also live all the days of his life, that my heir not throw him out of the house until he has died, because thus is my will.

Item. I desire and it is my will that a fifth of my property be used for my burial and Masses that are ordered said for my soul. I declare it thus, so that it is on record.

Item. I declare as my property a large trunk of Panamanian cedar with its lock and key.

Item. A table with its drawer and carved legs

Item. A copper pan, a large tray, and another, small one

Item. Also a black woman named María Isabel of *casta lucumí*

And heeding that I have no more heir than the said María de la Cruz, I name her as such my universal heir so that after my death, she may have and inherit my property with God's blessing and mine because this is my will.

And I name as the executor of my will and trustee the *licentiate* Don Ambrosio Girón de Estrada, cleric and priest, whose term of executorship I defer and extend the time needed for the completion of this, my will, to whom I give all my power that I rightly have, that is required for its execution. This is my will.

I revoke and annul and give as none and of no value or effect any other testaments, codicils, and powers to make a will and other last dispositions and wishes that I may have made and executed in writing or orally before this testament. I wish that any of the preceding have no value, nor serve as verification or proof in or out of court, except this my testament, which I now complete and execute before the present notary, which will be observed, fulfilled, and executed as my last will and testament, or by that document, in the best manner and form according to law, in testimony of which I execute this letter before the present notary.

I witness that I know the executor and I also witness that she is in her right mind according to the matters that she dealt with and communicated with me.[5]

She did not sign because she stated she did not know how to write. A witness signed at her request, which was witnessed by the aide-de-camp Juan Nevado, Alonso Gómez, and Joseph Márquez. Done in this city of Trujillo of Peru the twenty-fifth of this month of April of 1719. Before signing, the said Ana de la Calle said that she wanted and it is her will that a fifth of her property be set aside to be used for the good of her soul, as this is her wish. And the above said were witnesses at the executor's request, and as

---

5. Here, the notary inserts his witnessing statements.

witness Joseph Márquez. Before me, Felipe de San Román, public notary and [notary] of the municipal council.

[Codicil of Ana de la Calle][6]

In the city of Trujillo of Peru on [the] fourteenth day of the month of May of the year 1719, Ana de la Calle, free *morena*, appeared before me, the present public notary, and witnesses, who will be declared below. And she said that inasmuch as the twenty-fifth day of the past month of April, she executed her last will and testament, in which she disposed matters for the sake of her conscience. And because now she offers to remove and add and amend some dispositions of said will and she wishes to do so by means of a codicil or by such document as best conforms to the manner of the law, and putting it into effect, she executes and states that she wishes and it is her will that to her granddaughter be given and delivered a little black girl, her slave, named Teresa de Eduvigia, who is about a year and eight months old, who is a *criolla*, born of a slave in her household. Which child she wishes and it is her will that she be given and delivered by her executor to the said Juana de Silva, her granddaughter, once she has died, and that her heirs should not trouble or harass the said Juana de Silva in her possession of the little black girl. And this it is given to understand falls within the limits of the fifth [part of her possessions]. And she wishes also that this codicil and said testament be observed, fulfilled, and executed against any opposition. And the said executor, whom I, the notary, certify that I know and also attest that she is in her right mind, did not sign because she said she did not know how to write. At her request a witness signed it, which was witnessed by Felipe de los Reyes, Félix Nieto, and Alonso Gómez, all present.

Account of the Possessions That Were Left at the Death of María de la Cruz Cavero, My Mother, That Ended Up in the Hands of Baltasar de los Reyes[7]

First, a gourd adorned in silver that is worth about four *pesos*: four *pesos*

Item. A silver plate painted with the figure of Our Lady of Solitude with its glass cover that is worth about: four *pesos*

Item. A piece of the True Cross adorned in Prince's metal with its glass cover that is worth about: eight *pesos*

Item. A mirror that is worth about two *pesos*: two *pesos*

Item. A new copper frying pan that is worth about: three *pesos*

Item. A wheat-colored shawl that is worth about ten *pesos*: ten *pesos*

---

6. Expediente seguido por el Alférez don Faustino Vidaurre como marido legítimo de Juana de Silva, albacea, heredera, y teneder de bienes de María de la Cruz Cavero, su suegra difunta contra el Alférez Baltasar de los Reyes, pardo libre, vecino de Trujillo sobre que desocupe el cuarto de la casa situada en la calle del Postigo del Dean. Archivo Departamental de La Libertad, Cabildo, Causas Ordinarias, legajo 41, exp. 752 (1727), fols. 1–2. This is a legal document for additions or changes to a will.

7. Document created by Ana de la Calle's granddaughter, her spouse, Juana de Dios y Silva, and *Alférez* Don Faustino de Vidaurre.

Item. And a worn, iridescent skirt that is worth about: four *pesos*

Item. A length of lace underskirting that amounts to: twenty *reales*

Item. Also a small piece of false gold jewelry mounted with stones of amethyst, ruby, and diamonds of alchemy, that is worth about four *reales* with another four stones of alchemy that is worth about another four *reales*, and the two together amount to: one *peso*

Item. Also a bedstead that is worth twenty-five *pesos*: twenty-five *pesos*

Item. Also a canopy that is worth fourteen *pesos*: fourteen *pesos*

Item. Also a dais with its Holy Christ surrounded by engravings that is worth about: three *pesos*

Item. A spit that was my grandmother's with the value of one *peso*: one *peso*

Item. A small statue of the Most Pure Virgin with its little silver crown, that is mine, that is worth three *pesos*: three *pesos*

Item. In the possession of the said Baltasar de los Reyes, a snuff box with its silver fringe that is worth about three *pesos*: three *pesos*

Item. All the papers of bills, receipts, payments, and settlements executed by the said María de la Cruz Cavero for Ana, who they commonly call Mama Anica, who was mother of the said María de la Cruz Cavero. These papers were in a little wooden box.

Item. Accounting papers that the said Mama Anica had with the *Señor Licenciado* Don Ambrosio Girón de Estrada regarding the bread that she made for the sustenance of his family.

"El rey de los *congos*": The Clandestine Coronation of Pedro Duarte in Buenos Aires, 1787[1]

Patricia Fogelman and Marta Goldberg

Document translation by Joseph P. Sánchez, Angelica Sánchez-Clark, and Larry D. Miller

The Population of African Descent in Eighteenth-Century Buenos Aires and Its Organizations

In the eighteenth century, Buenos Aires grew as a result of both increased transatlantic trade and its own integration into the Peruvian economy. The growth of Buenos Aires was also spurred by contraband activities, which included the traffic of leather goods from the port's hinterland and cloth from the interior, and the response to the growing desire for European products not regularly supplied by the small Spanish fleets. Bourbon liberalization of the trade further stimulated the commercial exchange that tied Buenos Aires more closely to Alto Peru (Bolivia), now under the Río de la Plata jurisdiction. It also strengthened the Buenos Aires to Lima trade route, promoting trade in slaves, mules, and other merchandise, while much of the Andean metals that permeated regional economies flowed into the port.

Responding to complex factors, Buenos Aires' population grew almost fivefold at the end of the colonial period, increasing from 11,200 inhabitants in the 1744 census to around 50,000 in 1810, for an estimated annual growth rate of 2.2 percent. To explain this growth, historians have tended to highlight external immigration and the forced immigration of enslaved Africans from the Portuguese Atlantic, but later studies also give importance to internal migrations that included indigenous and *mestizo* populations (Díaz).

It is difficult to calculate precisely the population of African origin in Buenos Aires, though period iconography, literature, documentation from commercial houses in which blacks provided labor, and even militia records show their very real presence. Demographic sources account for their existence but omit important data regarding their origins and make errors in identifying their ethnicities. In 1810, blacks and *pardos*—six of every ten of whom were enslaved—constituted about 29 percent of the total census numbers. The distribution of the enslaved population in the city of Buenos Aires was not homogenous: the greatest density was found in the central zone integrated with the free population by virtue of their occupations in domestic service, petty commerce, laundry services, and the crafts they exercised.

---

1. See Maps 6 and 12. We wish to thank Marina Mansilla for her collaboration in composing the glossary for this chapter, which forms part of the Glossary for the volume.

Despite omissions and errors, the census lists (Goldberg, "La población" and "Los estudios") and parish registers (records of baptism, marriage, and death) are sources of enormous importance in helping us to understand the realities of the African-descent population of Buenos Aires during the colonial period, especially when the two are compared as synchronic and diachronic sources, that is, sources that provide both a demographic snapshot of a single moment and a picture of demographic change over time. Around 1778, when the census closest in time to the clandestine coronation presented in this chapter was taken, the population of Buenos Aires was around 24,754, about 30 percent of whom were *Afroporteños*.[2]

Doubtless, the idea that Buenos Aires lacked a population of African descent is a careless, often insidious, generalization in regard to their contributions to the socio-cultural development of Buenos Aires. The history of the Río de la Plata region counts those of African descent among its actors and documentary sources, which despite their limitations and lost information signal the evident influence of *Afromestizo*[3] social groups who participated in the city's growth. They also show the implantation of African cultural traditions through the mixing of religious and musical practices during the colonial period and well into the nineteenth century (see Goldberg, "Los africanos," "Los negros," and "Presencia").

This presence was wrought through, among others, the constitution of different social collectives. We can recognize three basic types of African communal groupings in Buenos Aires: confraternities, *nations*, and societies. Their existence and functioning from the final decades of the eighteenth through the end of the nineteenth centuries are relatively well documented, with sporadic later references.[4] Their history is one of a progressive search for autonomy, rarely realized until the end of this period.

The links between confraternities, societies, and *nations* at the end of the eighteenth century is not clear, but the *nations* were consolidated at a time when civil authorities assumed control of functions that had been in the Church's hands. The police replaced the Church in controlling these societies or *nations*, which began as simple associations and evolved into real organizations after independence. The societies took the names of the different African *nations* from which they were embarked or where their ancestors originated, such as *Angola, Banguela, Cambunda, Congo, Mina,* and *Mozambique,* among many others.

They began to acquire properties and establish headquarters. There they celebrated festivities and dances, during which they held collections and raffles. Among the aims of the societies were to help individuals of the same ethnicity to purchase their freedom and to organize festivities and processions, which at their height were attended by the governor of Buenos Aires and his family. Later, the viceregal administration rejected and often prohibited these celebrations.

---

2. We use the terms *Afroporteños* and *Afrorioplatenses* to refer to residents of African descent in Buenos Aires and the Viceroyalty of Río de la Plata, respectively, as the territory would not be called Argentina until after 1860.

3. The term *Afromestizo* is preferred in some regions, including Argentina, and among some scholars of Mexico, to refer to people of mixed African and European heritage.

4. See works by Andrews, Cirio, Fogelman, Goldberg, González, Mallo, and Rosal.

Afrorioplatense Confraternities

Religious brotherhoods and confraternities (*cofradías*) were corporations that served as instruments and vehicles of Christian consolidation in the colonial period. There were Marian[5] confraternities and confraternities dedicated to the Eucharist, the saints, or the souls of purgatory (Fogelman, "Coordenadas"). The confraternities played diverse social roles with two primary realms of activity, one material and the other strongly spiritual: they constructed and administered a confraternal patrimony, and they promoted religious practices and discourses. Clearly, they participated in the shared social space, creating alliances and defining group identities, offering support and collective solidarity to their members (Fogelman, "Una cofradía").

Scholars differ in their use and interpretation of the words "brotherhood" and "confraternity." In colonial Rioplatense sources, especially for Buenos Aires and its surroundings, both terms were generally used interchangeably (Fogelman, "Una cofradía," 179). Often their constitutions and minutes use both terms to refer to the same institution. Confraternities were among various institutions dedicated to promoting the Catholic religion. They were constituted by a body, or "association of the faithful," with religious aims, and they operated within the sphere of the Catholic Church, ordered by officially approved statutes (rules or constitutions). Often this approval was not obtained, or was delayed, and the confraternities functioned more or less informally.

To belong to a confraternity one paid a fee and, sometimes, fines. Each confraternity or brotherhood had an organizational, administrative, and functional structure presided over by the *mayordomo* (or *hermano mayor*, literally "elder brother"), accompanied by a representative council, often known as the "twenty-four brothers," independent of their real number (Fogelman, "Élite," 105–6).

Confraternities varied a great deal in their composition: they could be segregated by ethnicity, profession, or craft—the latter including an important number of black artisans; they could be reserved for members of the military or clergy, for men, or for women; or they could be mixed. They could be more or less socially inclusive. There were also confraternities composed exclusively of whites and those made up of only enslaved or free blacks. In the eighteenth century, there existed confraternities in which members of both African and European descent came together in devotion to a single patron saint.

The African confraternities reached their height in the colonial period. They brought together the aims of both their African members and the official Church; the former sought to gather those of like condition, whereas the latter sought to exercise control over any expression that could threaten the established order. These confraternities organized within churches and convents, similar to but apart from the model of white (European) lay religious brotherhoods. The confraternities in colonial Buenos Aires composed of people of African descent included the *Creole* Blacks of Our Lady of Luján, the Brotherhood of the Rosary, and the Brotherhoods of Saint Balthasar, Saint Benedict, and Saint Gaspar.

---

5. Dedicated to the Virgin Mary.

The favorite patrons of Afrorioplatense brotherhoods were saints considered black: Saint Benedict of Palermo and Saint Balthasar of the Magi. The brotherhoods also included Marian cults, such as those to Our Lady of Succor, of the Rosary, and of the Assumption. Members of Afrorioplatense brotherhoods identified strongly with these saints because they were thought to be black, but the Marian options also supported the search for protection in the passage from this life to the next. Identity and security were central characteristics of the discourses and practices of all colonial brotherhoods, where inclusion and exclusion were key to building group identity and solidarity; the Afroporteño brotherhoods were no exception.

The confraternities supported their activities with contributions from their members and collections taken at public dances; these allowed them to pay for masses, funerals, and aid to the ill. The membership fee in black and *mulatto* confraternities was about two *pesos*, and, in the case of enslaved blacks, registrants also needed permission from their owners. The *luminaria*, or annual fee, was four *reales*. The confraternities met once or twice a week, when they received instruction in Christian doctrine.

One weekly mass cost about three *pesos* in alms for the priest, whereas the *capellán* (chaplain) charged two *reales* to pray a chaplet.[6] Confraternities paid the priest about five *pesos* for a parish burial, with sung mass and body present, and additional prayed masses (González). Clearly there was a regular flow of money from the confraternity to the Church for the liturgy, in addition to the improper diversions that priests often made of confraternity funds.

If authority was nominally given to confraternities to elect internal leaders, they were always subject to strong external control by church and royal authorities, and often the *capellán*, syndic, and *mayordomo* elected successors without participation of the majority. Designation of leaders in the later black societies was carried out by election by the membership in the presence of a police delegate, from whom authorization was requested. The authorities in each confraternity consisted of a parish *capellán*, a syndic, and a black "elder brother," who were elected by the membership. The *capellán's* duties were to celebrate masses and other liturgies for the members. The syndic was charged with supervising the collection of alms at dances and *candombes*. The elder brother's duties were practically nominal, as important decisions were made by the white *capellán*.

The leadership structure, the presence therein of white colonial authorities, and the resulting tensions regarding decision-making power over confraternity activities produced a rich documentary record. In the Archivo General de la Nación Argentina (AGN) are found numerous complaints by African confraternities whose requests for masses and funerals were not properly attended to by the chaplains; that is, the service was not carried out with proper decency. There were even complaints because they were required to ask the priest's permission before speaking in their own meetings.

---

6. A series of prayers corresponding to prayer beads.

Dances and *Candombes* and Their Control
by Colonial Authorities

In the eighteenth century, dances and *candombes* were held on Sundays and feast days with the viceroy's permission. These were large gatherings of Afrorioplatenses. The Buenos Aires town council authorities demonstrated a fierce opposition to these *candombes* and did not authorize them, considering them indecent. In their reports to the viceroy, the councilors argued that these dances were lascivious and lewd and that in attending them slaves neglected their responsibilities. They also expressed fear of outbreaks of violence; some confrontations with authorities had been registered. Another concern frequently voiced by the councilors revolved around the origins of the monies that those of African descent collected to support their festivities. They argued that the money had to have been robbed from the slaves' owners.

As previously noted, the viceregal administration prohibited gatherings of Africans carried out without appropriate official supervision, for example in 1766, 1770, and 1790. Nevertheless, in two cases, the viceroy approved petitions to hold *candombes*. In 1795 he gave permission to the *Nación Congo* to hold dances on Sundays and feast days and, in 1799, he gave the same permission to the *Nación Cambunda*. What the viceroy did prohibit absolutely was the coronation of a participant, fearing that this might weaken his own authority. Such is the case of Pedro Duarte, an enslaved man bound to the *Nación Congo*, who apparently had been crowned king during a *candombe* in 1787 and was forced to resign (Goldberg, "Los negros," 6).

These dances undoubtedly preserved strong links to the original rituals of different African religious celebrations.[7] Their practices had to be secretive and reserved for the initiates, but, from the eighteenth century on, Afroporteños began to break the concealment of their dances and bring them into Catholic celebrations. The earlier secrecy can probably be explained because the early stage of the *candombe* coincided with the first communal organization of Africans in confraternities, under the unchallenged influence of the Church.

The later participation in Catholic ceremonies is relatively well documented from the last decades of the eighteenth until the end of the nineteenth centuries (Cirio, "Antecedentes" and "¿Rezan o bailan?"), with some later references. On certain days and times of the year, especially around Christmas and Epiphany but also during Carnival, during Easter, and for Saint John's Feast Day, sacred images surrounded by virtual gardens of artificial flowers were carried in processions through the streets to the sound and step of the *candombe*, among a multitude of Africans who danced their dances in public and before white onlookers.

The name *candombe* designated music, dance, and festivity. This last could be held behind closed doors, on the street, or at wakes; it could have a sacred or profane character. The principal moment was the enthroning of the statue of Saint Benedict or Saint Balthasar or another religious image, followed by the entrance of the "court" together with the king and queen. The brotherhoods held solemn processions through the streets, especially during Christmas festivities, accompanied by the image of the

---

7. See Cirio ("¿Rezan o bailan?") and Rodríguez Molas.

Virgin of Monserrat, patroness par excellence of the black *barrio*. She was carried on floats with candles and *candombes*, and often the government lent a troop escort.

The *Congo* Confraternity of Saint Balthasar Struggles for Autonomy in Choosing Its Leader

The Confraternity of Saint Balthasar in Buenos Aires achieved transcendence in historical memory in large part due to a conflict at the end of the eighteenth century regarding the selection of a king of the *Nación Congo*. The coronation occurred during a *candombe* that celebrated the Day of Our Lady of Assumption in an urban *hueco*, or open space, in 1787. Devotion to the Assumption of the Virgin was dear to the colonial confraternities, which were concerned with the passage from earthly existence to the Christian afterlife, signified by the moment of death.

The "good death," which one achieved by having carried out the sacraments and thus adequately prepared one's spirit, was a topic of special interest for the confraternities and brotherhoods. They dedicated themselves to providing services to ill members, aiding them in their suffering, and supplying the priest who would perform the last rites. The "spiritual economy of salvation" occupied an important place in the agenda of colonial confraternities (Fogelman, "Una 'economía'") and the inevitable entrance of the souls into purgatory—at least according to the imagination of the times—confronted faithful subjects with the weighing of their sins and good works (Fogelman, "Coordenadas" and "Una 'economía'").

The Virgin's "dormition," or "assumption"—terms that sought to elude the idea of death—was considered relevant to these beliefs and was commemorated according to the liturgical calendar. The Feast of Our Lady of Assumption must have been especially important for the confraternities of Saint Balthasar and the Souls of Purgatory, and it was one of these occasions, in 1787, that gave rise to the events that took the "king of the *Congos*" before the law. On this occasion, it was a black enslaved man named Pedro Duarte who was allegedly crowned king.[8]

The practice known as coronation appears to have been taken as a challenge to the viceregal authority, whose seat was in Buenos Aires. Beyond the personal tensions among the individual actors mentioned in the document, the colonial magistrate had motive to intervene, questioning witnesses, repressing the actions of the confraternity, and forcing Pedro Duarte to resign. The account, which is taken from the AGN, records the events reviewed by the colonial authorities. The document consists of various sections. The first is a report given to Viceroy Marqués de Loreto by the *sargento mayor* of the Company of Free Blacks Manual Farías (informer and party in the case against the free black Pablo Agüero for contempt). This report is followed by the testimonies of several witnesses of African origin (many of them identified as being from *Guinea* or African born), who report on conflicts between Farías and Agüero.

Among these appears the testimony taken from Pedro Duarte himself, black *mayordomo* of the Confraternity of Saint Balthasar and supposedly regarded as king of

---

8. In addition to the document in this chapter, see Bernand and Cirio, "¿Rezan o bailan?"

the *Congos*. Finally, the commissioner Francisco Rodríguez sought punishment for several of the parties in the cause. With some nuances, it seems that the colonial magistrate frowned on the Afroporteño parties, the informer, the man he has denounced, and several of the witnesses.

The people whose voices are recorded in the document are considered inclined to disorder and insubordination against Spanish rule in the city. The festive practices of the Africans, with their dances, elections, and rituals related to ethnic authorities, were seen as symptoms of the conflicts that overflowed the boisterous disorder of the festival with its dance and drink. These were practices and voices dangerous to the control that the Spanish Crown's regime exercised over its colonial subjects. The survival of ethnic identities and solidarities and the strengthening of social and cultural bonds they represented—in a somewhat underhanded way in the Christian celebrations—were a potential threat to colonial control.

*****

[Report by Manuel Farías against Pablo Agüero][9]

Most Excellent Lord Viceroy,

Manuel Farías, citizen of this city and *sargento mayor* of the *Compañías de negros libres* [Companies of Free Blacks], with the greatest respect and veneration that is due Your Excellency, presents the following:

That Pablo Agüero, commissioned to round up fugitive blacks and regulate their *tambos*, based on this *fuero* and without acknowledging that he himself is a soldier of the declarant's company, has completely refused to subordinate himself, refusing to obey [Farías] as required by ordinance. He has not reported for duty to the company and has not asked the petitioner [Farías] as *sargento mayor* for the aid he might need in certain cases for the fulfillment of his commission. Rather, without proper authority, he rounds up the blacks and takes them when he needs them. Without recognizing [Farías] as his immediate superior, [Agüero] treats him with complete scorn. He has even abused him verbally. For instance, on August 11 of last year, having seen [Agüero] near Don Manuel Warnes' estate, [Farías], for no reason other than to verify [what he had heard], told him about the *coronation* of the black man Pedro Duarte at a certain *tambo* by order and disposition of Agüero, [whereupon Agüero] called [Farías] a scoundrel, worthless, traitor, and other names, as [Farías] can prove, if Your Excellency considers it necessary.

The antagonism that he professes is so extreme that even the soldiers from [Agüero's] company, and with his protection, one of them, Manuel Jesús, availing himself of that protection at the corner store [*pulpería*] in the Plaza Nueva, had the audacity to call [Farías'] wife a whore, just because [she] was trying to collect four *reales* from an Indian who owed it to her. She begged [Manuel Jesús] to leave the Indian alone until she could collect from him, to which [Manuel Jesús] responded with said insult or profanity. If necessary, [Farías] also offers to verify this by way of the tavern keeper or owner of the tavern and some other witnesses who were present at this incident.

Lastly, if the declarant were to specify the various dealings he has had with Agüero and the many occasions and the trivialities [Agüero] seeks to provoke and offend, [aside from] failing to act as his subordinate, it would take forever. Moreover, it would serve as a distraction for Your Excellency, who, given your high office, has other serious matters equal to your prominent nature to consider, as all is left to your superior and wise understanding, more so as the *teniente del rey* of this *plaza* has verified some of the things that have been presented in this report and others, as the declarant understands them.

So that that they can be further certified, [the declarant] most humbly begs Your Excellency to consider it worthwhile to order an inquiry regarding all the foregoing and, with its documentation, proceed to give it [the] serious consideration that is justly commensurate with the circumstances of the related subjects, given Your Excellency's notable reputation for fairness.

Buenos Aires, January 16, 1787.

Manuel Farías.

---

9. Información hecha para esclarecer lo que expone Farías en su *memorial* contra Pablo Agüero, ambos dos *negros*, hecha en Buenos Aires a 23 de enero de mil setecientos ochenta y siete, Archivo de la Nación, Buenos Aires, Escribanía mayor de Gobierno, Sala IX, 36:4:3, legajo 75, exp. 10.

[Testimony of José García, Free Black]

Asked whether he [José García] has seen or heard that Agüero wished to crown some black as king, [he should declare] from what *nation*, what his name is, where, and when. He [García] responds that on the eve of the feast of *Nuestra Señora del Tránsito*, the witness [García] was at his home that night when some blacks, whom he says he did not know, passed in the vicinity. They were talking among themselves and saying that on the day of the *Tránsito* celebration, which was the following day, the black Pablo Agüero had arranged for the black Pedro Duarte to be crowned as King of the Congos.

Asked whether he knows or has heard that the *coronation* of said king has been confirmed on that day or any other day, he responds that he does not know if such a *coronation* has been confirmed on that day or any other day.

Asked whether he knows whether Agüero has failed to respect or subordinate himself to the aforementioned *sargento mayor* [Farías], he is to state the circumstances and when it occurred, he responds that he has heard Farías himself and other soldiers say that [Agüero] has never wished to obey him in anything, [that Agüero has] said he would not obey him in any way because the captains and the *sargento mayor* were soldiers just like him. These statements, and saying there was no other *sargento mayor* than he [Agüero], are frequent, as is verified by the manner in which all the *morenos* [blacks] treat him [Farías].

Asked whether he knows that the black Farías and Agüero hate each other or harbor ill will toward each other, he responds that it is so, because, leaving this city for his home one day—he does not remember which day—he encountered them two blocks before arriving at the *quinta* [estate] of *Don* Manuel Warnes, verbally tearing into each other. He heard the black Agüero saying to Farías that the reason the blacks were insolent and disobedient to the law and to him was because Farías himself advised them to be so. For this reason, [García] says that, seeing them so worked up, about to attack and hurt each other, he moved to separate them, which he managed to do, making each one leave in a different direction so that they would not continue to fight each other. They left immediately, as did the witness, and he did not see them again.

Asked whether he knows that the aforementioned Agüero had wanted to crown a black as king of some *nation*, he responds that he knows nothing about what is being asked.

[Testimony of José González, Native of *Guinea*]

Asked whether he knows the *sargento mayor de negros*, Manuel Farías, and the black Pablo Agüero, and what commission he has, he responds that he knows Manuel Farías, [his own] *sargento mayor* and obeys his verbal or written orders. He also knows Pablo Agüero and knows that he is commissioned with soldiers of the same *casta* by the *señor teniente del gobernador* to arrest black men and women who have fled their masters and to have them submit [to authority].

Asked whether he knows whether the black Agüero had made arrangements at one point for someone from the *castas* to be crowned as king, he responds that on one of the feast days when the blacks gather to dance at the *hueco*, the preselected site, the witness saw they were leading a black man named Pedro Duarte under a large parasol and that he was wearing a sort of crown. But once Agüero had seen the [crown], he immediately had them remove it. And that is what happened. The witness observed that all the other blacks of the *Congo nation* respected and obeyed all the orders that Pedro Duarte gave them as king.

Asked whether he knows or has heard that the aforementioned Duarte continues to act as such a king, he responds [that] he knows that on the day when the celebration of Saint Balthasar is held in the Church of La Piedad, they respect and obey him like a king of their *nation* and not as *mayordomo*.

[Testimony of Pedro Duarte, Native of the *Congo Nation*]

Asked whether he knows that the black Farías and Agüero have had words, have quarreled, or have fought, he responds that for many years they have been at odds, and they fight with one another whenever possible, since the aforementioned Farías told the *señor teniente del rey* and the *sargento mayor* that [there were still] kings in the various *nations*.

Asked how he knows for certain that the aforementioned Farías informed the *teniente del rey* and the *sargento mayor de la plaza*, he responds that when he was in the chapel of the Church of La Piedad with other black brothers of the *Cofradía* de San Baltasar, ready to go bury a deceased brother, Farías arrived with troops and arrested him near the chapel. Concerning Pablo Agüero, [Farías] went to look for him at his house and arrested [the rest of] them in the settlement, and from there they went to the royal jail.

Asked whether the blacks of his *nation* named him king last year and if on the Feast of the Assumption he went to the *hueco del tambo* so that they might recognize him as such, he responds that he has not gone to the *hueco* with insignias of a king. He went solely with the people of his *nation* with his cape, a hat, and a parasol made of a *pollera* [a rigid hoop wire], so that they might recognize him as *mayor*, but not as king.

Asked who arranged for the witness to be recognized as *mayor*, he responds that various blacks from his *nation* did so, but Pablo Agüero was not mixed up in this. Rather, he only became involved after he saw [Duarte] with the parasol, which he made him remove, and ordered that he be taken home. But Agüero did see that [Duarte] had already been recognized [as *mayor*].

[Testimony of Pablo Agüero, Native of *Guinea*]

. . . He responds that his name is Pablo Agüero, a native of *Guinea*, and that he is commissioned by the *señor gobernador intendente* to arrest black men and women, fugitives from their masters, and to keep them calm and quiet in their diversions and dances and that he lives in the neighborhood of Monserrat.

Asked what words he had with the wife of *Sargento Mayor* Farías [and that he] explain where and when, he responds that while he has known her, he has never spoken any offensive words to that woman.

Asked whether he recognizes Manuel Farías as his *sargento mayor* and if he obeys his orders concerning service to the king's and the public good, he responds that he has always obeyed him as his *sargento mayor* and so too his orders until he was given the commission, the one that he says he made [Farías] aware of when he was commissioned.

Asked whether, when he needs troops from his *nation* to arrest some fugitive, he asks the *sargento mayor* for the necessary troops to carry this out, he responds that he asked for them only once to arrest blacks who were dressing in *Cambunda* [style clothing] in the chapel of La Piedad on the day of Saint Balthasar. Because the *sargento mayor* refused to give [him the troops], he has never again counted on him. [Instead,] he has relied on veteran troops, as the *gobernador intendente* has mandated with the permission of the *Señor Virrey*.

Asked what other words were exchanged between the two blacks mentioned, he responds that he told Farías that what he said to him [was] not true. If anything is true, then it is that [Farías] himself went to look for the black Juan [de Belén], so that he might go to the house of the abovementioned *ayudante de la plaza* and tell him that the black Pablo Agüero wanted to crown [Duarte] king. As everything was uncertain, Farías also told [Agüero] that if he wanted, he would seek the same commission from the government, given that the city was large, that there was a great multitude of blacks, and that, in this way, they could be even more placated. To that [Agüero] responded that it would be very good and that he should request it [of the government].

[Testimony of Manuel de Jesús, Native of *Guinea*]

. . . He responds that his name is Manuel de Jesús, a native of *Guinea*, and he is commissioned under ordinance by the black Pablo Agüero, and he lives in his house.

Asked what salary he receives as an employee of the aforementioned Agüero and who pays him, he responds that he receives a salary of six *pesos* per month, which are paid by Agüero.

Asked from what source Agüero pays him, he responds that [Agüero] has work done on sheepskins at his house by laborers and from that, and from whatever the owners of the black fugitive slaves give him, he assumes that Agüero pays the six *pesos*.

Asked if he knows whether Agüero, when he needs soldiers from the same *nation* in order to arrest some blacks and in order to keep them orderly, asks for the appropriate assistance from his *sargento mayor*, he responds that he knows for a fact that, in order to arrest six blacks from different masters who were hiding in the woods of Valentín's estate, he asked for assistance to arrest them; but the [*sargento mayor*] did not give him any, saying that the companies did not have soldiers and that he himself should look for them, which is, in fact, what he did. They arrested the aforementioned blacks and delivered them to their masters, who gave him three to four *pesos* for each of them.

Asked whether he knows or has heard that the black, Agüero, has wanted to crown a particular black as king, he responds that at that time he was on Captain Bautista's ship on the Patagonian coast, but he has heard nothing about the black Agüero having arranged such a thing.

Asked with which woman he had words at Plaza Nueva and what words they were, he responds that when the witness [he, Manuel de Jesús] was in the said *plaza* looking for a fugitive black woman, he saw, at the door of a tavern, an inebriated Indian making a fool of himself, speaking impudently with a Spaniard. He approached him, telling him to get out of there and watch his rudeness with the Spaniards; otherwise he would arrest him. There, a black woman, whom he said he did not know, was selling turnovers or pastries. She told [him] that the aforementioned Indian owed her three *reales* and that he [Manuel de Jesús] should not arrest him. The witness stated that he replied to the black woman that if she returned for the Indian and defended him he would also arrest her. For that reason, the black woman called the witness "my [illegible]" and other rude words. Provoked at hearing such expressions from the black woman, he said it was true that he called her a "whore."

[Testimony of Juan de Belén, Native of *Guinea*]

. . . He responds that he knows Pablo Agüero through his commission to arrest black men and women who have fled their masters and to keep them calm as well as for the zeal he has for those of his color.

Asked what day, month, and year did *Sargento Mayor* Farías have a conversation [with him] and that he recount it, he responds that on the Feast of the Assumption, he went to the *hueco del tambo* to make an announcement. On the following day, Farías found [him] and told him he should come with him to the house of *Ayudante* Don Francisco Rodríguez to tell him that Pablo Agüero wanted to crown the black Pedro Duarte as king and that [he] should affirm that he had seen the crown. [Juan de Belén] said that he responded to Farías that he did not want to go to the house of the *ayudante* to tell him such a thing because he had not seen any crown to coronate Duarte, neither did he know nor had he heard tell such a thing, and that he could not in good conscience say so. Despite all these explanations, [Farías] made him go to the *ayudante's* house, telling him he would give him a document so that the authorities would not bother him. [Juan de Belén] responded to this [by] saying that he did not need any document, because he had not committed any crime for which the authorities could pursue and punish him. However, despite all that has been stated above, [Farías] made the witness accompany him to the dwelling of the *ayudante* at eleven o'clock at night. Not finding him there, Farías told him that they should go to the house of the *mayor de la plaza* and that he should tell him what he should tell him. . . .

In light of all [the testimonies], as the statements have neither been corroborated nor challenged, the truth is not entirely evident among all the witnesses. But they are [clear] in that the black Pablo Agüero has shown lack of the proper respect owed to Manuel Farías as *sargento mayor*, neither, at the very least, does he ask for assistance in the arrests he must make as part of his commission, thus abusing his own authority. He should be reprimanded or [dealt with] as Your Excellency might see fit. Farías should be admonished and punished for the influence he brought to bear on the free black Juan Belén, by making him go to the house of the *ayudante mayor* to tell him that the black Pablo Agüero wanted to crown Pedro Duarte, a free *moreno*, as king. Thus, everything appears questionable, as is evident by his and the rest of the testimonies.

The black Manuel de Jesús [should be] relieved of the commission because, without Pablo Agüero's [illegible], he tried to arrest the Indian without proper authorization.

He confessed in his statement that he called Farías' wife a whore and that Agüero did not have any part in this. This is proven.

The *tambos*, Sir, are very harmful, for I myself have seen the serious scandals that occur in their dances as well as how shameful they are, along with the unfortunate consequences that result from them. The first [ill consequence] is that many of the masters who have slaves cannot count on them on feast days, because they do not feel they are slaves on those days. The second is that they steal as much as they can from their masters in order to support and preserve their dances. And the last is that on those feast days many of them are drunk in the *tambos* and in the streets. For these reasons, the viceroys and governors previous to His Most Excellent Lord Viceroy Marqués de Loreto widely prohibited all these dances and *tambos* because several deaths and terrible things have occurred during these celebrations and, in particular, on the feast days of the Rosary and Saint Balthasar. Even the *alcaldes* Don José Gainza and Don Manuel Antonio de Warnes saw the same things as I did last Sunday. Moved by well-intended zeal and the proper administration of justice, they sought to inform themselves and concluded the same things. It seems to me that they testified about all of this to the *teniente gobernador* so that he might resolve this, which has not been carried out, well, on the following day.

Notwithstanding what has been said here, Your Lordship will make a determination in accordance with your supreme pleasure.

Buenos Aires, January 25, 1787

Francisco Rodríguez

PART III: RELIGIOUS BELIEFS AND PRACTICES

Religion was perhaps the most contentious sphere of cultural difference between Africans and Iberians. By 1502, Muslims and Jews who had not converted to Christianity were expelled from Spain, and converts and heretics under suspicion were punished by an active Inquisition. Religion and nationality built the foundations for racial differentiation and the social subordination of non-Christians. Africans were considered pagans who could be evangelized and saved, a purpose used to justify their enslavement, but when they continued to practice pagan beliefs or mixed them with Christianity, the Church felt threatened and prosecuted them as sorcerers, witches, and idolaters.

In times of high tension, colonials leveled accusations of witchcraft against Afro-Latinos as a social group out of fear of this more populous racial "inferior"; such fear may have played into the prosecution of Paula de Eguiluz (Chapter 11). In the Caribbean, Afro-Latinos were often caught between Catholic and Protestant worlds or navigated this European conflict to their advantage, as did many *Maroons* who aided Protestant pirates in their attacks on Spanish cities and wealth. In a contrary move, two *Beafada* men, slaves of a Cartagena woman, were captured by a Dutch citizen and taken to the English colony of Providence Island, where they sided with Catholicism and gave informative and condemnatory accounts of the Island's Puritan life to the Spaniards in Portobelo (Chapter 12).

Not all Catholic clergy thought alike, and, in the tradition of Saint Thomas Aquinas, Dominicans often saw pagan religious experience as preparation for Christian salvation. Perhaps this attitude provides some explanation for the survival in Sor Teresa Chicaba's as-told-to biography of syncretic elements of African religious belief, including a vision of a Holy White Lady in her West African homeland (Chapter 13). Many African religious societies in the Americas secretly sustained *transculturated* religious practices, but they could also proclaim orthodox Christianity to elevate themselves above other African *nations*, as did the leaders of the Confraternity of Saints Elesbão and Iphigenia in Rio de Janeiro, claiming superiority over the heathen *Angolans* (Chapter 14). All these stories show Afro-Latinos who adopted Catholicism continuing to live between religious worlds. Their stories allow glimpses into the ways that religion was a cultural space of transformation and a means to personal and communal survival and social standing.

11

The Witchcraft Trials of Paula de Eguiluz, a Black Woman, in Cartagena de Indias, 1620–1636[1]

Sara Vicuña Guengerich

Between 1623 and 1636, Paula de Eguiluz, a woman of African descent whose mother was of the *Biáfara* caste, was tried three times for witchcraft by the Inquisition in Cartagena de Indias on the northern coast of what is now Colombia. Paula was born on the Caribbean island of Santo Domingo but grew up serving different masters in Puerto Rico and Cuba. Her final master was Juan de Eguiluz, the royal treasury's accountant (*contador de la Real Hacienda de Su Majestad*) for the island of Cuba.

In 1620, Juan de Eguiluz took over the copper mines of El Cobre in Santiago del Prado, Cuba, as a private contractor and as *alcalde mayor* and he settled there with his household.[2] Arriving with him from Havana were his daughter Doña Paula de Eguiluz, his slave Paula de Eguiluz, and other servants. The enslaved black population of Santiago del Prado at that time consisted of 205 males and 110 females (Díaz, 33).[3] Unlike several other female slaves of El Cobre, Paula de Eguiluz was a slave who dressed well and who was given permission to visit her friends in Havana, from whom she learned spells to entice potential lovers. During the years prior to her arrest in Santiago del Prado, she was publicly known as a sorceress. The key suspicion that led to her arrest was that she had killed an Indian woman's child by means of witchcraft.

In 1623, Paula was accused of witchcraft (*brujería*), divination, and apostasy (declarations contrary to Church doctrine). In September of that year, the Inquisition prosecutor in Cartagena de Indias, Domingo Vélez de Asas y Argos, requested that the Inquisition authorities arrest her in Cuba, seize her goods, and transport her to the secret jails of the Cartagena Inquisition.[4] Paula de Eguiluz arrived in Cartagena in 1624 not yet informed of the specific charges she faced because of the secrecy with which the Holy Office conducted the inquisitorial proceedings. Eleven witnesses had accused Paula of numerous offenses, among them causing the death of an infant by sucking her navel,[5] transforming herself into a goat, appearing and vanishing in different places without leaving a trace, and selling love spells.

---

1. See Map 5.

2. These rich mines constituted one of the most important enterprises in the Caribbean in the early seventeenth century because they provided for the needs of the Crown's artillery. The title *alcalde mayor de minas* indicated both administrative and judicial responsibilities.

3. For a history of the ownership of this mine and the slaves who worked it, see Díaz and Chapter 8 of this volume.

4. According to Medina (108), the Inquisition tribunal in Cartagena de Indias built nine new cells to imprison their new offenders; among them was Paula de Eguiluz.

5. A common indictment in witchcraft trials in Europe as well as in Spanish America was infanticide by vampirism (Henningsen, 27).

Her alleged crimes fell into the categories of sorcery and witchcraft, which the Church condemned. According to Colombian historian Diana Luz Ceballos Gómez (86–90), the Cartagena Inquisition distinguished between the application of the terms *hechicería* (sorcery) and *brujería*. *Hechicería* was the label given to an individual who used spells and remedies for both good and evil purposes, often with the aid of natural materials. With its European, Amerindian, and African origins, *hechicería* often used magic to help a person attract a mate or resolve spousal conflicts. Conversely, *brujería* was a label that defamed an entire group or category of people. A witch—a *bruja*—was thought to reject God and the sacraments and instead worship the devil and observe the witches' Sabbath.[6] Consequently, *brujería* represented a much more serious charge.

Although Spanish inquisitors were much more concerned with maintaining religious orthodoxy than they were with prosecuting witches per se, the discourses of race and ethnicity were fused with those of witchcraft and thus brought the attention of the Inquisition to accusations of witchcraft among non-European racial groups. Africans and their descendants used a variety of charms, talismans, and rituals to bring themselves luck and to protect themselves from various maladies; hence, their practices were suspected of being the work of the devil (Sweet, 164–75). Charges of witchcraft and heresy were common among the African-descent communities.

From 1610 to 1660, more than four hundred people were tried by the Inquisition in Cartagena de Indias. Sixteen percent of the accused, imprisoned, and punished were classified as blacks and 11 percent as slaves. About 30 percent of the accused, including blacks transported from the Caribbean islands, were tried for witchcraft, sorcery, and divination (Splendiani, Sánchez Bohórquez, and Luque de Salazar). Paula de Eguiluz was counted among the fifteen black women enslaved and free accused of being a witch and having made a pact with the devil (Blázquez, 215).

The documents in this chapter belong to the dossier of Paula de Eguiluz's first trial, which in its entirety includes 111 folios. This documentation reveals the peculiarities of inquisitorial procedures such as the initial denunciation of the offender by the familiars and professional informers of the Inquisition, the confiscation of property, the refusal to divulge the reasons for arrest, the three warnings (*amonestaciones*), the formal accusation of the prosecutor, the permission to obtain legal help for the victim, and the conclusion of the case with the victim's sentence and punishment (Kamen, 164–97). Paula de Eguiluz's first trial was composed of a series of *audiencias*, or hearings, at which the prosecution and defense made their respective depositions of witnesses, and a series of interrogations carried out by the inquisitors in the presence of a notary.

The victim's confessions, such as Eguiluz's, in witchcraft trials offer a unique, if partial window into the life, religious beliefs, and supposed crimes of women of African descent. Paula's narrative, for example, employs a discursive strategy that speaks of a *transculturated* notion of Catholicism and upholds African cultural religious beliefs and practices often punished by the Church. Her confessions reveal her limited knowledge of Christian doctrine; yet, they expose her devotion to the Virgin.

---

6. The witches' Sabbaths or *aquelarres* were supposedly assemblies where witches gathered on the eve of the festivals of the Christian year to commit themselves to the devil (Henningsen, 71).

They disclose her herbal cures to heal the ill as well as her potions to attract men. Most interestingly, they bring to light the shared cultural practices and social and kin affiliations of the African-descendant communities in the colonial period.

When both prosecution and defense completed their duties, Paula's case concluded with her acknowledgment that the devil had persuaded her to follow him. However, she repented of her sins and pled to be reconciled with the Church, which was the fate of the majority of the penitents in the Spanish Inquisition (Kamen, 185). Following the basic inquisitorial procedure, Paula appeared in an *auto de fe*,[7] wearing the penitential robe or *sambenito*.[8] She abjured publicly while receiving two hundred lashes, and she was ordered to serve in the city hospitals for one year.

Once reconciled with the Church, Paula remained in Cartagena de Indias as a free woman (*negra horra*), having obtained her *manumission* during the period of her first trial. After completing her sentence in the city hospital, she continued practicing love-related magic (*arte de bien querer*), spells, and healing, from which she obtained an income. In 1632 and again in 1635, the Inquisition of Cartagena de Indias tried Paula under new witchcraft charges. Her second trial highlighted the offenses from the first, adding new accusations. The third trial was actually a retrial, mandated by the Inquisition's Supreme Council in Spain, because the Cartagena Inquisition had condemned Paula to be relaxed to the civil authorities to be executed. In these new trials, Paula was accused of having made an explicit pact with the devil, conjuring the souls of purgatory to attract men, and initiating several women—white, black, and of other *castas*—into the witches' sect (*la secta de las brujas*).

After repeatedly hearing in her trials the highly doctrinal discourse of the Church's accusations, Paula altered her testimony and explanations, which previously had been rooted in an oral popular culture. Understanding that the Inquisition classified her African beliefs and practices as heretical, Paula began to rework her narrative according to Catholic discourse. Her testimony shifted from a total denial of all the charges to the acknowledgment of her herbal healing, to which she gave Christian purposes.

As this did not satisfy the inquisitors' demands, Paula provided further confessions about her pact with the devil in which she admitted having committed aberrant sins. By the end of her third trial, not excerpted here, she provided the most symbolic images of witchcraft. She redefined the biblical concepts of the devil to provide a *transculturated* vision of the Catholic beliefs. As Paula de Eguiluz spoke with her inquisitors, and as her oral expressions were filtered through the bureaucratic discourse of the Inquisition, she left a narrative in which it is possible to hear her voice as she exercises agency in her own defense.

*****

---

7. Literally an "act of faith." It was a public expression of penance for sin and hatred for heresy (Kamen, 185).

8. The *sambenito* was usually a yellow penitential garment displaying one or two diagonal crosses; the penitent was condemned to wear it as a mark of infamy (Kamen, 186).

First Trial of Paula de Eguiluz, Accused of Witchcraft
and Reconciled with the Church, 1624[9]

[Paula de Eguiluz Appears for the First Time
before the Inquisitor: May 25, 1624]

In the afternoon hearing of the Holy Inquisition of Cartagena on May 25, 1624, the Lord Inquisitor Doctor Agustín de Ugarte Saravia being present, a dark-skinned woman was ordered to be brought from the secret jails. Her oath was taken as required by law, under which she swore to tell the truth and to keep in secret what was revealed in this hearing as well as in the rest of the hearings until the resolution of her case. The inquisitor asked her name, origin, age, and status, to which she answered that her name was Paula de Eguiluz and she was originally from Santo Domingo in Hispaniola.[10] She said that at the present she was the slave of Juan de Eguiluz, administrator of the mines of El Cobre near Santiago de Cuba, where she had been living for four years. She said she was about thirty-three years old. She was told that the *alcalde* reported her request for a hearing and now that she has one she should state why she requested it.

She said she requested it to declare her guilt. And having been told to declare it, she admitted the sin of incest, which she committed by carnal knowledge of two men who were relatives, but she does not know how they are related. She also accused herself of believing some of her dreams, such as the one she dreamed about some livestock that came from Báyamo to El Cobre, where she was at that time. The next morning, she saw livestock coming from Barajagua. Then she told everyone, "See how my dream came true: the livestock did come from Barajagua." Also, whenever she dreamed about a person, she happened to see this person the next day. Many other times she talked about what she saw without having dreamed it but bragged that she had dreamed it. . . .

Item. She said that one time her master [Juan de Eguiluz] had a high fever and she was looking for a remedy to heal him. Juana Gerónima, a single Spanish woman who lives in Juan[11] advised her to take some orange peels, place them on a grave and mix them with a little bit of ground bones from a dead person, along with rosemary leaves, and put them on the grave. Then the next day she was to mix all that with wine so her master would drink it and recover. Paula did as indicated because she wanted her master to feel better; however, her master did not allow it.

And because of the hour, the hearing ended. The inquisitor admonished Paula and sent her back to her prison. Before she left, the scribe read the content of this document,

---

9. Records of the three Paula de Eguiluz trials are preserved in the Archivo Histórico Nacional, Madrid. These documents are also available online through the Portal de Archivos Españoles (PARES). Procesos de fe de Paula de Eguiluz, Ministerio de Cultura, Archivo Histórico Nacional, Madrid, Inquisición 1620, exp. 10.

10. A note in the margin reads, "Age: thirty-three years."

11. This might be the name of a street or a neighborhood in colonial Havana. There are references to other geographical locations throughout the document that have masculine given names.

and she said it was recorded correctly. The inquisitor Agustín de Ugarte Saravia signed Paula's name because she did not know how to write. All this was done in my presence. I, the secretary Luis Blanco de Salcedo.

[The Second Hearing: July 4, 1624]

In the morning hearing of the Holy Inquisition of Cartagena—on July 4, 1624—the Lord Inquisitor Doctor Agustín de Ugarte Saravia being present...[Paula] was told to relate her genealogy. And complying, she said that as she has stated, she was born in Santo Domingo in the house of Diego de Leguízamo, who was her mother Guiomar's master. Her mother was a black slave of the *Biáfara* caste. She never knew her father or her grandparents on either side. She only knew that she had two sisters, Ana and Juana, living in Santo Domingo, and that Ana is free and Juana is Antonio de Jaques' slave in Santo Domingo, where Paula lived until the age of thirteen. Her master at that time gave her and other slaves to Juan Nieto, a *Creole* living in that city, as a payment for a debt. Juan Nieto, she said, sold her to Iñigo de Otazo, who took her to Puerto Rico, where she stayed as his slave for four years. After that, Otazo's wife, jealous of her, demanded that her husband send Paula to Havana, where her current master Juan de Eguiluz bought her, and she served him until the Holy Office arrested her.

Asked if she was baptized and confirmed in the Catholic faith, she responded that she is a baptized Christian, and she has heard she was baptized in the city of Santo Domingo, in the main church, and that the archbishop of Santo Domingo, Don Fray Agustín Dávila, confirmed her. She also said that she hears Mass on Sundays and feast days, and that she confesses and takes communion on the days the Holy Church commands, and that she did so this past Lent in the El Cobre mines, and that Padre Góngora received her confession and gave her communion.

She made the sign of the cross, correctly recited the Lord's Prayer, the Creed, the Salve Regina, and the Ten Commandments. She said she did not know the Articles of the Faith. Asked if she knows how to read and write, she responded she does not and she does not know who might possess prohibited books.

The inquisitors told her that the Holy Office does not arrest anybody without having enough information that this person has done, said, or committed or has seen someone else do, say, or commit acts that are or appear to be an offense against our Lord God or His blessed mother, the Holy Virgin Mary, or against the Holy Catholic Faith and the law of the Gospels, which is preached and taught by the Holy Mother Roman Catholic Church or against the free and right exercise of the Holy Office. Therefore, Paula should understand that she has been arrested because this Holy Office has received such information about her.

First Admonition

So she is admonished...and instructed to search her memory and to tell the whole truth of that for which she feels guilty or about which she knows of the guilt of others, without hiding anything and without giving false testimony. If she does so, her trial will be settled quickly and mercifully. Otherwise, justice will be done. She said she has told the truth and has nothing else to confess. And having been admonished, the defendant was sent back to her prison....

[Accusations of the Prosecutor of the Holy Office: July 11, 1624]

In the morning hearing of the Holy Inquisition of Cartagena on July 11, 1624, the Lord Inquisitor Doctor Agustín de Ugarte y Saravia being present....

Paula was advised that the prosecutor of the Inquisition wishes to accuse her and that it behooves her, first, to tell the truth. Otherwise, the prosecutor will be heard and justice will be done. She said she has told the truth and has nothing else to say. Then Domingo de Vélez de Asas y Argos presented the following accusation, signed in his name, and he swore in due form that he did not have evil intent, but because it was the truth. His accusation is the following: ...

I come before Your Lordship and criminally accuse the black woman Paula de Eguiluz, imprisoned in the secret jails of the Inquisition, who was born in Santo Domingo in Hispaniola . . . and is currently the slave of Juan de Eguiluz, the superior officer of the copper mines near Santiago de Cuba....

[First Accusation]

1   I state that [Paula], being a baptized and confirmed Christian... enjoying the mercies and immunities, privileges, and exemptions and indulgences of this state, without fearing God, harming her conscience, condemning her soul, and with little regard for the justice of this Holy Office, ungrateful for such mercies, has committed crimes against our Holy Catholic Faith. She has used spells and believed superstitions, mixing sacred objects with profane ones, calling on the devil, with whom she has a pact, and joining the witches' sect. And she has tried to foretell things that depend on the free will of man, attributing to human beings what belongs solely to the Creator.

[Second Accusation]

2   [I offer] as proof, that last year in August of 1623, this defendant established a pact with the devil for whom she had to commit crimes, without fear of God or her own conscience. When a certain person[12] had given birth, Paula took the newborn in her arms and uncovered her belly to suck the life out of her through her navel,[13] and she did all the harm that she could. And it was known that Paula did so, because the child was well before she took her in her arms, and because it is public opinion and well known that she is a witch and sorcerer and the child ended up dying....

[Fourth Accusation]

4   I offer as proof of her evil life and behavior and insincere Christianity that the accused went to a church with a certain person one day—about four years ago—because her master Juan de Eguiluz was ill. She started digging in a grave with a stick and took a couple of pieces of bone and carried them off secretly. And she said to the certain person who had gone with her that it was to cure her master. She ground [the bones] into a powder together with orange peels and rosemary leaves. Then she put

---

12. The words "a certain person" (*cierta persona*) are used to hide the identity of a witness, to maintain the secrecy demanded by the inquisitorial process.

13. Witches were sometimes thought to kill their victims by sucking that person's nose, ears, eyes, mouth, or navel so he or she would bleed to death (Splendiani, Sánchez Bohórquez, and Luque de Salazar, 140).

this mixture in a piece of cloth or paper and tied it with a red ribbon to use them for her spells and deceits. . . .

[Sixth Accusation]

6   And likewise, when Paula was still living in Havana with her master Juan de Eguiluz, he got upset at something she did and wanted to hit her with a saber, but Paula disappeared before his eyes. She threw herself through the window and fell on a rocky spot, where she should have been injured, but she received no injuries—which indicates that she did this with the alliance and pact she had with the devil—on this occasion he kept her from harm. . . .

[Eighth Accusation]

8   And likewise it was public knowledge in the mines that this defendant was imprisoned by order of the trial court [*por la justicia ordinaria*] because it was commonly held that she was a witch. And while she was imprisoned at the guardhouse, a certain person sent for her to punish her. And this defendant told the soldiers who were charged with her keeping that they should not let her be taken away, as she was imprisoned for a serious crime that she had committed, that of killing a child, as was imputed to her. . . .

[Twelfth Accusation]

12   And likewise, the accused used twigs and hairs from a man with whom she had committed indecent acts and has extracted liquid from the *yerba curia*.[14] Mixing all these things, she put them in a little white bag as if they were relics, or at least pretending they were. Then she put this mixture underneath his pillow. And using the root from the same *yerba curia* for her deceits, wherefrom it is evident this woman has departed from Our Lord God and our Holy Catholic Faith and has surrendered herself to the servitude and slavery of the devil. And although she has been admonished by Your Lordship many and various times to confess the whole truth, she has refused to do it and has silenced it, committing perjury. . . .

. . . Therefore, I humbly ask Your Highness to take my word as the truth and that Paula de Eguiluz be condemned to the greatest and most serious punishments that the law allows. . . . And that if it is necessary, she be tortured. And the torture be repeated until she confesses the whole truth regarding the matter for which I request justice. This I swear according to form and request from Your Lordship's Holy Office.

Domingo Vélez de Asas y Argos, prosecutor for the Inquisition.

After hearing the accusation, Paula de Eguiluz swore to respond and tell the whole truth. Each chapter was read to her again, to which she responded in the following way:

[Response to the First Accusation]

Chapter 1   . . . She said she has already responded to this one and that she is not a witch and has not used spells. She said she does not have a pact with the devil either and that these accusations were made by enemies who hate her.

---

14. Possibly an herb called *Justicia pectoralis*, or carpenter bush.

[Response to the Second Accusation]

Chapter 2   She said that her testimony is that one day when she was standing on the street, Leonor de Estrada who was Ana María's[15] neighbor called her inside because Ana María's daughter was dying and she was crying desperately. When Paula entered that house, the mother wanted to breastfeed the baby, but the girl was unable to feed. So, Ana María told Paula to unwrap the swaddling cloth to find out what was going on. When Paula did so, she saw that the baby's belly was swollen, but in order to calm her, she told Ana María not to worry about it. [She and Leonor] showed the mother the baby's navel, which was fine. Then Paula told her to look at the navel, and, warming a cloth infused with lavender and rosemary,[16] she applied it to the baby's belly and wrapped her up again, and gave her back to her mother. And immediately after that, Paula went home and did not see the baby again. And everything else in this chapter of the accusation is false, and they are accusations of people who hate her because her master loves her and they see her well dressed....

[Response to the Fourth Accusation]

Chapter 4   She said that the accusation refers to what she has already declared. Juana Gerónima told her to prepare a mixture made from a dead person's bones and a little rosemary and orange peels that have been on the grave and to give it to her master in a drink as a remedy for his fever. She was supposed to tell him what he was drinking so that with the repugnance he felt he would vomit. She said she had the intention to do so, but after she told her master about it, he told her off and did not allow her to do it. Though Paula did not get the bones, she still told the sacristan that she had been given these instructions as a remedy for her master and, telling her that she could not take a dead person's bone from the church, the sacristan said she should go to ask the hermit for a little piece. However, she decided not to go. She denies the rest of the charges in this chapter.

[Response to the Sixth Accusation]

Chapter 6   She said that her master did want to punish her... because she left the house without his permission. And fearing the punishment, she threw herself from the hallway of her house into the sea. And she was not hurt because she fell into the water, although her arm on the side she fell on was numb for a while. She denied the rest of the charges, saying everything was false.

[Response to the Eighth Accusation]

Chapter 8   ... She said her master got upset because everybody in the mines was saying that she had killed a child and sucked the baby's belly. Certain that this was a lie, he said that things should not be left as they were. If she had done as she was accused, then she should pay for her deeds, and if not, those who raised the false testimony should pay. So it was her master who had her arrested and placed in the guardhouse. While Paula was incarcerated, her master had to go to Santiago de Cuba to talk to the governor. Taking advantage of his absence, Doña Paula de Eguiluz [his

---

15. Elsewhere identified as "Ana Maria yndia."

16. *Alhucema*, or lavender, and rosemary leaves were used as natural remedies to heal injuries.

daughter] wanted to punish Paula because she was having indecent relations with her father. Doña Paula demanded Paula's release in order to punish her, but Paula, seeking her self-preservation, told the soldiers and the lieutenant that they should not release her because of the nature of the crimes for which she was imprisoned, and they let her stay. However, Doña Paula still ordered them to punish her inside the jail. She said all this was true and she denied the rest of the charges in this chapter....

[Response to the Twelfth Accusation]

Chapter 12   . . . She said she refers again to what she has already declared. She confesses that on many holy days she did not attend church or hear Mass, not because she lacked faith—she is a true Christian—but because she was busy cooking and taking care of her household duties, for she was in charge of all of them and could not neglect them.

[Response to the Thirteenth Accusation]

Chapter 13   And to the final accusation, Paula said that justice should be done, and she denied she committed perjury but in everything has told the truth. Then the scribe read her responses to the prosecutor's accusations and she said all of them were correct....

[Attorney Appointed for Paula]

The Lord Inquisitor ordered that Paula be given her written responses so she might discuss them with one of the attorneys who defend these types of cases in the Holy Office, who are *licenciados* Don Pedro de Silva and Don Francisco de Betancur. Paula was to choose one of them as her attorney. She chose Don Francisco de Betancur as her attorney. The Lord Inquisitor then accepted him as nominated and ordered him called. Paula was admonished and sent to her prison. Before me, Luis Blanco de Salcedo secretary.

[Confession: July 15, 1624]

In the morning hearing of the Holy Inquisition of Cartagena on July 15, 1624...the black woman Paula was brought from her prison....

She said she has requested [the hearing] to tell something else she has remembered: that about a year ago—and then she said that it was about two years ago—her master having beaten her because he was missing two bars of soap, and having injured her, certain people told him she was injured, to which he responded, "May the devil take her soul!"

Paula heard him and said, annoyed, "May all the devils and more take my soul!" Then she went to the garden and sat down under a plum tree.

While sitting there she heard a voice saying, "Did you not call me?"[17] Paula turned her head to see who it was and heard the same voice again saying, "Promise me something, and I will come every time you need me." Then this voice demanded her breath, which [Paula] understood to mean her soul.

She responded, "I will not give you my soul!"

---

17. In the margin: "Explicit pact with the devil."

And the voice said, "Well, then give me and offer me your fingernails." And when [Paula] was silent, the voice said again, "Then, give me the food you eat," to which she said,

"Yes, I will give you that!" She then understood . . . she had been speaking with the devil. And having gone home and forgotten what had happened with the devil, about an hour later, she was eating a piece of sugar cane. And on the second bite, one of her teeth hurt and she threw the sugar cane away. She said, "May the devil take you!" And then remembering her promise to the devil, she got up and looked for the sugar cane but could not find it.[18] . . .

[There follows a lengthy confession regarding the devil.]
[Paula concludes thus]:

Then, the devil said, "Look, if you want something, you had better follow me over there." He appeared to her later in the figure of a woman wearing a red skirt that was so long it dragged on the ground. He asked Paula to give him her soul, telling her that God did not even remember or love her because every time she called on Him, He never came as the devil did to see what she wanted and to favor her. And deceived by [the devil's] promise to always help her and to give her everything she needed, Paula offered him her soul saying, "I will give it to you."[19] . . .

Then Paula said the devil pursued her at every step. She confessed that when she gave her soul to the devil, he offered to give her everything she needed and that he would find her whenever she called or when she was upset or angry, and she believed him. And this is what moved her to give in to his demand for her soul, which she now regrets very much, and asks Our Lord to forgive her for these dreadful sins and errors, and requests that this Holy Office give her a merciful punishment. . . .

[On November 30, 1624, the Lord Inquisitor Agustín de Ugarte Saravia declared Paula de Eguiluz a heretical apostate, an idolater, and a witch and gave her the sentence described in the introduction to this chapter.]

---

18. A long line in the margin marks this section with the notation, "She offered him her sugar cane."
19. In the margin: "Her soul offered to the devil."

12

A Spanish Caribbean Captivity Narrative: African Sailors and Puritan Slavers, 1635[1]

David Wheat

Between Iberian and Protestant Worlds: Africans on the Spanish Main

In 1630, English Puritans colonized Providence Island (called Santa Catalina Island in Spanish sources), located slightly more than one hundred miles off the Caribbean coast of Nicaragua. Following unsuccessful efforts to cultivate profitable commodities for export, the colony turned to *privateering* and slave trafficking in the mid-1630s; its location in the western Caribbean gave northern European *privateers* a solid base from which to prey upon Spanish shipping. Less than a decade after the Dutch *privateer* Piet Heyn famously captured Spain's entire silver fleet, authorities in Cartagena de Indias[2] determined to eliminate this new threat.

The Puritan colony resisted attacks by Spanish forces in 1635 and 1640 but finally fell in 1641 (Kupperman). Enslaved Africans—as both profitable commodities and capable laborers who would enable either of the European powers to reinforce their efforts to colonize the Caribbean—were at the heart of the conflict. Each side sought to obtain them, but in notably different fashions: whereas Spanish authorities and would-be slave owners relied on Portuguese slave trade networks to supply enslaved laborers directly from Africa, English and Dutch newcomers sought to obtain Africans by preying on Iberian shipping and slave traffic in the region (Heywood and Thornton, 4–38).

Africans also occupied a central position in this imperial contest in a literal sense, as seen below. The same individual Africans were physically present on both sides of the religious-political frontier. The document presented here highlights the experiences of one extraordinary group of African sailors based in Cartagena who were captured by Dutch pirates in 1634 and resold to the English colonists on Providence Island. After experiencing slavery in two entirely different cultural environments, several of these men evidently preferred the former, and they managed to escape back to the Spanish-American mainland. In addition to indicating contrasts between Africans' position in the colonial Spanish Caribbean, on the one hand, and in the early Anglophone Atlantic, on the other, these testimonies demonstrate enslaved Africans' ability, literally and figuratively, to navigate them both.

---

1. See Maps 5 and 13.

2. Presently a major port and tourist destination in Colombia, in the colonial era Cartagena was the principal port city on the Caribbean coastline of South and Central America, a region known to contemporaries as *Tierra Firme* (or in English, "the Spanish Main"; Sauer, 1–4).

Within the larger structures of Spain's early modern empire, strategically located seaports along the Caribbean Sea and the Gulf of Mexico—the same ports frequented by our African protagonists—played critical roles as maritime hubs and centers of commerce. Heavily fortified during the late sixteenth century, Cartagena de Indias, Havana, Veracruz, and Nombre de Dios/Portobelo represented the principal stops along the *Carrera de Indias*, the ocean route that linked the *metropole* to its American colonies by means of annual convoys of Spanish galleons and merchant ships.

Simultaneously, these circum-Caribbean port cities served as major slave markets and redistribution centers for the transatlantic slave trade. Registered in Seville, Portuguese ships sailed to various African ports—Luanda, *Cabo Verde*, Cacheu, Arda, and *São Tomé*—transporting thousands of African captives to the Americas via the Caribbean. Cartagena de Indias in particular stands out as Spanish America's primary slave trade entrepôt during the late sixteenth and early seventeenth centuries. According to one official report that almost certainly failed to account for additional contraband slave trafficking, one hundred slave ships landed more than 17,500 Africans in Cartagena during the years 1615–1623 alone ("Certificaçion").

Too hot and humid for most Spanish emigrants, these low-lying Caribbean seaports and their hinterlands had been populated largely by Africans and people of African descent, both free and enslaved, since the late sixteenth century. Although Amerindian groups maintained a visible presence in the region, disease and conquest had drastically reduced the Caribbean's indigenous populations during the early colonial period. By 1634—one century after the city was founded—urban Cartagena de Indias contained a population of approximately fifteen hundred *vecinos* (i.e., heads of household), including "*mulatas* and freed blacks" (Córdoba Ronquillo).

This estimate did not include the seaport's fluctuating "floating population" of sailors, passengers, slaves, merchants, and others passing through. Nor did it include scattered Iberian *mayordomos* (overseers) living on rural or semirural farms and ranches, nor groups of *encomienda* Indians concentrated in several small villages. By far the most understated segment of Cartagena's population, however, comprised enslaved Africans and *Afrocreoles*, who made up the demographic majority. In 1621, Cartagena's governor estimated that black slaves in Cartagena and its province numbered around twenty thousand (Del Castillo Mathieu, 238–41). Given conflicts of interest, different parties had ample reason to either downplay or exaggerate the size of Cartagena's black slave population; estimates from the mid-1630s range from 12,000 to "over 25,000" (Wheat).

Slave labor in early colonial Latin America is most often associated with sugar mills and silver mines; yet the African sailors discussed below would have been unfamiliar with these forms of slave labor. In Caribbean port cities such as Cartagena, enslaved black populations worked at a wide variety of tasks that ensured the maintenance and defense of the urban seaport and the provision of its populace.

Enslaved men and women were commonly rented out by their masters for wages, working as cooks, laundresses, street vendors, nurses, domestic servants, porters, oarsmen, and town criers. Clergy, carpenters, caulkers, stonemasons, cobblers, and butchers alike either owned slaves or rented them. Operating fortresses built by royal slaves, local garrisons relied on support personnel consisting of African stable hands, janitors, cooks, and musicians. Enslaved Africans served in capacities ranging from seamstresses to warehouse guards, from shipwreck salvage crews to button makers.

Outside the urban center, literally thousands of black farmworkers raised livestock and food crops, particularly corn, yucca, and plantains. For example, corn grown by slave farmers in the village of Tolú was loaded on boats or rafts and then transported to Cartagena on vessels staffed by enslaved crews.

In addition to connecting Cartagena with these *estancias* (farms or ranches), boats powered by black sailors and oarsmen regularly plied the coastal and riverine passages, which allowed communication and trade between Cartagena and Santa Fé de Bogotá, capital of the New Kingdom of Granada.[3] Originally, Amerindians had been forced to provide labor for an organized system of canoe transportation known as the *boga*; but in the late sixteenth century, indigenous paddlers were replaced almost entirely by enslaved Africans and *Afrocreoles*. Enslaved boatmen and sailors also served on privately owned merchant vessels, as will be seen in these 1635 testimonies.

Though born in West Africa, the two Spanish-speaking *Beafada* men who testified in May 1635 in Portobelo were familiar with the world described above. As slave sailors, they knew the waterways of Cartagena's province and various ports of the southern Caribbean and Central America. In some respects, their Caribbean environment resembled the Guinea-Bissau region they had left behind.[4] On both sides of the Atlantic, they observed local economies oriented toward coastal and riverine commerce heavily reliant on canoes for transportation of food crops and commodities.

Furthermore, Iberian—especially Portuguese—merchants, mariners, exiles, and missionaries had been present on the Upper *Guinea* Coast since the mid-fifteenth century. Interactions between Iberians and West African societies over the following two centuries had created *Luso-African* populations that excelled as intermediaries, interpreters, and slave procurers; *Luso-Africans* often became merchants in their own right.

Like other West African groups in the region, many of the *Beafadas* captured, condemned, or sold into slavery in Spanish America may have already been exposed to Catholic traditions, and they may have already been familiar with Portuguese or with the Afro-Portuguese language, *Crioulo*. As indicated by their testimonies in Portobelo, Francisco *Biáfara* and Juan *Biáfara* spoke Spanish very well, and they knew how to present themselves as devout Catholics. Their high level of acculturation to the Iberian world may be attributed to evangelization efforts conducted in Cartagena, but their African background may have given them significant advantages in the Spanish-American colonial world as well.

The Testimonies of Juan *Biáfara* and Francisco *Biáfara*

The testimonies below are taken from court proceedings initiated when an unusual group of shipwrecked slaves and northern European deserters were delivered to the governor of Portobelo for questioning. In April 1635, Francisco Fernández Fragoso, a Spanish resident of the city of Granada, Nicaragua, found an Englishman plodding

---

3. The *Nuevo Reino de Granada* roughly corresponds in territory to what is now Colombia.

4. For more information on *Beafada* communities and their environment in precolonial Africa, see Brooks; Hawthorne; and Rodney. See also Map 13.

along the shoreline. Unable to speak Spanish, the stranger dropped to his knees, held up his hands, and placed them behind his head. Saying only "*Negro, negro,*" he pointed toward the mouth of the San Juan River, less than one league, or roughly two and a half miles, distant.

During dinner, and throughout the whole evening, Fernández could make out nothing more than "Catalina" and "*negros*," with the foreigner always pointing in the same direction. The following day, Fernández set out with two companions, each armed with a portable firearm called a harquebus, and with five Indians armed with bows. Arriving in two canoes at the mouth of the San Juan River, they found four Spanish-speaking African men and a young pock-faced "Englishman." As soon as Fernández arrived, the black men jumped up, saying, "Señor, we are peaceful! We are slaves owned by the widow of Amador Pérez, a citizen of Cartagena! We are the ones who were stolen by a Dutchman eight or nine months ago from our mistress' frigate, which was laden with wine, bound for the River Magdalena!"

And thus begins our story. Interviewed by government officials, each member of the motley group offered detailed testimony of their captivity, of collusion and escape, and of sickness, shipwreck, and murder. Along with their African co-workers, Francisco *Biáfara* and Juan *Biáfara* had been on Providence Island for approximately seven months, from October 1634 to April 1635. Questioned closely by Spanish officials, Francisco *Biáfara* and Juan *Biáfara* offered detailed descriptions of the Island's location and fortifications. They attempted to recall every ship they had seen visit the Island and the goods and passengers carried onboard, including a handful of Indians brought from the island of San Andrés. They listed the island's livestock and mention potatoes and corn grown for local consumption and tobacco cultivated for export.

With the possible exception of their assertion that "there were no other blacks on the Island" other than their companions, the details they provided corroborate not only each other's accounts but also information gleaned from English sources.[5] "Félix Beles," or rather Philip Bell, served as governor of Providence Island from 1630 to 1636. He had been governor of the Bahamas until 1629 and would take up the same post in Barbados in 1641. The man described below as "Captain Alfero," better known as Daniel Elfrith, admiral of Providence Island, had been a corsair operating in the Caribbean for the previous two decades. He was also Bell's father-in-law, and at one point Elfrith was reprimanded for inviting "Diego el *Mulato*," a famous Havana-born corsair who sailed under the Dutch flag, to visit the Island. Lieutenant William Rous, who appears here as "Captain Rus," was captured by the Spanish and briefly held captive in Cartagena, where he spoke with the itinerant priest Thomas Gage in 1638.

Francisco *Biáfara* and Juan *Biáfara* provided several troubling details without any prompting by Spanish officials. Both men voluntarily reported various "heresies" they had witnessed while on the island, including Bible readings, rosary stomping, and sermons delivered by a married preacher. Likewise, both mentioned that Francisco *Biáfara* was asked to marry an Indian woman who wore a red blanket for a skirt. Employing Amerindian and African words commonly used in Caribbean Spanish of

---

5. See especially Kupperman.

the time, both described English houses as *buhíos*, and Francisco *Biáfara* compared the small English forts on Providence Island to *palenques*. Their detailed account given in May 1635 surely helped to instigate the first Spanish assault on Providence Island two months later.

Significantly, these court proceedings constituted the only known account of daily life on Providence Island other than a diary kept by Governor Nathaniel Butler during the final years of the colony's existence. The entire document consists of twenty-six folios and opens with a brief report by Francisco Fernández Fragoso explaining his discovery of four Africans and two northern Europeans camped out at the mouth of the San Juan River.

The following declarations given by deponents Francisco *Biáfara* and Juan *Biáfara* are reproduced below, along with a very brief joint statement by Damián *Carabalí* and Gerónimo *Angola*; both essentially confirm Francisco *Biáfara*'s testimony. Two northern European men who had escaped Providence Island alongside the Africans, and who now likewise found themselves questioned by Spanish authorities in Portobelo, gave additional testimonies with the aid of an interpreter. A man identified only as "Herbatons" was a forty-year-old soldier from London, England. A twenty-three-year-old Flemish man, "Juan Yons," claimed to have deserted the English colony because he had grown weary of eating potatoes. Both claimed to be Catholic.

By the early seventeenth century, although Africans' roles in the English Atlantic colonies such as Providence Island were only beginning to materialize, Africans and Iberians had been interacting for more than a century in the Americas and for nearly two centuries in Africa and southern Europe. We cannot know the genuine motives that drove these two *Beafada* men, along with several of their colleagues, to escape back to slavery in the Spanish Caribbean, if that was indeed their actual intention. It is clear, however, that their familiarity with Catholicism and their ability to speak Spanish meant that *ladino* Africans such as Francisco *Biáfara* and Juan *Biáfara* were able to maneuver within the Spanish system to a far greater degree than the northern European deserters who accompanied them.

*****

Inquiry Carried Out by Captain Juan de Ribas, *Alcalde Mayor*, into the Population That [torn] the English Enemy on the Island of Santa Catalina. Portobelo, May 9, 1635[6]

[Declaration by Francisco *Biáfara*]

In the city of Portobelo on the ninth day of the month of May 1635, Captain Juan de Ribas, *alcalde mayor* and *capitán a guerra, teniente de capitán general* for His Majesty, for this investigation summoned to appear before him a black man from among those presented and brought by Francisco Fernández Fragoso, from whom His Mercy received his oath, which he swore by God and the cross as required by law, and by which he promised to speak the truth. And asked to state his name, his *nation*, and whose slave he was, and his age, and in what office he served his master, he said that his name is Francisco, and that he is of the *Biáfara* caste, and the slave of Doña Mariana de Armas Clavijo, widow of Captain Amador Pérez, *vecina* of the city of Cartagena de Indias. She owned a boat employed in traffic along the Río Grande [de la Magdalena],[7] on which Francisco *Biáfara* worked as a sailor alongside Pedro *Folupo*, Gerónimo *Angola*, Damián *Carabalí*, and Juan *Biáfara*. Other slaves were also on the boat, and its *arráez* [captain] was a Spanish man named Francisco Rodríguez. While making a trip to the Río Grande, with the boat loaded with wine, the boat was seized by a Dutch ship. All the slaves on board, Francisco *Biáfara*'s companions, were carried to the island called Santa Catalina. The pilot Francisco Rodríguez, who had been in charge of the boat named *Our Lady of the Rosary*, was left in Santa Marta about eight months ago more or less.

Asked what size the island was and whether it is low lying or high and how many days it took to arrive from where he was stolen to the island, he said that the island is high and mountainous and that it seemed to be about ten or eleven leagues in circumference. It took seven days to reach the island from where he was stolen, which was at Zanba.[8]

Asked the name of the captain who stole them, he said that his name was Captain Juan and that he was Flemish, approximately fifty years old, and small in stature. He brought no more than fourteen men in a ship with two decks.

Asked in what state the captain left them on the island of Santa Catalina, whether they were sold or not, to whom, and for what price, he said that eleven slaves were taken from Mariana de Armas Clavijo's ship, all eleven belonging to her. Upon arriving [at Santa Catalina], Captain Juan Flamenco sold them. The island's governor, named Captain Beles, bought Francisco *Biáfara* and several other companions for twenty-six pounds of tobacco and one pig each.

---

6. Ministerio de Cultura, Archivo General de Indias, Seville, Audiencia de Santa Fe 223, no. 34, fols. 5r–15v.

7. Primary commercial artery from Cartagena toward Santa Fe de Bogotá.

8. According to Francisco *Biáfara*, their boat was captured by Dutch *privateers* at Zanba, a small port located along present-day Colombia's Caribbean coast, just south of Santa Marta. The port of Zanba is mentioned in Francis (51). The boat's Spanish pilot was promptly left ashore in nearby Gaira (Gayra). "Gaira" appears on a map in Navarrete (17). Both locations appear in a travel account dated 1519, published in Urueta (54).

Asked if there are other blacks on the island, he said that there are none other than his companions.

Asked what kind of military force and civilian population are currently on the island, he said that there are approximately two hundred men plus or minus ten or fifteen, some boys, and perhaps twenty women. At present, the island is governed by Captain Félix Beles, as mentioned earlier. Two infantry captains with their lieutenant and two regiments are named Captain Rus, a robust young man, and another captain, Alfero. They carry neither swords nor daggers, and their arms consist entirely of harquebuses, muskets, cannon, and war drums.

Asked what forts they have, and what artillery, and what guard they keep by day and night in the forts, he said that they have nine small forts like *palenques*, some of which have two or three or four or five pieces of ordnance all of cast iron, some mounted on supports and others on the ground laid across wooden frames. These forts are under the care of the two captains and other people. The principal port is a bay, and there are several little fortresses along the bay's entrance, and another inside the mouth of the bay, and another next to the governor's house with one cannon. The other forts are on the outer coast, and in one place a little more than one league away is a fort where watch is kept, under the command of Captain Rus.

Asked if he saw them keep watch over the settlement or in some of the forts, he said no because all their arms are kept in one *buhío*. Francisco *Biáfara* saw them from up close, and they are very poorly maintained.

Asked what crops they have, he said that they sow great quantities of tobacco, small plots of maize, and very large plots of potatoes, which are their main sustenance. They raise chickens and swine and have three cows and two bulls to breed; the land has no wild pigs.

Asked if the island has many rivers and streams, he said that there are many streams and springs with very good water and that all over the island fish and turtles can be caught.

Asked what ships he has seen arrive at the island's port and from what *nations*, he said that about three months ago, an English ship with three decks arrived at the island carrying clothing, shoes, *aguardiente* [liquor] and beer, many fabrics and ribbons, and other things and sold them in exchange for tobacco. The ship left some people and women behind and took some local English people away. The ship left the island about one month ago. Before this big ship, another *patache* had arrived carrying beer and other things.

Asked whether they had a ship in the island's port at present, he said that they had no ship of their own, though they desired to have one in order to embark on corsair raids; Francisco *Biáfara* understood this to be the wish of the governor's father-in-law.

Asked in what manner he escaped from the island and with whom he left and in what type of vessel, he said that he, Francisco *Biáfara*, joined with Pedro *Folupo*, Gerónimo *Angola*, Damián *Carabalí*, and Damián *Biáfara*,[9] and with six Englishmen who were about to leave in a *chalupa* belonging to the governor. The Englishmen told them, "This place is no way to live; if you want to go back to your land, we're

---

9. Error (committed by scrivener?); should read "Juan *Biáfara*."

going"; and thus Francisco *Biáfara* embarked in their company. In two days' time, they reached the mainland and then traveled along the coast. After more than ten days, they reached the mouth of the river San Juan,[10] where they stopped and left behind their boat, which had been badly damaged by the sea.

Asked why only two Englishman arrived, because six had originally left the island with him and the other *morenos*, his companions, he said that after their second day at sea, his companion Pedro *Folupo*, who was his captain, died on land. In the port of San Juan, Juan Inglés, a robust young man, told Francisco *Biáfara*, "You must know, these Englishmen plan to attack you all and kill you." Francisco *Biáfara* and his companions took care that night. And on a different night, because they were warned again, they fought the Englishmen with clubs and killed one; three others fled and were nowhere to be found the next day. Francisco *Biáfara* and his companions reported this news to Master Francisco Fernández Fragoso, who found them camped out at the mouth of the San Juan. The remaining two Englishmen were always loyal to Francisco *Biáfara* and his companions, and so their lives were saved. About twenty days ago, they were discovered by Fragoso and brought to this city [Portobelo].

Asked if at any time he overheard the English and Dutch on the island mention a fleet of ships, he said that he overheard Captain Juan, who stole them, say that the following year he would come from his land with two large, new ships, to comb this coast and to load them with tobacco. Also, Francisco *Biáfara* notifies Your Mercy that they did not allow him to wear crosses or rosaries on the island, rather they were confiscated and stomped on. On the island, they had a *buhío* where they gathered to hear sermons and where he saw them gather very regularly. Returning from work, they all held a book, men, women, and children, and this is what he saw and was able to learn regarding the whole island.

Asked if he undertook or witnessed any voyage from Santa Catalina island to San Andrés [island], he said that neither he nor any of his companions left the island. During the time they were on the island, they saw a *tartana* with lateen sails cross over to San Andrés, and to other islands, for turtles. The ship brought back an Indian woman and two Indian men. The Indians suggested to Francisco *Biáfara* that he should marry the Indian woman, who came dressed in a red blanket worn as a skirt. He had no other news of these islands, and this is what he knows and is the truth, under charge of the oath given, which he affirmed and ratified. He is more or less twenty-eight years of age. He did not sign because he did not know how. I, the scribe, certify and attest that he is a *ladino*, who speaks the Spanish language well, and that he has provided capable, sufficient answers to the questions asked and to other relevant questions posed by the *Señor alcalde mayor*, and His Mercy signed it.

[Declarations by Damián *Carabalí* and Gerónimo *Angola*]

And His Mercy the *Señor alcalde mayor* asked Francisco *Biáfara* if his other companions knew how to declare and give testimony as he had given. Francisco *Biáfara* said that he did not take them to be as *ladino* as himself, but that even so, if summoned to appear before His Mercy with Francisco *Biáfara* being present as well, if they were shown his testimony, His Mercy would see whether they offer similar answers to the

---

10. The San Juan River forms the eastern boundary between present-day Nicaragua and Costa Rica.

same questions and whether they have anything else to declare. And then His Mercy summoned to appear before him Damián *Carabalí*, who appears to be thirty-five years old, and Gerónimo *Angola*, who appears to be thirty years old. From them he received an oath sworn by God and the sign of the cross as required by law, and they promised to tell the truth. Having read to each of them the questions asked of Francisco *Biáfara* and his answers, they said that Francisco *Biáfara* had satisfied and declared the full truth of what happened in each question, and that they had seen events unfold exactly as he had declared, and that if necessary they would make the same declaration. And not being as *ladino* [as he], they had doubts about some things and conferred about the time and finally agreed on what had already been declared [by Francisco *Biáfara*]. And with this agreement, His Mercy the *Señor alcalde mayor* accepted these two declarations from them and ordered that everything be duly recorded and certified and signed it. And because it was late, he left for tomorrow, the tenth of this month, the declaration of Juan Biáfara, because he is very *ladino*. Signed by Juan de Ribas before me, Juan de Medina Bejarano, public scribe.

[Declaration by Juan *Biáfara*]

In the city of Portobelo on the tenth day of the month of May 1635, the *Señor* Captain Juan de Ribas, *alcalde mayor* and *capitán a guerra*, *teniente de capitán general* of Portobelo on His Majesty's behalf, for the report and investigation went to the hospital[11] of San Sebastián in this city and summoned to appear before him a black man, from whom His Mercy received an oath, sworn by God and the cross, and Juan *Biáfara* promised to tell the truth.

Asked his name, his *nation*, his profession, and whose slave he was, and his age, he said that his name is Juan *Biáfara* and that he is the slave of Doña Mariana de Armas Clavijo, widow of Captain Amador Pérez, *vecina* of the city of Cartagena de Indias. He served as her sailor on a boat named *Our Lady of the Rosary*, engaged in river traffic along the Río Grande de la Magdalena. He worked as a sailor alongside Pedro *Folupo*, Gerónimo *Angola*, Damián *Carabalí*, and Francisco *Biáfara*, who are today in this city [Portobelo]; the remainder of the crew of eleven slaves are presently on the island of Santa Catalina. The boat's *arráez* was Francisco Rodríguez. During the course of their journey, they were stolen by an Englishman on a large boat, commanded by Captain Juan Nata, who left the pilot and his Spanish companions in Gayra in Santa Marta. From there, he took them with the boat and the cargo, which was mostly wine, to an island called Santa Catalina. The trip took seven days, and they reached the island in a large ship and the boat, and this happened a little more than eight months ago.

Asked in what manner the English captain who stole them left them on the island, he said that the island is peopled by Dutch and English, to whom the English captain sold them for twenty sheaves, or pounds, of tobacco and for one pig. At this price they were sold to the governor and captains, and Juan *Biáfara* was purchased by the island's governor along with Francisco *Biáfara*, Gerónimo *Angola*, and Pedro *Folupo*.

Asked if there are other blacks on the island, he said that he found no other blacks on the island.

---

11. The word "hospital" can refer to either a shelter for the sick or a shelter for the poor.

Asked what military force is currently on the island and if he knew or understood how long the island had been occupied, he said that it seemed to him there were roughly over two hundred men capable of bearing arms, and some boys, and approximately twenty women. There is a governor named Félix Beles and another two infantry captains with two regiments and their lieutenants. One captain is named Rus, a robust young man, and the other captain is named Alfero. They normally do not carry swords, and their arms consist of muskets and pikes, which are stored with the war drums, powder, and ammunition in a large *buhío* next to the governor's house. Nearby they also have a large *buhío* where they gather very regularly to hear sermons given by a young, married Englishman. When they finish their work, the men, children, and women all bring books. And they took away the crosses and rosaries brought by Juan *Biáfara* and his companions because they are all heretics. Juan *Biáfara* and his companions were forced to attend the sermons, but they neither understood nor wanted to know because they are Christians.

Asked what forts they have, with what artillery, and what guard they keep by day and night in the forts, he said that he saw no more than five forts but that his companion Francisco *Biáfara* found out that there were nine. Those that Juan *Biáfara* saw are inside the mouth of the port, and one [is] next to the governor's houses, and there is one fort on a point where they have a watchtower where they make signals with a cannon when a sail appears, and then they take up arms. The fortifications he saw were low, like platforms, with four or three pieces of ordnance each, some mounted on large wagons and others on wooden frames.

Asked if he saw them keep watch in the settlement as they do in the forts, he said no.

Asked what crops they have, and what size the island is, and if it has running water or rivers, and if there are wild pigs on the island, and if there is an abundance of fish and a variety of fruit-bearing plants, he said that they sow great quantities of tobacco, which they prepare in rolls, and many potatoes, which is what they mainly eat, and they mainly eat them raw. There is little corn, and they raise chickens, and they have three cows and two bulls for breeding. They have no wild pigs, but there are some plantains. The island is high and mountainous, more than four leagues wide and ten leagues in circumference. The port is a great bay with good anchorage, though it has some rocky outcroppings, and at each end there is a castle. There is much running water that crosses the island, and large streams, and the water is good to drink.

And asked what ships arrived on this island while he was there, and what merchandise and people they brought, and what they carried away, and the ships' nationalities, he said that a large ship from England arrived laden with beer, *aguardiente*, and other things. They left people on the island, and loaded tobacco in exchange for what they had brought. This ship brought women and left the island a little more than one month ago. And previously, a *patache* had arrived, which also left people on the island and loaded tobacco in exchange for many goods that it brought.

Asked if they have any ship on the island, large or small, to go out and do evil, he said that they do not have any vessel except *chalupas*, with which they go out to fish and which serve the settlement for other things. And the Englishman who stole them said that he would return the next year with large ships to scour these coasts. And Juan *Biáfara* heard the governor's father-in-law, a small and older man, say that he had sent to purchase a *patache* that he would use to travel along the coasts of Cartagena and Chagres.

Asked in what manner he and his companions fled from the island, and whether he knew of other islands in the area peopled by English or Indians, he said that many times he overheard the English say that nearby was an island that they call San Andrés populated by Indians. He saw that they went out in a small boat with a lateen sail to fish for turtles, and they brought back turtles and an Indian woman and two Indian men. And the two Indian men suggested to his companion Francisco *Biáfara* that he marry the Indian woman, who came wearing a red blanket as a skirt. And the English stay on the island [of San Andrés], and from what he has overheard, they communicate with the English on San Cristóbal [Saint Christopher] Island. And seeing that they were among infidels they agreed to flee, and for this purpose Juan *Biáfara* joined with Francisco *Biáfara*, Gerónimo *Angola*, Damián *Carabalí*, and Pedro *Folupo*, who was his captain. They were unable to bring out the other companions, who were Martín *Balanta*, Andrés Jolufo, Francisco *Angola*, Juan *Angola*, Baltasar *Folupo*, and Cristóbal *Arará*, who remained on the island. Having agreed to flee, they went down to the beach where there was the large boat belonging to an officer, which the governor used. Just as they were about to embark, they found six Englishmen on the beach, and they all agreed to escape together. And thus they embarked, and after sailing for two days and nights, they saw the mainland. From there they came along the coast, and his companion and Captain Pedro *Folupo* grew sick and crazed and died on land. And traveling along the coast, the sea broke the boat. They all went ashore, and after several days chanced to arrive at the mouth of the San Juan River, which drains from the [lake] of Nicaragua, near the mouth of the Taure River. Francisco *Biáfara* learned from an Englishman named Juan who is here in this city that the four Englishmen wanted to kill them at night. So they kept guard, and on another night, in order to save their lives, they attacked the English and killed one between them by blows. And the other three fled and could not be found. They reported this news to the *arráez* Francisco Fragoso, who arrived on a different day with his frigate, who looked for them and did not find them. And seeing Christian people in a vessel, Juan *Biáfara* and his companions joined them. And feeding them, Francisco Fragoso took them in his frigate to this city, along with the two Englishmen who always had been loyal to them.

Asked if he knew of or had heard anyone on the island talk of waiting for a fleet from Holland or England bound for these parts, he said that he never overheard anything regarding this topic, except that the Flemish captain who stole him publicly declared, as mentioned [in the question], that the following year he would return with two new ships to this coast and to the island to take revenge on general Don Antonio de Oquendo, who had captured a small ship full of Flemish men near the coast of Havana. He had heard nothing more. And that which he said and declared is the truth, and everything that he knew and saw and understood and happened in this case, and this he affirmed and ratified under the oath taken. By his appearance, he seems to be a man over thirty-five years old. He did not sign because he did not know how. The *Señor alcalde mayor* Juan de Ribas signed before me, Juan de Medina Bejarano, public scribe.

The Saint's Life of Sister Chicaba, c. 1676–1748: An As-Told-To Slave Narrative[1]

Sue E. Houchins and Baltasar Fra-Molinero

An Early Biography of an African Woman

The *Compendio de la Vida Ejemplar de la Venerable Madre Sor Teresa Juliana de Santo Domingo* (Salamanca, 1752) written by Father Juan Carlos Miguel de Paniagua was one of the earliest, if not the first, biographies of an African woman written in a modern European language. The *Vida* is the hagiography, a saint's life, of Sor Teresa de Santo Domingo (c. 1676–1748), an African *tertiary* nun who lived in a Spanish convent during the first half of the eighteenth century.

Although authored by the priest Paniagua, this text represents collaboration between an African woman and her Spanish biographer. The *Vida* is a hybrid text in which Chicaba, who is the subject of the hagiography, participates in the writing of the narrative by telling her story to the biographer. The *Vida* is a precursor to the African American as-told-to slave narratives of the nineteenth century.

The *Vida* tells the story of a remarkable Black woman who escaped slavery by exhibiting her extraordinary holiness. Sor Teresa attained a reputation for sanctity and healing, exercised some small power within the religious community that never accepted her in the upper ranks of its social hierarchy, and managed to publish her autobiography through the narrative of a priest writing in the third person. Her oral history was transcribed, edited, published, and disseminated to the Americas and throughout the Black Atlantic as a model of religious perfection for other Africans and people of African descent.[2]

Chicaba's Life Story According to Paniagua

Her biographer, Paniagua, claimed that Chicaba, or Sor Teresa, was the youngest daughter of the King of *La Mina Baja del Oro*, somewhere in the coastal area of eastern Ghana,

1. See Maps 4 and 14. Sue E. Houchins thanks the Woodrow Wilson National Fellowship Foundation for the Career Enhancement Fellowship that supported her research on this project at the Women's Studies in Religion Program at the Harvard Divinity School during 2007–2008.
2. See Paniagua's prologue to the *Compendio de la Vida* and his *Oración fúnebre* in honor of Sor Teresa, published a few months after her death. In 1757, a heroic poem in Sor Teresa's honor was written in manuscript form in Zaragoza, the *Vida de la venerable negra*. The only known copy is at the Schomburg Center for Research in Black Culture in New York City. The *Vida* itself was published twice, in 1752 and 1764, which is a testimony to its popularity. The excerpts in this anthology correspond to the 1764 edition.

Togo, and Benin.[3] Her captors concluded that she was a member of an important family because of the jewelry she was wearing when kidnapped. Her given name, *Chicaba*, meaning "golden child" or "divine gift," suggests that she was a member of the Ewe people, one of the ethnic groups of the region.[4] Following the Catholic custom with slaves, she was baptized upon capture and given a new, Christian, European name: Teresa.

Enslaved at the age of nine, Teresa/Chicaba was brought to Spain and purchased by the Marchioness of Mancera, Juliana Teresa Portocarrero. The marchioness' husband had been a protector of the Mexican writer Sor Juana Inés de la Cruz, during his tenure as viceroy to Mexico. As a member of the retinue of this aristocratic household, Teresa developed an unusually intense spiritual life that in time became her key to freedom.

Upon her death in 1703, the marchioness emancipated Teresa in her will with the request that she enter a convent, for which the mistress had bequeathed her a small but not insignificant annuity. The fact that Teresa was mentioned in the will twice indicates that this was less an imposition than an act of her own will.[5] After being rejected by several other religious communities, Teresa entered the Dominican *tertiary* convent of La Penitencia in Salamanca a year later. Her race and skin color put her at a disadvantage in the highly stratified social hierarchy of Spanish monastic houses. The community accepted her only in a marginal status, as a servant to the other nuns.

Her low status notwithstanding, admission to La Penitencia was an official mark of Chicaba's civil freedom. Although her monastic cell might not have been very different from the quarters she inhabited during her enslavement, and even though monastic life continued to limit her mobility, she was free. The papers she signed attesting to her act of profession as a Dominican *tertiary* also documented her freedom, and the convent was an institution that lived by these papers.

Despite this inferior status, Teresa/Chicaba's acts of charity, mystical experiences, and fame as a healer or miracle worker moved the Dominican Order soon after her death to initiate the process of beatification for which Paniagua's writings were an important step.[6] The text of the *Vida* claims to be making frequent references to Teresa's autobiographical writings, some of which appear in the book as direct quotations.

---

3. What Father Paniagua calls *La Mina Baja del Oro* corresponds to the coastal area east of *Elmina* Castle, which had been called *La Mina del Oro* by the Portuguese since 1482.

4. Spelled both Chicaba and Chicava by the hagiographer, the name is a compound word in Ewe, from *shika* or *sika* (gold) and *va* (to arrive), meaning the "gold has arrived" or the "golden child is here."

5. Testamento de Juliana Teresa Portocarrero, Meneses y Noroña, Marquesa de Mancera, otorgado el 10 de abril de 1703. 13977 fol. 135v. "Iten, después de los días de mi vida quiero y es mi voluntad que Teresa Juliana del Espíritu Santo, mi esclava, quede libre enteramente, y la ruego por lo mucho que la he querido, se entre religiosa en el convento de Santa Ana que antiguamente estuvo sujeto a los Padres Dominicos de la ciudad de Murcia y hoy está sujeto al obispo de dicha ciudad de Murcia. Y para su entrada se le dé de mis bienes todo lo necesario, y también todo lo necesario para su profesión. Iten, mando a Teresa Juliana que hoy es mi *criada* y esclava y la dejo libre en profesando de religiosa se le dé de mis bienes cincuenta *ducados* cada un año, para los gastillos y otras cosas que se le pueden ofrecer durante su vida."

6. Beatification is a formal ecclesiastical process resulting in permission to a local population of the faithful to venerate a Christian martyr or someone who in life had a reputation for sanctity and

The *Vida* recorded that Teresa/Chicaba enjoyed special favor with her mistress, who might have educated her as some European women did with their slave companions—especially those who entered the household as children. Therefore, it is entirely possible that this young woman learned to write enough to prepare her to undertake the customary projects of elite religious women: recording her spiritual life and writing religious poetry. Had she been illiterate, Paniagua would surely have noted it and would have chosen a different strategy for conveying her voice in the hagiography.[7]

With the exception of an autographed letter by Sor Teresa preserved in the Convent of Las Dueñas in Salamanca and her signature at the bottom of the document certifying her act of profession in June 1704, no other papers written by Sor Teresa Chicaba are known to exist.[8] In both documents, however, one can observe clear and firm handwriting, a sign of someone accustomed to using a quill pen with a certain frequency. The handwriting suggests a person who might well have produced the diary or notes her biographer used to produce the story of her life.

Hagiography and "As-Told-To" Life Stories: Two Related Genres

The *Vida* is an example of a hagiography, which is commonly defined as a life or legend of a saint. The genre "includes accounts of persons regarded as holy or exemplary in their own time, even if they were not formally canonized" (chapters 9 and 10).[9] In the words of Caroline Walker Bynum, saints are "socially constructed," and their legends are "fashioned and authenticated in a complex relationship between clerical authorities and the adherents who spread the holy person's reputation for virtues and miracles" (p. ix).

Hagiographies, therefore, are profoundly political. Paniagua's *Vida* is an example of an even more hybrid genre. Part hagiography—itself a bricolage of forms—and part as-told-to (auto-)biography/spiritual narrative, it is an instance of *pentimento*, or layered narrative, in which Chicaba's unique worldview and sometimes radical intent

---

miracles. Two portraits were also commissioned and painted of Sor Teresa with the aim of helping to disseminate her fame as a saint. One of them is displayed in the small museum created in her honor by the nuns of the convent of Las Dueñas of Salamanca, together with other documents and material testimonies of her life. The other remains in a deteriorated state in the Museo Provincial of Salamanca. For a commentary on these two portraits, see Fra Molinero.

7. The lives of several illiterate Black slave nuns were recorded by clergy in Spain (Magdalena de la Cruz), Mexico (Esperanza), and Brazil (Rosa Egipciaca). See Contreras; Gómez de la Parra and Ramos Medina; and Mott.

8. The Dominican convent of Las Dueñas in Salamanca is where Sor Teresa Chicaba is buried now. During the occupation of Salamanca by Napoleon's troops in 1810, the convent of La Penitencia, where she lived, was demolished. The nuns took Sor Teresa's remains with them as a precious possession together with several objects that belonged to her that had become relics as well as her autographed letter and the document certifying her act of profession. All these items are preserved now in the convent of Las Dueñas, a more aristocratic institution than La Penitencia at the time she lived in Salamanca.

9. For a view of sainthood outside the Catholic Church, see Wyschogrod.

peeks through the surface of her biographer's prose. As a result, Paniagua's representation of Chicaba's story exhibits its dual origins, African and European.

The priest was not Sor Teresa's confessor. He obtained the materials—both written and oral—for the hagiography through interviews with Sor Teresa Chicaba in the fall of 1748, during the last months of her life. If the manuscripts Paniagua claims to have consulted existed, Sor Teresa would be the first African-born woman known to us to have written in a modern European language.[10]

If read as the oral history of an ex-slave, however, the *Vida* bears a striking resemblance to another genre, the dictated biographies and spiritual narratives of freed African people or ex-slaves in the United States of the late eighteenth and nineteenth centuries. They are sometimes called "as-told-to slave narratives." The *Vida* would be the first example of this type of slave narrative in the Catholic tradition.

The spiritual narrative, the Protestant first cousin of the Catholic mystical autobiography and its sibling hagiography, is the genre from which the slave narrative evolved. First-person conversion accounts by Blacks of religious justification and sanctification lay "the necessary intellectual groundwork by proving that [Blacks] . . . were as much chosen by God for eternal salvation as whites" (Andrews, 7). Upon the foundation of this theological argument for racial equality, slave narratives made the case for emancipation—legal, political, and economic freedom for Americans of African descent. The first of these narratives, a dictated as-told-to spiritual autobiography, contains an abduction story strikingly similar to Sor Teresa Chicaba's.[11]

Race and Ethnicity in a Holy Woman's Life and *Vida*

Present-day readers may well question why an emancipated Black woman slave would choose a cloistered religious life. However, in Spain and the rest of the Catholic world of Europe and the Americas, female convents were sites of relative spiritual and intellectual freedom and of sexual safety as compared to the alternative of a secular life as a single woman. In France, a slave named Pauline Villeneuve avoided being sent back to the Caribbean by professing as a nun, a decision her Benedictine order successfully defended (Harms, 6–11). In Spanish America, this relative freedom operated both for white and Black women, although the case of women of African descent has received much less attention.

Race was an obstacle to Paniagua's producing a text that would support a case for an African woman's beatification; Blacks were not suitable subjects of Catholic hagiographies. Sainthood required nobility of lineage and birth from a legitimate marital union. Black slaves, lacking both, were not deemed adequate candidates for sainthood. The ideology of the era made the language of hagiography inadequate in

10. Úrsula de Jesús is the first woman of African descent known to date to have been credited with writing/dictating her spiritual autobiography. She lived in Lima in the first part of the seventeenth century (see van Deusen).

11. Joycelyn Moody traces this evolution in a book-length study of African American women's spiritual narratives (see Belinda; Moody).

this situation; the *Vida* needed to represent Chicaba's race positively against the contemporary negative discourse that was decidedly anti-Black.

Since the Middle Ages, the devil was represented in Spain as a Black man, and Black
men appeared in demonic visions of many Spanish and Spanish-American nuns since
the sixteenth century, including Saint Teresa of Avila herself. *Guinea* or Western Africa
was seen as a region close to hell (see Olsen). A close reading of the narrative reveals
a conflict between the dominant ideology of the day—beliefs sanctioning slavery and
racial inequality that Paniagua might have upheld—and an attempt to find textual space
for resistance, principles of gender and racial equality that Chicaba might have asserted.

The description of Chicaba's parents and siblings as members of her country's
royalty stands in tension with their Blackness and Africanness, but it serves to miti-
gate Chicaba's abject status as a slave by asserting her exceptional pedigree. However, Teresa/Chicaba's rejection by several convents that would not accept a Black in
their community—not even as a lay sister—was testimony to the impossibility of her
claims of legitimacy and high lineage to completely displace the negative aspects of
the doctrine of *limpieza de sangre*, or blood purity, that prevailed in her time.

In addition, most Spaniards subscribed to the belief in a symbolic relation between
skin color and paganism. The eighteenth-century reader of this hagiography/spiritual
narrative would have understood that slavery was the fortunate and providential inter-
mediate step through which Africans "transmigrated" on their Christian journey to
paradise. That is, the public instinctively justified the capture and bondage of Black
people as the means of expunging the moral stain inscribed as color across their bodies.

Thus, the exemplary depiction of Teresa/Chicaba's religious orthodoxy, grasp of
Catholic apologetics, sanctity, and compassion in her encounter with a fellow slave simply identified as the "Turkish girl" is an attempt on the part of the priest and the subject
of the story to problematize this ideology that demonized Blacks. Allegedly, the Muslim
woman became a weapon Satan attempted to wield against the innocent Chicaba.[12] But
Teresa's sanctity shielded her from the murderous attacks instigated by the devil.

When the assaults ceased, Chicaba befriended her assailant, who confided that a
Catholic priest had seduced and abandoned her, thereby turning her against Christianity. She had adamantly refused to convert despite the efforts of "many spiritual
and learned men"; however, "Grace" chose instead a lowly Black slave woman, Teresa/
Chicaba, as an instrument of salvation (chapter XIII, not anthologized here). A reader
in eighteenth-century Spain would have marveled at the unique sanctity that enabled
Teresa/Chicaba to prevail where European men had failed. The power of the incident
resides in the stark opposition of categories of difference, race and gender: whiteness
versus Blackness and men versus women.

Because Teresa/Chicaba was probably the last living witness to this episode in her
life, she might have had some part in this representation of her unusual spiritual and
intellectual superiority. In addition, occasionally her Blackness is transformed in the

---

12. There is documentary evidence that there were Muslim slaves in the *Mancera* household, as
attested by the sale of two Muslim men by the *Marquis of Mancera* a few years before Chicaba's
arrival to his home (Archivo Histórico de *Protocolos Notariales* de Madrid, 11.410 fol. 79, February
6, 1677).

narrative into a mark of divine choosing; for instance, during her journey to enter the convent in Salamanca, a blind man recognizes her skin color simply by touching her.

For the most part, slavery and the condition of Blacks under it were not a significant issue in the moral discussions of Paniagua's time. By 1685, the council of state advised King Carlos II, in response to radical *Capuchin* friars Francisco José de Jaca and Epiphane de Moirans' denunciation of slavery in the Americas, that the enslavement of Blacks was a matter of practical convenience and economic necessity for Spain (Pena González, liii). But the *Vida* betrays a conflicted view of slavery.

The prose exhibits stress when it describes the indignities and mistreatment of the slave Teresa/Chicaba. Yet, it cannot or will not condemn the institution of slavery that was the root cause of it. In other words, Chicaba's race becomes a site of this contradiction at salient points in the narrative. The mistreatment of Teresa/Chicaba by white servants of the *Mancera* household becomes an uncomfortable indictment of white racial violence that goes unpunished, and it becomes deflected in the text. On one occasion, Chicaba was thrown into the pond in Madrid's Retiro Park by some person first recognized as the marquis but later reidentified as the devil himself.

This narrative revision cautiously absolves members of the marquis' staff by displacing the crime into the demonic realm. The *Vida*'s narrative has to editorialize on these anecdotes that originate in Chicaba's conversations and papers in an attempt to present racial obstacles as a form of divine trial.

The *Vida* occasionally reveals interventions or narrative resistance to slavery. For example, immediately following the story of Chicaba's "gentle" kidnapping or abduction in Africa by a celestial being clothed like a Spaniard is the harrowing tale of her attempt to throw herself overboard only to be snatched from certain death by the intervention of a Holy White Lady, a syncretism of an African water deity and the Blessed Virgin. Further the protagonist describes how, while still in the *Middle Passage*, phantasmal blackbirds followed the slave ship. This vision or hallucination that the text attributes to satanic intervention is similar to the delirium recalled by other captives subjected to unbearable thirst and in a slave ship's hold (see Kiple and Higgins).

A modern audience alert to the double voice of the *Vida*'s narrative might detect Chicaba's voice in the assertion of her Africanness through the recollection of these events. The insistence on remembering her own African name and those of her relatives, as well as the insistence on her royal origins, might indicate an early form of racial consciousness. The framing of her mystical experience as beginning in Africa with the White Lady also implies an attempt to assert Africa as the place where her Christian spiritual quest originated prior to her abduction.

As evidenced by the anecdotes she must have related to Paniagua, the *Vida* appears to make a constant effort to construct and maintain Teresa/Chicaba's racial identity, her Africanness. Thus, in the aforementioned episode of her near drowning in the pond at the Retiro Park, when she experienced her submersion in the waters of El Retiro's pond as a journey back to her homeland—as *sankofa*—the text asserts that a return to her native land is a voyage to Africa, where she once enjoyed freedom and agency. The submersion/journey represents her as a diasporic African subject. She is someone who is aware of her African origins and ancestry as well as the historicity of her enslavement and social condition once she attains legal freedom.

The preservation of Sor Teresa/Chicaba's memories of Africa and her awareness of racial difference is exemplified with great originality in biblical exegesis in an unusual piece of convent poetry quoted in the *Vida* and attributed to Chicaba. In the poem, Jesus is depicted as a polygamist. The poem in chapter XXXV uses the biblical story of the competition between Mary and Martha to criticize the monastic hierarchy among *choir* nuns, lay sisters, and others. The unusual depiction of Christ as "go[ing] out with other women" seems to attest to the collaboration—oral or written—of Chicaba in the composition of the *Vida*.

One can argue that Paniagua's quotes from her spiritual autobiography, no matter how doctored, are more likely to have originated from her writings than not. Although such quotations cannot be accepted as faithful copies of the original text using today's standards of authenticity, they are marked in italics in the *Vida*. This was a typical practice in religious literature to mark the divine inspiration of the words of the subject of the hagiography. Among all the quoted passages in the narrative, the poem portraying Chicaba's spiritual jealousy of Christ most likely is a faithful representation of her voice.

The poem is striking in its interpretation of the story of Martha and Mary (Luke 10:38–42). In conventional Church exegesis, Martha and Mary are contrasting, hierarchical examples of contemplation and action in the Christian soul, which are translated to the relative status of nuns in a community. Sor Teresa/Chicaba combines the traditional representation of both women and applies their story to her own case.

Catholic theology has been at pains to explain away the idea of a polygamous Christ, the logical consequence of his mystical marriage to many nuns. The feeling of jealousy, which Paniagua rationalizes as a manifestation of Sor Teresa/Chicaba's intense love, might be a reflection of her lived experience in the convent. In the convent, she was relegated to the symbolic status of a "lesser wife," as indicated by the manual labor required of her. In this regard, the recrimination might well be a complaint against some perceived injustice visited upon her by the other sisters. The tension between Martha and Mary in the biblical story might point to this interpretation.

Sor Teresa/Chicaba's life is worthy of study as an extraordinary woman among other exceptional nuns in Spain and the Americas during the early modern era: Saint Teresa of Ávila, Sor María de Agreda, and Sor Juana Inés de la Cruz. Feminist scholars have been indispensable in discovering texts and establishing the importance of these early women writers. However, Black women remain invisible in most scholarly essays and monographs in spite of the abundant evidence of their presence as devout Catholics. Chicaba's case makes clear the importance of race in the analysis of the lives of monastic women in Spanish and Spanish-American convents.[13]

*****

13. Jodi Bilinkoff studies the anti-Jewish racial tension around the Carmelite reformation in sixteenth-century Spain. Racial relations between nuns of Spanish descent and *mestizas* and indigenous nuns are receiving increasing attention (see Bilinkoff; Myers; Rubial; and Sampson Vera Tudela).

[Exemplary Life of the Venerable Mother Sor Teresa Juliana de Santo Domingo][14]

Chapter I

Authors of the lives and deeds of heroes exert little effort and face even less difficulty finding out parents, country, family members, and other relatives of their subjects. But in the present case, our pen does not flow so easily. The unknown character of her native land and the remoteness of that region make information about her scarce. Had it not been for Mother Teresa herself, who supplied these details, they would have remained completely concealed from us. After the passing of those who brought her in the ship, as well as the Marquis of Mancera and his wife, all their servants, and the rest of their family, Teresa's land of origin and parents would have been forgotten. Only the color of her face would be left to trace her back to her native land. She was born in *Guinea* in 1676, according to the closest estimate. We do not know the day this fortunate creature saw the light of life. We know, though, that she was chosen among thousands by the Powerful Hand and for the glory of Divine Providence.

Guinea is one of the most extensive and vast provinces contained in the huge confines of Africa. It is divided into several kingdoms, each one governing itself independently. The Lower *Mina* off the *Gold Coast* [*La Mina Baja del Oro*] is among the most important ones. That was where this happy girl was born to a most illustrious family. Her parents were reigning princes. Their scepter ruled all that land in peaceful dominion. Time erased her father's name from her memory. She only remembered the shape of his body and the features of his face: *My father was*—she says in the account [*relación*] this venerable woman made of her origins—*a man of large and broad body, and with very thick eyebrows.*[15] Her mother was called Abar and was as important as her father in lineage and nobility. The venerable mother had three brothers, all of them older than she: one was called Juachipiter, Ensú was the second, Joachin, the third one. They all preceded this outstanding woman in birth. When she was born, they called her Chicaba in their language. This princess was born to be a joy to her parents and brothers and a consolation to the entire kingdom. Either because she was a girl or because she was the youngest, all care was lavished on her as if she were a precious jewel.

All the inhabitants of *Guinea* are of a dark, black color, as we frequently observe of those who come to our countries or read from histories of the greatest authority. Because such is the color with which wise nature painted all those from that region, parents and brothers and the girl herself could not help being adorned in the same fashion. However dark was their complexion, even darker was their situation. In their blindness, they worshipped the morning star.[16] They did not use temples for their

---

14. For this anthology, we use Paniagua, *Compendio de la vida.*

15. Father Paniagua uses italics only for quotations that he wants us to accept as being directly taken from Sor Teresa Chicaba's own writings. Otherwise, he represents the imagined speech of Chicaba and all other characters in a variety of typographical forms, and not always consistently.

16. The morning star, or Lucifer (Latin "bringer of light") has been interpreted since Saint Jerome (*To Eustochium* 22.4) as a reference to the devil. Thus, Chicaba's people were worshippers of the devil. Paniagua shows the tension between the moral and the biological discourse on Blackness of his time.

worship and sacrifices. Instead, as soon as they saw the star, they came out of their houses very early to adore it. What a superfluous vigil that was, because in the very act of seeking out the light, they remained in thicker and denser darkness. During their feast days, the people accompanied the king and queen and all their family. Following the customary ritual of their barbarous ceremonies, they bent their knees in humble recognition and sang praises to the star. These rites lasted until the zeal of the *Capuchin* missionaries, entering these lands not long ago, succeeded in planting the banner of the True Faith and banishing the shadows of idolatry.[17]

[Unable to accept the morning star as the creator of everything, Chicaba started on a personal search that took the form of contemplative walks in the meadows outside her palace. The people acknowledge her as a divine gift and a healer.]

Chapter III

...She went out one morning like any other with a reduced retinue of some female servants. Enjoying themselves for a while across the field, they left Chicaba alone. Suddenly she found herself assaulted by a barbarous army sent by an enemy of her *nation* and her father. They took her prisoner in order to tear her apart. The maids, anguished and seeing from afar the danger into which their lady had fallen, burst into the city shouting. They reached the palace in a confused melee; and with cries of alarm, they announced the peril. The father, as courageous as he was prompt to action, left for the field just in time, and his vassals, who had come at the call of the maids' voices, took courage with his presence. With valiant arms, they shatter and rout the barbarous enemies. After recovering her father's most precious treasure, they brought her back to him in celebration. They congratulated one another for having achieved this triumph because, though they had taken great risks, the girl's life assured their solace....

Chapter IV

...One day, distancing herself from them [her retinue] a good while, [Chicaba] arrived at a fountain of crystal waters. Completely taken by it, as was her custom, she saw what she saw, for she alone knew about it. What she said happened, happened; and she could not avoid it. I will tell about it in the very words that one of her *spiritual directors* used to testify about it.[18] "In one of these pauses"—he talks about how far Teresa walked to reach the object of her burning desire—"they baptized her as she stood by the fountain, and they gave her the name of Teresa, which later on she was given again, when she was baptized in *São Tomé*." Her *spiritual director* says no more. Who administered the sacrament, he does not say, nor does he explain.

---

17. This is historically inaccurate. An attempt was made by a *Capuchin* mission in 1658 sent by Spain, which produced a catechism in the Ewe language (see Labouret and Rivet; Law; and Olabiyi). Attempts were made by the bishops of *São Tomé* to send missions to the Kingdom of Benin and Whydah. *Capuchins* were very active in the Christian kingdom of Kongo around the time of its demise in 1688 (see Brásio; Thornton).

18. A Roman Catholic nun often seeks guidance about her spiritual life from a priest who meets with her outside the sacrament of penance or confession. The director is seldom her confessor.

Any learned person will have no doubt that this happened indeed. An angel must have done it because, at that time, there was no one in the entire kingdom yet who could have baptized her. After this incident Teresa returned more reassured, with more knowledge of the God for whom she was looking. However, as she was yet a child, this knowledge does not seem to have impressed itself enough on her to quench her long-felt desire. She did not stop going about the same business and continued looking for the One Whom she still did not know, even though she had Him within her. This God, so hidden to her, wished to show some clear sign that He was the one she sighed for with loving pain. He appeared to her as a tender Child in the arms of his Holy Mother. Teresa, stunned by the sight of such an uncanny vision, remained motionless in sweet contemplation, her eyes fixed on the Lady and Her Child, who was as peaceful as He was beautiful. Therefore, Teresa could understand better who He was. He had dangling from His hands a ribbon, as bright as it was pretty. He touched Teresa's head with it softly; and when she tried to take it, the Child withdrew His hand with grace, so that she could not reach it. The Child repeated this action a few times; and Teresa [repeated] her gesture to grab it, but she could never touch it. This mystical and miraculous game lasted for a while, after which the Lady and Her Son cast their benign eyes on the girl and disappeared from her sight. In spite of her young age, Teresa was left with all sorts of thoughts stirring in her imagination: the beauty of the Lady, the grace and sweetness of Her Son, the whiteness of their faces, when all she had ever seen were dark—these things became powerful incentives for her quick and alert understanding, despite her youth. She wanted to find out once and for all who this God was who was hiding under cover. When the marvel ended, she went back with her people. She did not reveal any part of the wonder to anyone. A few days later, she gave her brother alone some information, although vague, to calm his envy.

Chapter VI

...With the confidence and security of knowing that his orders and rules regarding the custody of his daughter would be observed to the letter, Teresa's father went off with his sons to take possession of his newly amassed provinces. Her mother was equally alert to enforce and execute the monarch's decree, because it was of utmost importance to obey it and thus ensure her daughter's security. Like a new Argos,[19] she would not allow Chicaba to leave her company. But what is human purpose in the face of divine decision? This loving vigilance and care lasted four days. The same love was the occasion for a lapse, which her mother would lament for a long time with inconsolable tears. Stealing herself away from her mother's watch—how she did so only God knows—and fooling the vigilance of the guards, Teresa was able to leave the house. Once out, she hurried toward her beloved meadow, where she hoped to see by the fountain the Lady with the white Child who had captured her affection so completely. When she could not find the compass that attracted her love, she was overtaken by her passion and continued walking far away from her household and court. Unable to find her way back and unaware of what was at the end of such a

---

19. Argos is a Greek mythological figure that has one hundred eyes.

long road, suffering in the heat of the sun and fatigued after such travail, she sat down under the shade of a tree.

Protected by the shadow from the sun's fierce heat, she wiped the perspiration from her face. Finding relief and rest, Teresa, although a child and in such desert solitude, remained unafraid, completely without fear. Doing what was appropriate for her years, she took the beautiful and precious bracelets [*manillas*] off her wrists and started playing with them. She was as calm and serene as if she were in her own house. . . .

. . . We left Teresa resting under a tree, when a Spanish vessel appeared on the shore. Suddenly a gallant young man grabbed her by the arm with the jewels she was wearing. He took her closer to the seashore, and those on the ship noticed her but did not see the man who was leading her. He was invisible to their eyes. One of them jumped overboard and carried her to the ship. The vessel took to the high seas without tending to any other concern or business. Teresa was frightened to see that they were taking her far from her land. With tears in her eyes and frightened to see herself among strange people, she was on the brink of death. Sadness and distress suffocated her, together with thirst. She moaned helplessly, and all the crew tried everything they could to quiet her. But the tears were caused more from her overwhelming thirst than from any other concerns, although so many of these gave her grief. Yet no one could calm her because they did not know what she wanted. By chance, she saw a glass of water, and thrusting herself toward it quickly, she was able finally to quench her thirst. [Chicaba] had restored herself to life, feeling refreshed and more at ease, when [the crew] began to comfort her, and little by little she started to recover from her fright, but not from the anguish of yearning to return to her land and to the company of her dear parents. It distressed her not to know how to swim because she thought that with this ability and skill, even though a small child, she might liberate herself from such painful slavery. Seeing herself denied this remedy, she reasoned childishly to herself, as she later explained: "*The vessel is sailing farther away against the current. If I jump into the water, it will take me to my land, because its waves go in that direction.*" As she finished her thought, she tried to put it into action. But as she was about to execute it, a Lady appeared to her whose majesty and grandeur made it clear that she was the same one she had seen on the happy occasion of the fountain back in her motherland. The Lady dried her tears with peaceful calm, and she also calmed her distress with her caresses. With this she completely freed Teresa from the affection for her motherland that she nurtured in her bosom and that had almost brought her to a most lamentable drowning.

[*She is baptized in* São Tomé. *From there she is taken to Spain. The devil in the form of blackbirds attacks her ship. She arrives in Cadiz and lives in Seville for some time. Finally she is presented to King Carlos II of Spain, who in turn gives her to the Marquis and Marchioness of Mancera.*]

Chapter X

. . . One afternoon the marchioness sent all the maidservants, including her little black girl, out for a walk, a decent and licit diversion. They obeyed the mistress' orders, and they went to the site of the Buen Retiro.[20] They planned to entertain themselves among its variety of beautiful fountains, gardens, and pools. As the sun was setting, they all approached the big pool and climbed onto its ledge. Some were standing on it, and others were sitting, and all were distracted by the soft noise of the waters, when they saw a man who looked by all the external signs to be the marquis' *mayordomo*. He approached them; and they did not think anything of it, because they saw him as a member of the household. Without a word, he went near Teresa, who was standing on the ledge unaware of his presence. The false *mayordomo* kicked Teresa into the water. They were all taken by surprise by such an unusual action in an individual they all considered a fellow member of the household. They were astonished at Teresa's danger and were paralyzed because they did not know how to handle the disaster. They remained confused for a long while. It was long enough for the water to have taken Teresa's life, were she not sheltered by Divine protection. She said that under the waves she was as contented as she had been in the little meadow back in her homeland. Once her companions recovered from the surprise and confusion, they started to discuss among themselves a solution; but they could not find any means to help her and they turned toward home in sorrow and tears. At the same time, Teresa was playing under the water with pleasure and contentment. A few steps away before leaving the Buen Retiro, they found a gallant and well-disposed young man. They informed him of the reason for their tears, and he obliged them to take him to the site. He recognized the place where Teresa had fallen in. The young man made no more effort than to stand by the shore, when the water placed Teresa reverently into his hands. She appeared happy, gay, and joyful as if she had never fallen into the water, and her clothes were not wet. He returned her to her fellow servants. They were so busy with their joy at seeing their dear Teresa restored to them that they neglected to ask who the young man was, just as in their fright, they had forgotten to find out what had happened to the one they believed to have been the *mayordomo* or where he had gone.

> [*After spending her youth in the house of the Marquis and Marchioness of Mancera, Teresa receives her freedom and enters a convent in Salamanca, after several failed attempts in other places due to her skin color.*]

Chapter XIX

... The nuns conferred among each other about the matter. Most of them had realized how opportune it would be for the convent to have such a special gem, more for her virtue and righteous life than for any other benefits. They were almost resolved to admit her. A lady belonging to the highest nobility in Spain heard the news of what was going on. She had renounced her high birth and lived as a poor nun in the same

---

20. The Buen Retiro was on the grounds of today's most popular urban park in Madrid. It had been used in the past by the kings of Spain as a place of retreat. It was in Paniagua's time that the park was opened to the public but not in Chicaba's time in Madrid. It may have happened that the household of *Mancera*, because the marquis was a member of the council of state, had privileges from the king to use the Buen Retiro.

convent. She had given up everything, yet she could not give up her own pride, so she barred Teresa's admission. Her vain pretext was that the postulant was black.

"A black woman!" she said. "In my convent! Not in my day. This house was not founded for blacks. So, ladies, stop the talking because I will do everything within my power to stop this from happening." And because she was a lady of such high standing and superior nobility, all the others had to be silent and agree. Teresa was excluded for being black. The same person who barred her admission later lamented her mistake. A few years after this event, she heard news of the heroic virtue that shone from Teresa. The lady was remorseful that her vain pride had made her reject Teresa for being black. She envied the nuns in La Penitencia for their fortune and good sense, as she explained repeatedly.[21] . . .

[Teresa gains admission as a tertiary in the convent of La Penitencia of Salamanca.]

Chapter XXII

. . . Once the ceremony came to an end, the bishop left. He was astonished at the piety shown by Teresa when he gave her the habit. All present, including his family, were no less astonished by the black woman's devotion. She had achieved her desired admission and gained her happiness, and this felicitous ceremony came to an end. Now we have Teresa in the harbor to which she had directed her sail for so long. Now we have seen how happily and joyfully the nuns received her at the door. But another community, invisible to those present yet noticeable to the black woman, received her with pleasure at the door of enclosure. As she entered the convent, Teresa noticed two *choirs* of nuns on each side. Together with the living ones, they were four. She looked at them carefully. At first, she could not believe her eyes. She thought that maybe her eyes were confused and she was seeing double. The four lines proceeded toward the *choir*. Paying closer attention now, Teresa noticed that two of them were more conspicuous than the others. Her soul was not disturbed; and in the midst of great calm and peace, looking at each of their faces and expressions, she felt an indescribable joy. She saw them behave with the modesty and composure that was appropriate to the ritual they were enacting and the life they led. But in these two rows every detail stood out much more than in the others. She saw cordiality without affectation, external composure devoid of the least atom of hypocrisy, and a joy in their faces that was markedly different from the rest because they were already in possession of that joy that will never disappear. The others' joy was mixed with many other things that could serve as obstacles to true happiness. The two extra lines of nuns that Teresa saw were those who had led virtuous lives in the convent and had found eternal rest in the Lord. These nuns, following a special command from God, came to receive her at the door in visible form and shape, and they accompanied her to the sacred ceremony of investiture. We owe this information to Teresa herself. Indeed, she told those still alive about the faces and particular features of those nuns who had already died before she had even entered the convent. Taking this incident

---

21. The convent of Santa María Magdalena de la Penitencia of Salamanca, commonly called *La Penitencia*, belonged to the Dominican Order.

into account, we have enough evidence to venerate her and not to question Heaven's secrets.

[Teresa helps poor women pay their dowries.]

Chapter XXXIV

. . . This is what happened to a nun, who after her postulant year found herself as short of money as she was rich and abundant in her desire to secure the harbor of religious life through the three vows.[22] She was very upset because neither she nor the others knew who could get her out of the predicament. Their only remedy would be to hope that the passage of time would play to her advantage. From the beginning, Teresa had covered all the expenses for the novice to be admitted. Trusting Divine Providence and putting all her hope in God, she proceeded with all the preparations necessary for the ceremony of religious profession. She went to kill two hens for next day's feast and said in good humor,

"We are already on the eve, and you are so tepid?"

The nun answered, "And what do we gain by killing the hens if the ceremony will not take place tomorrow because I lack the *dowry*. Where is it going to come from?"

To which Teresa said again, "Madam, you go and kill the hens; tomorrow the novice will profess without fail."

The nun had a hard time believing this. But her lack of faith served to show how much God was pleased by Teresa's hope. The next morning without fail, a person like many others who sought Teresa came to visit her. Liberal and pious, this person gave the convent all that was necessary for the novice's *dowry*, so before the end of the day the hens were served up, because that same day the nun made her profession. In this way and through a miracle, Divine Omnipotence showed how much He cherished the hope of His beloved spouse.

Chapter XXXV

. . . Her soul was eager to keep divine grace within itself as well as within the souls of all rational creatures. With that end, she promptly asked her Celestial Divine Spouse how to achieve this. She heard the following response: "*I felt*—she says—*inside my heart that everyone should love Him very much.*" And Teresa loved Him very, very much indeed, with all her heart, strength, and senses; and that is why she progressed so much in charity. "*I do not know*—the Venerable one goes on—*what it is to love God, or how to please Him; but it seems to me that He likes an attentive heart to be truthful in everything. The heart should be attached only to those things that pertain to His Glory, casting away from itself all worldly things and creature comforts. The heart should look at the Creator alone, as the Lord is the only thing the heart can call its own. Soul, life, and heart must spare nothing for His Majesty. I am well aware that I know this, but it still needs to be done.*" That is how it seemed to you, Teresa, but you did not hesitate for a moment to do what you felt and knew. If you think that you did not do enough, what then was all that eagerness of "I love you, I love you, I love

---

22. All religious women took vows of poverty, chastity, and obedience.

you," which on occasion burst from your chest, shaken uncontrollably by that very love? People heard it. If you did not know how to love, why were you so jealous when your spouse was absent?

Fine love has a certain element of jealousy that both is a faithful proclaimer of how active this volcano is and serves as a harbinger of the most intense affection. In chapter XXIX, we saw the Divine Lover a bit jealous of our venerable one when the Majesty of Christ reprimanded her for that slight lapse of admitting to her *cell* the priests who had said Mass at the convent.[23] This was a clear sign that He loved her because He was very jealous. Teresa's love for her Master wanted to take credit for its elevated nature by also being a little jealous. After one of her Master's absences, this jealousy made her exclaim spontaneously the following verses. The lack of artifice in them could well have been the ploy of a love expressing itself without restraint:

> Oh, Jesus, where are you gone?
> I cannot stand a moment
> without seeing you.
> Oh, Jesus of my soul,
> where are you gone?
> It seems you are not coming back
> and you are lost.
> Oh, Jesus, what shall I say?
> If you go out with other women,
> what shall I do?
> I will wail, I will cry
> till I see God,
> and if not, if not,
> I will die of love.
> And because I am so lonely
> I say
> that you have not come.
> And if you are with someone else,
> I have seen it before:
> Martha and Mary,
> you have loved them.
> O Jesus, where shall I find you?
> I feel giddy
> when I have you.
> Good-bye, good-bye, love,
> good-bye, Lord,
> good-bye, heart,
> no more, no more,
> no more.

---

23. The constitutions of cloistered orders prohibited direct contact between men and women. Only extern sisters and laypersons were allowed to socialize with visiting priests without the barrier of the iron grille between them.

These verses are evidence that love makes the lover intolerant. Teresa's love complains impatiently about her spouse's tardiness and that another soul detains Him. On the other hand, they express how well Teresa carried out the office of love when she laments, "I am well aware that I know this, but it needs yet to be done."

The impulse of divine love burning in this happy soul's breast was so fierce that the heaviness of her body could not contain the agility of her spirit. Her spirit lifted her up in rapture more than once, raising her off the ground. People saw her in this state only a few times because she hid herself and kept it as secret as she could. Once, however, they were able to see her without her noticing them. Impelled by her love, she was completely transported in her Celestial Divine Master, her face was resplendent, her *cell* was bathed in light, and she enjoyed her royal favors in solitude. She stitched this fine love to her breast and heart so securely that she felt deeply what His Supreme Majesty allowed no other pen but hers to tell.[24] No one but she could express even the slightest trace of what she felt: "*In this pain*—she speaks of an extraordinary pain that she felt in her heart—*I come to understand that the Lord is inside my heart always. Therefore, if I get upset, or I am not in conformity with Him, this pain goes away. So it is very painful when my heart is serene and calm. It becomes burning when my love rises excessively to the point of wishing to fulfill all my duties and obligations. But I am not saying it right, because it is not excessive, because it is reasonable. I am burning, I feel I am searing, I would shout aloud, but I scream inside myself.*"

And you shouted out too, oh fortunate soul, because you could not contain yourself. Is this the same person who knew love but did not practice it? Is this the same woman who accused herself of knowing how to love but not loving enough? Oh my God, and how tender You are with those who seek and love You. Let Teresa finish the explanation of the event: "*The pain I feel in my heart is so great,*" she says, "*that inside I feel as if it is covered in sweat. I do not know how to explain myself except in this manner. His Majesty will help Your Reverence understand everything I would like to say but cannot in this short explanation.*" So her pen wrote, but here is also where mine recoils from the fear of being seared by so much fire and flame, though I would be the happier. Those who are learned may reflect on this marvel, that although Church history records similar cases, hers is nonetheless magnificent. God performs these works to teach us.

---

24. This is internal evidence that she must have written about this experience herself.

The *Regent*, the Secretary, and the Widow: Power, Ethnicity, and Gender in the Confraternity of Saints Elesbão and Iphigenia, Rio de Janeiro, 1784–1786[1]

Elizabeth W. Kiddy

Black *Nações* and Their Confraternities in Eighteenth-Century Rio de Janeiro

In 1763, Rio de Janeiro became the capital of the colony of Brazil. Rio de Janeiro had risen in prominence during the mining boom in the neighboring captaincy of Minas Gerais, and it had quickly grown to be a bustling port city with a diverse population of Europeans, people of mixed descent, Brazilian-born blacks, and Africans from many different regions, both slave and free (Karasch, *Slave Life*). As in other cities in Spanish and Portuguese America, a wide range of confraternities served to organize this diversity in Rio de Janeiro and shape the religious and social life of the city.

Confraternities were Catholic lay religious associations organized around fidelity to a saint or a particular devotion; they fulfilled both religious and nonreligious functions within society.[2] Confraternity activities were often part of the domain of the street and included collecting alms, taking care of the bodies and souls of the deceased members, and both hosting and participating in feast day celebrations. Many Africans and their descendants, both slave and free, enthusiastically participated in the confraternity system, organizing their own devotions and engaging in the same sorts of activities that all confraternities sponsored.[3]

Black confraternities tended to divide along "ethnic" lines in Rio de Janeiro in the late eighteenth century. Portuguese and African inhabitants recognized these divisions, and they called them *nações* or *nations*, which can be understood to correspond roughly to what today are called "ethnicities" (Karasch, "Minha *nação*," 128). Different *nations* distinguished themselves with different clothing, hairstyles, and even scarification, and, in many cases, they would retain the language, foods, and devotional practices of their remembered homelands.

The main division among African groups, recognized by the Portuguese and the Africans, was between *Angolans* from West Central Africa and mostly transported from the ports of Luanda and *Benguela*, and *Minas*, who left from four main ports west of the Volta River in the Bight of Benin. Both of these terms collapse a wide variety of different ethnicities, some of which are elaborated in the document below

---

1. See Maps 2 and 6.

2. See also Chapters 6 and 10.

3. For some works on black brotherhoods in Brazil, see Kiddy, *Blacks of the Rosary*; and Soares, *Devotos*.

(Kiddy, *Blacks of the Rosary*, 43–49). Many Africans from both of these large regions became fervent Christians but practiced a Christianity that mixed, to varying degrees, with African traditions.[4] Much of the devotion of the African Christians, as well as their ethnic rivalries, came to be expressed through the confraternity system.

O Diálogo: The History of a Confraternity Dispute

It was in this context that the *"Diálogo"* was written.[5] Africans who had splintered from the Confraternity of Saints Elesbão and Iphigenia wrote this "Dialogue" in order to tell their side of the story of the conflicts that precipitated the break with the confraternity. Francisco Alves de Souza, the protagonist of the "Dialogue," was a freed black man from the *Maki* Kingdom on the *Mina Coast* (Bight of Benin).[6] Souza moved to Rio de Janeiro from Bahia, the port city for the vast sugar-growing region in the northeast of Brazil, in 1748, and joined the congregation of *Mina Maki.* The "Dialogue" relates the circumstances under which he became the *regent* of that congregation, which was a subgroup within the Confraternity of Saints Elesbão and Iphigenia.

Several other main characters appear in the story. Souza's fellow interlocutor, and the foil for his story, is Gonçalo Cordeiro, also a *Maki*, who had been Souza's friend from infancy. The antagonist of the story never speaks, nor is she named—she is referred to only as "the widow."[7] The widow was the wife of the recently deceased king of the congregation Captain Ignacio Gonçalves do Monte.

After his death, the widow surreptitiously had herself crowned queen of the congregation, keeping not only the power, but also the much contested safe with its contents and other belongings of the congregation. The main narrative thrust of the "Dialogue" is the escalating conflict between the two factions, one led by Souza and Cordeiro, the other by the widow. In the selections below, the other characters who speak include the bailiff's secretary, who arrives to compel Souza by law to assume the post of *regent*, and elders of the confraternity, notably Luiz Rodrigues Silva.

The original document, which is more than twice as long as the selections presented here, is excerpted in a way that preserves the action of the story. The entire text is, in fact, primarily in the form of a dialogue, which moves chronologically forward in time from 1784 to 1786. The dialogue format is not uncommon in sixteenth- to eighteenth-century Portuguese literature, especially religious works that used either dialogues or plays to help to convert non-Christians.[8] The dialogue form was also

---

4. On the concept of African Christianity, see Thornton.
5. The scholar who has worked most thoroughly with this document is Mariza de Carvalho Soares. Her work is an indispensable reference for anyone studying this document.
6. Soares identifies *Maki* as the Mahi, a people who inhabited the region that neighbored the Kingdom of *Dahomey* in the north ("Can Women Guide and Govern Men?" 81–82).
7. Soares identifies the widow as a *Coura* woman, from a region far inland from the Bight of Benin, who appears in her husband's will as Victoria Correa da Conceição ("Can Women Guide and Govern Men?" 80–81).
8. Soares discusses these forms in relation to this "Dialogue" ("Apreço e imitação," 111–15).

used, at least once, in a pamphlet in Portugal in the eighteenth century to argue for the abolition of slavery.[9] Perhaps some of these pamphlets also circulated in Brazil. Even with these examples, however, it is unclear where the creators of this "Dialogue" got the idea to tell their side of the story in this format.

Within the text itself, few clues indicate when one day has ended and another begins; in fact, these transitions are indicated only occasionally, by an opening comment asking, "Who is knocking on the door?" At times, it is also difficult to know where the "Dialogue" is taking place, but it seems the two main locations are Souza's home and the meeting room in the Church of Saints Elesbão and Iphigenia. The "Dialogue" is punctuated by two legal documents—the *termo* (entry) written to inaugurate Souza as *regent* and the statutes of the Congregation of the Devotion of the Souls in Purgatory. Both of these represent important legal documents for confraternities and serve as evidence of the legality of the actions of Souza and his compatriots.

Power Relationships in Black Confraternity Life

The "Dialogue" offers a unique look into three important relationships of power in confraternity life. First, the "Dialogue" demonstrates the ties between this congregation of blacks and the civil authorities of the city and the Portuguese state. In order to force Souza to accept the position of *regent*, his compatriots wrote a formal petition. Souza agreed to become *regent* only after he was visited by the bailiff and almost dragged before the magistrate as a result of this petition.[10]

The last part of the "Dialogue" is dominated by the lawsuit that the congregation brought against the widow and the news that Souza had lost the lawsuit. Souza and his group appealed to the *Relação*, or high court, but the court only confirmed the sentence. Finally, Souza was brought before the viceroy, together with the king of the rosary, to defend himself against the widow's claims that he was the leader of an uprising—a serious accusation against a black in eighteenth-century Rio de Janeiro.[11] In a strongly democratic retort, Cordeiro rejected the ruling, saying that Souza was *regent* by the will of the people and only that will had force.

Second, the "Dialogue" exposes power relationships within the confraternities and between different groups of Africans in the city of Rio de Janeiro. The largest conflict appears between the *Angolans* and *Minas*. The *Angolans*, who outnumbered *Minas* in Rio de Janeiro at the time the "Dialogue" was written, are presented in the "Dialogue" as the African "other," barbarians who did not know how to act in a

---

9. I refer here to the anonymous, mid-eighteenth-century Portuguese pamphlet discovered by Charles R. Boxer that was a dialogue about slaves and slavery between a Portuguese lawyer and a Brazilian miner (see Boxer).

10. Souza refused to accept the title of king, even though that was the title used by his predecessor, Captain Ignacio Gonçalves do Monte. Instead, he insisted on adopting the title of regent. His reasoning for this change is elaborated in the "Dialogue" itself.

11. The black kings and queens of the rosary brotherhoods were important figures in many colonial cities in Brazil (Kiddy, "Kings, Queens, and Judges").

civilized manner and gave all Africans a bad name. This conflict exposes the reality that Africans from vastly different regions did not see each other as a single people but as competing groups interacting within the unequal slave society of colonial Brazil. The "Dialogue" also highlights the story of the division between different groups from the *Mina Coast* and their eventual split into their own congregations. Despite these internal divisions, the *Angolans* remain the true "other."

Third, the document is not as much about ethnic differences as it is about a conflict with a woman who decided to take power and defend her right to that power. The document includes repeated diatribes against women, who were "disturbers of the peace and tellers of tales." Part of this antipathy certainly comes from the particular conflict with "the widow" in which Souza and his compatriots find themselves. In a more general sense, however, the "Dialogue" brings up interesting questions about the role of women and the extent of and limits on their power in the black confraternities to which they contributed significant sums of money (Soares, "Can Women Guide and Govern Men?" 80–81).

The document invites a careful reading between the lines of gender expectations as well as a history of Afro-Brazilian women's agency through the widow's perspective, which is presented here only through the eyes of her antagonists. In the end, the Portuguese state supported the widow's bid for power, and two years later the congregation of *Mina Maki* with Souza as their *regent* began its own confraternity dedicated to Our Lady of Remedies.

*****

[The Dialogue: Rules or Statutes That Are Practiced by the *Mina* Blacks and Their Kinsmen in the State of Brazil][12]

Between the speakers:

Francisco Alves de Souza, *regent* of the *Maki nation*

Second Lieutenant Gonçalo Cordeiro, secretary of the same *nation*...

[A Reluctant Souza Resists the Regency While the Deceased King's Widow Holds on to Power]

Cordeiro: . . . Yesterday you said you could not give me a response, so now I am waiting for it.

Souza: What response?

Cordeiro: Whether you will be our *regent* and be charitable toward the living and pray for the souls of the dead. . . .

Souza: Senhor Cordeiro, I find myself now less burdened by my passions and thus more unencumbered to ask you what the reason is that you and the others want to elect me as *regent* of this congregation although among you there is no lack of qualified people with whole, true, and just capabilities, when I do not have these qualities?

Cordeiro: What obstinacy. I have never seen anything like it. To scheme for so long about one thing, it seems more like impertinence than anything else. I already told you in the first part [of this dialogue] what I have to say, and now you force me to say again that we do not want any other leader than you, because in the time of the first *regent*, Captain Ignacio Gonçalves do Monte, you already governed, and when he was mortally ill he called you to his house and gave the regency to you, so that the association of our kinsmen, and its charity, would not be forsaken—and you promised to do it. Luiz Rodrigues Silva, Antônio da Costa Falcão, and Rosa de Souza de Andrade and other credible people who are here now witnessed that promise.

Souza: I do not doubt that what you say is true, but now they tell me that after Monte's death on December 25, 1783, and during the time I was away for fourteen days when I was sick with a skin infection [*erisipela*], his widow convoked our kinsmen and ordered them to go to the meeting room of the church of the Glorious Saints Elesbão and Iphigenia to ask for alms for the soul of her dead husband. And she had secretly taken measures beforehand with some of her faction, if it is permissible to say so, and, taking everyone by surprise, in the meeting room, had them put a crown on her head, announcing that she was queen, with such guile that everyone thought her manner of proceeding was strange and ran away from her the same day, because she called not only the *Maki* to go there but people from all over the *Mina Coast* and other *nations*. And everyone was astonished by such a calamity. It was all the work of

---

12. Regra ou estatutos, por modo de um diálogo onde se dá notícias das caridades, e sufrágios, das almas, que usam os pretos *Minas*, com seus nacionais no Estado do Brasil, especialmente no Rio de Janeiro por onde se hão de regerem, e governam, fora de todo o abuso gentílico, e supersticioso, composto por Francisco Alves de Souza, preto e natural do Reino de Maki, um dos mais excelente & potentados daquela oriunda Costa da *Mina*. Fundação Biblioteca Nacional, Rio de Janeiro, Seção Manuscritos 9, 3, 11, fols. 1, 12–14, 16–26, 29–36, 38, 41–44.

one *crioulo* from Bahia[13] who was in her house after the death of her husband. And consider yourself whether or not this is abuse and superstition, and this is one of the reasons that I have insisted that I do not want [to be *regent*] because I know that the widow does not want me to be without her consent.

Cordeiro: All of this is the plotting of the devil to pervert this good charity, but who consented to and approved this election?

Souza: I don't know, but as you know I was sick on that occasion, so I would not have even known about this tragedy if worthy and zealous people hadn't told me about it.

Cordeiro: What the widow should do is to govern her own house and take good care of the soul of her husband, fulfilling what his last will and testament commands and not meddling in other people's business. And if she has done this, it is not by the will of all of the people. As you well know, this congregation consists of more than two hundred people, men and women. I see no proof that she has been made *regent*, because that would have to be by the election and will of all the people, and what is more, no woman can occupy this position, which is to govern and rule over men....

[The Congregation Brings in the Law to Force Souza to be *Regent*]

Souza: Someone is knocking on the door.

Cordeiro: You can come in, the door is open. Oh, it's Senhor Luiz Antônio Ribeiro de Campos, secretary of the bailiff who is looking for you. I don't know why.

Souza: What the . . . secretary of the bailiff, what business does he have with me? I am at a loss to know what he might want.

Cordeiro: I don't know, but we will see—enter, sir, and have a seat.

Souza: May God keep you. Who are you looking for, sir?

Bailiff: Senhor Francisco Alves de Souza.

Souza: At your service.

Bailiff: I have come to notify you of the formal petition that Luiz Rodrigues Silva, Alexandre de Carvalho, and José da Silva and other *Mina* Makino blacks made to the honorable magistrate,[14] requesting that you be their *regent* and administrator of the alms and prayers for the souls of their kinsmen and of charity for the living, and if you do not want the position I will have to take you under guard to see the minister, as you see in the dispatch.

Souza: Such short notice! You can register that under guard I will not go speak to the minister.

Bailiff: Yes, sir, I will register the following: "I certify that I subpoenaed the supplicant Francisco Alves de Souza with this petition, which contains both an order and a declaration, and by the same supplicant it was said that 'I, without a doubt,

---

13. A *crioulo* was a Brazilian-born black. Bahia refers to the city of Salvador in the captaincy of Bahia. It was the first capital of Brazil and the center of the sugar-growing economy in the sixteenth and seventeenth centuries. It had an active slave trade, but after gold was found in Minas Gerais (see Map 6) in the early eighteenth century and the capital of Brazil was moved to Rio de Janeiro in 1763, many slaves, free blacks, and others moved south to find more economic opportunities. Salvador was also home to Souza before he moved to Rio de Janeiro.

14. Juiz de Fora: a magistrate named by the Portuguese Crown when there was no district court judge available.

accept the said post.' In verification of which I enacted the present [document]. In Rio de Janeiro on the ninth of March 1784, the bailiff, Judge Antônio Ribeiro de Campos."[15]

Souza: Is there any more doubt?

Bailiff: No sir, your part is finished; but I have to take care of other business included in the same petition.

Souza: What business is that?

Bailiff: I must notify the widow of Captain Ignacio Gonçalves do Monte to turn in the safe where the money of the congregation is kept, together with other articles and books. The blacks of this congregation told me that these things belong to the congregation because they were bought with their contributions and alms; so they requested the safe be returned, but the widow does not want to return it, saying that he [Monte] is her husband. That's what the blacks told me.

Souza: As far as that goes, it is of little importance to me.

Bailiff: Goodbye, sir. You can feel at ease; this matter will not be a problem.

Souza: Goodbye, Senhor Luiz Antônio....

Cordeiro: Didn't I tell you that we would obligate you to be our *regent*, but you were so stubborn that things had to come to this point.

Souza: What point is that?

Cordeiro: That you would be obligated and that you would have no other option.

Souza: I knew what had to happen... I promise you that when I am inaugurated as *regent*, I will make you secretary so that you can participate in the work that you talk so much about.

Cordeiro: You would honor me greatly by making me secretary to the *regent*.

Souza: You [Cordeiro], and all of you present, do not think that this will be a game.

Cordeiro: Be ready on the thirteenth of March, because we will come to get you so that you can be inaugurated in the meeting room of the church of the glorious Saints Elesbão and Iphigenia, as is customary and in the style preserved among us *Mina* blacks.

Souza: I am more than ready. It is also necessary to have a book for the official entry and with a record of what I say thereafter.[16]

Cordeiro: Everything is ready. Let's go because the blacks are already waiting in the meeting room....

Souza: May God watch over all of you in His Holy Peace, just as His Son said to His disciples when He appeared to them after His Holy Resurrection, placing himself among them, and saying, "May the peace of God be with you: *pax vobis.*"

All: May He come into our company to protect and rule us, as we desire it. We are here with more than forty people to inaugurate you.

---

15. This document and the other documents embedded in the dialogue are copies of historical documents.

16. Confraternities were supposed to keep books, which were then subject to oversight by state authorities. In order to make them legal, all important acts, as well as minutes of meetings, were to be entered into a book that was kept by the organization's secretary. Most confraternities had a book with their statutes (see below), accounting books, a book recording new members, and a book of meeting minutes or books with the certifications of masses celebrated for the souls of the dead.

Souza: Who are the elders of this congregation?

Cordeiro: Here are Alexandre de Carvalho, José Antônio dos Santos, Luiz Rodrigues Silva, and José da Silva, all freed blacks and the ones among us with the most authority, who are ready to inaugurate you with deference and gravity.

Souza: I have been inaugurated, and may God grant me health and wisdom to rule you with calm and peace, to pray for the souls of our kinsmen, giving charity to the living for the greatest honor of God and the salvation of our souls.

Everyone: Viva! ...

[The History of the *Mina Maki* Confraternity in Rio de Janeiro]

Souza: The blacks created this group, or corporation, because ever since the beginning of this land, they [the Portuguese] forcibly brought African blacks from the *Mina Coast* and *Angola*, and some of the masters who bought the Africans were inhumane. When the blacks fell ill with incurable diseases or when they became aged, these masters just threw them away and [left] them to die of hunger and cold, naked on the beaches without having anyone to bury them unless the Santa Casa de Misericórdia sent to bury the bodies with their zeal and charity.[17] Otherwise the abandoned corpses would just lie there. And for this reason the blacks themselves created this group, or corporation, in order to do good for their kinsmen, to let the community know when one of them died, to collect alms in order to bury them, and to order masses for their souls, and so that those who were poor could be assisted from time to time with a contribution.

Cordeiro: We are still missing some details.

Souza: Don't be in such a hurry, as I have not yet finished.

Cordeiro: Excuse me, I thought that you had forgotten and so I reminded you.

Souza: I certainly have not forgotten.

Cordeiro: Have the kindness to continue.

Souza: Yes, Sir. [Our practices are] contrary to those of the blacks from Angola, who not only collect alms to bury their deceased kinsmen but have the indecency to drag the cadavers that are going to the tomb of the Santa Casa [through the streets], placing them at the doors of their parishes in order to request alms from the faithful, to bury them with heathen and superstitious songs as I mentioned in the first chapter [of this dialogue]. However, when the most worthy criminal magistrate investigated this bad behavior, he imprisoned and punished them. And this is the reason that whites think that all of the blacks engage in the same practices as these individuals.

In 1748 I arrived in Rio de Janeiro from the city of Bahia, and I found this congregation already in existence, made up of *Mina* blacks from various *nation*s from that coast, such as *Dagome, Maki, Iano, Agolin, Sabaru*—all who used the lingua franca[18]—and they were united under their king, Pedro da Costa Mimoxo, who was

---

17. The Santa Casa de Misericórdia, literally "the Holy House of Mercy," was the confraternity designated by the Portuguese Crown to have the monopoly on burials in the Portuguese Empire. Although other confraternities also had their funeral biers and buried their dead, by law the *santas casas* actually had the right to control burials. They also were in charge of hospitals throughout the empire.

18. Mariza de Carvalho Soares identifies these names with the West African villages of *Agonli, Dassa,*

also from that *nation*. After he died they named Clemente de Proença to occupy that position, which he held for many years. As time went by, the blacks began to elect leaders of the *nations* among themselves and search for the preferences of the majority. Then there came the time when the *nations* of *Maki, Agolin, Iano*, and *Sabaru* left the rule of *Dagome*, scandalized and affronted by some of the sharp words that the *Dagomes* had said to them, and decided to name their own king, which they did with the person of Captain Ignacio Gonçalves do Monte in 1762, because he was a true *Makino*, and he was the first who was entered officially into the book and who improved and augmented this congregation....

Cordeiro: What I want is a continuation of the story.

Souza: I will continue it. With the passage of time, the other *nations* also distanced themselves—*Maki, Agolin*, and *Sabaru* each named their own king until the death of Ignacio Gonçalves on December 25, 1783, when you obligated me, using the law, to assume this position. And you never gave me the first thing that I requested: that this corporation never use the title of king.

All: But you govern and administer us, and we treat you like a father as we should, and, moreover, the title comes from the original founders.

Souza: Come from where it may, but I am not responsible for the mistakes of the founders, nor am I responsible in this matter. I am saying that this title will not be used anymore because it is dissonant in the ears of those who hear it, because it causes disruption in the harmony and devotion we have with those close to us. We must give a title that is suitable to our devotion.

All: What title can we give?

Souza: The title of *regent* is the appropriate one for what we are undertaking.

All: All right, but you should not take from us what is our right and our pleasure, that we have had for so many years.

Souza: What is the right that you say you have?

All: To not rid ourselves of our positions and titles that are an imitation of the nobles of the Kingdom of *Maki*, that we use among ourselves to distinguish the important from the less important, between the noble and the artisan, so that we maintain respect among ourselves.

[Souza Appoints the New Leadership]

Souza: Everything must be done with good harmony and order, without offending anyone. What you want is that I give titles like they do here in the land of the whites, isn't that it?

All: Yes, sir.

Souza: As you gave me power and faculty to do everything, I now name those who are the most zealous and caring, who foster hope among you and serve well the congregation.

All: We are all ready with good will to hear what you have to say.

Souza: Is Luiz Rodrigues Silva here?

Za, and *Savalu* ("Can Women Guide and Govern Men?" 85). Because these groups all came from the same region around the Bight of Benin, they had a common trading language, a lingua franca, that was used there and that could also be used in Brazil.

Silva: Sir, I am here, ready to obey the lord *regent*.

Souza: Raise the hand of Senhor Gonçalo Cordeiro.

Silva: For what post?

Souza: For secretary of this congregation.

All: Viva our *regent*, viva Senhor Secretary! May God preserve you for many years to fulfill your obligation.

Souza: José Antônio dos Santos will be *jacobû de Atoqquem*,[19] which is the same as duke here, and he is the first counselor with the first key to the safe.[20]

All: Well done! Viva and viva!

Souza: Alexandre de Carvalho will be *eceçûm valûm*, which is also like duke, and he will be the second on the counsel with the second key to the safe.

Marçal Soares will be *alolû belppôn lifoto*, also duke, and third on the counsel with the third key to the safe.

Boaventura Fernandez Braga will be *acolû cocoti de Daça*, duke, second secretary, and the fourth counselor with the key to the inner part of the safe.

José Luis will be *ajacôto chaûl de Zá*, which is like marques here, and fifth on the counsel.

Luiz da Silva will have the position of *ledô*, which is the same as count, and will be sixth counselor.

Luis Rodrigues Silva will be *aggaû*, which is the same as general.

And José da Silva will also be *aggaû*. Because it is already late and we would have only a short amount of time to finish the entry, we will finish the rest on another occasion.

All: Viva our regent for the wisdom he bestowed! ...

[The Legal Record of Souza's Installation]

Cordeiro: Official entry of obligation and inauguration of the freed blacks and subjects of the *Maki nation*, in which they elected Francisco Alves de Souza to be their *regent* and administrator, as we declare and sign below and at the same time inaugurate him. The inauguration, obligation, and nomination have been done in the following way:

Captain Ignacio Gonçalves do Monte was our *regent*, and the administrator of the alms that we use to celebrate masses for the souls of our deceased brothers of the *Mina nation*, and we subjected ourselves to all he decided. We elect to that position Francisco Alves de Souza, a freed black, married with possessions, and declare that he has all the necessary requisites to do a good job in the position, and also because he was second in command to the deceased and substituted for him, demonstrating his ability with zeal and promptness, that we name him *regent* and give to him all that

---

19. *Jacobû de Atoqquem, eceçûm valûm, alolû belppôn lifoto, acolû cocoti de Daça, ajacôto chaûl de Zá, ledô,* and *aggaû* appear to be terms for positions of authority derived from or in a West African language spoken by the *Mina Makis*.

20. The safes of the Brazilian confraternities held the most important possessions and the money of the organizations. The safes would often have several locks, each with different keys, to prevent one person from stealing the contents. The most important people in the organizations would keep the keys, but all had to be present to open the safe.

the deceased had, subjecting ourselves to all that he determines and taking away all the power and dominion that the wife of the deceased has or desires, because under no circumstances can she be *regent* and administrator, because it is against the laws. Nor can we ever be ruled over by a woman. It is our wish to concede to [Souza] all of our powers that by law are conceded to us, without coercion from anyone. We do this on our own so that our election and inauguration will be known for all time. We name you [Souza] and recognize you as our *regent* and as the good administrator of the souls of our departed brethren. All of us sign and ask the clerk Antônio Francisco Soares that he sign as witness, Rio de Janeiro, March 20, 1784; and I, Gonçalo Cordeiro, secretary of the *regent*, wrote [the entry] and signed below.

> As witness who made this and signed
> Antônio Francisco Soares
> Gonçalo Cordeiro
> Wherein all signed, as can be seen....

[The Official Statutes for the Devotion to the Souls of Purgatory][21]

Souza: Who is knocking? Come in, the door is open.

Cordeiro: How did you pass the night?

Souza: Very well. At your service.

Cordeiro: I come with pleasure, knowing that you have already finished the statutes.... I admire your energy and the way you get things done with such promptness.

Souza: In the name of the Holy Trinity, Father, Son, and Holy Spirit, three distinct persons in one true God, etc.

We, the *regent* and the important men of the congregation of the *Mina Maki* blacks, desiring this [congregation] to increase in the service of God and have its statutes by which it is governed, knowing each his obligation, in order to serve our fellow kinsmen with our devoted assistance and alms for their souls. The most loyal Christians would receive edifying impressions seeing how much we are able to do, knowing to be charitable to each other as commanded in the following statutes[22]:

Chapter One   There will be in this congregation one *regent* and one *regenta*[23] selected by a vote and by the will of all. There will also be a vice-*regent* who will sometimes take the place of the *regent*.

---

21. There is no clear break in the text preceding this section, but the date on the statutes indicates that two years have passed since Souza's installation.

22. Statutes were legal documents that officially incorporated the brotherhoods. They were a list of rules that after the Pombaline Reforms in the mid-eighteenth century were supposed to be authorized by the *Mesa de Conciência e Ordens* (Board of Conscience and Orders) in Lisbon, which was the branch of the government that oversaw church affairs. Statutes often postdated the actual formation of the organizations, as can be seen in this case, and sometimes brotherhoods never sent them to be reviewed.

23. Literally a female regent. Souza's wife, Rita Sebastiana, becomes *regenta* in this instance, but the statutes do not require that the *regenta* be the wife of the regent in future elections. In other black confraternities, the head female (often designated the queen) was not related to the king.

Chapter Two   The people who are elected to be *regent* will be from the *Mina* Coast and the Kingdom of *Maki*; no other nation can be elected.

Chapter Three   Every person who would like to join this congregation—except for blacks from Angola—will be examined by the secretary of the group and by the *aggaû*, which is the same as the general procurator, to make sure that they are not blacks that engage in abuses and heathen or superstitious practices. If it is found that they do engage in these practices they will not be allowed to join.

Chapter Four   All of the people in this congregation will be devoted to God and to His Holy Mother Mary and to the Saints of the Court of Heaven, especially the saints of their names, and the guardian angels of the souls in purgatory, for whom will be celebrated masses every day, especially Mondays, if possible, because they are the days dedicated by the church for their commemoration.…

Chapter Five   This congregation was created to offer charity to our kinsmen and with these foundations: it should be known that, first, we are obligated to accompany the burials of all who are from our *nation* and are members of this congregation, even if they are also members of another brotherhood.…

Chapter Six   Members who are freed but become sick will be helped by the congregation, first, by the *regent* and the *regenta* who will help, with charity and decency, and after them others will help. If the sick person is very poor, lacking money for whatever he needs, the *regent* will take necessary measures, calling together all of the important men of the congregation and the treasurer, so that they can vote on how much money to take from the safe to help our sick countryman. If the sick person is near death and the experts have given up, they will call the priests for confession and to prepare [them] to receive the Holy Sacrament, making his testament according to the Catholic Faith.

Chapter Seven   Slave members who want to buy their freedom with their own money but are missing part of their payment will tell the *regent* so that he can take measures to gather together the congregation to collect the necessary money to make a loan to buy the freedom. The secretary will make an entry in the book of obligation to pay back the loan.

Chapter Eight   The general procurator will be responsible for gathering news of [members of] the congregation, visiting them and seeing if they are sick, in order to tell the *regent*, also noting whether there are discords, making those people go before the *regent* in order to set things straight, because many times a little flare-up will become a huge fire and we desire among ourselves peace and unity, as Christ commanded His apostles.

Chapter Nine   There will be in this congregation one safe with two inside drawers, and for the good governance of this organization it will be locked with three keys. The *regent* will carry out an election of those most authorized in the congregation, giving a key to each [of those elected] with their titles of treasurer. The keys to the inside drawers belong to the *regent* or whoever substitutes for him. When it is necessary to open the safe, the *regent* will summon the treasurers so that each one can open it with his key, so that no one can open the safe without the others being there.

Chapter Ten   The position of *regent* in this congregation is the highest and most venerated, and for this reason we owe him obedience with total respect. Whoever does not demonstrate obedience will be punished according to the will of the *regent*, and the same will go for his wife and all that have titles in the organization.

Chapter Eleven   All of the members who miss a funeral of a fellow member will be fined. Those who are freed, who do not have a legitimate reason, will pay a fine of 120 *réis*,[24] which will be put in the safe as a punishment for their contempt and negligence; and those who are slaves who do not have a good reason will pay 60 *réis*. Those who have a legitimate reason because of their occupations will be required to pray an Our Father and a Holy Mary with a Gloria, offering these prayers to the Holy Passion of Christ for the souls of their deceased kinsman. On the other hand, a freed person who has a good reason for not accompanying the burial will pray the rosary of Christ's sacred death and passion for the soul of the deceased.

Chapter Twelve   When it is discovered that members of this congregation have engaged in bad behavior or been rebellious—either harming themselves, a third party, or others in the congregation—they will be called before a group that includes the *regent* and the other important men of the congregation. If they have been honestly warned three times and there have been no signs of improvement or obedience, they will be officially expelled. The expulsion will be entered in the book by the secretary and signed by the *regent* and the most important men and authorized by the entire congregation. This rule also holds true for the women, some of whom are proud, fond of intrigue, and disturbers of peace and quiet.

Chapter Thirteen   Because we have seen from experience that a festive royal court in the black brotherhoods is very useful, as much to lift the spirits of the blacks as to bring together again those from afar, we will have [a royal court] in our congregation. . . . We desire that on the day of Our Lady of the Rosary there be a festive royal court composed from this *Maki nation* that will accompany the King of Our Lady of the Rosary if he is from the *Mina Coast*, and if not [from that coast] the *Maki* court will not accompany him and will only be permitted to go to the palace of the most illustrious Senhor viceroy.[25] After these festivities, everyone

---

24. Portuguese currency used in Brazil in the eighteenth century.

25. Throughout Brazil, the biggest confraternity feast day celebration of the blacks was that of Our Lady of the Rosary. The rosary confraternities had a king and queen, often designated the King and Queen of *Congo* (although they often came from different African regions). The feast day celebration

will go back to their homes with complete quiet and calm, which is required at these functions.

Chapter Fourteen   All of us, except for the workers and the elderly, will fast every Monday during Lent. We will hear a mass, and those who can read will say the nine praises to Saint Gregory, which are commonly called the *Novena* for the Souls, and those who do not know how to read will pray nine Our Fathers and Ave Marias with the Gloria, all of them dedicated to the souls in purgatory.

Chapter Fifteen   This congregation will have four books. One book will be to list the membership of the group, one for certifications of the Masses, one for accounts, and one for statutes, and it is the secretary's obligation to keep them clean and clear, with all of the clarity and simplicity that is required.

Chapter Sixteen   Everyone who is a member of this congregation must be humble, because humility is one of the virtues that elevates [us] in the eyes of God, and one that our Lord practiced while in this world and commended to his sacred apostles, as you see in various places in the books....

These statutes were written in Rio de Janeiro on January 31, 1786, and I, Gonçalo Cordeiro, Secretary, sign them.

Gonçalo Cordeiro

The *Regent* Francisco Alves de Souza...

[The Widow Wins the Case against Souza and Cordeiro's Faction]

Cordeiro: Two years have passed that you have governed us.

Souza: Yes, they have. But the widow of the deceased, as far as I can see, has not returned anything that belongs to the congregation....

[Luiz Rodrigues] Silva: I am very upset....

Cordeiro: What is the matter and what happened to you?

Silva: I have come to give information to the *regent* that the lawsuit that we brought against the widow of Captain Monte came out in her favor. She does not have to return the safe or the other things that belong to our congregation, and I am appalled to see the hypocrisy that she practiced with us, knowing full well that it cost our money....

Souza: How did the sentence come out?

Cordeiro: The most important clause is that the entry we made [in our books] is without effect, and that she, the widow, will be treasurer or keeper of the safe, and you have no more powers at all.

Silva: I appealed to the high court; so we shall see.

Cordeiro: What happened at the high court, Senhor Luiz Rodrigues Silva?

Silva: The sentence was confirmed.

---

would include a long procession, often accompanied by different groups of "ambassadors" playing instruments and singing. The king would come accompanied by his court, or in Portuguese, his *estado*. In Rio, according to this testimony, it appears that they would end up at the house of the viceroy, where, if the king were not from the *Mina Coast*, the *Maki* would meet them.

Cordeiro: The sentence does not give her any more power than to be a worthy treasurer, to guard the money that they gave her, and not to say that she is the empress of the *Mina Coast*, as you have been hearing. Nevertheless, she wanted to demand that we all contribute our alms, prohibiting us from going here and there[26] without her consent, which put us in a great bind. In fact, she ordered a copy of the sentence and with it made a formal petition to the illustrious and excellent viceroy, saying that they [we] did not want to fulfill the sentence of the high court and that our *regent* impeded us from going to her house to give her the money to put in the safe. Worse, she claimed that he was the head of an uprising and that the entire congregation wanted her to be *regent*. The petition was sent, and His Highness [the viceroy] sent for the King of Our Lady of the Rosary and our *regent*. He can recount better what happened there because he is here.

Souza: I am astonished by the great imprudence of this widow and the sentence that she won against her brothers, as she should not act thus. As for me, she has done all of the harm that she can. She has fabricated lies [with] her hateful rancor. She sent me a summons various times without me having given her the least cause, to the extent that she did not want me to go to the church of Our Lady of the Rosary, nor to that of Saint Iphigenia, dressed and with my retinue. Tell me, is this a person who has reason? At the same time this lady knew well the upbringing and education that I have and the respect with which her deceased husband regarded me—and that he did nothing without my counsel and blessing. But her maliciousness reached such a point that she sought any way possible to make me lose. She put together a lawsuit against her brothers and, as I said above, made the sinister formal petition to the Illustrious and Most Excellent Viceroy, complaining that I did not want to fulfill the sentence of the high court, accusing me [illegible] that I did not want to understand and that I was the head of an uprising, and that everyone in the congregation was on her side, and that I impeded them from going there. Seeing these complaints, His Excellency thought it well to call the King of Our Lady[27] and me to come to a meeting. After we arrived that same gentleman ordered me to say that if I wanted to go [to the rosary celebration] that I would have to go to the widow's house, meaning that in order to participate in the feast day celebration of the rosary I would have to go talk with the widow. If I went without talking to the widow, I would be arrested and punished. This is the order that I received in the meeting, which I fulfilled without the least discrepancy. You all can see the falseness and the hatred with which she intended to beat me, [and] if not for the pure kindness and mercy of His Excellency, which I do not deserve, condescending to dispatch the formal petition—that they fulfill the sentence— perhaps imagining my insignificance and innocence, which everyone recognizes, perhaps would have had me punished....

Cordeiro: ... Considering that you are not guilty of anything nor can anyone place guilt on you, knowing full well that you are obligated by law to be *regent* of our congregation, and we all voted for you as you can see in our official record, it is [ridiculous] to accuse you of crimes. This congregation is a devotion made by the will of

---

26. Probably the text means "going here and there" to collect alms.
27. The king of the confraternity of Our Lady of the Rosary.

all, not an obligation, because there were never statutes. For her to be *regent* it would have to be by the will of all and not by only four, because as we all see in the sacred and human stories, and even the heathen ones, whoever is king, is king by the will of the people. And so I have said what needs to be said in regard to this congregation, because the time will come when there is wider recognition of her bad conduct and proud intent and how she intends to destroy this beautiful devotion that her husband willed to you.

PART IV: CLAIMING AND DEFENDING RIGHTS

As Afro-Latinos gained familiarity with both the European legal system and the lettered culture, they engaged with them to claim and defend their rights. In the four chapters of Part IV, Afro-Latino speakers express a sense that their actions and attitudes are morally upstanding according to the standards of European law and Catholic doctrine and that it is their mostly European abusers who have violated these norms. Before the Portuguese Inquisition in Lisbon, Pernambuco slave Luiz da Costa expresses repugnance at his abusive master's forced act of sodomy and clearly frames the event as one of violent domination (Chapter 15).

In Lima, both María del Carmen Ollague and Manuela *Zamba* position themselves as faithful wives who have fulfilled their duties within the Church-sanctioned institution of marriage (Chapter 16). In Ollague's case, it is her husband who has violated the sanctity of marriage by abusing her and treating her as a slave, whereas Manuela *Zamba* accuses her owner of having imposed divorce on her by selling her husband to an owner who lives forty leagues away, thus impeding her proper marital life. Both women use the ecclesiastical court system to defend their vision and exercise of proper family life.

The case of Javier, *esclavo*, against his master in San Juan de la Frontera (Chapter 17) also revolves around ownership and demonstrates how slaves engaged the legal system to negotiate improvements in their living situation by obtaining permission to seek their sale to a new owner. In Javier's case, his master frustrates this attempt; Javier flees, and upon returning receives a punishment so cruel that it exceeds the stipulations of the legal system. Javier is able to bring the weight of the law to his side for protection.

The final case shows a quite different type of petition (Chapter 18), as the Puerto Rican father and son Manuel and Antonio Pérez request proper rewards for their military service to the Crown in Spain; their argument stands on a concept of self-worth and honor as well as on legal documentation. In all five cases, individuals of African descent claim a place of belonging and social standing as subjects of the Iberian empires and, as such, demand protection and recognition of their rights.

15

Confessing Sodomy, Accusing a Master: The Lisbon Trial of Pernambuco's Luiz da Costa, 1743[1]

Richard A. Gordon

Luiz da Costa was barely twenty years old when he was transported from Brazil to Portugal in 1743 to stand trial for sodomy before the Tribunal of the Portuguese Inquisition in Lisbon. Yet, this was not Luiz's first forced transatlantic migration. He arrived in the northeastern Brazilian region of Pernambuco by way of the *Middle Passage*, having been taken captive years earlier. His native land was the Costa da *Mina* in the region of present-day Ghana, Togo, and Benin. When Luiz da Costa was brought from Africa to Brazil, he encountered in Pernambuco an old, relatively wealthy, and densely populated colonial territory.

During much of the colonial period, Pernambuco encompassed not only the present-day state of Pernambuco, but also what are now the Rio Grande do Norte, Ceará, Paraíba, and Alagoas. It was one of the original *capitanias*, or captaincies into which the Portuguese King Dom João III had divided Portugal's South American claim in 1534. João III acted in order to establish an official presence in Brazil and thereby forestall French poaching of Brazil's first export product, the coveted *pau-brasil*, a wood from which red dye was extracted for use in the European textile industries. By the time Luiz arrived in Brazil in the 1720s, Pernambuco was no longer a captaincy. In 1654, it had been incorporated by the Portuguese Crown into the so-called *Estado do Brasil*.

Since its founding nearly two hundred years earlier, the region had witnessed substantial economic and political changes starting in 1534, when the captaincy of Pernambuco was under the leadership of Duarte Coelho and from 1630 until 1654, when Pernambuco was occupied by the Dutch. When the Dutch took possession of the territory in 1630, the capital was moved from Olinda to Recife, a few miles away. The sugar industry that was introduced in the region by Duarte Coelho continued to expand during the Dutch occupation.

Just a few years after gaining their emancipation from Spain at the end of sixty years under their neighbor's control, the Portuguese regained Pernambuco from the Dutch in 1654 and began to rebuild Portugal's colonial economy there. Pernambuco's population grew steadily. In 1693, there were an estimated 62,415 people under Portuguese control in the region (this figure excluded nonsubjugated indigenous inhabitants). This number grew to 67,280 by 1700 and escalated to 363,238 by 1777 (Wadsworth, 8). Throughout the colonial era, sugar dominated the physical, social, and economic landscape of this Brazilian state and provoked an enormous influx of African slaves. Luiz da Costa thus lived in a Pernambuco of intense demographic and cultural change.

---

1. See Maps 1, 4, and 6.

170

Luiz da Costa was probably not one of the many slaves who worked in a sugar mill. We can deduce from his Inquisition confession that he was more likely a domestic slave and that he may have lived in the interior of Pernambuco. Even though the population in Pernambuco clustered principally in the *zona da mata*, or costal region, there were also settlements inland within the arid *sertão* (hinterlands) and the transitional morphological region that divides the hinterlands from the coast, called the *agreste*.

Luiz's *processo* (trial proceedings) lists Vila da Boa Vista as his place of residence. It is not clear where exactly that was; there is no surviving population center with that name, and the comprehensive four-volume *Diccionario chorographico, historico e estatistico de Pernambuco* does not list any town with that name at the time of the 1743 trial. This might refer to the Recife neighborhood called Boa Vista, which dates back to the seventeenth century (Galvão, 71–97), although the neighborhood was never designated as a *vila* (a small town). In support of this conjecture is the fact that more than 90 percent of denunciations in Pernambuco to the Inquisition came from the coastal regions (Wadsworth, 47). However, it is more likely that he lived in the interior of the captaincy. Consistent with this possibility, Luiz da Costa mentions in his confession that he went hunting with his master, Manoel Alves Cabral, in the *sertão* near what he calls Aldeia de Bode, which likewise does not appear in the *Diccionário* but would seem to be located in a region quite distant from Recife.

It was during the hunting trip on which Luiz accompanied his master that the offense for which he stood trial took place. In his testimony at trial, Luiz accused Manoel Alves Cabral of having sodomized him under threat of death. A priest who was also in the hunting party, Manoel de Lima, did not witness the act but found Luiz fleeing and heard his story. Lima brought the case to the attention of the Inquisition, possibly with the cooperation of Luiz da Costa. Luiz da Costa might have seen an investigation and trial as preferable to the sexual advances that continued after that first incident, especially given the likelihood that he would be transported to Lisbon to stand trial.

Although some cases that fell under the jurisdiction of the Inquisition were adjudicated in Brazil by bishops, many trials took place in the Tribunal of Lisbon, which retained jurisdiction over Brazil, the Atlantic islands, and Africa (see Wadsworth, especially chapters 1–3). In contrast with the Spanish Inquisition, which established tribunals in Mexico City (1571), Lima (1570), and Cartagena (1610; Wadsworth, 24), Brazil never had its own Inquisition tribunal (a distinction between Spanish America and Brazil that parallels the lack of universities and printing presses in Brazil and their long-standing presence in the Spanish-American colonies).

Rather, the Portuguese Inquisition sent representatives to Brazil several times to evaluate cases in the early years while Portugal was under Spanish control (for example, 1591–1595 to Bahia and Pernambuco; 1618–1620 to Bahia). Subsequently, in particular after the turn of the eighteenth century, the Inquisition developed a substantial network of lay and ecclesiastical representatives in Brazil.

In Pernambuco during Lent, the behaviors prohibited by the Inquisition were publicized, and residents were required to denounce transgressions and confess their own, information that would presumably be communicated to the Portuguese Inquisition. It was likely that Luiz da Costa's case was processed initially through these channels in Brazil and that the initiator of the case was the priest who Luiz states witnessed some of the events that he refers to in his confession. In some cases, the Lisbon tribunal sent back word that certain accused Brazilians were to be shipped to Portugal for trial, an eventuality that befell Luiz da Costa.

Notwithstanding the lack of Inquisition tribunals in Brazil during the period just preceding Luiz's trial (1709–1737), Brazilians represented more than 50 percent of those punished in Lisbon in *autos-da-fé* (Wadsworth, 47). This was the case, although the overall prosecutions of the Portuguese Inquisition had been declining. The Portuguese Inquisition, which lasted almost three centuries, from 1536 to 1821, carried out 22,481 investigations (with 863 executions) in the ninety years from 1584 to 1674; yet there were only 12,142 investigations (with 446 executions) in the same span from 1675 to 1767 (Wadsworth, 45).

The most common accusations in Pernambuco were, in order of frequency, Judaism, bigamy, witchcraft—a common accusation against African slaves, along with blasphemy—and heretical propositions (Wadsworth, 47). Although offenses such as bigamy and sodomy were not technically considered heresy, they were prosecuted by the Inquisition, as such acts were seen to compromise the sacrament of marriage (Vainfas, "Inquisição," 270–71) and thus constituted, by extension, *erros de fé* (crimes against faith). Formal heresy was defined as a baptized Christian voluntarily refusing to believe in some tenet of the Catholic Church and manifesting that conviction either mentally or externally (Mott, "Sodomia," 254).

Sodomy, which became part of the Spanish Inquisition's purview in 1509 (Vainfas, "Inquisição," 269) and the Portuguese Inquisition's in 1553 (Mott, "Sodomia," 254), accounted for around four hundred of the total full Inquisition trials (of around five thousand denunciations). Thirty of these defendants were burned in *autos-da-fé* by the river Tejo in Lisbon, after being *relaxados*, meaning they were turned over for execution to the civil authorities, who alone were allowed to carry out executions (Higgs, 113; for a description of the severe civil penalties for sodomy in Spain and Portugal beginning in 1603, see Lara, *Ordenações*, 91).

The Portuguese Inquisition prosecuted cases of *sodomia perfeita* or *consumada*—sodomy with phallic anal penetration as well as ejaculation—but not what was referred to as *molície*—all other homoerotic acts (see Vainfas, "Inquisição," 275; and Mott, "Sodomia," 255). Luiz da Costa refers to both *sodomia consumada* and *molície* in his confession. Luiz Mott ("Sodomia," 253) argues that after *New Christians*, sodomites were the social group most persecuted by the Portuguese Inquisition. It was not uncommon in colonial Brazil for Inquisition cases of sodomy to derive, as in Luiz da Costa's case, from abuses of disparate power relations, specifically that of slavery (Vainfas, "Inquisição," 277).[2]

Roughly one year passed between the attack on Luiz da Costa and his trial, but, once he reached the Inquisition jail in Lisbon, his prosecution was expeditious. This was not always the case; some trials lasted for months and even years. He was taken

---

2. For more information about sodomy as part of rape, as in Luiz da Costa's case, as well as extensive research on voluntary homoeroticism in Brazil and Portugal prosecuted by the Inquisition, see Higgs; Mott; Pieroni; and Vainfas.

into custody in Lisbon on July 23, 1743, tried on July 30, and sentenced on August 16. And his punishment, a reprimand and injunction to not commit such acts again, was extremely light. As his trial proceedings make clear, the tribunal took into consideration the extenuating circumstances of this case.

Inquisitors at the time sought testimony regarding whether or not sodomy was voluntary or forced, the age of the defendants, and the specific circumstances of the acts (Vainfas, "Inquisição," 275). Although a modern reader may abhor the notion that a rape victim would be prosecuted for the sexual act of the rape—or indeed for any offense to a moral *paradigm* (consider, however, that U.S. laws criminalizing sodomy remained in effect until 2003)—Luiz da Costa's treatment was relatively lenient; the 1603 secular law called for the burning of any sodomite under any circumstances. Even notwithstanding the particular circumstance of Luiz's case,[3] its outcome coincided with a general trend toward less severe punishments in cases of sodomy compared to those of the seventeenth century (see, for example, Higgs, 113).

Luiz da Costa's brief trials consisted of several key parts: the assignment of a guardian to him, as he was under the age of twenty-five; his confession; the tribunal's certification of the evidence; the reprimand of the defendant; and the swearing of the defendant to secrecy. All of these procedures were presided over by the inquisitor Manoel Varejão Távora and recorded by a scribe, Manoel Afonso Rebelo. Both the rigid structure of the trial and the relaying of all words and actions by the scribe influenced how Luiz was able to tell his story and how it ultimately was expressed in the document.

There was very little opportunity for the prisoner to speak. For the most part, the trial proceedings show him to be largely a mute variable in a well-established pattern. The scribe narrates how Luiz da Costa was brought before the court a week after arriving in Lisbon and mechanically records the several obligatory components of the trial. In almost every aspect of the trial, he speaks no more than a few words. The one notable exception is the confession. The inquisitorial conventions mediate the manifestation of Luiz's point of view almost exclusively through this part of the trial.

Within the parameters of this section, the prisoner is allowed to tell his story with some degree of rhetorical autonomy. However, he still has to recount the events that led him to this trial in the form of a confession, rather than, say, in the form of a defense. In other words, even within this section of the trial he does not have free rein on what he says or how he says it. The communication of Luiz da Costa's version of the story is further delimited by the fact that it comes to us as indirect discourse paraphrased in the third person by the scribe. The scribe presumably edited not only the form of the prisoner's discourse but also some of the content, perhaps based on what he deemed most relevant or acceptable for recording.

Nonetheless, in his confession, we can perceive something of Luiz da Costa's voice despite the filter of the scribe's own subjectivity and his use of formulaic language. Therein lies the importance of this document. Luiz's testimony allows us to glimpse something of the story and perspective of a young African slave living in eighteenth-century Brazil. In the confession section, Luiz recalls at some length the events for

---

3. Ronaldo Vainfas points out that the most severely punished sodomites were the ones who caused public scandal ("Inquisição," 275).

which he is on trial, prodded initially by the admonition to bring to mind every detail. How exactly he tells his story, the way that he maneuvers rhetorically within the formal confines of the confession, can give us some insight into his point of view.

The order in which Luiz recounts events, for example, and his decisions to include certain details and exclude others reveal something of his individual perspective. At the end of the trial, his testimony, as recorded by the scribe Rebelo, is read to him, and he is made to swear that the version he hears (and that we read in the document below) is accurate and that he would change nothing. By approving the trial proceedings, Luiz would seem to recognize at least some of his own voice in the mediated narration of the scribe. By looking carefully at those moments in which echoes of Luiz da Costa's words emerge from within the delimiting conventions of the trial proceeding, we can gain rare access into this enslaved man's life from his own perspective.

*****

Trial of Luiz da Costa, Black Male, Single, Slave of Manoel Alves Cabral, Native of Costa da *Mina*, Resident of Vila da Boa Vista, Diocese of Pernambuco[4]

Inquisition of Lisbon
Nº 6, trial 45
In custody on July 23, 1743
Register of Guardianship

On the thirtieth day of July 1743, in Lisbon in the Third Office of Hearings [*Estaos e Casa terceira das audiências*][5] of the Holy Inquisition, the inquisitor Manoel Varejão Távora, being present in the morning session, commanded that Luiz da Costa, imprisoned defendant in these proceedings and also present, appear before him. Because Luiz da Costa said that he was under twenty-five years of age, the *licenciate* Felipe Néri, chaplain of the Penitence Prison and also present, was commanded to appear before the board. He was told that because Luiz da Costa[6] was a minor,[7] they designated him as his guardian so that he might lend Luiz his authority and make it possible for the young man to stand trial, and so that in the trial his actions might be legally valid. And the *licenciate* declared that he accepted the guardianship and that he would lend Luiz his authority in all ways necessary so that he could stand trial. And he swore to perform these duties under the authority of an oath on the Holy Gospels, which he was administered.

I, Manoel Afonso Rebelo, wrote it.

Manoel Varejão Távora

Confession

On the thirtieth day of July 1743, in Lisbon in the Third Office of Hearings of the Holy Inquisition, the inquisitor Manoel Varejão Távora, being there in the morning session, commanded that a man come before him who on the twenty-third day of the current month and year was received into the custody of the prison of this Inquisition, ... and who had requested a hearing. And being present ... and having asked to confess his misdeeds, he was administered the oath of the Holy Gospels, on which he placed his hand, and under the authority of which he was commanded to tell the truth and to maintain secrecy, all of which he swore to fulfill.

And he said that he was called Luiz da Costa, black male, slave of Manoel Alves Cabral; no one knows who his parents were; native of Costa da *Mina* and resident of Vila da Boa Vista, Diocese of Pernambuco; more or less twenty years of age.

---

4. Arquivo Nacional da Torre do Tombo, Lisbon, Processos da Inquisição, Inquisição de Lisboa no. 6, processo 45, microfilm call number M.F. 2592.

5. The name designating the buildings in which the Lisbon Inquisition carried out its court sessions and where prisoners were kept.

6. To facilitate the reading, from here on I use the name "Luiz da Costa" or "Luiz" where the document repeats designations like "prisoner" or "confessant."

7. People who were under twenty-five years old.

And then he was advised that, because he had decided to follow such good counsel as to desire to confess his misdeeds, it would very much behoove him to recall all of them so that he might form from them a whole and true confession, not imputing, however, to himself or to others false testimony, for only the telling of the truth is proper for clearing his conscience, saving his soul, and satisfactorily resolving his case.

... To which he responded that he would tell only the truth, which was that more or less a year ago, while he was ... in Aldeia de Bode, in the hinterlands of Pernambuco, with his master Manoel Alves Cabral, they went hunting in the woods. And when they were alone his master induced him to commit acts of sodomy, threatening and intimidating him with the musket that he had, saying that he would kill him if he did not consent to what he intended to effectuate. And in spite of the repugnance that he felt, obliged by fear he consented to the turpitude, realizing with ... his master a consummated act of sodomy, there being ejaculation and penetration in his posterior orifice, ... performing Luiz the passive role and his master the active. And on many other occasions, and in diverse places [his master] had attempted to induce him into the same turpitude, though he had never again managed to practice it with him, ... due to Luiz's repugnance and his disinclination to consent to it. And only to see himself free from his master's harassment did he consent to practice with him other sinful sexual acts,[8] which he made on repeated occasions. And he additionally declares that on the above-mentioned occasion in which he went hunting with his master there was also in the party a priest called Manoel de Lima, who did not witness the referred incident due to the fact that he was hunting deep in the woods, which prevented him from seeing for himself the said fact, and observed only ... that Luiz was fleeing from his master around a dwelling, because of which he ... later asked Luiz what that was all about, and ... Luiz related to him the facts in the manner in which they are articulated above.

He also stated that ... while in the house of his master with another black called José, also a slave of the same master, and while they were both sleeping in a bed, his master came repeatedly to be with them at night while they were sleeping and got into the bed between them. Luiz clearly and distinctly perceived ... deeds with said black José, acts of consummated sodomy, which said black later declared to him to have been exactly what he had comprehended.

And these are the misdeeds that he has to confess to this board, misdeeds that he had committed ... because his master had coerced him and intimidated him in the way in which he has declared above and must have committed. He asks for forgiveness and that he be shown mercy and said no more.

He was told that he followed good counsel in initiating his confession of his misdeeds before this board, all of which he should recall so that he might form from them a whole and true confession. [The inquisitors] ... caution him and strongly recommend that he distance himself and flee the company of anyone who might pervert him and induce him in any way ... to commit again similar misdeeds, because if he does not mend his ways he will be punished with the full force of the law.

---

8. *Pecados de molície*, a term that referred to all sexual acts besides anal coitus (e.g., masturbation, fellatio).

And because he said that he had no more misdeeds to confess, he was once again advised...and sent to his prison after he was read this, his confession, which he heard and understood in the presence of his guardian and said that it was written truly and that he affirmed it, ratified it, and that he would say the same thing over again if necessary, and that he had nothing to add, remove, change, or correct,...under the authority of the same oath on the Holy Gospels, which he was again administered.

This was witnessed by the honest and religious people there present who saw and heard everything and swore to respond truly to anything they were asked under the authority of an oath on the Holy Gospels: the *licenciates* Francisco de Souza and Manoel da Silva Diniz, notaries of this Inquisition, who signed with...[Luiz da Costa], his guardian, and the inquisitor.

> I, Manoel Afonso Rebelo, wrote it.
> Manoel Varejão Távora
> Of Luiz [+] da Costa[9]
> Felipe Néri
> Francisco de Souza
> Manoel da Silva Diniz

And [Luiz da Costa] having left...for his cell, the above said *licenciates* were asked if it seemed to them that he spoke the truth and if his testimony deserved certification, and they said that it seemed to them that he spoke the truth and that his testimony deserved certification, and they once again signed with the inquisitor.

> I, Manoel Afonso Rebelo, wrote it.
> Manoel Varejão Távora
> Francisco de Souza
> Manoel da Silva Diniz

Certification of the Evidence

I, Manoel Afonso Rebelo, notary of the Holy Office of the Inquisition of Lisbon, who wrote the preceding confession of defendant Luiz da Costa, certify [that]...the inquisitor Manoel Varejão Távora [told me that] he certified [the confession], which I, the notary, also certify, and which I recorded by order of the inquisitor, and which I with him signed. Lisbon in the Holy Office on the thirtieth day of July 1743.

> Manoel Varejão Távora.
> Manoel Afonso Rebelo
> Being this trial recorded in these registers by order of the inquisitors, I concluded it.
> I, Manoel Afonso Rebelo, wrote it.
> [official mark]

The Board of the Holy Office of this Inquisition of Lisbon saw the directory of testimony, sent to it by the Diocese of Pernambuco, regarding the confessor Luiz da

---

9. The cross, Luiz da Costa's signature, is slightly taller than it is wide and appears in the indicated space between his first and last names as written by the scribe.

Costa, black, slave, single, native of Costa da *Mina*, resident of Vila da Boa Vista, Diocese of Pernambuco; and the confession that said man made to this board. And it seemed to all of the members of the board that taking into consideration the circumstances... and the confession, Luiz da Costa should be advised and reprimanded by this board and that he should atone for his misdeeds. Lisbon, meeting of the board, on the thirteenth day of August 1743.

     Francisco Machado
     Simão José
     Manoel Varejão
     Tiago [official mark]
     Silvio Lobo
     M. Távora
     Diogo Lopes [official mark]
     Joachim Jansen Moller [official mark]

Register of Reprimand

On the sixteenth day of the month of August 1743, in Lisbon in the Office of Sentencing of the Holy Inquisition, being there in the morning session, the inquisitors commanded that Luiz da Costa, imprisoned defendant in these proceedings, be brought from the custody prison and be made to appear before them. And being present and severely reprimanded by said inquisitors, he was told that he not commit again nor consent to these misdeeds... [for which] he was received into the custody of the prison of this Inquisition, nor other similar misdeeds under pain of being gravely punished, and that for now he can go wherever he liked, all of which... [Luiz da Costa] swore to perform in the manner in which they ordered under the authority of an oath on the Holy Gospels, which he was administered, from which I made this writ of the said inquisitors with whom Luiz da Costa signed with his guardian, in the presence of whom it was read to him, and by whom it was heard and understood.

     I, Manoel Afonso Rebelo, wrote it.
     Francisco Machado
     Simão José
     Manoel Varejão Távora
     Tiago [official mark]
     Silvio Lobo
     D[e] Luiz [+] da Costa
     Felipe Néri

Register of Secrecy

On the sixteenth day of the month August of 1743, in Lisbon in the Office of Sentencing [*Estaos e Casa do despacho*] of the Holy Inquisition, being there in the morning session, the inquisitors commanded that Luiz da Costa, imprisoned defendant in these proceedings, be brought from the custody prison and be made to appear before them. And being present he was administered the oath of the Holy Gospels, on which he placed his hand, and under the authority of which he was ordered to maintain in strict secrecy all that he saw and heard in these prisons and all that happened with him regarding his trial, and that he not reveal any of it by word or writing or by any other means, under pain of being gravely punished. He swore to perform all of this under the authority of said oath, from which this writ of the said inquisitors was made. He signed with them and with his guardian.

I, Manoel Afonso Rebelo, wrote it.

Francisco Machado

Simão José

Manoel Varejão

Tiago [official mark]

Silvio Lobo

M. Távora

De Luis [+] da Costa

Felipe Néri

A. Secret   240

Alcaide of Secrets   200

[illegible]   100

Cta [??]   036

Guardian Néri   400

      976

Lima [official mark]

16

Slavery, Writing, and Female Resistance: Black Women Litigants in Lima's Tribunals of the 1780s[1]

Maribel Arrelucea Barrantes

Document translation by Joseph P. Sánchez, Angelica Sánchez-Clark, and Larry D. Miller

A Historical Problem

Regardless of ethnicity, social status, and gender, everyone in colonial Lima came to court to solve diverse commonplace conflicts.[2] For this reason, it is revealing to analyze how Lima's black women, both slave and freed, used colonial law and in what cases and how they related to written documents. A focus on slave women and freed women as litigants allows us to see them as more than objects or victims. Women participated in their society and their time, learned to employ cultural codes without needing to read or write, and attempted in court to solve conflicts with other people, whether they were owners, husbands, or patrons.

In short, black female slaves and freed women who used the courts acted openly as historical agents with their own voices, ideas, and objectives. For colonial Quito, Kimberly Gauderman has demonstrated that not all women were victims of a social order based on patriarchal relations of power; many took independent actions, used the legal system to protect their social and economic interests, and punished men who abused them (Gauderman, 8). The documents in this chapter also challenge the prevalent view of colonial society as being so hierarchical and patriarchal that it prevented enslaved women from employing legal strategies on their own behalf.

Church and State as Normative Institutions

Both Church and state governed colonial society, dictating rules and punishments and often entirely confusing the lines of jurisdiction over the public and private affairs of clergy and lay people. Acting for Spain, the colonial state dictated the norms and laws, administered justice through the *Real Audiencia* (Lima's royal court), and publicly punished lawbreakers.[3] The Ecclesiastic Tribunal also heard cases brought by aristocrats and plebeians, men and women, whites and blacks. A large portion of the city's subaltern

---

1. See Maps 6 and 10.
2. In earlier publications, I noted a strong tendency to litigate especially among subaltern women (Arrelucea, "Esclavitud"; "Poder femenino"; "Poder masculino").
3. Punishments included whippings and mutilation in the public *plaza*, and prisoners worked in public works and in bakeries, wearing chains and with the doors open, because the colonial system believed that public punishments intimidated the rest of the population and discouraged rebelliousness. See Flores Galindo; Aguirre, "Mujeres delincuentes."

population appealed more frequently to the Ecclesiastic Tribunal than to the secular courts because the former was considered closer to God and, therefore, more just.

Slaves went to the Ecclesiastic Tribunal because it gave them an advantage. Unlike the secular courts, the ecclesiastic courts offered slaves an unusual equality with the free population: they were all considered children of God with souls. As such, slaves were evangelized and administered the sacraments, and their faith was monitored to prevent a return to idolatry. Consequently, in cases of excessive cruelty, slaves went first to the Church because there they could present themselves as defenseless creatures new to the faith and needing protection.[4]

In a similar fashion, the Church regulated marriage and sexuality for all individuals, including slaves, favoring free choice in marriage. The Church distinguished between the sacrament of marriage given by God and the institution of slavery created by human beings. Thus, in the face of owners' opposition to slaves' marrying, the Church often compelled owners to buy the other spouse in order to protect the marriage (Trujillo Mena, 297–333). Slaves converted this ecclesiastic protection of marriage into a legal weapon.

If an owner decided to sell a slave outside Lima, the spouse appealed to the Ecclesiastic Tribunal and engaged the power of the written word and the ecclesiastic law to block the sale. As María Emma Mannarelli points out, the Church also determined how people should lead their sexual lives—what was licit, under what conditions, and with whom. According to the Church, the principal function of sex was the configuration of the domestic and social order through the regulation of desire and the control of sexual conduct. In each parish, ecclesiastic investigators monitored these affairs ("Vínculos," 347–48). Thus, the Ecclesiastic Tribunal offered the best space to sanction those who broke the Church's own dictates.

Slaves' Rights

Spanish law considered slaves property without rights over their labor, bodies, earnings, or personal time. However, Spanish law also granted slaves two important rights: to seek *manumission* and to protect their personal safety. The first allowed slaves to buy their freedom, and the second prohibited *sevicia*, understood as excessive ill treatment that placed the slave's life in danger because of inadequate nourishment, clothing, or medicine or that prevented the slave from marrying and living a conjugal life.[5]

In addition, Spanish law made similar concessions to indigenous peoples, establishing tribunals and special functionaries such as the *protector de naturales* (legal advocate for indigenous people) to make separate laws for each social and ethnic group in colonial society. Native peoples also learned to use the special legislation, the legal maneuvers, written documents, and argumentation and tricks of the judicial system to defend, among other rights, their rights to communal land ownership, the

---

4. From an early date, Lima's church insisted that new slaves from Africa receive baptism, attend mass, confess, take communion, and participate in religious processions (*Segundo Concilio Provincial Limense*, 1567, chapters 126 and 127 in Trujillo Mena, 297–333).

5. These basic principles are found in the most ancient Spanish laws, such as, *Las Siete Partidas del rey Alfonso el sabio*, Partida IV, Título 21, Leyes 1–15 (see Alfonso el sabio) and are repeated in the *Recopilación de Leyes de Indias*, Libro VII, Título V, Leyes 1–10 (see *Recopilación Consejo de Indias*).

use of irrigation water and pastures, and marriage and to resist tribute payments and the *mita* labor drafts. Both indigenous people and slaves perceived these legal rights as opportunities; for this reason, from a very early moment, they developed a strong tendency to use legislation in the tribunals to defend their rights.

Even though the majority of the cases preserved in the Archivo General de la Nación (*Audiencia* cases) and the Archivo Arzobispal de Lima (ecclesiastical cases) were written and signed by notaries and secretaries, rather than by slaves themselves, this fact alone does not prove that slaves were ignorant of the judicial system. On the contrary, exhaustive analysis of the cases, the legal strategies, the declarations, the evidence, and the accusations themselves show that slaves litigated knowing what they could obtain (Jouve Martín, 185; Arrelucea, "Poder femenino," 86). The documentary evidence allows an analysis of the legal strategies employed by people who were unable to read or write, because one did not need formal academic skills to enter the judicial terrain. In addition, any literate person with access to ink and paper could write to the Ecclesiastic Tribunal because no expensive sealed paper or rigid formulas were required.

Ethnicity and Gender Difference before the Courts

The 173 cases presented between 1760 and 1820 by male and female slaves in Lima's *Real Audiencia* and the Ecclesiastic Tribunal fell into specific categories; 113 cases corresponded to women, revealing two principal concerns: petitions for freedom (twenty-six female slaves and nineteen male slaves) and the prevention of their sale or that of family members outside Lima (twenty-five female slaves and fifteen male slaves). The next most important concerns were cruelty by the master (twenty female slaves and eleven male slaves) and freedom to marry (eighteen female slaves and seven male slaves).

The cases suggest Lima's slaves most vigorously defended the right to buy their freedom, to control their own bodies, and to dispose of their labor and their time. The other issues litigated questioned the exercise of owners' authority by opposing excessive cruelty, sale outside Lima, and interference in conjugal life, any of which threatened the dense webs of social connections, family, and friends woven by Lima's slaves.

Cases	Litigants Men	Litigants Women	Total
Cruelty by the owner	11	20	31
Cruelty by the spouse	–	15	15
Sale outside Lima	15	25	40
Defense of marriage	7	18	25
Freedom	19	26	45
Retention of property	3	10	13
Retention of children	5	9	14
Total	**60**	**113**	**173**

Figure 3. Litigation by black slaves in the *Real Audiencia* and the Ecclesiastic Tribunal 1760–1820. Source: Based on the cases found in the Archivo Arzobispal de Lima (AAL), Causas de negros, and the Archivo General de la Nación (AGN), Real Audiencia, Causas Civiles.

Another problem litigated between masters and slaves involved slaves' property. According to the legal norms, a slave's earnings belonged to the slave owner.[6] But in practice, many slaves—especially wage earners—saved and bought with their own money a variety of items such as clothes, shoes, household goods, mules, and poultry.[7] When an owner decided to sell a slave, the problem arose of determining to whom these items belonged. Many slaves availed themselves of the courts to keep their personal property (ten female slaves and three male slaves).

Litigating over this issue meant questioning one aspect of slave owner power, and it appeared that female slaves were sometimes successful in keeping their property. For example, the *mulata* Josefa Escalé accused her master of spiritual cruelty and demanded the return of her furniture, jewelry, clothing, mattress, bed frame, and other household items. The slave owned a surprising number of luxury objects such as silk kerchiefs, shawls, and gloves.[8] These cases show that slave women distinguished clearly between the masters' property and their own, which they actively attempted to protect.[9]

By litigating, slave women questioned the norms governing property and a slave's earnings. These cases reveal that, to the extent that urban slavery relaxed the rules of bondage, flexible practices and rights humanized slaves and brought them closer to a semifreedom, which they used to press for more opportunities and to better conditions viewed as harsh and unjust.

Slaves also formed families. They had spouses and children, and they faced the same family problems as a free people, though these manifested certain characteristics imposed by slavery. Consequently, slaves developed strategies to defend familial bonds, such as securing the *manumission* of an enslaved wife before she conceived children, liberating small children before their price rose, looking for new owners closer to the household, and marrying residents of Lima so that attempts to separate the family could be appealed in court.

Twenty-five female slaves and fifteen male slaves opposed the sale of their spouses outside of Lima in court. Nine female slaves and five male slaves entered into litigation to block the sale of children or their separation from mothers. This documentary evidence reveals the concern of slaves, especially female slaves, for the protection of family, maternity, paternity, and affections. In addition, a gender analysis shows that female slaves turned to the courts with greater frequency than did male slaves, as they used the courts to combat the intrinsic problems of the institution of slavery: cruelty, deficient food, imprisonment in bakeries, excessive work days, and sale outside of Lima.

Women also approached the courts to demand more humane treatment, as when they complained of a husband's abuse, abandonment, or infidelity. Female slaves also denounced other slaves or freed blacks with whom they had conflicts, including those involving abuse, threats, fights, or insults. The tribunals were public spaces in which

---

6. Archivo General de la Nación, Lima, Causas Civiles, legajo 204, cuad. 2736, 1793.

7. Pioneering studies by Harth-Terré and Márquez Abanto ("El artesano negro"; "Historia de la casa") and Hünefeldt show that a relationship existed between slave wage earners, their capacity to accumulate savings, and the existence of effective strategies of action within the colonial system.

8. Archivo Arzobispal de Lima (AAL), Lima, Causas de negros, legajo 32, 1791.

9. Additional examples can be found in AAL, Lima, Causas de negros, legajo 32, 1792.

the problems between those of different status could be resolved when the parties could not find satisfactory solutions on their own.

A defense of ethnicity constituted another of the recurring arguments in the petitions presented by slaves. Many presented themselves as humble and poor, but when it was necessary to defend their honor or avoid being sold or punished, they claimed honor for their ethnic status: "It is difficult to grasp by what moral standard one can slander the character of a black just because of his [social] condition as a slave, simply because the information suits the *convento*'s purposes, and, because of some persons of status and character, such slander is declared in a public trial. And thus, from where the example should emanate, comes only our decline."[10] This case reveals how slaves could use the concept of black/slave (*negro/esclavo*) in different ways according to the circumstances. In this case, the slave questioned the common colonial stereotype that delinquency derived from race and social class.

Marriage and Abuse: The Voice of Female Litigants

The intermarriage of slaves and free blacks brought to light problems created by the differences of gender and ethnicity and the exercise of male power within marriage. An especially illustrative case (1787), featured in this chapter, involves María del Carmen Ollague, a recently freed black woman (*negra*) married to Manuel Cosío, a black (*negro*) slave.[11] In her complaint, María relates how, during twelve years of marriage, Manuel mistreated her: He beat her and forced her to work in the *pulpería* (shop) that belonged to both of them. Even though they had two slaves who worked for wages (*esclavos de jornal*), he made her do domestic work in front of everyone, humiliating her. Finally, he shut her up in a bakery to work in chains.

Her complaint reveals how black women articulated discourses by means of powerful concepts and images. María begins in a complaining tone, "During the prolonged period of our marriage, I have, of course, been nominally his wife, but in reality I have only been treated as a slave, because, far from the sacred treatment owed a legitimate wife, his actions have been the kind that a bad servant deserves." María compares the status of wife and slave for two reasons: first, because a wife was considered subject to the husband as a slave was to the master, and, second, because violence was permitted as part of conjugal relations just as it was in slave-master relations. For these reasons she compares her treatment to that deserved only by bad slaves.

Whether or not her arguments were truthful, María's objective was to stop the mistreatment by her husband. For this reason she requested to be "sent to a convent, where my aforementioned husband shall be obliged to support me with the required food and clothing. Otherwise, my life is uncertain." María was seeking to escape one prison by entering another. Even though the convent was a religious space with social prestige, it was perceived as a place of confinement, although some were in reality

---

10. From the case of Manuela, a slave belonging to Lima's Santo Domingo Convent, who presented a case to the Ecclesiastic Tribunal to block her husband's sale. AAL, Causas de negros, legajo 31, 1784.

11. AAL, Causas de negros, legajo 32, exp. 3, 1787.

spaces of female liberty because they allowed an escape from the exhausting rhythm of work, the pressure of daily labor, and the control of husband, father, or owner.[12]

María then added that she wished the judge to "make the most effective resolution to punish my avowed husband, giving him a harsh warning [and] ordering that he be notified to abstain from mistreating me under penalty of a fine, in conformity with Your Illustriousness' discretion. Or, considering natural law, I will separate from my said husband, and the marriage of so many years is abandoned. As such, I have resisted this, despite the horrible torments I have suffered, knowing and accepting that [matrimony] has been a work of Divine Providence." This paragraph clarifies María's real objective. She did not want separation or confinement in the convent; she wanted the Tribunal to reprimand her husband. So she sought the protection of men who wielded authority over her husband, given that she most likely lacked a father, godfathers, or brothers to do this.[13]

María finally adds, "I ask and plead that Your Illustriousness see fit to order that my said husband give me my letter granting me freedom, which I seek in this audience before Your Illustriousness. And, similarly, as I have been his day laborer for five years, giving him six *reales* daily, it is only right that I seek compensation." María ends the petition demanding her letter of *manumission*. She demands liberty on two levels: first, as an ex-slave she wants to be able to prove her personal liberty, and, second, as a woman, she wants a relationship without strife and violence.

Although more urban than rural women slaves litigated, some rural cases demonstrate a surprising argumentative capacity by rural black women who, for example, cite recent legal precedents as well as the medieval Spanish laws known as the *Siete Partidas* to argue their position. One such case, featured as the second document in this chapter, is the petition of Manuela, a *zamba* slave (of indigenous and African parentage) belonging to Lima's Santo Domingo Convent but living and working on its rural hacienda. In 1784, she went to the Ecclesiastic Tribunal to block her husband's sale.[14]

In her petition, she begins by citing the recent case of a slave woman named Juliana in which the Tribunal ordered the same convent to find a local buyer for the woman's husband in order to avoid breaking up the marriage. Manuela next asks to be sold to a Lima resident, citing the danger to her marriage that a separation from her husband has caused. She also astutely attempts to avoid turning over her wages and insists on the control over her own body, both of which are intrinsic rights not of a slave but of her owner. She then insists upon the sacred character of marriage and the protection that marriage should receive from the Church. The petition also cites the *Siete Partidas* to support her request. As it is difficult to say with certainty what

---

12. María's petition shows that the discourse of honor was not limited to elite women; subaltern women also used it. On honor, see van Deusen, *Entre lo sagrado*. For convents as places of female liberty, see Arias; Chambers.

13. Another element of María's discourse is how she describes the years spent in marriage as a personal investment. This proved a common characteristic in women's petitions for divorce during this period.

14. AAL, Causas de negros, legajo 31, 1784.

access Manuela had to this legal text, the references to the *Siete Partidas* point to the participation of a legal specialist on her behalf.

Many of the petitions presented before the courts are written with the tone of a supplicant, but Manuela's is different: she questions the actions of the Tribunal, reminds the Tribunal of earlier resolutions, and demands compliance with the law while at the same time expressing confidence in her rights and the law. Manuela's case reveals nuances that question some generalizations about rural slave women. For example, although they lived at a great distance from the courts and were subjected to tighter control on the haciendas, this did not mean that they were all entirely victims of the system. Several such rural women cited knowledge of laws and made use of argumentation and the legal process just as urban slave women did, though they did so in smaller numbers than their urban counterparts.

The ecclesiastic defense clashed with the rights of slave owners, who frequently intervened in their slaves' marriage choices. Owners tried to select spouses for their slaves from the same hacienda or a nearby street in order to control their slaves. Nevertheless, during the entire colonial period and the early republican period, slaves and freed people resisted and defended their personal decisions, appealing to the Church and creating a dynamic in which the Church became an intermediary between the state, the owners, and the slaves.[15]

*****

---

15. Aguirre (*Agentes*, 190), Flores Galindo (18), Hünefeldt (54), Jouve Martín (186), and Trazegnies (23).

Complaint Presented by María del Carmen Ollague, Free Black Woman, against Her Husband Manuel Cosío, Black Man, for Excessive Cruelty [1787][16]

Most Illustrious Lord Ecclesiastical Judge,

I, María del Carmen Ollague, a free black, in accordance with my legal rights, appear and testify to the best of my ability before Your Illustriousness. It has been more than twelve years that, according to the mandate of Our Holy Church, I married Mario Cosío, a black slave of Doña Isabel Solís, [thus] fulfilling, as God commands, the said [marital] status. [In that time], my husband has never had reason to suspect even the slightest impropriety on my part. On the contrary, his harmful and infamous behavior has given me good cause to bring before Your Illustrious Lordship this reverent appeal, summarized here to make Your Lordship aware of my sufferings, which are as follows:

During the prolonged period of our marriage, I have, of course, been nominally his wife, but in reality I have only been treated as a slave, because, far from the sacred treatment owed a legitimate wife, his actions have been the kind that a bad servant deserves.[17] Most Illustrious Lord, I have spent my years promoting only his interests, during which, absurdly, I found myself without the means to pay [even] a confraternity [fee]. I could, Most Illustrious Lord, give Your Lordship a report that supports [my case] against my said husband, exposing his abuses. However, seeing that it would only serve to distract you from your dutiful obligations, I will only say that if Your Illustriousness is satisfied, I am eager for Your Illustriousness to hear details concerning the aforementioned facts that I do not present now . . . [and to] order that I be sent to a convent, where my aforementioned husband shall be obliged to support me with the required food and clothing. Otherwise, my life is uncertain.[18]

[Case in point], Most Illustrious Lord, my said husband thinks himself a man when he makes me go to the tavern even though he has slaves. And when I fail to return home soon, either because I have not been quickly attended to or because, as I am master of my own freedom, I stay to talk with Alonza, a relative, this gives him enough of a reason to lock me outside of my dwelling, leaving me out on the street as is commonly known, where even thieves or any other evil people can harm me. So then, as he usually does, when he opens the doors of his residence, it is just to kick, punch, and bite me, etc.

---

16. Archivo Arzobispal de Lima (AAL), Causas de negros, legajo 32, exp. 3, 1787. I appreciate the help of Isabel Palomino and Ernesto Pajares in obtaining the paleographic version of these documents. The document is written in small, neat handwriting with a signature in the same style, which suggests it was written down by a notary or secretary, whom María possessed sufficient economic resources to pay.

17. María compares the image of "abused wife" with that of "bad servant." This was natural in colonial discourse. Punishment was viewed as corrective, even by subalterns themselves.

18. According to colonial discourse, women lost sexual honor in the street, in public; therefore, it was important to remain within enclosed spaces like the home or the convent. María's petition shows that subaltern women used this discourse too, even though elites considered them lacking honor.

Most Illustrious Lord, such are the insults I receive from my husband that even though I would clearly be justified to leave, I do not do it because I am incapable of leaving [him]. But there is more, Most Illustrious Lord. When he gets crazy like this (and that is what one must call it), he has become hostile and has had the nerve to put me in a bakery for as long as he wishes. All of this is permitted by his masters solely because it serves their interests and because he seems to want me dead, which would [allow his masters] to avoid giving him his freedom, which he clearly desires. Most Illustrious Lord, I dare say this because of what these experiences have taught me lately. Your Illustriousness, in your superior judgment, make the most effective resolution to punish my avowed husband, giving him a harsh warning [and] ordering that he be notified to abstain from mistreating me under penalty of a fine, in conformity with Your Illustriousness' discretion. Or, considering natural law, I will separate from my said husband, and the marriage of so many years is abandoned. As such, I have resisted this, despite the horrible torments I have suffered, knowing and accepting that [matrimony] has been a work of Divine Providence.[19] With these words, I ask and plead of Your Illustriousness that, in consideration of the grievances that I have expressed in making this most proper petition, you see fit to order it in the [name] of justice, which is what I ask and hope from Your Illustriousness who definitively grants it.

One more thing, I must say that my aforementioned husband purchased my freedom; but, regarding this, even though he made me pay him exactly the daily wage of six *reales*, I still do not know if I am a slave or free because, with the maliciousness that drives his behavior, he has kept it [the letter of *manumission*] to himself, without giving it to me. When he goes crazy, he throws me out of the house, thus it has been necessary to go the hospital because of my infirmities. They have not wanted to admit me because they did not have [this letter] before them. In this life, I ask and plead that Your Illustriousness see fit to order that my said husband give me my letter granting me freedom, which I seek in this audience before Your Illustriousness. And, similarly, as I have been his day laborer for five years, giving him six *reales* daily, it is only right that I seek compensation as expressed above.

María del Carmen Ollague

Complaint of Manuela, *Zamba* Slave, That She Be Sold in Lima [November 3, 1783][20]

Manuela, *zamba*, under the age of twenty-five, slave of the hacienda of Palpa, properly of the large Convent of Santo Domingo of this city, [and] legitimate wife of José Justo, a slave, formerly of the same hacienda and who today belongs to Don Joaquín

---

19. The writing in María's case reflects a key notion within colonial discourse related to marriage: marriage was a sacred sacrament and an unbreakable bond. To voluntarily leave this "sweet prison" challenged the foundations of society. For this reason, the petitions for divorce met general disapproval.

20. AAL, Causas de negros, legajo 31, exp. 19, 1783. The document consists of various loose sheets with small, rough lettering plus Manuela's own signature, indicating that she directed and understood the proceedings, the laws, and their reach.

de Oyague, supplier of bread, motivated by the action of this convent to sell him, by your leave, as is my legal right, I appear before Your Lordship and testify that more than three years ago my husband was removed from the hacienda and sold in this city, thus putting asunder our union and our conjugality, in which we were very content, through no fault of our own of which I am aware, and without any formal proceedings for similar separations, under these terms. The involuntary divorce was done against my will and conscience, leaving me in the same hacienda and my husband serving his master forty leagues away in this city. Desiring to see my said husband, whom I love as I am not only permitted but also commanded by divine and human laws, I decided to come to this city unbeknownst to the administrators of the hacienda, with the purpose of appearing before Your Lordship to seek a judgment so that the convent should sell me in this city, where my husband is located, in order for us to live and fulfill our union as our [marital] state requires. Each will serve his own master, as Providence has destined for us, with which I am in agreement.

My petition is supported by a precedent before you that Your Lordship has ruled on, which has been petitioned by Juliana, a slave of the same hacienda married to another slave [also] from there, whom the Church sold to the same Don Joaquín, thus splitting apart the marriage. [Your Lordship] has ordered that the convent proceed with her sale at a reasonable price and under good terms, as she was not at fault, and that the sale take place in this city, allowing her sufficient time to seek a master who might buy her. The case is identical in all circumstances; this gives me hope in Your Lordship's fairness, that your judgment will be the same.

And, therefore, having made a most suitable petition before Your Lordship, I ask and plead, given the reasoned facts, which I swear are true by God, Our Lord, and by this sign of the cross +, that you see fit to order that the father prior of said convent proceed to sell me in this city at a reasonable and fair price, under good terms, so that this involuntary divorce, which I have been made to suffer during the referenced time period, can come to an end. And thus, I will be able to continue marital life in union with the aforementioned José Justo, with each of us serving our respective masters. Grant me sufficient time in order to petition whoever can accommodate me and [grant that] meanwhile the party of the convent not disturb or pursue me, as I understand they are eagerly trying to find me in order to arrest me, and I am frightened by the threat. I ask for justice and hope to obtain it from Your Lordship's sense of impartiality.

Manuela *Zamba*

[The Ecclesiastical Tribunal's Sentence]

In the Ciudad de los Reyes [Lima] on November 7, 1783:

I, the Illustrious Lord Doctor Don Francisco de Santiago Concha, canonical doctor of this Holy Metropolitan Church, provincial and vicar general of this archbishopric, having reviewed the proceedings pursued by Juliana, a black slave of the Hacienda de Palpa, properly of the Convent of Santo Domingo, concerning her sale in this city, so that she and Valentín, her legitimate husband, a slave of Don Joaquín de Oyague, could live together in marriage, which are pertinent to and used by the present case, order that the most illustrious father prior of the Convent of Predicadores [Dominican convent] be notified to proceed immediately to sell the *zamba* [Manuela] referred to in this petition. This shall be done in this city, setting a fair and customary price for her, and giving the said slave the period of nine days to carry this out. In the meantime, [I order that] no harm be done to the *zamba* who has testified here. Signed,

Concha
Before me
Manuel del Bado Calderón

In the Ciudad de los Reyes [Lima] on October 10, 1783, I personally notified and made aware of the preceding decision, to which I attest, the Reverend Father Fray Domingo Ruedas of the Order of the Preachers, current prior of the Convent Grande de Santo Domingo.

José de Cárdenas, Notary Public

Lima, February 6, 1784

Manuela, *zamba*, under the age of twenty-five, slave of the Hacienda de Palpa, properly of the Convent Grande de Santo Domingo of this city, legitimate wife of José Justo, a black slave who belonged to the same hacienda and, now, after being sold by the same convent, [belongs] to Don Joaquín Oyague. The decrees provided that I would be sold in this city at a fair price and under good terms, so that there would be no division in or encumbrances to our marriage. In responding, without prejudice, to the copy of the document given to me, in which the party of the convent requests it be provided a copy of my petition, I say that, in the interests of justice, Your Lordship should see fit to order that the decree on folio 14 provided on November 7, of this past year, 1783, be obeyed and fulfilled. [Your Lordship should] declare that the convent's petition to examine this matter does not have merit, and [Your Lordship] should impose silence on them and order them to pay the costs [incurred], which I would consider to be just. Once the facts are known [and] the law and the ruling made clear, the quickest resolution is the most just, as delays cause risk. These are the terms of the present case.

The present father prior of the convent confesses in his statement that he only conceded to what was favorable [to him] from my testimony in my written document, [which] prompted Your Lordship's decision. In order to uphold [the decision], it is necessary to know that we were both slaves of the hacienda, that we [were] married with the knowledge and consent of the administrator in charge of its management. [Although] separated by a matter of leagues, [we as] married slaves of one master, according to the wisest morality approved by jurists, [such] married slaves cannot be separated nor sold at such a distance that may prohibit or impede the communication and the practice of matrimony, and under disposition of the law, the master who thus alienates his ownership of one must be compelled to transfer the other to the same place. The same is ordered by *Ley* 7, *Título* 5, *Partida* 4 to avoid the danger of fornication, which is, no doubt, common among the young people, in which age group we both belong. Thus, the timely decision pronounced by Your Lordship is based on the facts, the law, and the particular case and should be upheld, as nothing to the contrary is alleged that will weaken this [decision].

The father prior says he sold my husband and Valentín, a slave of the same hacienda married to the black woman, Juliana, for being depraved criminals, with the stipulation that they would always be imprisoned. Their bill of sale says nothing about their vices or the condition of imprisonment. The party of the convent has been petitioned to present the document of sale in which is clearly stated what Your Lordship ordered, but it has not been presented. If it were produced, the signature found on the bill of sale would be that of the scribe Alejandro Cueto, whose meticulousness and trustworthiness are well known.

Now the party of the convent says the slaves are depraved in order to cover up the excesses committed in the sale when they separated the spouses. If it is enough to [simply] accuse a man of being a criminal in order to deem him as such, then no one would be innocent and without any accusations. In order for these vices to be credible, it is necessary to prove each one specifically because the law, which is above all prudent and fair, has established that according to judicial practice, no one should be presumed malicious until he is proven to be so.

It is difficult to grasp by what moral standard one can slander the character of a black just because of his [social] condition as a slave, simply because the information suits the convent's purposes, and, because of some persons of status and character, such slander is declared in a public trial. And thus, from where the example should emanate, comes only our decline.

The notarized document presented by the court's scribe Don Martín Julián Gamarra is not relevant [because it] does not include the slaves the convent sold to Don Joaquín Oyague, but only those sold to Don José Pomiano. [Those slaves'] crimes were later proven. Thus, the superior government granted permission for their sale because they were malicious and depraved. [In order] for those to state that these [slaves, Valentín and José Justo,] are [malicious and depraved], it would be necessary for all [slaves] to have the same character. For that reason, one can see that it is absurd for them to present such a notarized document, given all that I have favorably testified about here.

I ask and plead that Your Lordship see fit to provide and order according to my request in the opening statement of my written testimony, which is to me just. I attest to the necessity of your costs.

     Manuela *Zamba*
     Slave of the Convent of Santo Domingo

                        Lima, February 4, 1783

These proceedings have been reviewed, taking into consideration the poverty and paucity of the interested parties in this litigation, who lack the wherewithal to sustain the pending dispute argued by the party of the Convent of Santo Domingo. What has been ordered in the decrees of folios 5 and 14 before us, however, has not up to now had the desired effect. In the opinion of the general public prosecutor of this archbishopric, who has undertaken all that is referenced above, the response shall be legally binding.

     Signature, Concha

17

The Case of Javier, *Esclavo*, against His Master for Cruel Punishment, San Juan, Argentina, 1795[1]

Ana Teresa Fanchin

Document translation by Joseph P. Sánchez, Angelica Sánchez-Clark, and Larry D. Miller

A Denunciation in San Juan de la Frontera

On Christmas Eve, 1795, a court in San Juan de la Frontera held hearings on a denunciation of abuse made by an enslaved man named Javier. For four consecutive days, Javier's master Don Juan de Echegaray had kept him imprisoned in stocks, unleashing his rage against him with countless beatings.

The hearings took place in a city located to the east of the Andean range, in the southern territories of the vast Spanish colonial empire, in what is today Argentina, distant from the political centers of colonial domination. The region is characterized by a mountainous landscape and arid plains and valleys irrigated by the rivers born in the Andes. In 1562, Spanish colonizing forces had crossed the Andes from the Kingdom of Chile and founded the city of San Juan at two thousand feet above sea level on the southern bank of the San Juan River. The San Juan River is one of the largest rivers of the Tulum Valley, which lies between the Andes to the west and the Sierra Pie de Palo to the east in San Juan Province. The designation of "Frontera," which was added to the city's name, indicates its delimitation with the lands of the indigenous Chalchaquis to the north, a people conquered by the Spanish forces who emanated southward out of Peru.

The city of San Juan together with Mendoza (1561) and San Luis (1594) fell under the administration of the Reino de Chile and comprised one of its eleven *corregimientos*, until the creation of the Viceroyalty of Río de la Plata in 1776, when the district was transferred to the latter's governmental jurisdiction. From its beginnings in the mid-sixteenth century, San Juan represented a colonial outpost and an essential overland link between Rio de la Plata and Chile.

It was across the dusty pampa trails and rugged mountainous paths of the San Juan region that *sanjuanino* muleteers drove their mule trains transporting merchandise. They departed the area carrying skins filled with wine, liquor, grape juice, and vinegars and bags of locally produced dried fruit, together with goods acquired in Chile and other neighboring areas. They would return later with products that satisfied local demands or that they resold in other markets.

A good portion of this stock was sold in public *plazas*, stores, and corner shops and came and went as contraband supplied directly by troop captains and wagoners

---

1. See Maps 6 and 12.

(Fanchín, "Protagonistas," 69). Documentary evidence suggests that it was also through contraband that most enslaved blacks were introduced into the region, and so it is difficult to quantify the number of people of color transported in this wretched traffic.[2] What is certain is that the inhabitants of the region did not just watch as people of color passed by in their caravans of horror and death, but also acquired them, principally as status symbols to employ in domestic tasks.

Enslaved Blacks in San Juan and Their Legal Controls and Protections

In the 1777 census, 16 percent of the inhabitants of San Juan were registered as African born or of African descent.[3] It is likely that the percentage was actually higher because about half the population was listed as either *mestiza*, which might include people with African ancestors, or without a particular ethnic identity.[4] When the 1777 census was carried out, Don Juan de Echegaray declared that he owned four male slaves, one female slave married to an *indio*, and three minor children. Among the named slaves, three are protagonists of the events related here: the same Javier, Manuel, and Cayetano who testified before the judge. Don Juan de Echegaray was a prominent *hacendado* and the son of a man who founded towns and villages in the area, as instituted by action of the *Junta de Poblaciones de Chile* in the mid-eighteenth century. Thus, along with his wealth, Don Juan de Echegaray had inherited prestige and honor.

When he meted out his cruel punishment to Javier, beating him with four quince rods, he did so with the backing of Spanish colonial law. The *Consejo de Indias, reales audiencias, cabildos*, viceroys, and governors were constantly engaged in creating legislation on the most varied aspects of the activities of black slaves in Spanish America. The regulations regarding escaped slaves, which were sanctioned by the king and incorporated into the *Recopilación de leyes de los reinos de las Indias* (1680), constituted the definitive procedures to be employed in combating *marronage*. The number of lashings to be given to an escaped slave varied according to the length of his or her absence, the slave's distance from home, and the place to which the slave had fled. For a weeklong desertion, a slave was to receive one hundred lashings and was to wear an iron shoe on one foot (Mellafe, *La esclavitud*, 83).[5]

Nevertheless, the law also protected slaves. The thirteenth-century *Siete Partidas* (Part 7, Title 8, Law 9) set penalties against the owner who inflicted mortal injury on his slave. The *real cédula* (royal decree) of 1789 reiterated in chapter X that in the

---

2. The certificates of births, marriages, and deaths of blacks and *mulattoes* are recorded in the parochial records (kept in the city from 1665 on) in the "Libros de 'no españoles,'" which mention their origins—principally *Angola, Guinea*, the Portuguese colonies of Brazil, or this jurisdiction (these last had the usual designation of "*criollo*"). The Archivo Histórico de la Provincia also preserves contracts of purchase and sale of slaves carried out between individuals.

3. See López-Chávez, who examines slavery in the city's Jesuit haciendas.

4. For more information on the region's population, see Fanchin, "Los habitantes."

5. See also Lucena Salmoral.

case of mortal injuries, contusions, wounds, and mutilations, the owner should suffer "the punishment corresponding to the crime committed if the injured were free" (*la pena correspondiente al delito cometido como si fuese libre el injuriado*; Goldberg, 5).

In addition he should lose the slave through a change of ownership. If the cruelty led to a permanent handicap, the slave could claim freedom. In other words, had it been verified that Javier had been rendered "gravely ill and on the verge of dying" (*gravemente enfermo y en término de fallecer*), as the doctor stated in his first testimony, his owner would have been obliged to grant him a letter of *manumission*. But this possibility was lost when the doctor certified Javier's physical recovery.

The Case of Slave Javier versus Don Juan de Echegaray

In his declaration, Javier testified that his master had given him a document of sale that allowed him to seek a new owner. But, as generally occurred in such cases, Don Juan de Echegaray had set the price too high to make the sale possible. Moreover, Don Juan threatened Javier with a beating if he persisted in his request to be sold. Javier must have known that his master would be true to his word, and he chose to flee. But ten days later, he presented himself voluntarily in the same court that had aided him in producing the document of sale. Thus it was the judicial authority who returned Javier to his owner and recommended a "moderate correction of this minor offense" (*moderada corrección a este corto delito*).

This ambiguous wording does not specify what the appropriate punishment was, nor does it name the exact offense for which Javier was to be punished. Of course, it is important to remember that this wording was recorded by the scribe who took Javier's declaration in the investigation of the circumstances that provoked the master's rage. The only witnesses to the incident were the master's other slaves, and all of them specified the number of lashings. Even Manuel knew what had happened, despite having only witnessed the beatings on the last day, as he had been out working in the fields. Finally, despite making determinations in favor of Javier, the judge was benevolent toward the master, restoring his condition of honorable citizen (*vecino honorable*).

In other colonial territories the *manumission* of slaves was more frequent, at least in particular circumstances, as in Santiago de Cuba after the proclamation of the free entry of slaves in 1789. Where large slave markets existed, owners could accede more readily to grant freedom to slaves because they could more easily purchase replacements (Belmonte Postigo, 8). In contrast, in San Juan de la Frontera, the social sector that had sufficient material wealth to buy this type of merchandise had fewer opportunities to do so, and slaves constituted an important investment for commercial development.

The regulation of free trade occasioned very different effects in the interior to those seen in and around large port cities. In the last quarter of the eighteenth century, Buenos Aires saw a significant rise in *manumissions* by purchase as increased urban development corresponded to an increase in the opportunity for slaves to earn income with which to purchase their freedom (Johnson, "La manumisión en el Buenos Aires," 645). San Juan de la Frontera's response to the economic growth in

Buenos Aires was an intensification of its viticulture, or wine-growing, activity. Thus wine producers such as Don Juan de Echegaray would have been motivated to keep their slave labor, even more so if they had already recuperated the initial purchase cost through the slave's work.

In reading the testimonies in the case, it is important to keep in mind factors that shape the testimony. I will name just three. First, there is the question of mediation. Although there was no interpreter who translated the slaves' words, as Javier and his fellow slaves spoke Spanish, their testimony was a reelaboration of their words composed by a "lettered" Spanish court official, who would have modified the slaves' language according to his understanding and legal and linguistic training. Second, this episode exposes a strategy commonly adopted by slaves, who used to their benefit a subterfuge offered by the judicial system. This formal system of justice gave slaves the opportunity to solicit their freedom or, as happened concretely in this case, to petition a document of sale for the purpose of being transferred to a new owner and hopefully to an improved living situation. Thus, the testimonies open a window on to a strategy by which enslaved blacks sought to negotiate better circumstances through the court system. Finally, the case reaffirms the meanings that slavery gave and still gives to its human victims in the concept of the enslaved body: It is well known that the African population and their descendants were perceived as body merchandise. This combination of coordinates is still sustained in our own time in so many renewed forms of slavery.

*****

Proceedings Concerning the Physical Abuse Inflicted by Don Juan de Echegaray on His Slave Javier[6]

[Denunciation of the Corporal Punishment Given to the Mulatto Javier, Slave of Don Juan de Echegaray]

In the city of San Juan de la Frontera on December 21, 1795, Don Francisco Ortega y Ramos, *alcalde ordinario de segundo voto* of this city, and [other] witnesses, as there is not a public scribe available, I say that...yesterday, the twentieth of the present [month and year], it has been reported that Don Juan de Echegaray of this city has, with a *novenario* of lashes,[7] cruelly punished his slave named Javier, a *mulatto*. Due to this punishment, the aforementioned slave is gravely ill and on the verge of dying. And, as this is an offense against God and against royal decrees that deal with the punishment of servants, therefore, I should and do order that, for the clarification of the incident recorded in the customary manner in these proceedings...that the witnesses knowledgeable about the incident be questioned....Let the first [statement] be that of Don José Casamadrid, doctor of medicine....

[Medical Certification Issued by Don José Brizuela y Casamadrid, Doctor of Medicine of the City]

Don José Brizuela y Casamadrid, doctor of medicine in this city and in fulfillment of the previous decree:

In fulfillment of the above decree of His Lordship, the *alcalde [ordinario] de segundo voto*, I certify to the best of my ability, and as the law permits me, that I went to the house of Don Juan de Echegaray of this city. There, I examined his slave who was ill....According to what I observed, his back and buttocks are battered and bruised and he is suffering from an inflammatory fever caused by the violence brought on by the very serious punishment inflicted on him by his master....

[Statement of the Slave, Javier, Mulatto, Thirty Years of Age]

In the city of San Juan de la Frontera on December 21, 1795, for the clarification of the incident that prompts the initial proceedings of criminal investigation, I, Don Francisco Antonio de Ortega, *alcalde ordinario de segundo voto*, ordered to appear in [this] tribunal a *mulatto* named Javier, a slave of Don Juan de Echegaray of this vicinity. From him, before me and the witnesses, I received his oath made in the customary manner, in the name of God, Our Lord, and by the sign of the cross, by which he swore to tell the truth....

Asked if he is ill, what caused his illness, and why his master has him in this evidently precarious state, he answers that he is ill primarily because of his [injured] back and buttocks, caused by the four-day punishment...the last one taking place

---

6. Archivo General de la Provincia de San Juan, Argentina, Fondo Tribunales, caja 18, carpeta 75, coc. 15, fols. 1–6v.

7. Although the expression *novenario* refers to a series of events over the course of nine days, the witnesses recount that Javier's punishment was carried out over four days.

on the day before yesterday, the nineteenth of the present [month],... carried out by his master's own hand. [He says] that the device used to whip him was a switch made of four quince sticks and that he does not remember exactly how many lashes he was given but only knows that the first afternoon of the punishment was followed by a long period of time, [whereas] the other three, carried out during the morning, were done with four breaks. After punishing him for a while, his master stopped, smoked a cigarette, and again gave him another beating lasting as long as the previous one. Once finished, he took a break and [then] again continued the punishment. He carried it out in this manner in four sessions on each of the three days, as has been stated.... His shackles were [put] on him by his master before he began the punishment he experienced. That is why he is still wearing them, today.

Asked what crime or injury he committed against his master that resulted in this punishment and who is knowledgeable about the punishment, he responds that the crime he committed, for which he has suffered the punishment that has been reported [was that he] had run away for ten days. The reason for his flight was that, on the night that he ran away, he knew that his master wanted to punish him simply because he had asked for a document of sale [but] had not yet found a [new] master, the reason being the exorbitant price [his master] had put on him. All this should be evident to the tribunal.[8] Similarly, on the last day of the flight... he turned himself in to the same tribunal so that it would return him to his master, which was immediately carried out. [The tribunal] told [Echegaray that] he should impose a moderate punishment for this minor offense. Those who have knowledge about the punishment inflicted on him are the rest of his master's slaves who happened to be present and whose names are Pascual, Eusebio, Cayetano, Manuel, [and] Damián. This is the truth about what has occurred in this matter....

[Statement of Cayetano, Forty Years of Age, Slave of Don Juan de Echegaray]

In the city of San Juan de la Frontera on December 22, 1795, in preparation of the proceedings... regarding the clarification of the crime that prompts the initial criminal investigation, I, Don Francisco Antonio de Ortega, *alcalde ordinario de segundo voto*, ordered Cayetano, a slave of Don Juan de Echegaray, to appear in [this] tribunal, from whom, before witnesses, lacking a scribe, I received the oath that he made before God, Our Lord, and a sign of the cross, under which he swore to tell the truth about what he would say and be asked....

As to what concerns the proceedings mentioned, he answers that he knows, because he saw it, that his master Don Juan de Echegaray has punished, with his own hand, one of his slaves named Javier... for four days, the first day in the afternoon and the rest in the morning. On each of these days, he has given him four sessions of twenty-five lashes in each one with four quince sticks, and this is all the truth about which he knows....

---

8. This is the same court in which Javier entered his petition for his master to grant him the document of sale.

[Statement of Damián, Thirty Years of Age,
Slave of Don Juan de Echegaray]

On the same day [the proceedings continue], I had Damián, a slave, appear, [who] responds as follows: that he knows, because he saw it, that his master Don Juan de Echegaray punished his slave named Javier, a *mulatto*, with his own hand for four consecutive days. On each of the said days, he gave him a large number of lashes with some quince sticks until he got tired. He states that this is the truth, under oath . . . in which it is affirmed and ratified. . . .

[Statement of Eusebio, Twenty Years of Age,
Slave of Don Juan de Echegaray]

On the same day, I, the presiding judge, had Eusebio, a slave of Don Juan de Echegaray, appear before me and witnesses [and] had him take an oath . . . he swore to tell the truth about what he might know and be asked. Doing so, in accordance with the proceeding and initial criminal investigation, he answered the following: that he knows, because he saw it, that his master, Don Juan de Echegaray, has punished with his own hand another *mulatto*, also his slave, named Javier, [whom] he beat for four days, the first day in the afternoon on which he gave him a great many lashes with some quince sticks and then for three days in the morning. The punishment was not as cruel as the first day, but always [inflicted] with the sticks. He states that this is the truth, under the oath he has made. . . .

[Statement of Manuel, Twenty Years of Age,
Slave of Don Juan de Echegaray]

In the city of San Juan de la Frontera on December 22, 1795, I, Don Francisco Antonio de Ortega y Ramos, *alcalde de segundo voto* of this city, in continuance of the above proceedings, had Manuel, a slave of Don Juan de Echegaray, appear in [this] tribunal. Before me and witnesses, I received his oath . . . by which he swore to tell the truth about what he might know and be asked. . . .

He responds that it is evident to him, because he had seen his master punish the said slave named Xaviel [Javier] in his presence that one day . . . he beat him with quince sticks, giving him, it seems, twenty-five lashes. As [Manuel] is the one who takes care of his master's vineyard, he was not present for the punishment that he also heard the other slaves, his companions, say that his master meted out on the three days before the one [day] he witnessed. . . .

[Judge's Verdict, Sentencing of the Master]
San Juan, December 24, 1795

[Judicial Decree and Findings]

Based on the [evidence presented in the] proceedings, the excessive punishment meted out by Don Juan de Echegaray to his slave, Xaviel [Javier], and the tribunal having been properly informed by Doctor Casamadrid, in charge of treating the aforementioned *mulatto*, . . . Don Juan de Echegaray is hereby sentenced to a specific deadline of three days in which to assign the said slave to find a master with the document of sale he gave him, among [the candidates] the said Echegaray must select a person to whom he will sell him.[9] Let it be understood that if this is not carried out because of procrastination on his part, official proceedings will be initiated and he will be given the punishment that corresponds to disobedience. Upon receipt of this order, the shackles will be removed immediately from the said slave. Also, [Echegaray] is sentenced to pay for the slave's care and medicine until he is completely healed, for this he owes Doctor Casamadrid. [He must also pay] the costs of these proceedings and other related consequences that have arisen. He is also warned that if, henceforth, [he] goes too far in his punishments, the full force of the law will be applied against him. At present, it is waived, given that this is the first incident [and] taking into consideration that he is one of the principal citizens, honored and honorable. . . .

---

9. The wording in the original is confusing and might also mean that Don Juan de Echegaray is to find the purchaser within the same three-day time limit that he had originally given Javier to do the same.

18

In the Royal Service of Spain: The *Milicianos Morenos* Manuel and Antonio Pérez during the Napoleonic Invasion, 1808–1812[1]

Jorge L. Chinea

Paul Gilroy's *The Black Atlantic* (1993) challenges scholars to look beyond the dominant *paradigm* of the African diaspora that privileges colonial or national particularities isolated from hemispheric and intercontinental events. He advocates a multidimensional approach linking local, regional, and global developments, one that is consonant with the extensive dispersion of Africans across Europe, Asia, and the Americas through the slave trade.

Gilroy also reminds us that Africans circulated both coercively and voluntarily in the flow of people, goods, ideas, and institutions that shaped the early modern Atlantic world: "The history of the black Atlantic since then, continually crisscrossed by the movement of black people—not only as commodities but engaged in various struggles toward emancipation, autonomy, and citizenship—provides a means to reexamine the problems of nationality, location, identity, and historical memory" (16).

The free and enslaved black sailors that navigated across the many cultures, religions, languages, and political struggles of the Atlantic world were at the forefront of these changes. By embracing a flexible, *diasporic identity*, they witnessed and participated in events taking place on the ocean and the many lands it touched (Bolster, 38–41; Pettinger, ix). Mariners figured prominently in these transatlantic exchanges by virtue of their indispensable role in operating or maintaining ships.

But they were certainly not the only ones, nor were they alone in these endeavors. During the age of slavery and in the postemancipation era, their sea vessels transported a wide assortment of Afro-Latinos and other non-Europeans from all walks of life—among them servicemen. Narratives of their experiences overseas and overland may be found buried in the mass of documents housed in governmental, business, and private repositories. Within these archives lie their hidden, frozen voices waiting for the patient researcher to "bring them back into the sun" (Sánchez González, 7).

The submerged voices of the Afro-Puerto Rican soldiers Manuel and Antonio Pérez exemplify this archival entombment. Until recently, Afro-Latinos had been all but overlooked, understudied, or silenced in the canonical scholarship documenting the clashes and encounters involving Iberians, Africans, and "New World" colonials despite ample evidence of their significant participation in many of those historical developments (Andrews; Scott).

The previously unknown or ignored deeds of the Afro-Latino duo highlighted here is a case in point. Though born in Puerto Rico, they sailed through the Atlantic

---

1. See Maps 4 and 15.

during a tour of duty in the Spanish military. Eventually, they joined the anti-French opposition in the Andalusian city of Seville when Napoleon invaded Spain in the early 1800s. By doing so, they repositioned themselves to demand better treatment and other tangible gains in order to improve their social and economic conditions.

If one were to judge by the colonial library—or that body of work built by or reflecting the interests of *Eurocreole* colonial elites—their experiences represent a historical anomaly.[2] For much of the past century, this exclusionary scholarship held that Iberians and *Eurocreoles* were the key protagonists of Puerto Rico's history.

Fortunately, research over the past three or four decades has shown that the so-called *clases vulgares*, the poor, racially ostracized groups that comprised the majority of the population in Spanish America, were not the powerless, inert mass that previous writers had once suggested (see Dávila; Sued Badillo, "Theme of the Indigenous"; and Sued Badillo and López Cantos, *Puerto Rico Negro*). Instead, scholars now see them as *subaltern agents* operating under extremely harsh conditions. Thus, the case involving our two militiamen questions the merit of Eurocentric historical analyses while highlighting the malleability of the black Atlantic as a fluid space wherein the idealized neat boundaries separating colonial subject and metropolitan overseer and the oppressed and the oppressor are often blurred, contested, and overturned.

Afro-Latinos in Spanish Colonial Puerto Rico, c. 1650–1800

Following the exodus of Spanish colonists from the Greater Antilles and the virtual cessation of European immigration and trade triggered by the depletion of alluvial mineral deposits after about 1600, the Africans left behind became a greater share of the population. Along with *cimarrones* and *mestizos*, nonwhites retained this demographic edge over the next two centuries. Subsistence farming, cattle ranching, and seafaring—including fishing, whaling, salt racking, salvaging damaged or sunken ships, piracy, *privateering*, and maritime *marronage*—afforded them the chief means of survival (Chinea, "A Quest"; Morales Carrión, *Puerto Rico*).

The Puerto Rican ship carpenter Alonso Ramírez, who journeyed to Havana, Mexico, and the Far East in the late 1670s, touched on this dismal economic reality.[3] According to this native of San Juan, the gold-mining bust and a string of destructive hurricanes wiped out the cacao exporting business that had been a major source of income. As shipwright work began to dry up, he "determined to steal my body from my very homeland in order to secure in [other places] a better way of life" (Sigüenza y Góngora, 17). So did many others, but not always permanently.

Since at least 1650, "ship carpenters, caulkers, blacksmiths, lumberjacks, and sawyers became common trades in San Juan and other coastal areas" (López Cantos, 168). Woodworkers often carved local trees, whose timber had been highly sought after by the Spanish naval industry, into small boats and canoes that serviced a lucrative

---

2. The phrase "colonial library" is borrowed from Schmidt and Patterson (5).

3. Although scholars have long conjectured that Sigüenza might have "invented" the *Infortunios of Alonso Ramírez*, a recent study by López Lázaro offers new evidence about the historical veracity of the late seventeenth-century account.

contraband trade with the nearby non-Hispanic Caribbean (López Cantos, 169). The *mulatto* Miguel Enríquez reaped a fortune from his seafaring exploits, mainly illicit trade, shipbuilding, pillaging nearby Danish, Dutch, French, and British colonies in the Caribbean, and sacking enemy vessels (López Cantos; Morales Carrión, *Puerto Rico*, 69–70).

The clandestine business persisted through the eighteenth century, as documented by the Spanish clergyman-historian Fray Agustín Iñigo Abbad y Lasierra. In the 1770s, he reported that the local inhabitants of the western seaside town of Arecibo built rudimentary watercraft capable of transporting up to twenty-five men to barter in French Saint Domingue on the western tip of Hispaniola.[4]

Most of these dealings entailed short sailing trips and rarely extended outside the archipelago; therefore, one can only speculate about the circumstances surrounding our two *afroboricuas'* sojourn in Spain in the early 1800s. It is possible that they either sought out work or were impressed into the Spanish armed and naval services to replenish vacancies caused by the shortage, desertion, death, or incapacitation of Iberian personnel destined for the Hispanic Caribbean.

Field Marshall Alexander O'Reilly, whom the Spanish Crown dispatched to the Indies in response to the 1762 British occupation of Havana, was troubled by the large number of Spanish soldiers, stowaways, ship boys, and seamen who jumped ship and remained underground on the Island ("Memoria," 387). Some two thousand deserted between 1769 and 1776 alone (Ortiz, 196). In 1786, the Crown offered incentives to anyone who helped in locating and apprehending them.[5] By the end of the century, metropolitan authorities tied desertion to the spread of idleness and criminality in Puerto Rico. Compulsory or voluntary impressment of local men and boys between the ages of fourteen and sixty via the creation of the *gremio de marina* in 1795 was expected to compensate for the large-scale losses of manpower and simultaneously lessen the growing social "problem" of vagrancy.[6]

As part of his overhaul of the Island's defense system, O'Reilly assembled nineteen infantry and five cavalry companies. One of the infantry units was composed of *morenos libres* (Martín Rebolo, 96). The origins of the nonwhite detachment date as far back as the 1660s when *Maroons* fleeing to Puerto Rico from the non-Hispanic Caribbean were required to embrace Catholicism and pledge allegiance to Spain before they could be granted sanctuary or set free.

Since then, *Maroon* males were placed in military installations, or conscripted into the Spanish armed forces, or both (Chinea, "A Quest," 61–67). A *moreno* military detachment was in place as early as 1700 (Stark, 557). In 1718 and 1752, elements of the free black corps were successfully deployed against foreign colonists occupying the adjacent island of Vieques (Chinea, "A Quest," 65; Stark, 557). *Mestizos, pardos,* and *morenos libres* may have also served on other units after O'Reilly's 1765 reorganization.

---

4. See his description of the town of Arecibo in *Diario* (unpaginated).

5. Archivo General de Puerto Rico, San Juan, Fondo de los Gobernadores Españoles de Puerto Rico, Asuntos de Marina, 1782–1811, caja 272, Circular, Capital [San Juan], December 20, 1800.

6. Instrucción aprobada por el Rey para el establecimiento y gobierno de un gremio de gente de mar matriculada, en la isla de San Juan de Puerto-Rico y sus aguadas, año 1796, Archivo General de Indias, Santo Domingo 2330.

According to his plan, only peninsular and foreign troops loyal to Spain were to be assigned to San Juan's fixed garrison, or *fijo*. This arrangement proved impractical due to difficulties with keeping the garrison manned at full strength. After 1790, it was decided to replace the European forces with local draftees (Martín Rebolo, 207). Given the long history of *racial miscegenation* in Puerto Rico, particularly during the *preplantation period*, the soldiery certainly would have included many nonwhites (Chinea, "Fissures," 185–86).

These nonwhite units soon proved their worth on the battlefield. The *milicianos* out-maneuvered a superior British expeditionary force that attempted to take over Puerto Rico in 1797. Although understated in the official accounts of the combat, the active role played by the *morenos libres* in repelling the attack continues to be celebrated by their descendants to this day (Guisti Cordero). The Puerto Rican militia also saw action in Hispaniola, first to keep the slave rebellion that sparked the Haitian Revolution in 1791 from spreading to Santo Domingo and later to expel French occupation forces during the early 1800s (Artola, 451–63; Morales Carrión, "El reflujo," 25).

After Spain reluctantly ceded Santo Domingo to France in the 1795 Treaty of Basle, about 1,500 ex-slaves and free coloreds from Haiti who crossed into the Span-ish lines were resettled in Florida, Honduras, Yucatan, Panama, and Cadiz (Geggus, 180–200). Spanish fighting units, including *morenos libres* within their ranks, escorted the Haitians to their new destinations in Central America and Spain, which explains the presence of Manuel and Antonio in Seville in the years leading to the Napoleonic invasion. Or perhaps the father and son were taken to Europe to perform certain specialized jobs within the military that required knowledge of the leather, metal, and woodworking trades, occupations traditionally relegated to slaves and free coloreds. Manuel's employment as a blacksmith in the *maestranza de artillería* (artillery corps) encamped in Seville prior to the French attack seems to support the last scenario.[7]

"In defense of the just rights of Your Majesty"

So states the *memorial* or petition that Manuel and Antonio addressed to His Royal Highness, Ferdinand VII. Likely penned by a trained scribe, the petition followed a well-established format wherein the supplicants explained their grievances and implored the king for redress. Manuel identified himself and his son Antonio as former black officers who had served in an 1808 military mission against the French invaders who attempted to permanently unseat the reigning Spanish emperor.

Next, he declared that the *Supreme Junta*, acting in the name of the deposed Span-ish king, had endorsed Manuel's request for a job promotion in Puerto Rico and monetary payment in compensation for "his good services." He went on to explain how some ill-intentioned Spaniards refused to honor the aforementioned conces-sions and, worse still, had him exiled to a remote Spanish *presidio* in Africa, where he worked without pay for two years. The petition concluded by pleading for royal inter-cession to ensure that the junta's favorable ruling on their behalf be fully carried out.

---

7. Certification issued by Julián Francisco Senesen y Buendía, Capitán del Regimiento de Caballería de Texas y Secretario de la Suprema Junta de esta capital, Seville, November 16, 1808, Ministerio de Cultura, Archivo General de Indias, Ultramar, legajo 446, nos. 1–2.

A cursory reading of this case could lead to the conclusion that this was just a major misunderstanding resulting from the confusing state of wartime affairs or, at worse, another instance of a miscarriage of justice. Even though that may true, the petition also reveals the Afro-Latino pair as active agents who seized an opportunity to counter the socioeconomic barriers stacked against people of color in Spain and the Americas. The standard treatment of the French occupation of Spain in Latin American studies rarely delves deeply into specific Iberian developments.

Rather, it overwhelmingly stresses the breakdown of the colonial bond and the ensuing rise of independence movements across the Indies. Although colonials pledged their lives and material possessions to restore the Spanish Crown to power, few apparently crossed the Atlantic to fight the French.[8] The noticeable silence that surrounds the possible involvement of Amerindians, Africans, or any of the *castas* in the peninsular conflict itself considerably enhances the *memorial's* historical importance. In an inversion of roles, it tells the story of heroic Afro-Latino soldiers on Spanish soil willingly taking up arms "in defense of the just rights of Your Majesty." And they were not alone. A detachment of twenty-three veteran Haitian auxiliaries who had been relocated to Cadiz around 1796 also volunteered to fight the French, vowing to "spill the last drop of our blood" in defense of Ferdinand VII (Parrilla Ortíz, 195–97).

It is also important to note that Manuel and Antonio Pérez did not act on specific orders from the military chain of command to which they supposedly reported. Instead, they took matters into their own hands by spontaneously organizing a company of armed free colored men that went out to confront the foreign invaders. The fact that Manuel was elected captain and his son second lieutenant of the improvised unit is a strong indication that they possessed vital leadership and fighting skills that perhaps higher-ups in the military had failed to notice, acknowledge, or promote.

Manuel not only decided to join the Spanish resistance movement of his own free will, but also did so at no cost to the government. He furnished uniforms to twelve of the soldiers *a su costa*, that is, "at his expense," as opposed to using public or state funding. Moreover, his armed party subsequently engaged the enemy at the Battle of Bailén (July 19–22, 1808) without ever taking salary or remuneration of any kind.

Manuel also played a role in mobilizing the local Sevillean population against the subjects of France in their districts. Manuel confirmed this when he declared that Field Marshall Joachim Murat Loubieré (the Duke of Berg), who oversaw the Napoleonic offensive in Spain, singled him out as the person responsible for drumming up the anti-French backlash in the city. Berg jailed him and sentenced him to death. However, after seventeen painful days behind bars, Manuel managed to break free and rejoin the Spanish forces.

Upon learning of Manuel's selfless sacrifice, courage, and determination, Julián Francisco Senesen y Buendía, secretary of the *Junta Suprema* of Seville, praised his "most active fervor and patriotism in the service of the just cause."[9] He also wrote that

---

8. The Puerto Rican *Creoles* Antonio Valero Bernabé, a leader of the independence movement of Latin America, and Demetrio O'Daly y de la Puente, a liberal who advocated constitutional government under Spanish rule, also fought in Spain against the French. See Quintana (53) and Ribes Tovar (60–61).

9. Certification issued by Julián Francisco Senesen y Buendía.

Manuel had "subsequently distinguished himself in an [unspecified] important service, which made him worthy of this *Supreme Junta*'s recommending him to the governor and captain general of Puerto Rico for an officer position that he has requested in one of the vacant posts of the free colored military regiments."[10] The secretary ordered that Manuel be compensated with one hundred ducats on his departure to Puerto Rico. He directed Manuel to forward his request for medals bearing the bust of Ferdinand VII for himself and his son through Puerto Rico's captain general when he returned to the Island.

Despite Manuel's steadfast dedication to the royal cause, unidentified "spiteful and bad Spaniards who have prevailed over the good and loyal ones" deported him to Spanish *presidios* in Ceuta and Alhucema (located in northern Africa), where he toiled without pay for two long years.[11] Despite the setback, Manuel's persistence, sharp powers of observation, excellent memory, and literacy served him well. He had the presence of mind to document or obtain written legal copies (referred to as numbers 1 and 2 in the *memorial*) of any information that could help clear his name in the future.

His *memorial* tells us that his exile in Ceuta ran from March 29, 1810 through January 6, 1812, and from January 7 through September 2, 1812 at Alhucema. He served gratis as a master blacksmith and locksmith in the artillery and royal arsenal's furnace room in both places, "leaving in one and the other a net benefit to the royal exchequer of a soldier's daily wages and the seven *reales* [illegible] per diem that the master [blacksmith and locksmith] assigned to the post should have drawn, of which he has kept legalized documents to support the truth of all he claims."[12]

The episodes narrated by Manuel open a fascinating window to the past in which Africans (as represented by the Haitian auxiliaries exiled in Spain) and Afro-Latinos played major roles. Their actions took place not just in Latin America, but also in one of its metropolitan centers. Moreover, their active involvement in the convoluted revolutionary conflicts of the Atlantic world of the late eighteenth century and first decade of the nineteenth, as Bolster has suggested, debunks the pervasive Euro-American belief that blacks "were acted on, rather than acting [on local, regional, hemispheric, and global affairs]" (2).

The *memorial* presented by Manuel and Antonio Pérez supports this view of Afro-Latinos playing important roles in the Atlantic world by revealing the self-actualizing ethos that led them to confront job discrimination, death threats, and differential justice. Future research about the historically neglected contributions of Afro-Latinos in the Iberian peninsula and elsewhere in Europe may well lead to additional insights about this underexplored intercontinental dimension of the African diaspora in the Caribbean.

*****

10. Certification.

11. Archivo General de Indias, Ultramar, legajo 446, Manuel and Antonio Pérez to King, Madrid, November 26, 1814.

12. Manuel and Antonio Pérez to King, Madrid, November 26, 1814 (see note 11 above).

Petition of Manuel and Antonio Pérez[13]

Sir,

Manuel Pérez, and in the name of his son Antonio, free blacks, former officers of the colored militias of the company that was being organized in the city Seville in the year 1808 in defense of the just rights of Your Majesty and recommended for a job in Puerto Rico, his homeland, by the Supreme Junta of Seville in recognition of their good services, in reverent submission to Your Majesty states:

In 1808 he organized a colored company in the city of Seville in which he was elected captain, and his son sublieutenant, having furnished uniforms to twelve soldiers who fought at the Battle of Bailén,[14] never drawing salary or any gratification during all the time they have served; he also suffered a rigorous imprisonment for seventeen days at the hands of the Duke of Ver,[15] who ordered his execution for leading a conspiracy against the French in Seville, and managed to escape. Moved by the noble sentiments of this black man, the Junta Central granted him (in the name of Your Majesty) the concessions shown in copies numbered 1 and 2, but the spiteful and bad Spaniards who have prevailed over the good and loyal ones have blocked the dispensation, exiling him to one of the minor *presidios* in Africa with the original note indicated in copy 3 that he now places in Your Royal Hands. He did not stop claiming justice through multiple petitions from which he has not yet heard back; had the paternal and tireless mercy of Your Majesty not granted him the reprieve of the past September 2, he would still be in exile.

He has been quartered at the Ceuta fortress from March 29, 1810 to January 6, 1812, during which time he has been assigned to the artillery and royal arsenal's furnace room. From the seventh of the said month and year when he was taken to the Alhucemas one, he worked as a master blacksmith and locksmith of that arsenal, leaving in one and the other a net benefit to the royal exchequer of a soldier's daily wages and the seven *reales* [illegible] per diem that the master [blacksmith and locksmith] assigned to the post should have drawn, of which he has kept legalized documents to support the truth of all he claims.[16]

Therefore, they plead submissively before Your Majesty that on account of your well-known kindness and justice the services of this hapless black man who has not omitted anything possible to support the just cause [of His Majesty] be accredited and on their merits command that he be given new documents to leave for his destiny (the island of Puerto Rico) as previously determined, likewise be paid (by order of Your Majesty) the one hundred *ducados* that the said junta ordered to undertake his voyage, whose instructions should be in the Ministry of War and Navy and the government [office] of Cadiz.

Considering His Majesty that the stated services were carried out in Spain, in defense of the homeland, they ask that His Majesty award them medals bearing the

---

13. Ministerio de Cultura, Archivo General de Indias, Seville, Ultramar 446.
14. Battle of Bailén (Province of Jaén), where in 1808 Spanish forces first defeated the French army.
15. Field Marshall Joachim Murat Loubieré (Duke of Berg), who led Napoleon's forces in Spain.
16. The *presidios* of Ceuta and Alhucemas were located in modern-day Spanish Morocco, northern Africa.

Royal bust of His Majesty and that their passage [to Puerto Rico] be on a military ship due to their inability to defray the costs for such a prolonged trip.

In return for all [entreated], upon arrival at their destiny father and son promise to spare no effort within their reach to demonstrate an eternal appreciation to the beneficent and most dignified of monarchs.

They so expect of the Paternal Clemency of Your Majesty, praying at all times that the Supreme Being reward his efforts with a happy and long life, triumphant always against his enemies.

Madrid, November 26, 1814

A.L.R.P.D.S.M.[17]

Manuel Pérez

Antonio Pérez

---

17. *A los reales pies de Su Majestad*: Spanish abbreviation for "at the Royal Feet of Your Majesty."

GLOSSARY

It is with trepidation that we include and define in the Glossary some of the African names used in the documents. **Ethnonyms** used during the Atlantic slave trade era are complex and can be misleading (see "Historical Protagonists and Questions of Identity" in the Introduction). Apparent ethnic designations when used to refer to enslaved Africans might designate the port from which they were embarked, a "brand name" that described desirable or undesirable qualities in a slave, or American re-creations of social bonds. Even when they accurately name an origin or language, they do not refer to static cultural identities but often to identities constructed within historically shifting political alliances and oppositions. Without some explanation of these terms, however, it is very difficult to sort out the different general areas from which the identified speakers came and thus the different alliances and conflicts among African-descent groups in the Americas. We recommend the work of Robin Law (see Bibliography) as a starting point to better understand the complexity of how **ethnonyms** were used during the Atlantic slave trade.

Abbreviations used in the Glossary are as follows: E = English; P = Portuguese; Sp = Spanish. These language designations refer to either the language to which the term belongs or the language context in which it is used in this book.

África (Sp, P): in early colonial times, the northern part of the continent on the Mediterranean coast.

Afroboricua (Sp): a Puerto Rican of African descent; "Boricua" is from Borinquen, the Taino name for the island before the 1492 Columbian invasion.

Afrocreole (E): an individual of African descent born in the colonial Iberian world, including Africa, identified in documents as "**criollo/criolla**" rather than by African **ethnonym**.

Agolin/Agonli (P): Gbe village west of the Zou River in the Zou province of today's Benin.

agreste (P): transitional morphological region dividing arid hinterlands (**sertão**) from the coast.

aguardiente (Sp): "burning water"; strong rum-like alcohol, usually from sugarcane.

ajuste (Sp): account adjustment.

alcalde (Sp): royal municipal authority who executed edicts to maintain order and exercised some police power.

alcalde mayor (Sp): mayor, superior officer, or provincial governor.

alcalde ordinario de segundo voto (Sp): town council authority who administered justice as a trial court judge.

alférez (Sp): member of the city council who could preside in the absence of the justice of the peace; also a military rank, something like "second lieutenant"; standard bearer in church or civil ceremonies.

alguacil (Sp): judicial officer of a town or municipality.

alvara (P): a decree.

Anchico (Sp): Also known as Anzicu, Téké, or Bateke: a people who lived north of the Zaire or Congo River, near the Malebo Pool and the Kingdom of Kongo, in the Democratic Republic of Congo, the Republic of Congo, and to a lesser extent Gabon.

Angola (P, Sp): Portuguese derivation from *ngola*, referring to an object made of iron, which symbolized political authority supported by spiritual forces. Slave traders used the name to refer to people embarked in the Portuguese colony of **Angola**, regardless of their specific ethnic origin.

apoderado (Sp): legal representative with proxy powers.

aquelarre (Sp): from the Basque *akelarre*, meaning "meadow of the male goat"; the witches' assemblies.

Arará (Sp): Allada or Arda; Bight of Benin; powerful Kingdom of Aja-Gbe speakers prior to the rise of Dahomey. A town in the Beninese province of Atlantique now claims the name.

arte de bien querer (Sp): the practice of preparing ointments, concoctions, and charms to bind lovers or unfaithful husbands.

asiento (Sp): royal monopoly granted to export slaves to the Americas.

audiencia (Sp): the hearing at which the prosecution and the defense made their depositions. See also **Real Audiencia**.

auditor general (Sp): the principal royal magistrate who heard criminal and civil cases.

auto (Sp, P): an official act or a legal proceeding; a decree or judge's determination; a dossier detailing the legal actions of a judicial process.

autos-da-fé (P), **auto de fe** (Sp): a generally public ceremony that concluded some trials of the modern Portuguese and Spanish Inquisitions in which the penitents were read their sentence, renounced their errors, and, in some cases, suffered corporal punishment or execution.

ayudante de la plaza (Sp): subordinate officer of an urban militia who followed the orders of a superior general.

Balanta (P, Sp): ethnic group from the upper Guinea Coast; Guinea-Bissau region.

Bañón (Sp): Also known as Bainuk or Banyun; ethnic group from Senegal and Guinea-Bissau. Their language today is closely related to that of the **Biáfara**.

banza: see **mbanza**.

banzo (P): in West Africa, a package of goods exchanged for some other good, used to set standards where there is no shared monetary system.

barrio (Sp): a division of a city, town, or district.

Benguela: a province and a port city in Angola; also a related ethnonym.

Biáfara (Sp): Also known as Beafada or Biafada; a major ethnolinguistic group in West Africa, between the Senegal and Gambia rivers, in the sixteenth and seventeenth centuries.

boga (Sp): literally "paddle"; an organized system of canoe river transportation for a variety of goods and passengers, particularly along the Magdalena River, connecting the New Kingdom of Granada with the Caribbean. It originally relied on involuntary indigenous laborers, but by the close of the sixteenth century they were replaced by enslaved Africans.

bozal, pl. bozales (Sp): a person recently enslaved and brought from Africa to Europe or the Americas who did not speak a European language.

Bran (Sp): ethnic group from today's Guinea-Bissau and Senegal.

buhío (Sp): also bohío, from Taíno, a type of thatched hut made from wood and mud.

cabildo (Sp): governing council of a town or city.

Cabo Verde (Sp): the Cape Verde islands, an important center of the slave trade, west of Senegal and Mauritania in Atlantic Africa. By extension, it designates a slave sent from that location independent of his or her ethnic origins.

Camangala (Sp): a present-day Angolan stream in the province of Benguela; **ethnonym** may refer to this area.

Cambunda (P, Sp): place-name associated with the Kimbundu region of what is today Angola; Cambunda **nations** were active in the Río de la Plata region (Argentina and Uruguay). In Brazil, members of colonial confraternities were identified as Cambunda.

candombes (Sp): music and dance style with lively rhythms from the Río de la Plata region, created by African descendants; also refers to celebrations where dances are practiced.

capellán (Sp): chaplain; ecclesiastic charged with performing masses and other liturgical tasks at a chapel.

capellanía (Sp): foundation in which money or goods are given to the Church or a priest to fund the celebration of masses or other pious acts that are beneficial for the salvation of the soul of the grantor.

capitán (Sp): a ranking officer, generally above a first lieutenant and below a major.

capitán a guerra (Sp): a civil authority trained in issues of war; in colonial times these were mayors and governors.

capitania (P): captaincy.

Carabalí (Sp): in Spanish colonial documents Carabali refers to people exported from the ports of the Niger Delta.

carrera de Indias (Sp): trade route used by Spanish fleets to come and go to the Americas.

cartas de libertad (Sp): deed of **manumission**; written document given to a slave as proof that she or he had been granted freedom.

Casa de Contratación (Sp): the House of Trade; created in Seville in 1503, it supervised commercial affairs, communication, and emigration to the Americas.

casta (Sp): caste; the position of an individual within the hierarchical social system of Spanish-American colonial society, which based rights and obligations on the identification of an individual's ancestry as being European, African, indigenous, or a combination of them. (See also the Introduction.)

chalupa (Sp): a small boat or launch, usually with one deck and two masts for sails.

chichería (Sp): a small shop where *chicha* (an alcoholic corn beverage) and other beverages and foods were sold.

cimarrón, pl. cimarrones (Sp): **Maroon** or runaway slave. The word was first used to name livestock that had escaped from its owner to the hilltops and connotes an indomitable or wild nature.

clases vulgares (Sp): poor people. In the Latin American context, the term was often applied to **castas**, or racially ostracized groups.

coartación (Sp): a Spanish system of **manumission**, by which a master and slave agreed on a purchase price; after an initial down payment, the slave could purchase his or her freedom in installments over a set period of time.

cobrero/a (Sp): native of the town of El Cobre, Cuba. A term that denotes origin, not slave status.

cocoliste/coliste (Sp): from Náhuatl *cocoliztli*, epidemic disease or typhoid fever.

cofradía (Sp): a confraternity, or religious fraternity, that practices pious acts.

compañías de negros libres (Sp): militia made up of African descendants, **mulattoes**, and people of brown complexion.

confesor (Sp): confessor; the priest to whom a Catholic habitually confesses sins and moral transgressions in the Sacrament of Penance. See **director**.

Congo (E, P, Sp): from Central West Africa, lower Congo River basin, in modern Angola; a general designation rather than specific ethnicity.

Consejo de Indias (Sp): council that dealt with affairs related to the overseas possessions of the Spanish empire.

coro (Sp), **choir** (E): place in a convent connected to the chapel but divided by a grille from the people, where nuns say their communal prayers. The name also indicates the highest status among nuns, those who perform the daily prayer of the Church. Sor Teresa Chicaba (Chapter 13) was not expected to participate in the coro.

Coura: region far inland of the Bight of Benin; possibly related to the Beninese town of Aledjo-koura in the Donga province where the people speak a Yoruba dialect.

covacha (Sp): hovel or small dwelling; literally, "a small cave."

Creole (E), **criollo/a** (Sp), **crioulo/a** (P): in Central Africa, the mixed culture that had evolved from the interactions between the Portuguese and the Kimbundu, including language, Christianity, naming patterns, and the like. In Spanish America, someone born in the Americas who was not of indigenous ancestry; used to refer to people of both African and European descent.

criado/a (Sp): laborer; servants or slaves who normally lived in the homes of their masters.

cuarterón (Sp): in theory, someone who was of one-fourth African origin and therefore considered "whiter" than a **mulatto**. In practice, **mulatto** and **cuarterón** were used interchangeably because the designations did not imply a change in rights and obligations.

Dagome/Dahomey (E, P, Sp): West African kingdom of Fon speakers; now the Republic of Benin and its related ethnonym (Dagome).

Dassa/Za (E): Yoruba village inside Mahi land. Today the name designates a city in the Zou province of Benin.

depositario (Sp): the title of an office of someone who kept slaves or other possessions or goods that were the subject of litigation.

desamparado (Sp): defenseless, unprotected.

diasporic identity (E): cultural markers that are reshaped by a person's or group's history of migration or dispersion outside their original homelands.

director (Sp), **spiritual director** (E): a spiritual advisor—not necessarily a confessor—who is familiar with the experiences a soul commonly encounters in developing a close relationship with God and who can provide counsel in the spiritual process of seeking transcendence.

Dominican Order (E): the Order of Preachers, founded in 1216 by Saint Dominic Guzman to promote the conversion and salvation of souls through dynamic and informed preaching that conformed to Catholic doctrine.

dote (Sp), **dowry** (E): as in traditional marriages, nuns—who will become brides of Christ—donate money, goods, or real estate to the general fund (endowment) of the convent.

ducado (Sp): gold coin of varying monetary value used in Spain and its American colonies.

Elmina (E, P, Sp): port city located in the central coast of today's Ghana. See also **Gold Coast**.

encomendero (Sp): Spaniard who holds the grant of an Indian town or its labor.

encomienda (Sp): literally "assignment"; errand. During colonial times in the Americas, this term was used for the assignment in which indigenous peoples were forced to work as tributaries to the Spanish authorities, who in turn were charged with their evangelization.

escribanía (Sp): notary office. In colonial cities, these offices were frequently situated in or near the town's main square because most colonial administrative institutions occupied this social and symbolic central space.

escribano (Sp), **escrivão** (P): notary or clerk; a person authorized to document civil, religious, or commercial formalities and legalize documents. *Escribanos de número* were assigned to a specific town or city, and *escribanos reales* had royal permission to work in different parts of the realm. Specific colonial institutions also had notaries assigned to them.

estancia (Sp): a small farm that grew food crops for market, especially to transport to urban areas.

estaos e casa (P): the buildings where the Lisbon Inquisition carried out its court sessions and where prisoners were kept.

Ethiopia (E): During the sixteenth and seventeenth centuries, the word "Etiopía" (Ethiopia) simultaneously described Africa to the south of the Sahara and what was known in the medieval imagination as the Kingdom of Ethiopia, which embraced Christianity in the fourth century AD. Although in religious and historical literature the term *etíope* (Ethiopian) sometimes describes a person from this kingdom, it was mostly used in the colonial setting as a learned synonym for "negro" (black).

ethnonym (E): a name attributing ethnic identity, but in the Black Atlantic often imposed by slave traders based on port of embarkation.

Eurocreole (E): "white" Spanish-Americans belonging to either the **Creole** or Iberian social group.

fidalgo (P): a noble person. In Kongo, as in Portugal, nobility was determined by birth, but position and authority more generally depended on royal favor.

Folupo/a (E, P, Sp): a small ethnicity located in the Guinea-Bissau region.

fuero (Sp): jurisdictional codes granted to a religious, military, or political entity.

geração (P): probably the Portuguese translation of the Kikongo word *kanda* (pl. *makanda*), which often means "lineage" or "clan." In Kongo, *makanda* were complex sets of alliances including political clients and slaves. It has a secondary meaning of faction; brothers and their followers might form two separate *makanda*.

gobernador intendente (Sp): person in charge of the city council.

Gold Coast or **Mina Coast** (E), **Mina Baja del Oro** (Sp), **Costa da Mina** (P): For Paniagua (Chapter 13), the Mina Baja del Oro is the area east of Elmina Castle (São Jorge da Mina) in Ghana roughly to the Volta River, where the Slave Coast begins. In Portuguese, the Mina Coast is the Slave Coast.

gremio (Sp): guild; association of people of the same trade or occupation ruled by norms and statutes, formed to protect mutual interests and maintain standards.

gremio de marina (Sp): naval guild.

grumete (Sp): a Spanish sailor learning the trade, ranked below a full sailor and above the younger *pajes*, who were dedicated to serving the officers and crew and cleaning.

Guinea (Sp, P): first used by Portuguese navigators to refer to coastal West Africa; later loosely applied to the general area of sub-Saharan West Africa connected to the slave trade until the late eighteenth century.

hacendado/a (Sp): owner of estates or ranches.

hato (Sp): open cattle ranch.

horro/a (Sp): a manumitted slave.

hueco (Sp): vacant plot of land.

in solidum (Latin), **in sólidum** (Sp): legal term referring to a jointly held responsibility in which each party is fully responsible for payments or duties.

indio (Sp): label for indigenous people in the Americas; for the Spanish this was a legal category with assigned rights, such as communal land rights, and assigned obligations, such as paying tribute and providing draft labor.

indulgence (Sp): indulgence. In Roman Catholic theology, an indulgence is the total or partial remission of the spiritual punishment associated with a sin. In the context of a will, testators express their wish to use their remaining earthly possessions after they die to obtain such indulgences, and hence they declare their soul universal heir of those possessions.

inquisidor fiscal (Sp): prosecuting attorney of the Inquisition.

inventory (Sp): inventory; in the context of a will, a complete list of items that were the property of the testator.

item (Sp): the same as something previously mentioned, used to note every new entry in a list.

Jaga (P): a warlike people from Africa's inland who invaded the Kingdom of Kongo and conquered its capital city Mbanza Kongo in 1568. Several years later, they were defeated by a Portuguese expedition, sent in response to the Bakongo king's request for military assistance from the Portuguese monarch in a war that lasted a year and a half. By the seventeenth century, they had become one of several states joined in a coalition headed by Queen Njinga.

Jolofo/a (Sp): also known as Wolof; a confederation of Senegambia states that broke up into several different kingdoms during the mid-sixteenth century.

jornal (Sp): wage.

junta de poblaciones (Sp): board or council whose policy was to attract indigenous populations into nuclear settlements to found towns.

justicia ordinaria (Sp): the administration of justice within a specific geographical jurisdiction.

La Mina Baja del Oro (Sp): see **Mina Coast**.

ladino (Sp, P): "latinized"; person acculturated to Iberian social norms. The term is primarily used to refer to non-Iberians who became conversant in Spanish or Portuguese. The term also implies adherence to the Catholic faith and loyalty to the Iberian monarchies; cf. **bozal**.

letrado (Sp): a person of letters, usually related to the legal profession.

licentiate (E): title addressing someone who holds a university degree.

limpieza de sangre (Sp): purity of blood, a social and quasi-legal concept that excluded people who did not have "old" Christian ancestry. Among those excluded were descendants of Jews, Muslims, indigenous people in the Americas, and people of African descent.

Lucumí (Sp): The term is supposed to have appeared through the Yoruba greeting *oluku mi* (my friend!). However, it was used over time to refer to various neighboring peoples of Yoruba. In seventeenth-century Spanish America, it referred to a speaker of Yoruba or suggested noble or elite characteristics associated with the Dahomey or Oyo kingdoms within the interior of the Bight of Benin.

Luso-African (E): African-born and, generally, familiar with Catholic practices and Portuguese language and other cultural attributes such as food and dress. Sometimes used to refer to Portuguese men who had lived for many years in Africa, it especially applied to their mixed-race descendants born of African mothers.

maese de campo (Sp): field commander, chief administrative officer of the province, with the status of commander general of all royal troops within the province.

Maki/Makino (P): people of the Maki Kingdom on the Mina Coast (Bight of Benin), neighboring Dahomey to the northeast.

Malemba (Sp): port city of the Kakongo Kingdom, also the area west of the Luando River valley. Enslaved people referred to as Malembas likely came from this area.

Mancera, Marquis of (E): Antonio Sebastián de Toledo (1608–1715). His third wife, Juliana Teresa Portocarrero y Meneses, was the legal owner of Sor Teresa de Santo Domingo (Chicaba). Mancera was a member of the Council of State under Carlos II of Spain and had been viceroy of Mexico (1664–1673), where his second wife was the protector of writer Sor Juana Inés de la Cruz.

mandadores (Sp): appointed officials; also used in some **Maroon** communities to refer to leadership positions.

mani (Kikongo): sixteenth-century spelling of the Kikongo word *mwene*, a person holding authority or a title. It is followed by the name of the territory the **mani** was deputed to govern or the office the **mani** fulfills.

manillas (Sp): bracelets, normally made of bronze and used as currency in West Africa for the purchase of slaves. They are frequently mentioned in documents as cargo for slave ships en route to West Africa.

manumission (E): the formal act of freeing someone from slavery.

Maroon (E): see **cimarrón**.

marronage (E): flight from enslavement.

mayor (Sp): superior or leader of a community.

mayordomo (Sp): head servant of a household or member of a confraternity charged with administering funds and overseeing functions.

mbanza (Kimbundu): a communal compound.

memorial (Sp): document in which something is petitioned.

mestizo/a (Sp): a person of mixed European and Amerindian ancestry.

metropole (E): the parent state of a colony.

Middle Passage (E): the journey of captive Africans from their homelands to the Americas.

milicianos (Sp): members of an armed militia.

Mina (E, P, Sp): name used to refer to people brought to the Americas from **Elmina** and the **Gold Coast** or Slave Coast areas; in Brazil the term refers to the Ewe-Fon group from modern Benin.

Mina Coast or **Lower Mina** (E), **Mina Baja del Oro** (Sp), **Costa da Mina** (P): see **Gold Coast**.

monterías (Sp): hunting grounds.

moreno/a (Sp): in colonial Spanish America, a person of African descent, possibly enslaved but usually signifying a person who has freed herself or himself.

morenos libres (Sp): free blacks.

morisco (Sp): a Moor who has converted to Christianity and his or her descendants.

muenho (P): Kimbundu word meaning "life," "life soul," or "spirit." Among the Mbundu, the title probably referred to an official spokesperson.

mulatto (E): an individual of mixed European and African origins. *Mulattoes* had a social and legal status that was usually more permissive than that assigned to *negros*.

nação, pl. nações (P), **nación, pl. naciones** (Sp), **nation** (E): place of origin or linguistic group of a slave or a slave's family. Frequently this term was assigned to the area where the person had been enslaved according to the geographical divisions established by Europeans as part of the slave trade. These identities are not accurate indications of specific African ethnic groups; nevertheless, in the Iberian colonies they played an important role in the cultural and social organization of black communities. For Africans in Brazil, *nações* were more or less constructed identities and reflected alliances specific to certain contexts and not necessarily to a specific geographic territory.

narrative agency (E): the control exercised by a speaker or writer over the content and form of the story he or she tells.

negro/a, negrito/a (Sp): an individual of African descent; often used to refer to black slaves as distinct from free blacks (*negros horros*). The diminutive *negrito/a* is used to refer to black people with a sense of familiarity—whether welcome or not. Sor Teresa Chicaba (Chapter 13) is still referred to as La Negrita today in the literature published by the Dominican Order.

new Christians (E): descendants of Jews converted to Christianity under duress in 1492 in Spain and shortly thereafter in Portugal and later the target of accusations of Judaism.

novenario/novena (Sp): a liturgical act referring to a nine-day period of worship and sermons dedicated to a saint.

Oyo (E, P, Sp): Yoruba empire (fifteenth through nineteenth centuries) established in what is now Nigeria, Togo, and Benin.

palenque (Sp): literally "palisade" or defensive fence made of stakes. The term refers to clandestine **Maroon** communities where homes were built and food crops were planted.

paradigm (E): interpretation or model.

pardo/a (Sp): brown, **mulatto**; can also refer to a **zambo**. In mid-colonial Spanish America, a person of color born or raised as a free person.

patache (Sp): packet boat, a service boat normally used to ferry passengers or supplies between a larger ship and the shore.

patria (Sp): homeland; literally, "fatherland."

peso (Sp): a standard currency in colonial Spanish America worth eight **reales**.

plaza (Sp): garrison, fortress, or town/city square.

pombeiro (P): slave-trading agents who traveled the interior of Angola.

preplantation period (E): historical period generally associated with the absence of large landed estates known as *haciendas* or plantations in a particular colony or country.

presidio (Sp): correctional facility; fortress.

privateer (E): an armed ship owned by private individuals holding a government commission and authorized for use in war.

processo (P): legal proceedings.

protocolos notariales (Sp): collection of files kept by public notaries where documents and legal transactions among individuals were recorded.

pueblo (Sp): a village; legal category for a population settlement constituting a corporate community.

pulpería (Sp): store that sold various goods such as food, liquor, textiles, and tools.

quilombo (P): from the Kimbundu word *kilombo*, referring to a military encampment.

Quisama (Sp): a large district south of the Kwanza River in Angola.

racial miscegenation (E): interracial mixture.

real, pl. reales (Sp): silver coin and standard currency in colonial Spanish America, with eight *reales* equaling one **peso** in the seventeenth century.

Real Audiencia (Sp): judicial body, high court of appeal, and viceregal council; in the absence of a viceroy, it could govern a territory.

real cédula (Sp): royal decree.

regent (E): a regent; one who rules in place of a king or queen when absent or unable to rule.

Relação (P): the highest court in Brazil; the appellate court.

relación (Sp): a narrative; in the religious context, a document written about one's life and spiritual experiences following the command and under the guidance of a spiritual **director**.

renda (P): a revenue-bearing property; in Kongo **rendas** could be freely given and withdrawn by the king or other high officials.

royal slaves (E), **esclavos del rey** (Sp): slaves owned by the king or the state.

Sabaru (P): Gbe village inside Mahi land, which is today in the Zou province of Benin.

sankofa (Akan): literally, "go back and take." It represents the need to return to the past and reclaim what was good and worthwhile. Among some people of African descent exiled in the diaspora, it also represented a return to one's ancestral homeland after death.

São Tomé (P): former Portuguese island colony in the Gulf of Guinea that acted as a clearinghouse for slaves coming from Angola, Kongo, and the Lower Mina region.

sargento mayor (Sp): often translated as "sergeant major"; a senior operating officer second in command to the **maese de campo**.

sargento mayor de la plaza (Sp): subordinate officer of an urban militia, superior to a sergeant.

secta de las brujas (Sp): witches' sect; used in an accusatory manner to refer to a group of men and women who allegedly rejected God and the sacraments and worshipped the devil.

sertão (P): an arid, inland region (hinterlands).

sevicia (Sp): juridical term that refers to physical and psychological cruelty.

subaltern agents (E): in postmodernist and postcolonial studies, refers to the oppressed, voiceless, or marginal elements of a society.

Supreme Junta (E), **Junta Suprema** (Sp): regal council that took over the governmental functions of Spain and its overseas colonies during the Napoleonic invasion.

tambo (Sp): in Río de la Plata, dance of African descendants; hidden place where they gathered to perform dances.

tambuquado, tambuquara (P): from the Kikongo word *tambuka*, meaning "to remove from office." The verb was conjugated according to Portuguese rules in this text (Chapter 1), as was the custom for all borrowed words.

tartana (Sp): sailing vessel with one mast and a lateen sail.

teniente de capitán general (Sp): military officer appointed to undertake the duties of the field marshal during his absence.

teniente del rey (Sp): governor deputy; cf. **teniente gobernador**.

teniente general (Sp): general deputy; an office of wide colonial power, the appointment to which was ratified by the viceregal government; abbreviated as *teniente*.

teniente gobernador (Sp): deputy governor; person appointed to undertake the duties of the governor in his or her absence.

termo (P): an entry; a record of one of the acts of an organization; a written declaration that forms part of a trial.

Terranova (Sp): person who came, usually, to Peru as a slave from the East Guinea Coast.

tertiary (E): third-order nun; a tertiary nun; one who belongs to one of the tertiary orders of a religious institute (Dominicans, Franciscans). Sor Teresa de Santo Domingo, Chicaba (Chapter 13), is referred to as a *tercera*, but her status in the convent was more like the black *donadas* of Spanish America, who entered the religious community in service to the ranking members. Tertiaries were laity—the faithful outside the ranks of the clergy—who, influenced by the spiritual practices and piety of a monastic Catholic religious congregation, entered into a formal relationship with that order and lived lives in accordance to the rule. In 1285, Munio de Zamora united disparate groups of laity who called themselves the Order of Penance under a rule titled the Penance of Saint Dominic. This third order, unlike many others, includes a few cloistered convents of nuns as well as some active congregations of sisters and laity organized in fraternities. Teresa Chicaba was a member of an enclosed community of nuns; however, her status in that convent was unique. Paniagua refers to her as a tertiary, as if she were a lay person who had taken vows and was attached to La Penitencia in Salamanca. His description would make her a tertiary of the Tertiary Order of Penitence. His inability to clearly define her status among Dominicans accentuates her marginality among her sisters.

transculturated/transculturation (E): coined by Cuban sociologist Fernando Ortiz in 1940 to describe the process of selective cultural transformation in areas of intercultural contract.

vecino/a (Sp): neighbor; a long-term inhabitant of a particular town or city; generally refers to property holders or heads of household and signifies a reputable person. When used as a legal term, *vecino* is akin to the word "citizen" but on a local level. *Vecinos* were entitled to rights and privileges not enjoyed by outsiders, and they had corresponding responsibilities to the community.

vega (Sp): in the Caribbean, a tobacco farm.

villa (Sp): a town; legal category for a large incorporated population settlement.

virrey (Sp): viceroy, the highest political officer in Spanish America; one who represented the power and authority of the king of Spain. There were two viceroyalties originally—Mexico and Peru.

zambo/a (Sp, P): individual of mixed indigenous and African descent. From a legal point of view, **zambos** were considered part of the **mulatto** caste. Socially, however, they occupied a more difficult position as the offspring of two castes that were considered morally and intellectually inferior to Spaniards. Some **zambos** lived closer to indigenous communities than to European society, which also led them to occupy a unique cultural space.

Zape (Sp): a people from what is modern-day Sierra Leone.

BIBLIOGRAPHY

Introduction

Andrews, George Reid. *Afro-Latin America, 1800–2000*. New York: Oxford UP, 2004.

Butler, Judith. *Gender Trouble: Feminism and the Subversion of Identity*. New York: Routledge, 1999.

García Canclini, Néstor. *Hybrid Cultures: Strategies for Entering and Leaving Modernity*. Introduction by Renato Rosaldo. Trans. Christopher L. Chiappari and Silvia L. López. Minneapolis: U of Minnesota P, 2005.

Gilroy, Paul. *The Black Atlantic: Modernity and Double Consciousness*. London: Verso, 1993.

Klein, Herbert S. *The Atlantic Slave Trade*. Cambridge: Cambridge UP, 1999.

Lienhard, Martín. "De mestizajes, heterogeneidades, hibridismos y otras quimeras." In *Asedios a la heterogeneidad cultural: Libro en homenaje a Antonio Cornejo Polar*, 57–80. Edited by José Antonio Mazzotti and Ulises Juan Zevallos Aguilar. Philadelphia: Asociación Internacional de Peruanistas, 1996.

———. "Padrões da cosmologia congo e sua adaptação-recriação na América escravista." *Anais de História de Além-Mar (Lisboa)* 1 (2000): 245–72.

———. "Una tierra sin amos: Lectura de los testimonios legales de algunos esclavos fugitivos (Puerto Rico y Brasil, siglo XIX)." *América Indígena* 54, no. 4 (1994): 209–27.

Lorenzo Cadarso, Pedro Luis. *La documentación judicial en la época de los Austrias: Estudio archivístico y diplomático*, 2nd ed. Caceres, Spain: Plaza, 2004. [The first edition of this book (1998) can be read online at the Web site of the Facultad de Biblioteconomía y Documentación, Departamento de Historia, Universidad de Extremadura (Badajoz), http://alcazaba.unex.es/~plorenzo/publicaciones/libros/docaust.html. Accessed Jan. 7, 2009.]

Modern Language Association Ad Hoc Committee on Foreign Language. "Foreign Languages and Higher Education: New Structures for a Changed World." Modern Language Association. 2007. http://www.mla.org/flreport. Accessed Jan. 7, 2009.

Ortiz, Fernando. *Contrapunteo cubano del tabaco y el azúcar*. Caracas, Venezuela: Biblioteca Ayacucho, 1978.

Rama, Ángel. *Transculturación narrativa en América Latina*, 2nd ed. Mexico City: Siglo Veintiuno, 1985.

Restall, Matthew. "A History of the New Philology and the New Philology in History." *Latin American Research Review* 38, no. 1 (2003): 113–34.

White, Hayden. *The Content of the Form: Narrative Discourse and Historical Representation*. Baltimore, MD: Johns Hopkins UP, 1987.

Chapter 1

Balandier, Georges. *Daily Life in the Kingdom of Kongo: Sixteenth to Eighteenth Centuries*. Trans. Helen Weaver. New York: Pantheon, 1968.

Bontinck, François. "Ndoadidiki Ne-Kino a Mubemba, premier évêque Kongo (c. 1495–c. 1531)." *Revue africaine de théologie* 3 (1979): 149–69.

Brásio, António, ed. *Monumenta missionaria africana*. 11 vols. Lisbon: Agência-Geral do Ultramar, 1952–1971.

Cardoso, Mateus. *Historia do Reino de Congo*. First published 1624. Edited by António Brásio. Lisbon: Centro de Estudos Históricos Ultramarinos, 1969.

Cavazzi da Montecuccolo, Giovanni Antonio. *Istorica descrizione de' tre' regni Congo: Matamba ad Angola*. Bologna, Italy: Giacomo Monti, 1687.

Heywood, Linda. "Slavery and Its Transformation in the Kingdom of Kongo, 1491–1800." *Journal of African History* 50, no. 1 (2009): 1–22.

Heywood, Linda, and John Thornton. *Central Africans, Atlantic Creoles, and the Foundation of the Americas, 1585–1660*. Cambridge: Cambridge UP, 2007.

Hilton, Ann. *The Kingdom of Kongo*. Oxford: Oxford UP, 1985.

Lopes, Duarte, and Filippo Pigafetta. *Relazione del Reame di Congo et della Circonvince Contrade*. Rome, 1591. Edited by Giorgio Cardonna. Milan: Bompiani, 1978.

Paiva Manso, Levy Maria Jordão, Visconde de. *História do Congo*. Lisbon: Academia Real das Sciencias, 1877.

Thornton, John. *Africa and Africans in the Making of the Atlantic World, 1400–1800*, 2nd ed. Cambridge: Cambridge UP, 1998.

———. "The Development of an African Catholic Church in the Kingdom of Kongo, 1491–1750." *Journal of African History* 25, no 2 (1984): 147–67.

———. "Early Kongo-Portuguese Relations: A New Interpretation." *History in Africa* 8 (1981): 183–204.

———. "Elite Women in the Kingdom of Kongo: Historical Perspectives on Women's Political Power." *Journal of African History* 47, no. 3 (2006): 437–60.

———. *The Kingdom of Kongo: Civil War and Transition, 1641–1718*. Madison: U of Wisconsin P, 1983.

———. "The Origins and Early History of the Kingdom of Kongo, c. 1350–1550." *International Journal of African Historical Studies* 34, no. 1 (2001): 89–120.

Vansina, Jan. *Kingdoms of the Savanna*. Madison: U of Wisconsin P, 1966.

———. *Paths in the Rainforest: Toward a History of Political Tradition in Equatorial Africa*. Madison: U of Wisconsin P, 1990.

Vansina, Jan, and Téofile Obenga. "The Kongo Kingdom and Its Neighbors." In *Africa from the Sixteenth to the Eighteenth Century*, 546–87. Edited by B. A. Ogot. Vol. 5 of the *UNESCO General History of Africa*. Berkeley: U of California P, 1992.

Chapter 2

Alcina Franch, José. "Penetración española en Esmeraldas tipología del descubrimiento." *Revista de Indias* 36, nos. 143–244 (1976): 65–121.

Andrien, Kenneth J. *The Kingdom of Quito, 1690–1830: The State and Regional Development*. New York: Cambridge UP, 1995.

Bailyn, Bernard. *Atlantic History: Concept and Contours*. Cambridge, MA: Harvard UP, 2005.

Beatty-Medina, Charles. "Between the Cross and the Sword: Religious Conquest and Maroon Legitimacy in Sixteenth- and Early Seventeenth-Century Esmeraldas." In *Africans to Spanish America: Expanding the Diaspora*, 95–113. Edited by Sherwin K. Bryant, Rachel Sarah O'Toole, and Ben Vinson III. Urbana-Champaign: U of Illinois P, 2014.

————. "Caught between Rivals: The Spanish-African Maroon Competition for Captive Labor in the Region of Esmeraldas during the Late Sixteenth and Early Seventeenth Centuries." *The Americas* 63, no. 1 (2006): 113–36.

————. "Rebels and Conquerors: African Slaves, Spanish Authorities, and the Domination of Esmeraldas, 1563–1621." PhD diss., Brown University, 2002.

Bryant, Sherwin K. "Finding Gold, Forming Slavery: The Creation of a Classic Slave Society, Popayán, 1600–1700." *The Americas* 63, no. 1 (2006): 81–112.

Cabello Balboa, Miguel. "Verdadera descripción y relación larga de la Provincia y tierra de las Esmeraldas" In *Obras*, Vol. 1, 7–76. Edited by Jacinto Jijón y Caamaño. Quito, Ecuador: Ecuatoriana, 1945.

Calero, Luís Fernando. *Chiefdoms under Siege: Spain's Rule and Native Adaptation in the Southern Colombian Andes, 1535–1700*. Albuquerque: U of New Mexico P, 1997.

Elliot, J. H. "The Spanish Conquest." In *Colonial Spanish America,* 1–59. Edited by Leslie Bethell. Cambridge: Cambridge UP, 1987.

Genovese, Eugene D. *From Rebellion to Revolution: Afro-American Slave Revolts in the Making of the Modern World*. New York: Vintage Books, 1981.

Lane, Kris E. *Quito 1599: City and Colony in Transition*. Albuquerque: U of New Mexico P, 2002.

Newson, Linda A. *Life and Death in Early Colonial Ecuador*. Norman: U of Oklahoma P, 1995.

Ortiz de la Tabla Ducasse, Javier. *Los encomenderos de Quito, 1534–1660: Origen y evolución de una élite colonial*. Seville: Escuela de Estudios Hispano-Americanos, 1993.

Parris, Scott V. "Alliance and Competition: Four Case Studies of Maroon-European Relations." *Nieuwe West-Indische Gids* 55 (1981): 174–224.

Phelan, John Leddy. *The Kingdom of Quito in the Seventeenth Century*. Madison: U of Wisconsin P, 1967.

Pike, Ruth. *Aristocrats and Traders: Sevillian Society in the Sixteenth Century*. Ithaca, NY: Cornell UP, 1972.

Powers, Karen Vieira. *Andean Journeys: Migration, Ethnogenesis, and the State in Colonial Quito*. Albuquerque: U of New Mexico P, 1995.

Price, Richard, ed. *Maroon Societies: Rebel Slave Communities in the Americas*, 3rd ed. Baltimore, MD: Johns Hopkins UP, 1996.

Restall, Matthew, ed. *Beyond Black and Red: African-Native Relations in Colonial Latin America*. Albuquerque: U of New Mexico P, 2005.

————. "Black Conquistadors: Armed Africans in Early Spanish America." *The Americas* 57, no. 2 (2000): 171–205.

————. *Seven Myths of the Spanish Conquest*. Oxford: Oxford UP, 2003.

Rueda Novoa, Rocio. *Zambaje y autonomía: Historia de la gente negra de la provincia de Esmeraldas, siglos XVI–XVIII*. Quito, Ecuador: Abya-Yala, 2001.

Savoia, P. Rafael, ed. *El negro en la historia*. Quito, Ecuador: Ediciones Afroamerica, Centro Cultural Afroecuatoriano, 1992.

Szaszdi, Adam. "El Transfondo de un cuadro: 'Los mulatos de Esmeraldas' de Andrés Sánchez Galque." *Cuadernos Prehispánicos* 12 (1986–1987): 93–142.

Williams, Caroline. *Between Resistance and Adaptation: Indigenous Peoples and the Colonisation of the Chocó, 1510–1753*. Liverpool, UK: Liverpool UP, 2005.

Chapter 3

Birmingham, David. "Central Africa from Cameroun to the Zambezi." In *The Cambridge History of Africa,* Vol. 4, 325–83. Edited by J. D. Fage and Roland Anthony Oliver. Cambridge: Cambridge UP, 1986.

Brásio, Padre António, ed. *Monumenta missionaria africana: África Ocidental.* 15 vols. Lisbon: Agência-Geral do Ultramar, 1971.

Cadornega, António de Oliveira de. *História geral das guerras angolanas: 1680.* Annotated and edited by José Matias Delgado. Vol. 2. Lisbon: Agência-Geral do Ultramar, 1972.

Heintze, Beatrix. *Fontes para a história de Angola do século XVII.* Vol. 1. Stuttgart, Germany: Franz Steiner Verlag, 1985.

Heywood, Linda M., ed. *Central Africans and Cultural Transformations in the American Diaspora.* Cambridge: Cambridge UP, 2002.

Heywood, Linda, and John Thornton. *Central Africans, Atlantic Creoles, and the Foundation of the Americas, 1585–1660.* Cambridge: Cambridge UP, 2007.

Miller, Joseph Calder. *Kings and Kinsmen: Early Mbundu States in Angola.* Oxford: Clarendon, 1976.

Montecuccolo, Giovanni Antonio Cavazzi de. *Istorica descrizione de' tre' regni Congo, Matamba, et Angola.* Bologna, Italy: Giacomo Monti, 1687.

Napoli, Antonio Gaeta da. *La maravigliosa conversione alla Santa Fede di Cristo della Regina Singa e del svo Regno di Matamba nell'Africa meridionale.* Naples, Italy: Passaro, 1669.

Njinga of Ndongo, Rainha. Letter to António de Oliveira de Cadornega, June 15, 1660. In *Histórica geral das guerras angolanas.* First published 1680. Vol. 2, 172–73. Annotated and edited by José Matias Delgado. Lisbon: Agência-Geral do Ultramar, 1972.

———. Letter to Bento Banha Cardoso, March 3, 1625. In *Fontes para a história de Angola do século XVII*, Vol. 1, 244–45. Edited by Beatrix Heintze. Stuttgart, Germany: Franz Steiner Verlag, 1985.

———. Letter to Luís Mendes de Sousa Chicorro, Governor General of Angola, December 13, 1655. In *Monumenta missionario africana; África ocidental (1651–1655).* Vol. 11, 524–28. Edited by Padre António Brásio. Lisbon: Agência-Geral do Ultramar, 1971.

———. Letter to Propaganda Fide (The Sacred Congregation for the Propagation of the Faith), August 15, 1651. In *Monumenta missionaria africana: África ocidental (1651–1655).* Vol. 11, 70–71. Edited by Padre António Brásio. Lisbon: Agência-Geral do Ultramar, 1971.

———. Letter to Serafino da Cortona, August 15, 1657. In *Monumenta missionario africana: África ocidental (1651–1655).* Vol. 12, 131–32. Edited by Padre António Brásio. Lisbon: Agência-Geral do Ultramar, 1971.

Chapter 4

Ares Queija, Berta, and Alessandro Stella, eds. *Negros, mulatos, zambaigos: Derroteros africanos en los mundos ibéricos.* Seville: Escuela de Estudios Hispano-Americanos, 2000.

Franco Silva, Alfonso. *La esclavitud en Sevilla y su tierra a fines de la Edad Media.* Seville: Diputación Provincial de Sevilla, 1979.

Garofalo, Leo J. "The Case of Diego Suárez: Defining Empire through Afro-Iberian Incorporation and Movement in the Early Ibero-American World." Unpublished manuscript.

———. "The Shape of a Diaspora: The Movement of Afro-Iberians to Colonial Spanish America." In *Africans to Spanish America: Expanding the Diaspora*, 29–49. Edited by Sherwin K. Bryant, Rachel Sarah O'Toole, and Ben Vinson III. Champaign: U of Illinois P, 2014.

Gerhard, Peter. "A Black Conquistador in Mexico." *Hispanic American Historical Review* 58, no. 3 (1968): 451–59.

González Díaz, Antonio Manuel. *La esclavitud en Ayamonte durante el Antiguo Régimen (siglos XVI, XVII y XVIII)*. Huelva, Spain: Diputación provincial de Huelva, 1996.

Lobo Cabrera, Manuel. *La esclavitud en las Canarias orientales en el siglo XVI (negros, moros y moriscos)*. Las Palmas, Canary Islands: Ediciones del Cabildo Insular de Gran Canaria, 1982.

Martín Casares, Aurelia. *La esclavitud en la Granada del siglo XVI*. Granada, Spain: Universidad de Granada, 2000.

Pike, Ruth. "Sevillian Society in the Sixteenth Century: Slaves and Freedmen," *Hispanic American Historical Review* 47 (1967): 344–59.

Restall, Matthew. *Seven Myths of the Spanish Conquest*. Oxford: Oxford UP, 2003.

Saunders, A. C. de C. M. *A Social History of Black Slaves and Freedmen in Portugal, 1441–1555*. Cambridge: Cambridge UP, 1982.

Stella, Alessandro. *Histoires d'esclaves dans la péninsule ibérique*. Paris: Editions de l'Ecole des Hautes Etudes en Sciences Sociales, 2000.

Sweet, James H. *Recreating Africa: Culture, Kinship, and Religion in the African-Portuguese World, 1441–1770*. Chapel Hill: U of North Carolina P, 2003.

Chapter 5

Aguado, Fray Pedro de. *Recopilación historial de Venezuela*. First published 1581. Vol. 2, Chs. 9–13, 599–630. Caracas, Venezuela: Academia Nacional de la Historia, 1963.

Arrázola, Roberto. *Palenque, primero pueblo libre de América: Historia de las sublevaciones de los esclavos de Cartagena*. Cartagena, Colombia: Hernández, 1970.

Borrego Plá, María del Carmen. *Palenques de negros en Cartagena de Indias a fines del siglo XVII*. Seville: Escuela de Estudios Hispano-Americanos de Sevilla, 1973.

Friedemann, Nina S. de. *Ma ngombe: Guerreros y ganaderos en Palenque*. Bogota, Colombia: C. Valencia, 1979.

Heywood, Linda, and John Thornton. *Central Africans, Atlantic Creoles, and the Foundation of the Americas, 1585–1660*. Cambridge: Cambridge UP, 2007.

Landers, Jane G. "*Cimarrón* and Citizen: African Ethnicity, Corporate Identity, and the Evolution of Free Black Towns in the Spanish Circum-Caribbean." In *Slaves, Subjects, and Subversives: Blacks in Colonial Latin America*, 111–45. Edited by Jane G. Landers and Barry M. Robinson. Albuquerque: U of New Mexico P, 2006.

Lienhard, Martín. *O mar e o mato: Histórias da escravidão (Congo-Angola, Brasil, Caribe)*. Salvador, Brazil: EDUFBA/CEAO, 1998.

———. "Una tierra sin amos: Lectura de los testimonios legales de algunos esclavos fugitivos (Puerto Rico y Brasil, siglo XIX)." *América Indígena* 54, no. 4 (1994): 209–27.

Lovejoy, Paul E. "Identifying Enslaved Africans in the African Diaspora." In *Identity in the Shadow of Slavery*, 1–29. Edited by Paul E. Lovejoy. London: Continuum, 2000.

McKnight, Kathryn Joy. "Confronted Rituals: Spanish Colonial and Angolan 'Maroon' Executions in Cartagena de Indias (1634)." *Journal of Colonialism and Colonial History* 5, no. 3 (2004). Project MUSE. Unpaginated.

———. "Gendered Declarations: Testimonies of Three Captured *Maroon* Women, Cartagena de Indias, 1634." *Colonial Latin American Historical Review* 12, no. 4 (2003): 499–527.

Movimiento Nacional Cimarrón. Colombia. 2007. http://www.movimientocimarron.org. Accessed March 11, 2015.

Navarrete, María Cristina. *Cimarrones y palenques en el siglo XVII*. Cali, Colombia: Universidad del Valle, 2003.

Price, Richard, ed. *Maroon Societies: Rebel Slave Communities in the Americas*. Garden City, NY: Anchor, 1973.

Renacientes PCN Colombia. Proceso de Comunidades Negras de Colombia. Hosted by galeotas.org. 2009. http://www.renacientes.org. Accessed May 10, 2009.

Rodríguez, Frederick Marshal. *Cimarrón Revolts and Pacification in New Spain, the Isthmus of Panama and Colonial Colombia, 1503–1800*. PhD diss., Loyola University of Chicago, 1979.

Ruiz Rivera, Julián B. "Cimarronaje en Cartagena de Indias: Siglo XVII." *Memoria (Bogotá: Archivo General de la Nación)* 8 (2001): 10–35.

Salgado, Paulino. *Batata y Su Rumba Palenquera*. (compact disc). Network, 2003.

Simón, Fray Pedro. *Noticias historiales de las conquistas de Tierra Firme en las Indias Occidentales*. First published 1625. Vol. 8, Chs. 22–23, 165–74. Edited by Manuel José Forero. Bogota, Colombia: Biblioteca de Autores Colombianos, 1953.

Thornton, John. *Africa and Africans in the Making of the Atlantic World, 1400–1800*, 2nd ed. Cambridge: Cambridge UP, 1998.

Chapter 6

Blackburn, Robin. *The Making of New World Slavery from the Baroque to the Modern, 1492–1800*. London: Verso, 1997.

Bristol, Joan Cameron. *Christians, Blasphemers, and Witches: Afro-Mexican Ritual Practice in the Seventeenth Century*. Albuquerque: U of New Mexico P, 2007.

Eire, Carlos M. N. *From Madrid to Purgatory: The Art and Craft of Dying in Sixteenth-Century Spain*. Cambridge: Cambridge UP, 1995.

Gomez, Michael A. *Exchanging Our Country Marks: The Transformation of African Identities in the Colonial and Antebellum South*. Chapel Hill: U of North Carolina P, 1998.

Larkin, Brian. "Confraternities and Community: The Decline of the Communal Quest for Salvation in Eighteenth-Century México City." In *Local Religion in Colonial Mexico*, 189–214. Edited by Martin Nesvig. Albuquerque: U of New Mexico P, 2006.

Lovejoy, Paul E. *Identity in the Shadow of Slavery.* London: Continuum, 2000.

Lovejoy, Paul E., and David V. Troutman. *Transatlantic Dimensions of Ethnicity in the African Diaspora.* London: Continuum, 2003.

von Germeten, Nicole. *Black Blood Brothers: Confraternities and Social Mobility for Afro-Mexicans.* Gainesville: UP of Florida, 2006.

————. "Death in Black and White: Testaments and Confraternal Devotion in Seventeenth-Century Mexico City." *Colonial Latin American Historical Review* 12, no. 3 (2003): 275–301.

————. "Routes to Respectability: Confraternities and Men of African Descent in New Spain." In *Local Religion in Colonial Mexico*, 215–34. Edited by Martin Nesvig. Albuquerque: U of New Mexico P, 2006.

Chapter 7

Aguirre, Carlos. *Agentes de su propia libertad: Los esclavos de Lima y la desintegración de la esclavitud, 1821–1834.* Lima, Peru: Pontificia Universidad Católica del Perú, 1993.

Alfonso X [King of Castile and Leon, 1221–1284]. *Siete partidas.* Edited by Licentiate Gregorio López. First published 1555. Facsimile edition. 3 vols. Madrid: Boletín Oficial del Estado, 1985.

Bowser, Frederick P. *The African Slave in Colonial Peru, 1524–1650.* Stanford, CA: Stanford UP, 1974.

Brockington, Lolita Gutiérrez. *Blacks, Indians, and Spaniards in the Eastern Andes: Reclaiming the Forgotten in Colonial Mizque, 1550–1782.* Lincoln: U of Nebraska P, 2006.

Charún-Illescas, Lucía. *Malambo.* Trans. Emmanuel Harris, II. Chicago: Swan Isle Press, 2004.

Eire, Carlos M. N. *From Madrid to Purgatory: The Art and Craft of Dying in Sixteenth-Century Spain.* Cambridge: Cambridge UP, 1995.

Gaspar, David Barry, and Darlene Clark Hine, eds. *Beyond Bondage: Free Women of Color in the Americas.* Urbana: U of Illinois P, 2004.

Gauderman, Kimberley. *Women's Lives in Colonial Quito: Gender, Law, and Economy in Spanish America.* Austin: U of Texas P, 2003.

Graubart, Karen B. *With Our Labor and Sweat: Indigenous Women and the Formation of Colonial Society in Peru, 1550–1700.* Stanford, CA: Stanford UP, 2007.

Herzog, Tamar. *Mediación, archivos y ejercicio: Los escribanos de Quito (siglo XVII).* Frankfurt am Main, Germany: Vittorio Klostermann, 1996.

Hünefeldt, Christine. *Paying the Price of Freedom: Family and Labor among Lima's Slaves, 1800–1854.* Berkeley: U of California P, 1994.

Irolo Calar, Nicolás de. *La política de escrituras.* First published 1605. Edited by María del Pilar Martínez López-Cano. Mexico City: Universidad Autónoma de México, 1996.

Jouve Martín, José Ramón. *Esclavos de la ciudad letrada: Esclavitud, escritura y colonialismo en Lima (1650–1700).* Lima, Peru: Instituto de Estudios Peruanos, 2005.

Kellog, Susan, and Matthew Restall, eds. *Dead Giveaways: Indigenous Testaments of Colonial Mesoamerica and the Andes.* Salt Lake City: U of Utah P, 1998.

Le Goff, Jacques. *The Birth of Purgatory*. Chicago: U of Chicago P, 1984.

Portocarrero Lazo de la Vega, Melchor Antonio, and Conde de la Monclova. *Numeración general de todas las personas de ambos sexos, edades y calidades que se ha hecho en esta ciudad de Lima*. First published 1700. Edited by Noble D. Cook. Lima, Peru: Comide, 1985.

Powers, Karen Viera. *Women in the Crucible of Conquest: The Gendered Genesis of Spanish American Society, 1500–1600*. Albuquerque: U of New Mexico P, 2005.

Socolow, Susan Migden. *The Women of Colonial America*. Cambridge: Cambridge UP, 2000.

Torres, Carmen. "Los asientos como sistema del comercio negrearo en América: El Real Asiento inglés de 1713." *Boletín de la Academia Nacional de la Historia de Venezuela* 77, no. 307 (1994): 117–22.

van Deusen, Nancy E., ed. and trans. *The Souls of Purgatory: The Spiritual Diary of a Seventeenth-Century Afro-Peruvian Mystic, Ursula de Jesús*. Albuquerque: U of New Mexico P, 2004.

Vila Vilar, Enriqueta. "Los asientos portugueses y el contrabando de negros." *Anuario de Estudios Americanos* 30 (1973): 557–609.

Chapter 8

Aguirre, Carlos. *Agentes de su propia libertad: Los esclavos de Lima y la desintegración de la esclavitud*, 181–210. Lima, Peru: Pontificia Universidad Católica del Perú, Fondo Editorial, 1993.

Andrews, George Reid. *Afro-Latin America, 1800–2000*. Oxford: Oxford UP, 2004.

Cáceres, Rina. *Negros, mulatos, esclavos y libertos en la Costa Rica del siglo XVII*. Mexico City: Instituto Panamericano de Geografía e Historia, 2000.

Chaves, María Eugenia. "Slave Women's Strategies for Freedom and the Late Spanish Colonial State." In *Hidden Histories of Gender and the State in Latin America*, 108–26. Edited by Elizabeth Dore and Maxine Molyneux. Durham, NC: Duke UP, 2000.

Deschamps Chapeaux, Pedro. *Los batallones de pardos y morenos libres*. Havana, Cuba: Editorial Arte y Literatura, Instituto Cubano del Libro, 1976.

Díaz, María Elena. "Conjuring Identities: Race, Nativeness, Local Citizenship and Royal Slavery in a Frontier Location (Revisiting El Cobre, Cuba)." In *Imperial Subjects: Race and Identity in Colonial Latin America*, 197–224. Edited by Andrew B. Fisher and Matthew D. O'Hara. Durham, NC: Duke UP, 2009.

———. *El Cobre, Cuba: Images, Voices, Histories*. Department of History, University of California, Santa Cruz. http://humweb.ucsc.edu/elcobre. Accessed Jan. 1, 2009.

———. "Of Life and Freedom in the (Tropical) Hearth: El Cobre, 1709–1773." In *Beyond Bondage: Free Women of Color in the Americas*, 19–36. Edited by D. B. Gaspar and D. Clark. Chicago: U of Illinois P, 2004.

———. "Mining Women, Royal Slaves: Copper Mining in Colonial Cuba, 1670–1780." In *Mining Women: Gender in the Development of a Global Industry, 1700–2000*, 21–39. Edited by Laurie Mercier and Jaclyn Viskovatoff. New York: Palgrave MacMillan Press, 2006.

———. "Rethinking Tradition and Identity: The Virgin of Charity of El Cobre." In *Cuba, the Elusive Nation*, 43–59. Edited by D. J. Fernández and M. Cámara Betancourt. Gainesville: UP of Florida, 2000.

————. *The Virgin, the King, and the Royal Slaves of El Cobre: Negotiating Freedom in Colonial Cuba, 1670–1780.* Stanford, CA: Stanford UP, 2000.

Granda, Germán de. "Orígen, función y estructura de un pueblo de negros y mulattos libres en el Paraguay del siglo XVIII (San Agustín de la Emboscada)." *Revista de Indias* 43 (1983): 229–64.

Klein, Herbert. "The Colored Militia of Cuba: 1568–1868." *Caribbean Studies* 6, no. 2 (1966): 17–27.

Landers, Jane. "Gracia Real de Santa Teresa de Mose: A Free Black Town in Spanish Colonial Florida." *American Historical Review* 95 (1990): 9–30.

Patterson, Orlando. *Slavery and Social Death: A Comparative Study.* Introduction, 1–14. Cambridge, MA: Harvard UP, 1982.

Pérez, Louis. *Cuba: Between Reform and Revolution.* New York: Oxford UP, 1988.

Salas, Esteban, composer. *Esteban Salas: Un barroco cubano.* Performed by Coro Exaudi de La Habana. Conducted by Maria Felicia Perez. Milan Records, 2003. (compact disc). [Period music by the Cuban baroque composer Esteban Salas (1725–1803), who was choirmaster of the Cathedral of Santiago de Cuba from 1764 to 1803. His music may have even been heard in the Marian Sanctuary of El Cobre, barely ten miles away from Santiago.]

Taylor, William B. "The Foundation of Nuestra Señora de Guadalupe de los Morenos de Ampa." *The Americas* 26 (1970): 442–46.

Vinson, Ben, III. *Bearing Arms for His Majesty: The Free-Colored Militia in Colonial Mexico.* Stanford, CA: Stanford UP, 2000.

Chapter 9

Afro-Peru. (compact disc). London: World Music Network, 2002.

Anguiano, Mateo de. *Vida, y virtudes del Capuchino español, el Venerable Siervo de Dios Fray Francisco de Pamplona.* Madrid: Lorenzo García, 1685.

Burns, Kathryn. "Notaries, Truth, and Consequences." *American Historical Review* 110, no. 2 (2005): 350–79.

Charún-Illescas, Lucía. *Malambo.* Trans. Emmanuel Harris II. Chicago: Swan Isle, 2004.

Chaves, María Eugenia. "Slave Women's Strategies for Freedom and the Late Spanish Colonial State." In *Hidden Histories of Gender and the State in Latin America*, 108–26. Edited by Elizabeth Dore and Maxine Molyneux. Durham, NC: Duke UP, 2000.

Cimarrón. "El Quinto Suyo: Afrodescendientes en el Perú," http://www.cimarrones-peru.org/reel.htm. Accessed Sept. 12, 2008.

"Demanda del Capitán don Gerónimo de González, vecino de Trujillo, contra Martín Ximenez, maestro de carpintería; sobre redhibitoria de la venta de una negra Mariana de casta *mina*." (1685). Ms. Leg. 206. Exp. 1489. Archivo Departamental de La Libertad. Trujillo, Peru.

Estenssoro, Juan Carlos. *Los cuadros de mestizaje del virrey Amat: La representación etnográfica en el Perú colonial.* Lima, Peru: Museo de Arte de Lima, 1999.

Graham, Sandra Lauderdale. "Honor among Slaves." In *The Faces of Honor: Sex, Shame, and Violence in Colonial Latin America*, 201–28. Edited by Lyman L. Johnson and Sonya Lipsett-Rivera. Albuquerque: U of New Mexico P, 1998.

Hanger, Kimberly S. *Bounded Lives, Bounded Places: Free Black Society in Colonial New Orleans, 1769–1803*. Durham, NC: Duke UP, 1997.

———. "Landlords, Shopkeepers, Farmers, and Slave-Owners: Free Black Female Property Holders in Colonial New Orleans." In *Beyond Bondage: Free Women of Color in the Americas*, 219–36. Edited by David Barry Gaspar and Darlene Clark Hine. Urbana: U of Illinois P, 2004.

———. "'The Most Vile Atrocities': Accusations of Slander against Maria Cofignie, *Parda* Libre (Louisiana, 1795)." In *Colonial Lives: Documents on Latin American History, 1550–1850*, 269–78. Edited by Richard Boyer and Geoffrey Spurling. New York: Oxford UP, 2000.

Higgins, Kathleen J. *"Licentious Liberty" in a Brazilian Gold-Mining Region: Slavery, Gender, and Social Control in Eighteenth-Century Sabará, Minas Gerais*. University Park: Penn State UP, 1999.

Hünefeldt, Christine. *Paying the Price of Freedom: Family and Labor among Lima's Slaves, 1800–1854*. Berkeley: U of California P, 1994.

Karasch, Mary. *Slave Life in Rio de Janeiro 1808–1850*. Princeton, NJ: Princeton UP, 1987.

Law, Robin. *The Kingdom of Allada*. Leiden, Netherlands: Research School CNWS. School of Asian, African, and Amerindian Studies, 1997.

———. *The Slave Coast of West Africa, 1550–1750: The Impact of the Atlantic Slave Trade on an African Society*. Oxford: Clarendon, 1991.

Littlefield, Daniel. *Rice and Slaves: Ethnicity and the Slave Trade in Colonial South Carolina*. Baton Rouge: Louisiana State UP, 1981.

Mills, Kenneth, William B. Taylor, and Sandra Lauderdale Graham, eds. "Two Brazilian Wills (1793 and 1823)." In *Colonial Latin America: A Documentary History*, 375–83. Lanham, MD: SR Books, 2002.

Morgan, Jennifer L. *Laboring Women: Reproduction and Gender in New World Slavery*. Philadelphia: U of Pennsylvania P, 2004.

Obregón, Julio Luna. *Efigenia, la negra santa: Culto religioso de los descendientes africanos en el valle de Cañete. Sabino Canas, gestor de la tradición afroandina*. Lima, Peru: Centro de Articulación y Desarrollo Juvenil "Mundo de Ébano," Centro de Desarrollo de la Mujer Negra Peruana (CEDEMUNEP), 2005.

Olwell, Robert. "'Loose, Idle and Disorderly': Slave Women in the Eighteenth-Century Charleston Marketplace." In *More Than Chattel: Black Women and Slavery in the Americas*, 97–125. Edited by David Barry Gaspar and Darlene Clark Hine. Bloomington: Indiana UP, 1996.

O'Toole, Rachel Sarah. "To Be Free and *Lucumí*. Ana de la Calle and Making African Diaspora Identities in Colonial Peru." In *Africans to Spanish America: Expanding the Diaspora*, 73–92. Edited by Sherwin K. Bryant, Rachel Sarah O'Toole, and Ben Vinson III. Urbana: U of Illinois P, 2012.

Peru Negro. 2006. http://perunegro.net. Accessed Sept. 12, 2008.

Reis, João José. *Death Is a Festival: Funeral Rites and Rebellion in Nineteenth-Century Brazil*. First published 1991. Chapel Hill: U of North Carolina P, 2003.

Schafer, Daniel L. *Anna Madgigine, Jai Kingsley: African Princess, Florida Slave, Plantation Slaveowner*. Gainesville: UP of Florida, 2003.

Thornton, John K. *The Kongolese Saint Anthony: Dona Beatriz Kimpa Vita and the Antonian Movement, 1684–1706*. Cambridge: Cambridge UP, 1998.

van Deusen, Nancy E., ed. and trans. *The Souls of Purgatory: The Spiritual Diary of a Seventeenth-Century Afro-Peruvian Mystic, Ursula de Jesús*. Albuquerque: U of New Mexico P, 2004.

von Germeten, Nicole. *Black Blood Brothers: Confraternities and Social Mobility for Afro-Mexicans*. Gainesville: UP of Florida, 2006.

Chapter 10

Andrews, George Reid. *Los afroargentinos de Buenos Aires*. Trans. Antonio Bonanno. Buenos Aires, Argentina: La Flor, 1980.

Bernand, Carmen. "Un sargento contra un rey, ambos a dos negros." In *Negros, mulatos, zambaigos: Derroteros africanos en los mundos ibéricos*, 149–73. Edited by Berta Ares Queija and Alessandro Stella. Seville: Escuela de Estudios Hispano-Americanos, 2000.

Cirio, Norberto P. "Antecedentes históricos del culto a San Baltasar en la Argentina: La Cofradía de San Baltasar y Ánimas (1772–1856)." *Latin American Music Review (Austin)* 21, no. 2 (2000): 190–214.

———. "¿Rezan o bailan? Disputas en torno a la devoción a San Baltazar por los negros en el Buenos Aires colonial." In *Actas de la IV Reunión Científica: Mujeres, negros y niños en la música y sociedad colonial iberoamericana*, 88–100. Edited by Víctor Rondón. Santa Cruz de la Sierra, Bolivia: Asociación Pro Arte y Cultura, 2002.

Díaz, Marisa. "Las migraciones internas a la ciudad de Buenos Aires, 1744–1810." *Boletín del Instituto de Historia Argentina y Americana "Dr. Emilio Ravignani." (Buenos Aires)* 3, nos. 16–17 (1997): 7–31.

Fogelman, Patricia. "Coordenadas marianas: Tiempos y espacios de devoción a la Virgen a través de las cofradías porteñas coloniales." *Trabajos y Comunicaciones (La Plata)* 2, nos. 30/31 (2004–2005): 118–38.

———. "Élite local y participación religiosa en Luján a fines del período colonial: La Cofradía de Nuestra Señora del Santísimo Rosario." *Cuadernos de Historia Regional (Luján)* 20–21 (2000): 103–24.

———. "La población de color en la frontera bonaerense: Los negros y pardos de la Villa de Luján." *Revista Signos Históricos (México)* 2 (1999): 9–33.

———. "Una cofradía mariana urbana y otra rural en Buenos Aires a fines del período colonial." *Andes: Antropología e Historia (Salta)* 11 (2000): 179–207.

———. "Una 'economía espiritual de la salvación': Culpabilidad, Purgatorio y acumulación de indulgencias en la era colonial." *Andes: Antropología e Historia (Salta)* 15 (2004): 55–86.

Goldberg, Marta. "La población negra y mulata en la ciudad de Buenos Aires." *Desarrollo Económico (Buenos Aires)* 61, no. 1 (1976): 66–84.

———. "Las afroargentinas." In *Historia de las mujeres en la Argentina*, Vol. 1, 68–85. Edited by Fernanda Gil Lozano. Buenos Aires, Argentina: Taurus, 2000.

———. "Los africanos de Buenos Aires, 1750–1880." In *Rutas de la esclavitud en África y América*, 269–88. Edited by Rina Cáceres. San Jose: Editorial de la Universidad de Costa Rica, 2001.

———. "Los estudios sobre castas en la demografía histórica argentina." In *Cambios Demográficos en América Latina: La experiencia de cinco siglos*, 715–23. Córdoba, Argentina: Universidad Nacional de Córdoba, 2000.

———. "Los negros de Buenos Aires." In *Presencia africana en Sudamérica*, 529–607. Edited by Luz María Martínez Montiel. Mexico City: Consejo Nacional para la Cultura y las Artes (CONACULTA), 1995.

———. "Presencia africana en la historia y cultura argentina." *Con eñe: Revista de Cultura Hispanoamericana (Badajoz)* 11 (2000): 19–24.

———. "Vida cotidiana de los negros en Hispanoamérica." In *Tres grandes cuestiones de la historia de Iberoamérica*. Edited by José Andrés-Gallego. (CD-ROM). Madrid: Fundación Ignacio Larramendi, Tavera, 2005.

González, Ricardo. *Imágenes de la Ciudad Capital. Arte en Buenos Aires en el siglo XVIII*. Buenos Aires, Argentina: Minerva, 1998.

Mallo, Silvia. "El color del delito en Buenos Aires." *Revista Memoria y Sociedad: Diásporas Afroamericanas (Bogotá)* 7 (2003): 111–124.

———. "Negros y mulatos rioplatenses viviendo en libertad." *Rutas de la esclavitud en África y América Latina*, 305–22. Edited by Rina Cáceres. San Jose: Editorial de la Universidad de Costa Rica, 2001.

Rodríguez Molas, Ricardo. "La música y la danza de los negros en el Buenos Aires de los siglos XVIII y XIX." *Historia* 2, no. 7 (1957): 103–26.

Rosal, Miguel Ángel. "Algunas consideraciones sobre las creencias religiosas de los africanos porteños (1750–1820)." *Investigaciones y Ensayos (Buenos Aires)* 31 (1981): 369–83.

Chapter 11

Behar, Ruth. "Sex and Sin: Witchcraft and the Devil in Late-Colonial Mexico." *American Ethnologist* 14, no. 1 (1987): 34–54.

Blázquez, Juan. *La Inquisición en América (1569–1820)*. Santo Domingo, Dominican Republic: Editora Corripio, 1994.

Ceballos Gómez, Diana Luz. *"Quyen tal haze que tal pague": Sociedad y prácticas mágicas en el Nuevo Reino de Granada*. Bogota, Colombia: Ministerio de Cultura, 2002.

Díaz, María Elena. *The Virgin, the King, and the Royal Slaves of El Cobre: Negotiating Freedom in Colonial Cuba, 1670–1780*. Stanford, CA: Stanford UP, 2000.

Franco, José Luciano. *Las minas de Santiago del Prado y la rebelión de los cobreros, 1530–1800*. Havana, Cuba: Editorial de Ciencias Sociales, 1957.

Henningsen, Gustav. *The Witches' Advocate*. Reno: U of Nevada P, 1980.

Kamen, Henry. *The Spanish Inquisition*. New York: New American Library, 1965.

Marrero, Levi. *Los esclavos y la Virgen del cobre: Dos siglos de lucha por la libertad*. Miami, FL: Universal, 1980.

Maya Restrepo, Luz Adriana. "Paula de Eguiluz y el arte del bien querer: Apuntes para el estudio de la sensualidad y el cimarronaje femenino en el Caribe, siglo XVIII." *Historia Crítica* 24 (2002): 101–24.

Medina, Toribio. *La Inquisición en Cartagena de Indias*. Bogota, Colombia: Carlos Valencia Editores, 1978.

Monter, William. "The New Social History and the Spanish Inquisition." *Journal of Social History* 17, no. 4 (1984): 705–13.

Navarrete, María Cristina. *Prácticas religiosas de los negros en la colonia.* Cali, Colombia: Universidad del Valle, 1995.

Splendiani, Anna María, José Enrique Sánchez Bohórquez, and Emma Cecilia Luque de Salazar. *Cincuenta años de inquisición en el Tribunal de Cartagena de Indias, 1610–1660.* Santa Fe de Bogotá, Colombia: Pontificia Universidad Javeriana, Instituto Colombiano de Cultura Hispánica, 1997.

Sweet, James H. *Recreating Africa: Culture, Kinship, and Religion in the African-Portuguese World, 1441–1770.* Chapel Hill: U of North Carolina P, 2003.

Tejado Fernández, Manuel. *Aspectos de la vida social en Cartagena de Indias durante el seiscientos.* Seville: Escuela de Estudios Hispano-Americanos, 1954.

Vidal Ortega, Antonio. "Entre la necesidad y el temor: Negros y mulatos en Cartagena de Indias a comienzos del siglo XVII." In *Negros, mulatos, zambaigos: Derroteros africanos en los mundos ibéricos*, 89–104. Edited by Berta Ares Queija and Alessandro Stella. Seville: Escuela de Estudios Hispano-Americanos, 2000.

Chapter 12

Andrews, Kenneth R. *The Spanish Caribbean: Trade and Plunder, 1530–1630.* New Haven, CT: Yale UP, 1978.

Borrego Plá, María del Carmen. *Cartagena de Indias en el siglo XVI.* Seville: Escuela de Estudios Hispano-Americanos, 1983.

Brooks, George E. *Landlords and Strangers: Ecology, Society, and Trade in Western Africa, 1000–1630.* Boulder, CO: Westview Press, 1993.

Carreira, António. *Os Portuguêses nos Rios de Guiné (1500–1900).* Lisbon: Litografia Tejo, 1984.

"Certificaçion de los negros que han entrado en Cartaxena desde primero de mayo de 1615 hasta 20 de marzo deste presente año de 1623. Cartagena, 28 marzo 1623." Archivo General de Indias, Seville. Santa Fe 74, no. 6.

Córdoba Ronquillo, Obispo fray Luis de. "Obispo fray Luis de Córdoba Ronquillo a S. M. Cartagena, 10 agosto 1634." Archivo General de Indias, Seville, Santa Fe 228, no. 97.

Del Castillo Mathieu, Nicolás. *La llave de las Indias.* Bogota, Colombia: El Tiempo, 1981.

Francis, J. Michael. *Invading Colombia: Spanish Accounts of the Gonzalo Jiménez de Quesada Expedition of Conquest.* University Park: Penn State UP, 2007.

Games, Alison. "'The Sanctuarye of our rebell negroes': The Atlantic Context of Local Resistance on Providence Island, 1630–1641." *Slavery and Abolition* 19, no. 3 (1998): 1–21.

Hawthorne, Walter. *Planting Rice and Harvesting Slaves: Transformations along the Guinea-Bissau Coast, 1400–1900.* Portsmouth, NH: Heinemann, 2003.

Heywood, Linda, and John K. Thornton. *Central Africans, Atlantic Creoles, and the Foundation of the Americas, 1585–1660.* Cambridge: Cambridge UP, 2007.

Kupperman, Karen Ordahl. *Providence Island, 1630–1641: The Other Puritan Colony.* Cambridge: Cambridge UP, 1993.

Landers, Jane. *Black Society in Spanish Florida.* Urbana: U of Illinois P, 1999.

Navarrete, María Cristina. *Historia social del negro en la colonia: Cartagena, siglo XVII.* Santiago de Cali, Colombia: Universidad del Valle, 1995.

Newson, Linda A., and Susie Minchin. *From Capture to Sale: The Portuguese Slave Trade to Spanish South America in the Early Seventeenth Century.* Leiden, Netherlands: Brill, 2007.

Pargellis, Stanley, and Ruth Lapham Butler, eds. "Daniell Ellffryth's Guide to the Caribbean, 1631." *The William and Mary Quarterly* 1, no. 3 (1944): 273–316.

Phillips, Carla Rahn. *Six Galleons for the King of Spain: Imperial Defense in the Early Seventeenth Century.* Baltimore, MD: Johns Hopkins UP, 1986.

Rodney, Walter. *A History of the Upper Guinea Coast, 1545 to 1800.* New York: Monthly Review Press, 1970.

Sandoval, Alonso de. *Un tratado sobre la esclavitud.* First published in Seville, 1627. Edited by Enriqueta Vila Vilar. Madrid: Alianza Editorial, 1987.

Sauer, Carl O. *The Early Spanish Main.* Berkeley: U of California P, 1966.

Urueta, José P. *Documentos para la historia de Cartagena.* Cartagena, Colombia: Araújo, 1887.

Vidal Ortega, Antonino. *Cartagena de Indias y la región histórica del Caribe, 1580–1640.* Seville: Escuela de Estudios Hispano-Americanos, 2002.

Vila Vilar, Enriqueta. *Hispanoamérica y el comercio de esclavos.* Seville: Escuela de Estudios Hispano-Americanos, 1977.

Wheat, David. "África no desenvolvimento da terceira cidade das Índias." Paper presented at the conference "Cortes, cidades, memórias." Universidade Federal de Minas Gerais, Belo Horizonte, Brazil, Nov. 13, 2007.

Chapter 13

Andrews, Williams L. *To Tell a Free Story: The First Century of Afro-American Autobiography, 1760–1863.* Urbana: U of Illinois P, 1986.

Belinda. "Petition of an African Slave, to the Legislature of Massachusetts." First published 1787. In *American Women Writers to 1800*, 253–55. Edited by Sharon M. Harris. New York: Oxford UP, 1996.

Bilinkoff, Jodi. *The Avila of St. Teresa: Religious Reform in a Sixteenth-Century City.* Ithaca, NY: Cornell UP, 1989.

Brásio, Antonio. *Monumenta missionaria africana: Africa Ocidental.* Vols. 13–14. Lisbon: Agência Geral do Ultrmar, Divisão de Publicações e Biblioteca, 1958.

Bynum, Caroline Walker. Foreword. In *Gendered Voices: Medieval Saints and Their Interpreters*, ix–xii. Edited by Catherine M. Mooney. Philadelphia: U of Pennsylvania P, 1999.

Contreras, Pedro de. *Sermón fúnebre en las honras de la Venerable Magdalena de la Cruz, negra de nación.* Seville: Imprenta de los Gómez, 1735.

Fra Molinero, Baltasar. "Baltasar Fra Molinero: Su blog." Wordpress.com. http:// bframoli.wordpress.com/chicaba-en-imagenes. Accessed Jan. 1, 2009.

Gómez de la Parra, José, and Manuel Ramos Medina. *Fundación y primero siglo: Crónica del primer convento de carmelitas descalzas en Puebla, 1604–1794.* Puebla, Mexico: Universidad Iberoamericana, Comisión Puebla V Centenario, 1992.

Harms, Robert. *The Diligent: A Voyage through the Worlds of the Slave Trade.* New York: Basic Books, 2002.

Kiple, Kenneth F., and Brian T. Higgins. "Mortality Caused by Dehydration during the Middle Passage." *Social Science History* 13, no. 4 (1989): 421–37.

Labouret, Henri, and Paul Rivet. *Le Royaume d'Arda et son évangélisation au XVIIe siècle.* Paris: Institut d'ethnologie, 1929.

Law, Robin. "Religion, Trade and Politics on the 'Slave Coast': Roman Catholic Missions in Allada and Whydah in the Seventeenth Century." *Journal of Religion in Africa* 21, no. 1 (1991): 42–77.

Moody, Joycelyn. *Sentimental Confessions: Spiritual Narratives of Nineteenth-Century African-American Women.* Athens: U of Georgia P, 2001.

Mott, Luiz. *Rosa Egipcíaca: Uma santa africana no Brasil.* Rio de Janeiro, Brazil: Bertrand Brasil, 1993.

Myers, Kathleen A. "Testimony for Canonization or Proof of Blasphemy? The New Spanish Inquisition and the Hagiographic Biography of Catarina de San Juan." In *Women in the Inquisition: Spain and the New World*, 270–95. Edited by Mary E. Giles. Baltimore, MD: Johns Hopkins UP, 1999.

Olsen, Margaret M. *Slavery and Salvation in Colonial Cartagena de Indias.* Gainesville: UP of Florida, 2004.

Paniagua, R. P. don Juan Carlos Miguel de. *Compendio de la vida ejemplar de la Venerable Madre Sor Teresa Juliana de Santo Domingo, tercera profesa en el convento de Santa María Magdalena, vulgo de la Penitencia, Orden de Santo Domingo, de la ciudad de Salamanca*, 2nd ed. Salamanca, Spain: Eugenio García de Honorato y San Miguel, impresor de dicha ciudad y Real Universidad, 1764.

———. *Oración fúnebre en las exequias de la Madre Sor Teresa Juliana de Santo Domingo, de feliz memoria, celebradas en el día nueve de enero en el Convento de Religiosas Dominicas, vulgo de la Penitencia.* Salamanca, Spain: Eugenio García de Honorato y San Miguel, impresor de dicha ciudad y Real Universidad, 1749.

Pena González, Miguel Anxo. *Francisco José de Jaca: La primera propuesta abolicionista de la esclavitud en el pensamiento hispano.* Salamanca, Spain: Publicaciones de la Universidad Pontificia de Salamanca, 2003.

Rubial, Antonio. *La santidad controvertida.* Mexico City: Fondo de Cultura Económica, 1999.

Sampson Vera Tudela, Elisa. "Fashioning a Cacique Nun: From Saints' Lives to Indian Lives in the Spanish Americas." *Gender and History* 9 (1997): 191–206.

Soler y las Balsas, Luis. *Vida de la venerable negra, la madre sor Theresa Juliana de Santo Domingo, de feliz memoria.* Zaragoza, Spain: Schomburg Center for Research in Black Culture. Ms. Sc Rare F 81–6, 1757.

Tardieu, Jean-Pierre. "Du bon usage de la monstruosité: La vision de l'Afrique chez Alonso de Sandoval (1627)." *Bulletin Hispanique* 86, no. 1 (1984): 164–78.

Thornton, John. *The Kongolese Saint Anthony: Dona Beatriz Kimpa Vita and the Antonian Movement, 1684–1706.* Cambridge: Cambridge UP, 1998.

van Deusen, Nancy E., ed. and trans. *The Souls of Purgatory: The Spiritual Diary of a Seventeenth-Century Afro-Peruvian Mystic, Ursula de Jesús.* Albuquerque: U of New Mexico P, 2004.

Vauchez, Andre. *Sainthood in the Later Middle Ages.* Trans. Jean Birrell. Cambridge: Cambridge UP, 1997.

"Venta de dos esclavos moros, otorgada por Sebastián Antonio de Toledo y Molina, Marqués de Mancera, a favor de Juan de Artieda. 6 de febrero de 1677." Archivo Histórico de Protocolos Notariales de Madrid. Libro 11.410, fol. 79.

Wyschogrod, Edith. *Saints and Postmodernism: Revisioning Moral Philosophy.* Chicago: U of Chicago P, 1990.

Yai, Olabiyi Babalola. "From Vodun to Mawu: Monotheism and History in the Fon Cultural Area." In *L'Invention religieuse en Afrique: Histoire et Religion en Afrique Noire,* 241–65. Edited by Jean-Pierre Chrétien. Paris: Karthala, 1993.

Chapter 14

Boxer, Charles R. "*Nova e Curiosa Relação*: Negro Slavery in Brazil: A Portuguese Pamphlet (1764)." *Race* 5 (1964): 38–47.

Conrad, Robert Edgar. *Children of God's Fire: A Documentary History of Black Slavery in Brazil.* State College: Penn State UP, 1994.

Curto, José, and Paul E. Lovejoy, eds. *Enslaving Connections: Changing Cultures of Africa and Brazil during the Era of Slavery.* Amherst, NY: Prometheus/Humanity Books, 2004.

Heywood, Linda M., ed. *Central Africans and Cultural Transformations in the American Diaspora.* New York: Cambridge UP, 2001.

Karasch, Mary C. "Minha *nação:* Identidades escravas no fim do Brasil colonial." Trans. Angela Domingues. In *Brasil: Colonização e escravidão,* 127–41. Edited by Maria Beatriz Nizza da Silva. Rio de Janeiro, Brazil: Nova Fronteira, 2000.

———. *Slave Life in Rio de Janeiro, 1808–1850.* Princeton, NJ: Princeton UP, 1987.

Kiddy, Elizabeth W. *Blacks of the Rosary: Memory and History in Minas Gerais, Brazil.* State College: Penn State UP, 2005.

———. "Kings, Queens, and Judges: Hierarchy in Lay Religious Brotherhoods of Blacks, 1750–1830." In *Africa and the Americas: Interconnections during the Slave Trade,* 95–125. Edited by Renée Soulodre-LaFrance and José Curto. New Brunswick, NJ: Africa World Press, 2005.

Reis, João José. "Identidade e diversidade étnicas nas irmandades negras no tempo da escravidão." *Tempo* 2, no. 3 (1997): 7–33.

Russell-Wood, A. J. R. *The Black Man in Slavery and Freedom in Colonial Brazil.* New York: St. Martin's, 1982.

Schwartz, Stuart B. "Magistracy and Society in Colonial Brazil." *Hispanic American Historical Review* 50 (1970): 715–30.

Soares, Mariza de Carvalho. "A 'nação' que se tem e a 'terra' de onde se vem: Categorias de inserção social de africanos no Império português, século XVIII." *Estudos Afro-Asiáticos* 26, no. 2 (2004): 303–30.

———. "Apreço e imitação no diálogo do gentio convertido." *Ipotesi: Revista de Estudos literários Juiz de Fora* 4, no. 1 (2000): 111–23.

———. "Can Women Guide and Govern Men? Gendering Politics among African Catholics in Colonial Brazil." In *Women and Slavery, Vol. 2: The Modern Atlantic,* 79–99. Edited by Gwyn Campbell, Suzanne Miers, and Joseph Calder Miller. Athens: Ohio UP, 2007.

———. *Devotos da cor, Identidade étnica, religiosidade e escravidão no Rio de Janeiro, século XVIII.* Rio de Janeiro, Brazil: Civilização Brasileira, 2000.

———. "O Império de Santo Elesbão na cidade do Rio de Janeiro, no século XVIII." *Topoi* 4 (March 2002): 59–83.

Thornton, John K. *Africa and Africans in the Making of the Atlantic World, 1400–1680.* Cambridge: Cambridge UP, 1992.

Chapter 15

Azulay, Jom Tob, producer-director. *O Judeu.* A&B Producoes, 1996. [Film about the Brazilian *converso* António José da Silva, who was burned at the stake in 1739.]

Bethencourt, Francisco. *História das Inquisições: Portugal, Espanha e Itália—Séculos XV–XIX.* São Paulo, Brazil: Companhia das Letras, 2000.

Boxer, C. R. *Race Relations in the Portuguese Colonial Empire, 1415–1825.* Oxford: Clarendon, 1963.

Buarque, Chico, and Ruy Guerra. *Calabar: O elogio da traição.* Rio de Janeiro, Brazil: Civilização Brasileira, 1975. [Play about a seventeenth-century Dutch/Portuguese conflict in which the black soldier Henrique Dias fights on the Portuguese side.]

Diegues, Carlos, director. *Quilombo.* CDK, 1984. [Film about Afro-Brazilian slave resistance in seventeenth-century Pernambuco.]

Ferlini, Vera Lúcia Amaral. "Pobres do açucar: Estrutura produtiva e relações de poder no Nordeste colonial." In *História econômica do período colonial,* 2nd ed., 21–34. Edited by Tamás Szmrecsányi. São Paulo, Brazil: Hucitex/Associação Brasileira de Pesquisadores em História Econômica/Editora da Universidade de São Paulo/Imprensa Oficial, 2002.

Freyre, Gilberto. *The Masters and the Slaves (Casa-Grande & Senzala): A Study in the Development of Brazilian Civilization.* Berkeley: U of California P, 1986.

Galvão, Sebastião de Vasconcello. *Diccionario chorographico, historico e estatistico de Pernambuco.* 4 vols. Rio de Janeiro, Brazil: Imprensa Nacional, 1908.

Higgs, David. "Lisbon." In *Queer Sites: Gay Urban Histories since 1600,* 112–37. Edited by David Higgs. London: Routledge, 1999.

Images of Seventeenth-Century Pernambuco by the Dutch Painter Franz Post (c. 1612–1680). "Frans Post e o Brasil Holandês na Coleção do Instituto Ricardo Brennand, Recife. http://www.institutoricardobrennand.org.br/pinacoteca/fpost/index.html. Accessed March 11, 2015.

Jones, Gayl. *Song for Anninho.* Detroit, MI: Lotus, 1981. [North American poetic evocation of the destruction of Palmares, a large community of escaped slaves in Pernambuco, from a woman's point of view.]

Julião, Carlos, and Lygia da Fonseca Fernandes da Cunha. *Riscos illuminados de figurinhos de brancos e negros dos uzos do Rio de Janeiro e Serro do Frio (c. 1740–1811 or 1814).* 1960. [Paintings representing African slaves in eighteenth-century Brazil. Some images available online: http://hitchcock.itc.virginia.edu/Slavery/returnKeyword.php?keyword=Juliao. Accessed Jan. 1, 2009.]

Klein, Herbert. *The Atlantic Slave Trade.* Cambridge: Cambridge UP, 1999.

Lara, Sílvia Hunold. *Campos da violência.* Rio de Janeiro, Brazil: Paz e Terra, 1988.

———, ed. *Ordenações Filipinas: Livro V.* São Paulo, Brazil: Companhia das Letras, 1999.

Lima, Walter, Jr., director. *Chico Rei.* Brazil: Embrafilme, 1985. [Film about the Portuguese slave trade, and slavery in eighteenth-century Brazil. The film lacks subtitles and is hard to obtain but provides the best available evocation of eighteenth-century Brazilian slavery.]

Mattoso, Kátia M. de Queirós. *To Be a Slave in Brazil, 1550–1888*. New Brunswick, NJ: Rutgers UP, 1986.

Menard, Russel R., and Stuart B. Schwartz. "Por que a escravidão africana? A transição da força de trabalho no Brasil, no México e na Carolina do Sul." In *História econômica do período colonial*, 2nd ed., 3–19. Edited by Tamás Szmrecsányi. São Paulo, Brazil: Hucitex/Associação Brasileira de Pesquisadores em História Econômica/Editora da Universidade de São Paulo/Imprensa Oficial, 2002.

Mott, Luiz. *O sexo proibido: Virgins, gays e escravos nas garras da Inquisição*. Campinas, Brazil: Papirus, 1988.

———. "Sodomia não é heresia: Dissidência moral e contracultura." In *A Inquisição em xeque: Temas, controvérsias, estudos de caso*, 253–66. Edited by Ronaldo Vainfas, Bruno Feitler, and Lana Lage da Gama Lima. Rio de Janeiro, Brazil: EdUERJ, 2006.

Palacios, Guillermo. *Campesinato e escravidão no Brasil: Agricultores livres e pobres na capitania geral de Pernambuco (1700–1871)*. Brasilia, Brazil: Editora Universidade de Brasília, 2004.

Pieroni, Geraldo. *Os excluídos do Reino: A Inquisição portuguesa e o degredo para o Brasil Colônia*. Brasilia, Brazil: Editora Universidade de Brasília; São Paulo, Brazil: Imprensa Oficial do Estado, 2000.

Souza, Laura Mello e. *The Devil and the Land of the Holy Cross: Witchcraft, Slavery, and Popular Religion in Colonial Brazil*. First published 1986. Trans. Diane Grosklaus Whitty. Austin: U of Texas P, 2003.

Sweet, J. H. *Recreating Africa: Culture, Kinships, and Religion in the African-Portuguese World, 1441–1770*. Chapel Hill: U of North Carolina P, 2003. [Award-winning history of the cultural lives of African slaves in Portugal and Brazil.]

Vainfas, Ronaldo. "Inquisição como fábrica de hereges: Os sodomitas foram exceção?" In *A Inquisição em xeque: Temas, controvérsias, estudos de caso*, 267–80. Edited by Ronaldo Vainfas, Bruno Feitler, and Lana Lage da Gama Lima. Rio de Janeiro, Brazil: EdUERJ, 2006.

———. *Trópico dos pecados: Moral, sexualidade e Inquisição no Brasil*. Rio de Janeiro, Brazil: Editora Campus, 1989.

Wadsworth, James E. *Agents of Orthodoxy: Honor, Status, and the Inquisition in Colonial Pernambuco, Brazil*. Lanham, MD: Rowman & Littlefield, 2007.

Chapter 16

Aguirre, Carlos. *Agentes de su propia libertad: Los esclavos de Lima y la desintegración de la esclavitud. 1821–1854*. Lima, Peru: Pontificia Universidad Católica del Perú, 1993.

———. "Mujeres delincuentes, prácticas penales y servidumbre doméstica en Lima (1862–1930)." In *Familia y vida cotidiana en América Latina, siglos XVIII–XIX*, 203–31. Edited by Scarlett O'Phelan, Fanni Muñoz, Gabriel Ramón, and Mónica Ricketts. Lima, Peru: Pontificia Universidad Católica del Perú, Instituto Riva Agüero, Instituto Francés de Estudios Andinos, 2003.

Alfonso X. *Las Siete Partidas del rey don Alfonso el sabio*. Paris: Lecointe y Lasserre, 1843.

Aránguiz, Horacio, ed. *Lo público y lo privado en la historia americana*. Santiago, Chile: Fundación Mario Góngora, 2000.

Archivo Arzobispal de Lima (AAL). Lima, Peru.

Arias, Ybeth. "Economía y sociedad de los monasterios limeños durante la época borbónica: La Encarnación y la Concepción (1750–1821)." Licentiate Thesis, Lima, Peru: Universidad Nacional Mayor de San Marcos, 2008.

Arrelucea, Maribel. "Esclavitud, sexo y seducción en Lima, 1760–1820." *Revista del Archivo General de la Nación* 26 (2006): 167–92.

———. "Poder femenino, sexo y seducción: Esclavas en el recinto doméstico. Lima, 1760–1820." *Diálogos en Historia (Lima)* 4 (2006): 73–105.

———. "Poder masculino, esclavitud femenina y violencia doméstica en Lima, 1760–1820." In *Mujeres, familia y sociedad en la historia de América Latina, siglos XVIII – XXI*, 147–70. Edited by Scarlett O'Phelan and Margarita Zegarra. Lima, Peru: Pontificia Universidad Católica del Perú, Instituto Riva Agüero, 2006.

Chambers, Sara. *De súbditos a ciudadanos: Honor, género, y política en Arequipa, 1780–1854*. Lima, Peru: Red para el Desarrollo de las Ciencias Sociales, 2003.

Cosamalón, Jesús. *Indios detrás de la muralla: Matrimonios indígenas y convivencia interracial en Santa Ana (Lima, 1795–1820)*. Lima, Peru: Fondo Editorial de la Pontificia Universidad Católica, 1999.

Flores Galindo, Alberto. *Aristocracia y plebe: Lima 1760–1820*. Lima, Peru: Mosca Azul, 1984.

Gauderman, Kimberly. *Women's Lives in Colonial Quito: Gender, Law, and Economy in Spanish America*. Austin: U of Texas P, 2003.

Gonzalbo, Pilar, and Cecilia Rabell, eds. *La familia en el mundo Iberoamericano*. Mexico City: Instituto de Investigaciones Sociales de la Universidad Autónoma de México, 1994.

Harth-Terré, Emilio, and Alberto Márquez Abanto. "El artesano negro en la arquitectura virreinal limeña." *Revista del Archivo Nacional (Lima)* 25 (1961): 360–430.

———. "Historia de la casa urbana virreinal de Lima." *Revista del Archivo Nacional (Lima)* 26, no. 4 (1962).

Hünefeldt, Christine. *Mujeres, esclavitud, emociones y libertad: Lima 1800–1854*. Lima, Peru: IEP, 1987.

Jouve Martín, José Ramón. *Esclavos de la ciudad letrada: Esclavitud, escritura y colonialismo en Lima (1650–1700)*. Lima, Peru: Instituto de Estudios Peruanos, 2005.

Lauderdale Graham, Sandra. *House and Street: The Domestic World of Servants and Masters in Nineteenth-Century Rio de Janeiro*. Austin: U of Texas P, 1992.

Lavrin, Asunción, ed. *Las mujeres latinoamericanas: Perspectivas históricas*. Mexico City: Fondo de Cultura Económica, 1985.

———. *Sexualidad y matrimonio en la América hispánica, siglos XVI–XVIII*. Mexico: Grijalbo, 1991.

Macera, Pablo. "Sexo y coloniaje." In *Trabajos de historia*, Vol. III, 297–352. Lima, Peru: Instituto Nacional de Cultura, 1977.

Mannarelli, María Emma. *Pecados públicos: La ilegitimidad en Lima, siglo XVII*. Lima, Peru: Flora Tristán, 1993.

———. "Vínculos familiares y fronteras de lo público y privado en Perú." In *La familia en Iberoamérica, 1550–1980*, 327–67. Edited by Pablo Rodríguez. Bogota, Colombia: Convenio Andrés Bello, Universidad Externado de Colombia, 2004.

O'Phelan, Scarlett, ed. *Etnicidad y discriminación en el Perú.* Lima, Peru: Instituto Riva Agüero, Banco Mundial, 2003.

O'Phelan, Scarlett, Fanni Muñoz, Gabriel Ramón, and Mónica Ricketts, eds. *Familia y vida cotidiana en América Latina, siglos XVIII–XX.* Lima, Peru: PUCP, Instituto Riva Agüero, IFEA, 2003.

O'Phelan Godoy, Scarlett. "Entre el afecto y la mala conciencia: La paternidad responsable en el Perú borbónico." In *Mujeres, familia y sociedad en la historia de América Latina, siglos XVIII–XXI,* 37–56. Edited by Scarlett O'Phelan Godoy and Margarita Zegarra Flórez. Lima, Peru: Pontificia Universidad Católica del Perú, Instituto Riva Agüero, 2006.

Price, Richard, ed. *Sociedades cimarronas: Comunidades esclavas rebeldes en las Américas.* Mexico City: Siglo XXI, 1981.

Real Consejo de Indias. *Recopilación de Leyes de los Reynos de las Indias, mandadas imprimir y publicar por la Magestad Católica del Rey Don Carlos II, nuestro señor.* Madrid: Gráficas Ultra, 1943.

Reyes Flores, Alejandro. *La esclavitud en Lima.* Lima, Peru: Universidad Nacional Mayor de San Marcos, 1985.

Stern, Steve. *The Secret History of Gender.* Chapel Hill: U of North Carolina P, 1995.

Trazegnies, Fernando de. *Ciriaco de Urtecho, litigante por amor.* Lima, Peru: Pontificia Universidad Católica del Perú, 1982.

Trujillo Mena, Valentín. *La legislación eclesiástica en el virreynato del Perú durante el siglo XVI.* Lima, Peru: Lumen, 1980.

van Deusen, Nancy E. "Determinando los límites de la virtud: El discurso en torno al recogimiento entre las mujeres de Lima durante el siglo XVII." In *Mujeres y género en la historia del Perú,* 39–58. Edited by Margarita Zegarra. Lima, Peru: CENDOC-Mujer, 1999.

———. *Entre lo sagrado y lo mundano: La práctica institucional y cultural del recogimiento en la Lima virreinal.* Lima, Peru: Instituto de Estudios Peruanos, Instituto Francés de Estudios Andinos, 2007.

Wiesner-Hanks, Merry. *Cristianismo y sexualidad en la Edad Moderna: La regulación del deseo, la reforma de la práctica.* Madrid: Siglo XXI, 2001.

Chapter 17

Alfonso X, King of Castile and Leon, 1221–1284. *Siete partidas del rey don Alfonso, el sabio, cotejadas con varios códices antiguos por la Real Academia de la Historia.* Madrid: Imprenta Real, 1807. http://www.archive.org/details/lassietepartidas01 castuoft. Accessed May 10, 2009.

Ansaldi, Waldo. "Cuestión de piel: Racialismo y legitimidad política." In *Calidoscopio latinoamericano.* Buenos Aires, Argentina: Ariel Historia, 2004.

Belmonte Postigo, José Luis. "Con la plata ganada y su propio esfuerzo: Los mecanismos de manumisión en Santiago de Cuba, 1780–1803." *Revista del Grupo de Estudios Afroamericanos (Universidad de Barcelona) EAVirtual* 3 (2005): 1–33.

Fanchin, Ana. "Los habitantes: Una visión estática." In *Espacio y población: Los Valles Cuyanos en 1777,* 47–89. San Juan, Argentina: UNSJ-Academia Nacional de la Historia, 2004.

————. "Protagonistas de un intercambio cotidiano, desde y hacia Chile por San Juan (Siglo XVIII)." *Estudios Trasandinos* 6 (2001): 67–79.

Goldberg, Marta B. "Negras y mulatas de Buenos Aires 1750–1850." Paper presented at the Forty-Ninth Congreso Internacional de Americanistas (ICA). Quito, Ecuador, July 7–11, 1997. http://www.naya.org.ar/congresos/contenido/49CAI/Goldberg.htm. Accessed Nov. 21, 2008.

González Undurraga, Carolina. "Los usos del honor por esclavos y esclavas: Del cuerpo injuriado al cuerpo liberado (Chile, 1750–1823)." *Nuevo Mundo Mundos Nuevos* 6 (Nov. 19, 2006). http://nuevomundo.revues.org/document2869.html. Accessed Nov. 21, 2008.

Johnson, Lyman L. "La manumisión de esclavos en Buenos Aires durante el Virreinato." *Desarrollo Económico* 16, no. 63 (1976): 331–48.

————. "La manumisión en el Buenos Aires colonial: Un análisis ampliado." *Desarrollo Económico* 17, no. 68 (1978): 637–46.

López-Chávez, Celia. "Microhistoria de la esclavitud negra en el siglo XVIII: El caso de la residencia jesuita de San Juan de la Frontera." *Colonial Latin American Historical Review* 5, no. 4 (1996): 441–74.

Lucena Salmoral, Manuel. *Los códigos negros de la América española.* Alcala, Spain: Unesco-Universidad de Alcalá, 1996.

Mellafe, Rolando. *La esclavitud en Hispanoamérica.* Buenos Aires, Argentina: Editorial Universitaria de Buenos Aires, 1984.

————. *La introducción de la esclavitud negra en Chile: Tráfico y rutas.* Santiago, Chile: Universidad de Chile, 1959.

Recopilación de leyes de los reinos de las Indias: Mandadas imprimir y publicar por la Magestad Católica del Rey Don Carlos II, Nuestro Señor. First published 1681. 4 vols. [5th ed. published Madrid, 1841.] [The *Título Quinto*, "De los mulatos, negros, berberiscos, é hijos de indios," is found in Vol. 3, available on Google Books.]

Rodríguez Molas, Ricardo. "El negro en el Río de la Plata." *Polémica* 2 (1970):38–56. [First published in *Historia integral Argentina, Vol. 1: De la independencia a la anarquía.* Buenos Aires, Argentina: Centro Editor de América Latina, 1970.]

Zuluaga, Rosa María. "La trata de negros en la región cuyana durante el siglo XVIII." *Revista de la Junta de Estudios Históricos de Mendoza* 2, no. 1 (1970): 39–66.

Chapter 18

Abbad y Lasierra, Fray Agustín Iñigo. *Diario del viaje a la América.* Caracas, Venezuela: Banco Nacional de Ahorro y Préstamo, 1974.

Andrews, George Reid. *Afro-Latin America, 1800–2000.* New York: Oxford UP, 2004.

Artola, Miguel. "La guerra de reconquista de Santo Domingo (1808–1809)." *Revista de Indias* 21, no. 45 (1951): 447–84.

Bolster, W. Jeffrey. *Black Jacks: African American Seamen in the Age of Sail.* Cambridge, MA: Harvard UP, 1997.

Chinea, Jorge L. "Fissures in *El Primer Piso*: Racial Politics in Spanish Colonial Puerto Rico during Its Pre-plantation Era, c. 1700–1800." *Caribbean Studies* 30, no. 1 (2002): 169–204.

————. "A Quest for Freedom: The Immigration of Maritime Maroons into Puerto Rico, 1656–1800." *Journal of Caribbean History* 31, nos. 1–2 (1997): 51–87.

————. *Race and Labor in the Hispanic Caribbean: The West Indian Worker Experience in Puerto Rico, 1800–1850*. Gainesville: UP of Florida, 2005.

Dávila, Arlene. "Local/Diasporic Taínos: Towards a Cultural Politics of Memory, Reality and Imagery." In *Taino Revival: Critical Perspectives on Puerto Rican Identity and Cultural Politics*, 11–29. Edited by Gabriel Haslip-Viera. New York: Centro de Estudios Puertorriqueños, Hunter College, CUNY, 1999.

Dungy, Kathryn R. "Live and Let Live: Native and Immigrant Free People of Color in Early Nineteenth Century Puerto Rico." *Caribbean Studies* 33, no. 1 (2005): 79–111.

Geggus, David Patrick. *Haitian Revolutionary Studies*. Bloomington: Indiana UP, 2002.

Gilroy, Paul. *The Black Atlantic: Modernity and Double Consciousness*. Cambridge, MA: Harvard UP, 1993.

Giusti Cordero, Juan A. "Piñones sí se acuerda: 200 años de la participación negra en la victoria sobre la invasión inglesa (1797–1997)." *Revista de Genealogía Puertorriqueña* 1, no. 2 (2000): 33–41.

González, José Luis. *Puerto Rico: The Four-Storeyed Country and Other Essays*. New York: Markus Wiener Publishing, 1993.

Kinsbruner, Jay. *Not of Pure Blood: The Free People of Color and Racial Prejudice in Nineteenth-Century Puerto Rico*. Durham, NC: Duke UP, 1996.

Landers, Jane G., and Barry M. Robinson, eds. *Slaves, Subjects, and Subversives: Blacks in Colonial Latin America*. Albuquerque: U of New Mexico P, 2006.

López Cantos, Ángel. *Miguel Enríquez: Corsario boricua del siglo XVIII*. San Juan, Puerto Rico: Puerto, 1994.

López Lázaro, Fabio. "La mentira histórica de un pirata caribeño: El descubrimiento del trasfondo histórico de los *Infortunios de Alonso Ramírez* (1690)." *Anuario de Estudios Americanos* 64, no. 2 (2007): 87–104.

Martín Rebolo, J. F. Isabelo. *Ejército y sociedad en las Antillas en el siglo XVIII*. Seville: Ministerio de Defensa, 1988.

Morales Carrión, Arturo. "El reflujo en Puerto Rico de la crisis dominico-haitiana, 1791–1805." *Revista Eme-Eme: Estudios Dominicanos* 27 (1976): 19–39.

————. *Puerto Rico and the Non-Hispanic Caribbean: A Study in the Decline of Spanish Exclusivism*. Río Piedras: U of Puerto Rico P, 1952.

Moreno, Isodoro. "Festive Rituals, Religious Associations, and Ethnic Reaffirmation of Black Andalusians: Antecedents of the Black Confraternities and Cabildos in the Americas." In *Representations of Blackness and the Performance of Identities*, 3–17. Edited by Jean Muteba Rahier. Westport, CT: Bergin & Garvey, 1999.

Olsen, Margaret M. "Negros Horros and Cimarrones on the Legal Frontier of the Caribbean: Accessing the African Voice in Colonial Spanish American Texts." *Research in African Literatures* 29, no. 4 (1998): 52–72.

O'Reilly, Alexander. "Memoria de D Alexandro O'Reylly sobre la isla de Puerto Rico." First published 1765. In *Antología de lecturas de historia de Puerto Rico (siglos xvi–xviii)*, 387–88. Edited by Aida R. Caro Costas. San Juan, Puerto Rico: M. Pareja, 1972 (unpublished).

Ortiz, Altagracia. *Eighteenth-Century Reforms in the Caribbean: Miguel de Muesas, Governor of Puerto Rico, 1769–76*. Rutherford, NJ: Farleigh Dickinson UP, 1983.

Parrilla Ortíz, Pedro. *La esclavitud en Cádiz durante el siglo XVIII*. Cadiz, Spain: Diputación de Cádiz, 2001.

Pettinger, Alasdair. *Always Elsewhere: Travels of the Black Atlantic*. London: Cassell, 1998.

Picó, Fernando. "Esclavos, cimarrones, libertos y negros libres en Río Piedras, P.R., 1774–1873." *Anuario de Estudios Americanos* 43 (1986): 25–33.

Quintana, Jorge. "La biografía del general Valero escrita por Vicente Dávila." *Revista del Instituto de Cultura Puertorriqueña* 7, no. 25 (1964): 52–57.

Ribes Tovar, Federico. *100 Outstanding Puerto Ricans*. New York: Plus Ultra Educational Publishers, 1976.

Sánchez González, Lisa. *Boricua Literature: A Literary History of the Puerto Rican Diaspora*. New York: New York UP, 2001.

Schmidt, Peter R., and Thomas C. Patterson, eds. *Making Alternative Histories: The Practice of Archaeology in Non-Western Settings*. Santa Fe, NM: School of American Research, 1995.

Scott, Julius S. "The Common Wind: Currents of Afro-American Communication in the Era of the Haitian Revolution." PhD diss., Duke University, 1986.

Sigüenza y Góngora, Carlos de. *Infortunios de Alonso Ramírez*, 3rd ed. First published 1690. Puebla, Mexico: Premiá, 1989.

Stark, David M. "Rescued from Their Invisibility: The Afro-Puerto Ricans of Seventeenth- and Eighteenth-Century San Mateo de Cangrejos." *The Americas* 63, no. 4 (2007): 551–86.

Sued Badillo, Jalil. "The Theme of the Indigenous in the National Projects of the Hispanic Caribbean." In *Making Alternative Histories: The Practice of Archaeology in Non-Western Settings*, 25–46. Edited by Peter R. Schmidt and Thomas C. Patterson. Santa Fe, NM: School of American Research Press, 1995.

Sued Badillo, Jalil, and Angel López Cantos. *Puerto Rico Negro*. Rio Piedras, Puerto Rico: Editorial Cultural, 1986.

Torres, Arlene. "La gran familia puertorriqueña 'ej prieta de beldá' (The Great Puerto Rican Family Is Really Black)." In *Blackness in Latin America and the Caribbean: Social Dynamics and Cultural Transformations*, Vol. 2, 285–306. Edited by Arlene Torres and Norman E. Whitten, Jr. Bloomington: Indiana UP, 1998.

Zenón Cruz, Isabelo. *Narciso descubre su trasero: El negro en la cultura puertorriqueña*. 2 vols. Humacao, Puerto Rico: Furidi, 1975.

Glossary

Law, Robin. "Ethnicities of Enslaved Africans in the Diaspora: On the Meanings of 'Mina' (Again)." *History in Africa* 32 (2005): 247–67.

———. "Ethnicity and the Slave Trade: 'Lucumí' and 'Nago' as Ethnonyms in West Africa." *History in Africa* 24 (1997): 205–19.

Resources for Teaching Early Modern Afro-Latino Experiences and Their Legacies

Additional Publications of Afro-Latino Voices

Baquaqua, Mahommah Gardo. *The Biography of Mahommah Gardo Baquaqua: His Passage from Slavery to Freedom in Africa and America*. Edited by Robin Law and Paul E. Lovejoy. Princeton, NJ: Markus Wiener, 2001. [Biography based on

Baquaqua's (b. 1820s; last documented 1857) own words. Baquaqua was born in what is today Benin and lived in slavery in Brazil, escaping when in the United States and then traveling to freedom in Haiti.]

Barnet, Miguel. *Biografía de un cimarrón*. Havana, Cuba: Academia de Ciencias de Cuba, Instituto de Etnología y Folklore, 1966. [Writing from interviews, anthropologist Miguel Barnet composed as autobiography the life story of the ex-slave Esteban Montejo, whose life spanned the late nineteenth and early twentieth centuries.]

Boyer, Richard, and Geoffrey Spurling. *Colonial Lives: Documents on Latin American History, 1550–1850*. New York: Oxford UP, 2000. [Six chapters present, in English translation, documents in which Afro-Latinos speak.]

Brásio, Padre António, ed. *Monumenta Missionaria Africana: África Ocidental*. 15 vols. Lisbon: Agência-Geral do Ultramar, 1971. [All but one of Njinga's known surviving letters are published in Brásio's works.]

Conrad, Robert Edgar. *Children of God's Fire: A Documentary History of Black Slavery in Brazil*. University Park: Penn State UP, 1994. [Includes a few nineteenth-century narratives by black slaves.]

"Digest of Documents in the Archives of the Indies, Seville, Spain, Bearing on the Negroes of Cuba and Especially Those Employed in the Minas de Cobre." *Journal of Negro History* 12, no. 1 (1927): 60–99.

Equiano, Olaudah. *The Interesting Narrative of the Life of Olaudah Equiano, or Gustavus Vassa, The African, Written by Himself*. New York: Norton, 2000. [In his abolitionist account of his life, Equiano (c. 1745–1797) tells of being born in "Eboe" (in what is now Nigeria) and being enslaved at about age eleven and taken to the West Indies. Although he moved mostly in the Anglophone world, he did spend time in the Spanish Caribbean.]

Jopling, Carol F., ed. *Indios y negros en Panamá en los siglos XVI y XVII: Selecciones de los documentos del Archivo General de Indias*. Trans. Margarita Cruz de Drake. Antigua, Guatemala: Centro de Investigaciones Regionales de Mesoamérica, 1994. [Includes a few testimonies by Afro-Latinos.]

Latino, Juan. *La Austriada de Juan Latino: Introducción, traducción inédita y texto*. Edited by José A. Sánchez Marín. Granada, Spain: Instituto de Historia del Derecho, Universidad de Granada, 1981. [Writings by a black Spanish Renaissance humanist and ex-slave.]

Manzano, Juan Francisco (1797–1854). *The Autobiography of a Slave*. Introduction and modernized Spanish version by Ivan A. Schulman. Trans. Evelyn Picon Garfield. Detroit, MI: Wayne State UP, 1996.

McKnight, Kathryn Joy. "Gendered Declarations: Testimonies of Three Captured Maroon Women, Cartagena de Indias, 1634." *Colonial Latin American Historical Review* 12, no. 4 (2003): 499–527.

Peabody, Sue, and Kelia Grinberg. *Slavery, Freedom, and the Law in the Atlantic World: A Brief History with Documents*. Boston: Bedford/St. Martin's, 2007. [Includes some slave petitions for freedom in nineteenth-century Ibero-America.]

Redworth, Glyn. "Mythology with Attitude? A Black Christian's Defence of Negritude in Early Modern Europe." *Social History* 28, no. 1 (2003): 49–66. ["Carta a unas monjas"—which is housed in Biblioteca Nacional, Madrid (Ms. 6149, item 83, fols. 236r–237v)—is reproduced in this article.]

Schwartz, Stuart B. "Resistance and Accommodation in Eighteenth-Century Brazil: The Slaves' View of Slavery." *Hispanic American Historical Review* 57, no. 1 (1977): 69–81. [Includes a translation and the original Portuguese of a remarkable late-eighteenth-century peace treaty, which escaped slaves from the Engenho Santana in the captaincy of Bahia proposed to their master.]

Splendiani, Anna María, and Tulio Aristizábal, eds. *Proceso de beatificación y canonización de San Pedro Claver.* Trans. Anna María Splendiani and Tulio Aristizabal. Bogota, Colombia: Centro Editorial Javeriano, 2002. [Some of the witnesses quoted in this work were Africans or Afro-Latinos. Their testimony was translated into Latin during the beatification and canonization process and was translated back into Spanish by the editors.]

Splendiani, Anna María, José Enrique Sánchez Bohórquez, and Emma Cecilia Luque de Salazar. *Cincuenta años de Inquisición en el Tribunal de Cartagena de Indias, 1610–1660.* Bogota, Colombia: Pontificia Universidad Javeriana, Instituto Colombiano de Cultura Hispánica, 1997. [Includes a few summaries of testimonies by Afro-Latinos.]

van Deusen, Nancy E., ed. and trans. *The Souls of Purgatory: The Spiritual Diary of a Seventeenth-Century Afro-Peruvian Mystic, Ursula de Jesús.* Albuquerque: U New Mexico P, 2004.

Films

[These films are listed by title. Abbreviations for languages listed: E (English), Sp (Spanish), P (Portuguese).]

A Dios Momo [Goodbye Momo]. Director Leonardo Ricagni. Mojo Films, 2005. [Feature film. Story of a young Afro-Uruguayan boy's magical encounters with the Murgas during the Montevideo carnival. Sp with E subtitles.]

Bahia, Africa in the Americas. Director Michael Brewer. Berkeley: University of California, Extension, Media Center, 1988. [Documentary film. P with E subtitles.]

Black in Latin America. Written by Henry Louis Gates, Jr. Directed by Ricardo Pollack, Diene Petterle, and Ilana Trachtman. PBS, 2011. [Documentary series covering slavery, emancipation, and present-day black experience in Cuba, Brazil, Peru, Mexico, Dominican Republic, and Haiti. E and Sp and P with E subtitles]

Candombe. Director Rafael Deugenio. ArtMattan Productions, 1993. [Documentary about the preservation of Afro-Uruguayan music and dance traditions brought by slaves. Sp with E subtitles.]

Candombe: Tambores en Libertad. Directors Carlos Paez Vilaró, Hassen Balut, and Silvestre Jacobi. Mistika Films, 2006. [Documentary about the Afro-Uruguayan music and dance traditions brought by slaves. Sp with E subtitles.]

Chico Rei. Director Walter Lima, Jr. Embrafilme, 1985. [Portrays the legendary Galanga, king of Kongo, who was enslaved and taken to Minas Gerais, Brazil, in the eighteenth century, where he found gold, bought his freedom, and became a landowner. P.]

Garifuna Journey. Directors Andrea E. Leland and Kathy L. Berger. New Day Films, 1998. [Documentary. Present-day Garifunas tell of their people's history of resistance and their culture. E and Garifuna with E subtitles.]

Gorée: Door of No Return. Directors Ann E. Jonson and Robin Klein. Même Chase
Production, 1992. [History of the slave trade. E.]

Hands of God. Director Delia Ackerman. ArtMattan Productions, 2004. [Documentary
about Afro-Peruvian percussionist Julio "Cholote" Algendones (1937–2004), who
played a mix of traditional and contemporary styles. Sp with E subtitles.]

Îlé Aiyé [The House of Life]. Director David Byrne. Little Magic Films, 2004.
[Documentary and poetic evocation of Afro-Brazilian Candomblé. E.]

La raíz olvidada [The Forgotten Root]. Director Rafael Rebollar. Writers Antonio
Noyola and Beatriz García. Producciones Trabuco, 2001. [Documentary on the
history and cultural traditions of Afro-Mexicans. Sp with E subtitles.]

La última cena [The Last Supper]. Director Tomás Gutiérrez Alea. Writers Moreno
Fraginal and Constante Diego. Instituto Cubano de Arte e Industrias Cinematográ-
ficos (ICAIC), 1977. [Feature film recreating an eighteenth-century slave uprising
following a master's reenactment of the Last Supper with twelve slaves. Sp with E
subtitles.]

Maluala. Director Sergio Giral. Instituto Cubano de Arte e Industrias Cinematográ-
ficos (ICAIC), 1979. [Feature film portraying nineteenth-century Cuban
Maroon communities in negotiations and armed confrontations with Spanish
colonial government. Sp with E subtitles.]

Negro che, los primeros desaparecidos. Director Alberto Masliah. 2006. [Documentary
about the official erasure of Afro-Argentine culture and the struggle of Afro-
Argentineans to preserve their cultural heritage. Sp.]

Quilombo. Director Carlos Diegues. New Yorker Films, 1984. [Feature film depicting
the autonomous *Maroon* republic in seventeenth-century Brazil in conflict with
the Portuguese landowners and military under its legendary leaders Ganga Zumba
and Zumbi. P with E subtitles.]

Quilombo Country. Director Leonard Abrams. Moving Eye Productions, 2006.
[Documentary on the history and traditions of Brazil's Quilombo communities,
who descended from *Maroon* communities. P with E subtitles.]

The Slave Kingdoms. From *Wonders of the African World.* Director Henry Louis
Gates, Jr. PBS, 1999. [Documentary in which Gates visits Elmina, Abomey, and
Asante to interview descendants of slave traders and explore the history of the
slave trade. E.]

Sons of Benkos. Director Silva Lucas. Palenque Records & Les Films Du Village,
2003. [Documentary on Colombia's African musical culture, particularly in the
rural town of *Palenque* de San Basilio, which was formerly a *Maroon* settlement.
Sp with E subtitles.]

Susana Baca: Memoria Viva. Director Marc Dixon. 24 Images, Karma Productions,
2003. [Documentary on Susana Baca, cofounder of the Instituto Negrocontinuo, which supports research and performance of Black Peruvian musical culture.
Sp with E subtitles.]

Voices of the Orishas. Director Alvaro Pérez Betancourt. University of California,
Extension, Center for Media and Independent Learning, 1993. [Docudrama
of Yoruba cultural and religious heritage in Cuba. Sp and Yoruba with E
subtitles.]

Music

Andy Palacio & the Garífuna Collective. *Watina*. Cumbancha, 2007. (compact disc). [Garífuna music from Belize with indigenous Arawak and Carib as well as West African roots.]

Antología del candombe Vol. II. Bizarro, 1995. (compact disc). [Afro-Uruguayan drum-based processional music.]

Baca, Susana. *Espíritu vivo*. Luaka Bop, 2002. (compact disc). [Baca is an Afro-Peruvian singer and the founder of the Instituto Negrocontinuo.]

Cáceres. *Murga Argentina*. Mañana, 2005. (compact disc). [Afro-Argentine Candombe-carnival-style music.]

Capoeira Angola from Salvador, Brazil. Smithsonian Folkways, 1996. (compact disc).

Ecuador & Colombia: Marimba Masters and Sacred Songs. Music of the Earth, 1998. (compact disc).

Fariñas. *Cajón al muerto*. Camaján, 2002. (compact disc). [Afro-Cuban rumba music in honor of the spirits.]

Grupo Afro Boriqua. *Bombazo*. Blue Jackel Entertainment, 1998. (compact disc). [Afro-Puerto Rican call-and-response music in the bomba tradition.]

Grupo Siquisirí. *En Vivo desde el Rialto Center for the Arts*. Grupo Siquisirí, 2007. (compact disc). [Son Jarocho music from Veracruz, Mexico.]

Ilê Aiyê. *Canto Negro*. Warner Music Brazil, 2003. (compact disc). [Afro-Brazilian ritual music.]

Les joyeuses ambulances, musique funéraire afro-colombienne. Buda, 2004. (compact disc). [Funeral music from the Palenque de San Basilio, Colombia.]

Los Gaiteros de San Jacinto. *Un fuego de sangre pura*. Smithsonian Folkways, 2006. (compact disc). [Colombian gaitero music.]

Millan, Angelica, & Grupo Costa y Sierra. *African Influences in Mexico*. Agave records, 1998. (compact disc).

Perú negro. *Jolgorio*. Times Square, 2004. (compact disc).

Ros, Lázaro. [All his many albums are recommended. Afro-Cuban Regla de Ocho music rooted in Yoruba culture.]

Soul of Angola Anthology: 1965–1975. Lusafrica, 2001. (compact disc set).

The Soul of Black Perú: AfroPeruvian Classics. Luaka Bop, 2000. (compact disc).

Spiro, Michael, and Mark Lamson. *Batá Ketú: A Musical Interplay of Cuba & Brasil*. Bembe, 1996. (compact disc).

Totó la Momposina y Sus Tambores. *La candela viva*. Real World Records, 1993. (compact disc). [Colombian singer of music of Afro-Latino and indigenous roots.]

Valdés, Merceditas & Yoruba Andabo. *Aché IV*. Egrem, 1995. (compact disc). [Afro-Cuban spiritual music.]

Wemba, Papa. *Papa Wemba*. Stern's, 1994. (compact disc). [Congolese rumba or soukous musician.]

Afro-Latino Legacies in Art

Araújo, Emanoel, curator. *A divina inspiração, sagrada e religiosa. Sincretismos*. Exhibit curators Carlos A. C. Lemos and Vagner Gonçalves da Silva. São Paulo, Brazil: Museu Afro-Brasil, 2008.

Araújo, Emanoel, curator. *Para nunca esquecer. Negras memórias. Memórias de negros.* Rio de Janeiro, Brazil: Museu Histórico Nacional, 2002.

Assunção, Matthias Röhrig. *Capoeira: A History of Afro-Brazilian Martial Art.* London: Routledge, 2005.

Beumers, Erna, and Hans-Joachim Koloss, eds. *Kings of Africa: Art and Authority in Central Africa. Collection Museum für Völkerkunde Berlin.* Utrecht, Netherlands: Foundation Kings of Africa, 1992.

Centro Cultural de España. *Aportaciones culturales haitianas: VIII Festival Antropológico de Culturas Afroamericanas.* Santo Domingo, Dominican Republic: Centro Cultural de España, 2002.

Grimaldi Forum. *Arts of Africa: 7000 Years of African Art.* Monaco: Grimaldi Forum, 2005.

Herreman, Frank, ed. *In the Presence of Spirits: African Art from the National Museum of Ethnology, Lisbon.* New York: Museum for African Art, 2000.

Hurst, Norman. *Ngola. The Weapon as Authority, Identity, and Ritual Object in Sub-Saharan Africa.* Cambridge, MA: Hurst Gallery, 1997.

Lam, Wifredo. *Wifredo Lam.* Introduction by Graziella Pogolotti. Havana, Cuba: José Martí, 1997.

Mexican Fine Arts Center Museum. *The African Presence in México: From Yanga to the Present.* Chicago: Mexican Fine Arts Center Museum, 2006.

National Museum of African Art. *Selected Works from the Collection of the National Museum of African Art.* Washington, DC: Smithsonian National Museum of African Art, 1999.

Price, Sally, and Richard Price. *Maroon Arts: Cultural Vitality in the African Diaspora.* Boston: Beacon, 1999.

Visonà, Monica Blackmun. *A History of Art in Africa.* New York: Harry N. Abrams, 2001.

NOTES ON CONTRIBUTORS

Maribel Arrelucea Barrantes is a researcher and teacher at the Universidad Nacional Mayor de San Marcos and the Universidad de San Ignacio de Loyola, in Lima, Peru. She is the author of *Replanteando la esclavitud: Estudios de etnicidad y género en Lima borbónica* (2009), and has published on slavery and marronage in Peru, with a focus on gender, in the *Revista del Archivo General de la Nación, Visión Histórica, Perspectivas, Diálogos en Historia*, and *Summa Historiae*. She has also contributed to several books, including *Mujeres, familia y sociedad en la historia de América Latina, siglos XVIII–XXI.*

Charles Beatty-Medina is associate professor of Latin American history at the University of Toledo. He specializes in the history of colonial Latin America, the African diaspora, and the southern Atlantic and circum-Caribbean region. His articles include "Caught between Rivals: The Spanish-African Maroon Competition for Captive Indian Labor in the Region of Esmeraldas during the Late Sixteenth and Early Seventeenth Centuries" in *Americas: A Quarterly Review of Inter-American Cultural History* and "Between the Cross and the Sword: Religious Conquest and Maroon Legitimacy in Colonial Esmeraldas" in *Africans to Spanish America: Expanding the Diaspora*, edited by Ben Vinson III, Sherwin K. Bryant, and Rachel Sarah O'Toole. He is co-editor with Melissa Rhinehart of *Contested Territories: Native Americans and Non-Natives in the Lower Great Lakes, 1700–1850 (2012).*

Jorge L. Chinea specializes in colonial Latin American history. His book, *Race and Labor in the Hispanic Caribbean: The West Indian Immigrant Worker Experience in Puerto Rico, 1800–1850*, received Wayne State University's Board of Governors Faculty Recognition Award in 2006. His work has appeared in the *Journal of Latin American Studies* and *Caribbean Studies*, among others. A past contributing editor for the *Handbook of Latin American Studies*, he is currently associate professor and director of the Center for Chicano-Boricua Studies at Wayne State University.

María Elena Díaz is associate professor of history at the University of California, Santa Cruz. Her research on the Atlantic world, colonial Latin America, the colonial Caribbean, and Cuba is interdisciplinary and focuses on slavery and freedom, colonialism, and legal, political, popular, and religious cultures. She is the author of *The Virgin, the King, and the Royal Slaves of El Cobre: Negotiating Freedom in Colonial Cuba, 1670–1780*. Her essays have appeared in *Latin American Research Review, Latin American and Caribbean Ethnic Studies, and Hispanic American Historical Review.*

Ana Teresa Fanchin is professor of history at the Universidad Nacional de San Juan (Argentina), where she directs research at the Instituto de Geografía Aplicada and teaches colonial history, history of demographics, and Latin American women's history in the Department of History and the Department of Graduate Studies. She is academic advisor for International Publications and corresponding foreign member of the Academia de Estudios Hispanoamericanos in Cadiz, Spain.

Patricia Fogelman is a historian and researcher at CONICET (Argentina). She earned her doctorate in history at the EHESS (France) and the Facultad de Filosofía y Letras at the Universidad de Buenos Aires. Her research is on religiosity, culture, and power in the colonial Americas. She is the editor of *Religiosidad, cultura y poder: Temas y problemas de la historiografía reciente* (2010) and co-editor of *El culto mariano en Luján y San Nicolás: Religiosidad e historia regional* (2013). She coordinates the Grupo de Estudios sobre Religiosidad y Evangelización, and she teaches history at the Universidad de Buenos Aires and the Universidad Nacional de Luján (Argentina).

Baltasar Fra-Molinero is professor of Spanish at Bates College. He is the author of *La imágen de los negros en el teatro del Siglo de Oro* as well as a number of essays on the representation of blacks in Spain and Latin America from the Renaissance to today. He is working on a critical edition and English translation of the *Vida ejemplar* of Sor Teresa Chicaba in collaboration with Sue E. Houchins.

Leo J. Garofalo is associate professor of history at Connecticut College, where he teaches Latin American and Caribbean history and the history of race and gender in colonial Latin America and directs the Center for the Comparative Study of Race and Ethnicity. He is the author of *Taverns, Witches, and Marketplaces: Ethnicity and Race in Colonial Peru*, and co-editor of *Más allá de la dominación y la resistencia: Estudios de historia peruana, siglos XVI–XX*, and an issue of the *Journal of Colonialism and Colonial History* devoted to constructing difference in colonial Latin America, and he has published articles and chapters on colonial Peru and the African diaspora in the Atlantic world.

Marta Goldberg is a historian, researcher, and full professor at the Universidad Nacional de Luján (Argentina), where she directs the master's program in social sciences, with a specialization in social history. Her research is on the social history of blacks and mulattoes in Río de la Plata from the late colonial period through the early decades of independence. She is a member of the ALADAA and the Comité Científico Internacional del Programa de la UNESCO "La Ruta del Esclavo."

Richard A. Gordon is professor of Brazilian and Spanish-American Literature and culture and Director of the Latin American and Caribbean Studies Institute at the University of Georgia. He researches primarily Brazilian- and Spanish-American historical cinema and eighteenth-century Luso-Brazilian culture. He is author of *Cannibalizing the Colony: Cinematic Adaptations of Colonial Literature in Mexico and Brazil* and *Cinema, Slavery, and Brazilian Nationalism*.

Sara Vicuña Guengerich is assistant professor of Spanish at Texas Tech University. Her research centers on the discursive production of colonial women, particularly indigenous women, in colonial Peru. She has published in the *Colonial Latin American Review*, *Hispania*, the *Journal of the Southwest*, and the *Journal of Spanish Cultural Studies*.

Linda Heywood is professor of history at Boston University, where she teaches African, African-American, and women's history. She is the author of *Contested Power in Angola, 1840s to the Present*, editor of *Central Africans and Cultural Transformations in the American Diaspora*, and coauthor, with John K. Thornton, of *Central Africans,*

Atlantic Creoles, and the Foundation of America, which was awarded the Herskovits prize by the African Studies Association. She is also co-author of *Njinga, reine d'Angola, 1582–1663: La relation d'Antonio Cavazzi da Montecuccoli, 1687*. She has consulted for museum exhibitions, including African Voices at the Smithsonian Institution and Against Human Dignity sponsored by the Maritime Museum.

Sue E. Houchins is associate professor at Bates College, where she chairs African American Studies and also teaches courses in Women and Gender Studies. Her research focuses on the intersection of race, gender, and sexuality among women of the Black Atlantic. She edited *Spiritual Narratives*, a collection of African-American women's writings, and is completing a book on representations of Black lesbians in women's literatures of Africa and the Americas, co-editing a collection of essays on W. E. B. Du Bois, and co-editing a translation of the eighteenth-century hagiography of Sor Teresa Chicaba.

Elizabeth W. Kiddy (d. 2014) taught history and directed Latin American and Caribbean Studies at Albright College. She authored the book *Blacks of the Rosary: Memory and History in Minas Gerais, Brazil* and several articles and book chapters on Africans in confraternities in Brazil.

Luis Madureira holds a degree in comparative literature and is professor in the Department of Spanish and Portuguese at the University of Wisconsin–Madison. He has published two books, *Imaginary Geographies in Portuguese and Lusophone-African Literature: Narratives of Discovery and Empire* and *Cannibal Modernities: Postcoloniality and the Avant-Garde in Caribbean and Brazilian Literature*, and several articles on Luso-Brazilian literature and postcolonial theory. His current research focuses on Mozambican theater and the politics of time in contemporary Lusophone fiction.

José R. Jouve Martín is associate professor in the Department of Hispanic Studies at McGill University. His research focuses on seventeenth-century colonial lettered culture, the intersection between writing and religious practices, and the use of written documents by slaves and their descendants in Spanish America. He has authored *Esclavos de la ciudad letrada: Esclavitud, escritura y colonialismo en Lima (1650–1700)* and *The Black Doctors of Colonial Lima: Science, Race, and Writing in Colonial and Early Republican Peru* as well as articles in journals such as *Colonial Latin American Review, Canadian Review of Hispanic Studies, Theatralia*, and *Hispanófila*.

Kathryn Joy McKnight is associate professor of Spanish at the University of New Mexico. Her book, *The Mystic of Tunja: The Writings of Madre Castillo, 1671–1742*, won the Modern Language Association's Kovacs prize in 1998. She has published on Afro-Latino documentary narratives in the *Colonial Latin American Review, Colonial Latin American Historical Review, Revista de Estudios Hispánicos*, and the *Journal of Colonialism and Colonial History*.

Larry D. Miller (d. 2009) was a research historian at the Spanish Colonial Research Center, University of New Mexico (UNM), and was on the editorial staff of the *Colonial Latin American Historical Review*. He interpreted the history and demonstrated the art of blacksmithing at Rancho de las Golondrinas and Bent's Old

Fort National Historic Site. He earned his B.A. and M.A. in Spanish at UNM. For eighteen years he worked as a compiler, paleographer, and translator on the Vargas Project's publication of the journals of Don Diego de Vargas. He coauthored *Martineztown 1823–1950: Hispanics, Italians, Jesuits & Land Investors in New Town Albuquerque.*

Rachel Sarah O'Toole is associate professor of the early modern Atlantic world and colonial Latin America in the Department of History at the University of California, Irvine. Her book *Bound Lives: Africans, Indians, and the Making of Race in Colonial Peru* (2012) won the 2013 Perú Flora Tristán prize from the Latin American Studies Association. She is also co-editor of *Africans to Spanish America: Expanding the Diaspora.* Other publications include "From the Rivers of Guinea to the Valleys of Peru: Becoming a *Bran* Diaspora within Spanish Slavery" in *Social Text* and "Danger in the Convent: Colonial Demons, Idolatrous *Indias,* and Bewitching *Negras* in Santa Clara (Trujillo del Perú)" in the *Journal of Colonialism and Colonial History.*

Joseph P. Sánchez is superintendent of the National Park Service's Petroglyph National Monument and the Spanish Colonial Research Center at the University of New Mexico. He is the founding editor of the *Colonial Latin American Historical Review.* He has published studies on the Spanish colonial frontiers in California, Arizona, New Mexico, Texas, and Alaska, including *Between Two Rivers: The Atrisco Land Grant in Albuquerque's History, 1691–1968.*

Angelica Sánchez-Clark is a National Park Service linguist historian with the Spanish Colonial Research Center at the University of New Mexico (UNM). Since 1995, she has been the managing editor of the *Colonial Latin American Historical Review.* She holds a PhD from the Department of Spanish and Portuguese at UNM and is co-editor of *Set in Stone: A Binational Workshop on Petroglyph Management in the United States and Mexico.*

John K. Thornton is professor of history at Boston University, where he teaches African and Atlantic history. He is the author of *The Kingdom of Kongo: Civil War and Transition, 1641–1718; Africa and Africans in the Making of the Atlantic World, 1400–1680; The Kongolese Saint Anthony: Dona Beatriz Kimpa Vita and the Antonian Movement, 1684–1706; Warfare in Atlantic Africa, 1500–1800, A Cultural History of the Atlantic World, 1250–1820* coauthor, with Linda Heywood, of *Central Africans, Atlantic Creoles, and the Foundation of the Americas, 1585–1660,* which was awarded the Herskovits prize by the African Studies Association, and co-author of *Njinga, reine d'Angola, 1582–1663: La relation d'Antonio Cavazzi da Montecuccoli, 1687.*

Nicole von Germeten holds a PhD in history from the University of California, Berkeley, and is associate professor of history at Oregon State University. She has published three books: *Black Blood Brothers: Confraternities and Social Mobility for Afro-Mexicans, Treatise on Slavery,* an annotated translation of Alonso de Sandoval's 1627 *De instauranda Aethiopum salute,* the earliest known book-length study of African slavery in the Americas, and *Violent Delights, Violent Ends: Race, Sex, and Honor in Colonial Cartagena.*

David Wheat is an assistant professor of history at Michigan State University. His research centers on migration and diaspora. His first book, *Atlantic Africa and the Spanish Caribbean, 1570–1640*, is forthcoming with University of North Carolina Press for the Omohundro Institute of Early American History and Culture. He is also co-author of *African Laborers for a New Empire: Iberia, Slavery, and the Atlantic World*, a Lowcountry Digital History Initiative, launched in 2014.

INDEX

Note: All italicized words are defined in the Glossary. We have also added English-language cross-references in the Index to facilitate its use as a tool for considering themes for further investigation.

abuse: of power, 172, 180; of slaves, xviii, 36, 57, 86–87, 108, 160, 169, 192, 196; of spouse, 183, 184, 187, 187n.

Afonso, King of Kongo, 2, 3, 4, 6, 6n, 7, 8

Africa, xiv, xv, xvi–xvii, xix–xx, xxv, 1–19, 26–34, 35–36, 44n, 45–47, 55, 56–57, 93–94, 115, 126, 127, 128, 128n, 130, 141–42, 144–47, 145n, 153–54, 156, 200, 203, 205, 206

Afroboricua, 202

Anchico (ethnonym), 43, 46, 48–49

Angola (ethnonym), 43, 46–52, 54, 93, 102, 115, 130, 131–34, 136, 153, 155–56, 160, 164

Angola (Portuguese colony), 3, 26, 45, 193n; Bantu languages spoken in, xx; Benguela, xvii; as center in slave trade, xvi–xvii, 1, 27, 28, 29, 31, 33n, 34n, 45; conquered by Dutch, 27, 32n; culture of, 28, 45n; history of, 1, 3; Njinga siege against, 27, 28, 30n; and wars with Ndongo, 30n, 45

Arará, 94, 136

Argentina. *See* Río de la Plata, Viceroyalty of

argumentation, 181, 186

armed militia members. See *milicianos*

artisans, xvii, 93, 103

asiento. See slave trade, monopoly on

as-told-to biographies, 115, 137–40

Audiencia. See Real Audiencia

Audiencia of Quito, the, 25; Esmeraldas, 20–25; Quito, xvii, 21–23, 25, 180

Bahia (Brazil), xvii, xx, 154, 158, 158n, 160, 171

Bañón (ethnonym), 52, 54

baptism, 26, 31, 39, 92, 102, 181; required of new slaves, 181n

Battle of Bailén, 204, 206, 206n

Biáfara (ethnonym), 116, 120, 128–36

Black Atlantic, The, xvi, 200

bonded subjects, 81, 82

bozal, xxi, 22, 48

Bran (ethnonym), 49, 52, 71, 74

Brazil, xvi, xv, xvii, 27, 28, 32n, 36, 139n, 155, 155n, 156, 157, 158n, 161, 165n, 170, 171–72, 173, 193n; Afro-Latino communities in, xiv, xix, 28, 44, 46n, 95, 153–58; confraternities in, xix, 95, 153n, 153–56, 155n, 162n, 165n; demand for slaves in, xiii, xvi, xvii, xviii, 28, 36; enslaved indigenous people in, xvii, xviii; export orientation of, xviii, 269; Goiás, xvii; Minas Gerais, xvii, 153, 158; Pernambuco, xvii, 169–72, 175–78; plantations in, xiii, xvii, 36, 154; Portuguese Inquisition adjudicated in, 171–73, 172n; Rio de Janeiro, 153, 154, 158n, 170–73

Buenos Aires. *See* Río de la Plata, Viceroyalty of

cabildo, 45, 81, 83, 193

Cabo Verde (Islands), 127

Caboverde (ethnonym), 71

Cadiz (Spain), 147, 203, 204, 206

candombes (*Afro-Rioplatense* dance style and celebrations), 104–6

Capuchins, 145, 145n; missionaries in Matamba, Angola, 27, 30, 31, 34, 145n

Carabalí (ethnonym), 52, 74, 78, 130–36

Cardoso, Bento Banha, 30, 30n

Caribbean, xiii, xvii, xix, 69, 116, 116n, 117, 126; Afro-Iberians in, xvii, 22, 36, 37, 40, 41, 205; non-Hispanic colonies in, xiv, 44, 82, 82n, 115; pirating in, 44, 115, 126, 129, 131, 131n, 132, 201, 202

Carlos II, King, 142, 147

Carmelite Order, 31, 143n

Cartagena de Indias (New Kingdom of Granada or present-day Colombia), 38, 40–45, 48, 49–50, 54, 127, 131, 134, 136; African religious practices in, 116, 117, 128; Inquisition tribunal of, 85, 116, 116n, 171; persecution of *"brujas"*

(witches) in, 85, 116–25; and privateering, 126, 129; as slave port, xvii, 1, 127
castas, xxi, 41, 49, 69–71, 77n, 93, 109,
116, 118, 120, 131, 204; *Anchico*, 43,
46, 48, 49; *Biáfara*, 116, 120, 128, 131;
interactions among, 69, 70; *Lucumí*, 93,
95, 97, 98
castes. See *castas*
Catholic brotherhood. *See* confraternities
Catholic Church, xix, 23, 36, 59, 73, 77,
90, 97, 73, 77, 104, 105; authority
of, xix, 7, 7n, 19, 30, 60n, 103, (*see
also* Inquisition); authority of vs. civil
authorities, 7, 7n, 19, 22, 27, 30, 102,
103, 118, 169, 172, 180, 181, 18 (*see
also* Ecclesiastic Tribunal); crimes against
faith, 120, 172, 116–21, 123, 172; laws
of, 3, 41, 72, 117, 120, 121, 172; prohibited books, 120; as space of political
power, 10, 19, 24, 30, 36, 38, 103, 104,
105, 110, 117, 155, 157, 180; structure
of, xviii, 103, 104, 163n. *See also* confraternities; convents; Pope; priests;
saints
Catholicism, 1, 36, 55, 58, 103; beatification, 138n, 139n, 143; beliefs, 35,
54n, 56, 59, 73, 77, 86, 106, 115, 117,
124, 141, 143, 165, 186, 188n (*see also*
Christians, old vs. new); conversion to,
1, 3, 32, 33, 35n, 105, 115, 117, 140,
141, 139n, 154, 181, 202 (*see also* missionaries and evangelizing); doctrine,
59, 73, 104, 116–18, 141, 143, 169;
giving Christian name, 12, 138; imagery,
57, 75, 96, 100, 105–6; miracles 86,
137–39, 139n, 146, 150, 152; practices,
3, 27, 68, 70, 90, 105, 120, 137, 146n,
164; religious feast days and holidays,
105–6, 110, 113, 120, 145, 153, 165n,
166n, 167; religious processions, 82,
102–3, 105–6, 165, 166n, 181n (*see also*
confraternities: festivals and celebrations); sacraments, 27, 39, 41, 59, 60,
62, 66, 73, 91, 92, 97, 106, 117, 120,
146, 146n, 165, 181 (*see also* baptism;
Communion; confession, sacrament of;
funerals; marriage; mass); understanding/
knowledge of, xxi, 59, 117–18, 128, 130,
141; Virgin Mary, 59, 73, 74n, 82, 84,
84n, 86, 103, 104, 106, 118, 142–43.

See also confraternities; *indulgencia;* wills
and testaments
Ceballos Gómez, Diana Luz, 117
Central Africa, xiv, xv, 26, 46; in relations
with Europeans, xvi, 1, 27, 28, 45; in
slave trade, xvi, xx, 27, 28, 35, 36, 44n,
45, 56, 57, 93, 153
chicherías, 69
Christian, identity as, 35, 82, 86, 104
Christianity, xxi, 27, 33–34, 41, 55, 82, 95,
96, 115; claiming Christian status, xxi,
33–34, 36, 55, 56, 59, 73, 77, 82, 86,
96, 124; identifying as Christianity for
protection, xix, 27, 115, 128, 181, 182,
202; identifying as Christianity for social
status, 115; as justification for slavery,
xvi, 115, 141 (*see also* missionaries and
evangelizing); and racial differentiation,
115, 140, 141; used in argumentation
to achieve goals, 22, 23, 24–25, 29, 30,
36, 38, 40, 41, 169. *See also* Christian,
identity as; Protestants; Puritans
Christians, old vs. new, 38, 41
cimarrones. See *Maroons*
cities, xvii, xviii, 21, 69, 82, 115, 127, 153,
155n, 194; Afro-Latinos in, xvii, xviii,
55, 115, 169, 205
citizenship, 81, 132, 196, 200
civil litigation, 61–67, 72, 83–88, 89–92,
106–7, 108–13, 154–56, 157–68,
180–86, 180n, 187–91, 192–95, 196–99,
206–7. *See also* gender differences
coartación, 86
cobrero/cobrera, 84, 86, 87, 90, 91, 92
cofradía. See confraternities
Colombia. *See* New Kingdom of Granada
Colombia, present-day, xix, 1, 24n, 43, 116,
126, 128n, 131n
colonization, xxii, 3, 22, 23, 41, 127, 170,
192, 204; of Ecuador (*Audiencia* of
Quito), 1, 20, 22, 23; of Providence
Island, 126, 130; role of Afro-Iberians
in, xiii, 20, 35, 36, 126; structure of,
81, 82, 127; time period of, xiv, xix,
21, 26
commerce, xvi, 35, 36, 127, 128
Communion, 120, 181n
compañías de negros libres, 108
confession, sacrament of, 13, 13n, 120,
145n, 164

confessions, Inquisition, 117–18, 120, 124, 171–78

confessors, 28, 72, 140, 145n

confraternities, xviii, 36, 45, 56, 58, 74, 74n, 105–7, 153–56; based on ethnicity, xviii, 57, 103, 153; based on mulatto race, 57; disputes between, 154, 155; festivals and celebrations, 95, 102, 103, 105, 106, 109, 110, 113, 153, 165, 165n, 167–68; funeral and burial duties of, 70, 160n; organization and administration, 102, 103, 159n, 160n, 163n; patron saints of, 104, 153; practice of coronation, 106–7, 154, 155n, 163n, 165n; religious role of, 103, 115, 153, 154; social role of, 55, 103, 153. *See also* confraternity of . . .

confraternity of *Mina* Maki, 154–56, 158, 160–63

confraternity of Saint Balthasar, 103–6, 110–11, 113

confraternity of Saint Elesbão and Iphigenia, 154–55, 157, 159

confraternity of the *Zape* nation (confraternity of the Immaculate Conception), 57–58, 61–66

Congo, xx, 2–3, 105–7, 109

Congo (ethnonym), 49, 51, 52, 55, 79, 101, 102, 105, 106–7, 109–10, 165n. *See also* Kongo, Kingdom of

conscription, 202, 203

Consejo de Indias, 181n, 193

convents, 140, 143, 151n, 185, 187n; confraternities within, 103; and Manuela *Zamba*, property of the Convent of Santo Domingo, 184n, 185, 188, 189, 190, 191; mentioned in wills, 59, 73, 74, 75, 77; and Sor Teresa de Santo Domingo, 137–39, 139n, 141–51

corsairs. *See* pirates

Costa Rica, present-day, 133n

Coura (ethnonym), 154n

Council of the Indies. See *Consejo de Indias*

Creoles (*criollos/criollas*), xxi, 43, 44, 45, 49–54, 91, 120, 158, 158n, 193n, 201; Afrocreole, 127, 128; in Buenos Aires, 104; in Cartagena, 127; culture of in Central Africa, 27; Eurocreoles in Spanish America, 201; in Puerto Rico,

201, 204; as royal slaves in Cuba, 85, 89–90

criminal litigation, 116–18, 119–25, 170–79

cuarterón, 71

Cuba: anti-Spanish violence in, 43, 44, 87, 90–92; free black communities in, 44, 55, 56, 81–88, 89–92; manumission in, 89–90, 194; mining in, 555, 116, 119, 121, 124; negotiations between Afro-Latinos and Spanish authority in, 44, 81–88, 89–92; as slave center, xviii, 57; views of slavery in, 89

Dagome (ethnonym referring to *Dahomey*), 160–61

Dahomey, Kingdom of, 94, 154n

dances, 102, 104, 105, 107, 110, 111, 113

dialogue, written, 22, 154, 155, 155n, 157–68

diaspora, xvi, xvii, xix, xx, 143, 200, 205; diasporic identity, xx, 94, 143, 200; diasporic religion, 95, 96

Diogo I, King of Kongo, 2–9, 4n, 7n, 10–19, 11n, 13n

disease, xvii, 21, 127, 160

domestic servants, xvi, xvii, xviii, 21, 22, 36, 45, 69, 101, 116, 127, 138, 142, 144, 145, 148, 171, 193

Dominicans, 115, 138, 138n, 148n, 189n

double consciousness, xviii, xxii, 46–47, 142, 174

drinking, 119, 123, 187

Duarte, Pedro, 55, 101, 105, 106, 108–12

Dutch, the: in Africa, xvii, 27, 32n; in the Americas, 28, 133, 134–35, 170, 202; as pirates, 126, 129; as privateers, 126, 131, 131n, 133; and the slave trade, 27–28, 126; stealing slaves, 126, 129

Ecclesiastic Tribunal, 180, 181, 182, 184n, 185

Ecuador, present-day, xix

education, 3, 22, 28, 58, 167

Eguiluz, don Juan de, 84, 85, 89, 89n, 116–15

Eguiluz, Paula de, 85, 89, 89n, 115, 116–25

Elfrith, Daniel (Captain Alfero), 129, 132

encomendero, 45

encomienda, 127

erros de fé. See Catholic Church
esclavos del rey. See royal slaves
escribanía, 71
Esmeraldas (*Audiencia* of Quito), 20, 21, 22, 23, 24, 24n
estancia, xix, 52n, 53, 91, 127, 128, 201
ethnicity, xvi, xix, xxi, 56, 57; of Angolans and Minas, 153; and confraternities, xix, 57, 102, 103, 107, 153; differences, xiv, 183–84; Ewe, 138, 138n, 145; labeling of, xx, 57, 101, 193; laws related to, 182; rivalries, 154; and status, 184; and witchcraft accusations, 117; *Zape,* 56
ethnonym, xxi, 45, 208
Ethiopia, 77
Europe: African descent peoples in, xvi, xvii, 35, 36, 130, 200, 205; Catholic Church and, 23; convents in, 140; shipping from, 101; witchcraft trials in, 116n

family, xviii, 37, 38, 57, 93, 96; African royal families, 3, 138, 144; bearing and raising children, xviii, 27, 184; buying freedom of family members, xviii, 70; in Europe, 35; families in El Cobre, 82, 86, 87, 90; financial support, xv, 93; forming and securing, xviii, 35, 36, 37, 55, 169, 182–85; relation to identity, xv, xxi, 55, 94, 95; role of in cultural beliefs, 55; role of in determining Kongo's ruler, 5; roles of family members, 95; slavery transmitted matrilineally, 69. *See also* marriage
farm overseers, 44, 127
farm workers, xvi, 128, 201
Ferdinand VII, 203, 204, 205
festivals and celebrations, 82, 107, 117n, 204. *See also* Catholicism: practices; confraternities
fishing, xix, 27, 201
Folupo/Folupa, 77, 77n, 78–79, 131, 132, 133, 134, 136
formulaic language, xxii, xxiv, 71, 86, 96, 173, 182
forts, xvi, 27, 30, 39, 90, 90n, 127, 129, 130, 132, 135, 206
free black corps, 202
free black militias, see *compañías de negros libres*
free black towns, xix, 44

freedmen/freedwomen, 84, 95. See also *horro/horra* (Spanish), *morenos/morenas*
French, the, 203, 204, 206, 206n. *See also* Napoleonic invasion
funerals, 57, 57n, 70,71, 104, 160n, 167

Gauderman, Kimberly, 180
gender, 29, 54; and black community, 55, 68, 72; expectations, 156, 158; power relations, 58, 65, 154–56, 157, 180, 185
gender differences, 24, 142; in litigation, 182–85; in manumission, 69; in population numbers, 69; in preparing wills and testaments, 55, 68, 70; in privileges, 69, 70; in social and economic participation, 69, 70
Gilroy, Paul, xiv, 200
gobernador intendente, 110, 111
Goiás (Brazil), xvii
government authorities, 29, 86, 103, 112, 129, 159n, 186, 202; *alcalde mayor,*116. 116n, 119, 121, 131, 133–36; *alcaldes,* 113, 196, 197, 198 (see also *alcalde de minas*); *ayudantes,* 111, 112, 113; civil authorities, 72, 102, 155, 172; colonial authorities, xix, 20, 21, 68, 70, 71, 104, 105–6; Council of Indies, 87; governors, 1, 22, 29, 83, 90, 103, 113, 127, 128, 129, 130, 132, 133, 135, 193, 205; magistrates, 2, 10, 11–12, 13–14, 16–19, 39, 106, 107, 155, 158, 158n, 160; *mandadores,* 89; *mayor de la plaza,* 110, 112; *mayordomo,* 103–4, 106, 110, 127, 148; police, 102, 104; Portuguese Crown, 158n, 160n, 170; royal authorities, 21, 22, 35, 38, 104; Spanish authorities, 1, 21, 22, 37, 43, 45, 126, 130; Spanish Crown, 1, 22, 35, 36, 81, 82n, 84, 107, 202, 204; Supreme Council of Justice, 87; *tenientes,* 48, 49, 110, 124, 131, 134; town and municipal councils, xviii, 45, 81, 83, 98, 99; tribunals, 84, 92, 171, 180–82. See also *cabildo;* Inquisition; *Protector de Naturales; Real Audiencia;* Spain: *Casa de Contratación;* Spain: Council of State; Spain: Supreme Junta; viceroyalty
Granada (Nicaragua), 128
gremios, xxvii, xviii, 202, 202n
guilds. See *gremios*

Guinea, 45, 46, 48–51, 51n, 53, 77, 106, 109, 110, 111, 112, 128, 141, 144, 193n
Guinea-Bissau, 128

hacendado/hacendada, 193
haciendas, xix, 94, 185, 186, 188–90, 193n
hagiographies, 137–43, 144–52
Haitian Revolution (1791–1804), 203
herbalists, 118, 122
heresy, 35, 36, 172, 117, 118n, 172; and witchcraft trial of Paula de Eguiluz, 118, 125
horro/horra, 71, 85, 89

Ibero-Atlantic, xiii–xv, xvi–xix, xxii, xxiii, xxv, 1, 28
identity, xx, 55, 58, 106; ethnic, xiv, xix, xx, xxi; maintenance of, 35, 56, 57, 107; racial, 142, 143; as subjects of the Crown, 38. *See also* Christian, identity as; slave, identity as
Illescas, Alonso de, 1, 20–23, 24–25, 24n, 44
Imbangala. See *Jagas*
imprisonment, 43, 48, 145, 161, 180n, 206; by the Inquisition, 116n, 117, 121, 122, 173, 175n; in Kongo, 5, 14, 14n, 18, 29; of slaves by owners, 191, 192; by spouse, 184
indigenous peoples, 82, 170, 182, 185, 193, 204; Chalchaquis, 192; in convents, 143; culture of, 117; decimation of, xvii, 20, 21, 127; enslavement of, xvii, xviii, 128; forced relocation of, 68; languages of, xxi, 130; miscegenation, xxi; occupations of, 93; population of, xviii, 56; *Protector de Naturales,* 181; relations with Afro-Latinos, xiv, xix, 20–23, 24, 44, 45, 50–54
indulgence. See *indulgencia*
indulgencia, 59, 78, 121
Iñigo Abbad y Lasierra, Fray Agustín, 202
inquest, judicial, 1–9, 4n, 10–19, 48–54, 55, 59–67, 108–13, 131–36, 196–99
Inquisition, the, 115, 116, 117, 118, 121n, 172; *auto de fe,* 118, 170; of Cartagena de Indias, 85, 116, 116n, 117; *inquisidor fiscal,* 51, 52, 53; of Luiz da Costa, 169, 170–74; of Paula de Eguiluz, 116–18, 119–25; Portuguese, 169, 170, 171;

Spanish, 36, 118, 171, 172; trial proceedings, xiii, 119–25, 171–74
interpreters, 13, 13n, 14, 46–47, 48, 49, 128, 130, 195; role as narrative mediators, 46–47

Jagas, 26, 27, 29, 31, 33, 45
Jesuits, 7, 8, 28, 48, 77, 193n
João III, King Dom, 170
Jolofo (ethnonym), 58
jornalero/jornalera (wage laborer, slave as), 184

Kikongo governor. See *mani*
Kissama. *See* Quissama
Kongo, Kingdom of; archiving in, 8; bureaucratic language, 11n; capital of (Mbanza Kongo), 2, 6; Catholicism in, 1, 3, 7, 8, 11n, 144n; diplomatic mission to Rome, 7, 7n, 11n, 19, 28; electoral process, 6, 6n; elite in, 3, 6, 8, 9, 28; external political alliances, 27; family ties in, 5, 5n, 15; geography of, 1, 2, 3; history of, 2, 3, 4, 7, 144n; involvement in slave trade, 3, 15n, 27–28; judicial inquests, 1–9, 10–19; kings of Kongo, 1, 3, 4, 5, 6, 6n, 7 (*see also* Afonso, King of Kongo; Diogo I, King of Kongo); legal system, 8, 15n; letters, internal, 8; letters between Kongo and Ndongo, 28; letters between Kongo and Portugal, 3, 8, 18–19; plots to overthrow king, 3, 4, 5, 7, 8, 9; politics, 1–8, 5n, 9, 12; population size, 3; Portugal, relations with, xvi, 1, 3, 7n, 8, 28; *rendas* in, 4, 5, 6, 12; royal succession, 3, 4, 4n, 8; schools in, 3, 28; treason, 1, 2, 4, 9, 11, 19; wars in, 3, 6, 12, 13, 28. *See also* literacy; *mani;* Mani . . . ; Nkanga a Mvemba, Dom Pedro; papal bull in Kongolese politics.

ladino, xvi, 22, 35n, 48, 62, 130, 133, 134
languages used: *Anchico,* 48; Bantu languages, xx; *Crioulo* (Afro-Portuguese), 128; Kikongo, 4n, 12n; Kimbundu, 28, 29, 33; Portuguese, xxi, 3, 28, 128, 154;

Spanish, xxi, 22, 128–30, 133; Yoruba,
    94
"latinized" or acculturated person. See *ladino*
laundry workers, 101, 127
legal systems: and Afro-Latino organizations,
    55, 155, 164, 167, 168; Afro-Latinos'
    access to mediation in the Americas,
    81–84, 83n, 88, 170–74, 174–79, 175n,
    180–86, 187–91, 192–95, 196–99,
    200–205, 206–7 (*see also* wills and testa-
    ments; women, Afro-Latino); in Europe,
    36, 37–38, 39–42; European colonial,
    46–47, 70, 81–84, 83n, 87, 88, 117,
    128, 158n; in Kongo, 7, 8, 15n, 23
letters, 4, 5, 83, 89, 139, 139n; of diplo-
    macy, 27–29, 30–34; of negotiation, 1,
    22–23, 24–25, 44; official, 3, 8, 18–19,
    28; personal, 84–85, 89; of petition,
    20–23, 24–25, 37–38, 37n, 39–42, 39n,
    85–88, 90–92, 185–86, 187–91, 206–7
Lima (Peru), xviii, xiv, 55, 93, 101, 171,
    181n; Afro-Latino women litigants in,
    181–91; Afro-Latino women's legal
    testaments in, 68–80
Limón, Palenque del, 1, 28, 43–54
limpieza de sangre (purity of blood), 38, 41n,
    81, 141, 214,
lineage: xxi, 41, 140–41, 144; and *limpieza
    de sangre,* 141; requirements for saint-
    hood, 140; as unit of political organiza-
    tion, 5, 5n, 18–19, 213
literacy, xiv, 83–84, 87–88, 182, 205; in
    Central Africa, 3, 8, 28; of nuns, 139,
    139n; preparing wills and testaments,
    70–72, 96
Luanda (Angola), xvi, 26, 27, 28, 93, 127,
    153
Lucumí (ethnonym), 55, 93–98, 214
Luso-African, 8, 128, 214

magistrate of mines. See *alcalde de minas*
Maki (ethnonym), 154–66, 214
Malemba (ethnonym), 45, 49, 51, 51n, 52,
    54, 214
Mancera, Marquis and Marchioness of, 138,
    138n, 141n, 142, 144, 147–48, 214
Mandé, 57
mani, 12n
Mani Mpangala, 6, 9, 15, 17,
Mani Mpemba, 5, 6, 9, 12, 12n, 13, 15–17

Mani Vunda, 6, 9, 12, 13, 15, 18
manumission, 69, 74, 78, 78, 83n, 118,
    181, 183, 185, 188, 194, 210, 211, 214;
    deed of manumission 37, 37n, 69, 74,
    78, 79, 185, 188; freedmen/freedwomen;
    gender differences; *horro/horra;* women,
    Afro-Latino
Maroon communities, xix, 1, 20–25, 43–54,
    82, 90; authorities' searches for, 90; crim-
    inal litigation and,43, 45–46; culture of,
    20–23; livelihood of, xviii, 43–44; nego-
    tiations with colonial authorities, 54. *See
    also* (specific) *palenques;* politics; slavery
Maroons, pirating, in Puerto Rico. See also
    Maroon communities
marriage, 38–39, 40–41, 59–60, 62–63, 97,
    187–91, 191, 193; bigamy, 172; Catho-
    lic Church sanction of, 27, 157, 185;
    Church regulation of, 181; defending
    rights of, 38–39, 182–85; and divorce,
    72, 157, 184n, 188n, 189; per *Imbangala*
    custom, 27; owner intervention in slaves'
    marriage, 182–85; pueblo affiliation and,
    82, 89–90; records, 102, 193n; relation
    to identity, xx, 55; view of marriage, 157,
    172, 185, 188n; wife's duty within, 157,
    183–84. *See also* abuse; family; racial
    miscegenation
mass, 79, 104, 120, 124, 151, 164, 166;
    attendance required of slaves, 181n; for
    souls of deceased, 57, 59, 70, 73, 78, 98,
    104, 160, 162
memorial, 108n, 203–7, 215
merchants, xvi, 3, 21, 22, 36, 93, 128
mestizo/mestiza, xxi, 101, 102n, 143n, 193,
    201, 202, 215
Mexico, present-day Black communities, xix
Mexico City (New Spain), xvii, xviii, xix,
    xxxv, 37, 39n, 55–67, 138, 171, 214
milicianos, 200–207
Mina (ethnonym), 93, 94, 102, 153–67, 215
Mina Coast (*Mina Baja del Oro*; *Costa da
    Mina*), xl, 154, 156, 167, 160, 164–67,
    213, 214
Minas Gerais (Brazil), xvii, 153, 158n
missionaries and evangelizing, 8, 27–29,
    31n, 128, 145, 145n
morenos/morenas, 37, 39, 73n, 77n, 93, 95,
    97, 97n, 99, 109, 112, 133, 200, 202,
    203, 215

morenos/morenas libres, 73n, 77n, 97n, 202, 203, 215
morisco, 52–54, 215
Mozambique, xx, 102, 215
muenho, 29, 30, 215
mulato/mulata (mulatto/mulatta), xxi, 22, 37, 39, 40, 41, 41n, 42, 57, 60, 61, 62, 64, 65, 66, 68, 68n, 69, 70, 71, 89, 104, 127, 129, 183, 193, 196, 198, 202, 211, 215
muleteers, xvii, 21, 93, 192
Murga of Cartagena, Governor Francisco de, 44, 48, 54

nación (nation), xx, xxi(n), 56, 61–66, 71, 74, 77–79, 94, 102, 105–6, 109, 111, 115, 131, 132, 134, 145, 153, 157, 160–62, 164–65, 215
Napoleonic invasion, 139n, 200–204, 206n, 217
narrative agency, xxii, xxiv, 46, 47, 118, 137, 141, 215. *See also* textual mediationnation. See *nación*
Ndongo, xiv, xxviii, 1, 3, 26, 29, 30, 34; Christianity in, 26, 27, 28, 30, 33, 34; internal conflict, 1, 26, 27; language of (Kimbundu), 28, 29, 33; negotiations with Portugal, 1, 26, 27, 28, 29; population of, 26; Portuguese conflict with, 3, 26, 27, 28, 34n, 45; reign of Queen Njinga, 1, 26, 29, 30, 34; religion of (Kimbundu), 26; size of, 26; slave trade in, 1, 27, 28, 30, 34, 34n
negro/negra, 37, 37n, 39, 59n, 68, 68n, 71, 72, 77n, 108, 108n, 109, 118, 129, 137n, 182, 183n, 184, 184n, 185, 187n, 188n, 211, 212, 215
New Kingdom of Granada (*Nuevo Reino de Granada*)/Colombia, xiv, 1, 28, 43, 116, 128, 128n, 131n, 209; Cartagena de Indias, xvii, xxxiv, 1, 38, 40, 41, 41n, 42, 43–54, 85, 93, 115, 116–25, 126, 126n, 127–29, 131, 134, 136, 171. *See also* Colombia, present-day
New Spain (Mexico), xiv, 36, 37, 39n, 40, 44, 56–67
Nicaragua, 126, 128, 133n, 136; Granada, 128
Nigeria (Biafra), xx, 94, 216
Njinga, Queen (Dona Ana de Sousa), 1, 26–34, 45, 213

Nkanga a Mvemba, Dom Pedro, 2–19
North Africa, xxx, xli, 205–6
notaries, xxiii, 10, 19, 38, 39, 39n, 60, 62–67, 68–71, 75, 77–80, 93, 95, 96, 98, 99, 117, 177, 182, 187n, 190, 191, 212, 216

oarsmen, 127–28, 209
occupations, of Afro-Latinos, xiii–xviii, xx, xxi, 21, 35–36, 48–50, 54, 69, 81, 82, 85, 88, 90, 96, 101, 127, 128, 131, 134, 171, 184, 185, 201, 202, 203, 213
oral narratives in the lives of religious women, 137, 140, 143
oral tradition/oral culture, xxi, 29, 46, 83, 96, 118
orality, xxiv, 70, 71

*palenques,*xix, xxxiv, 1, 43–54, 130, 132, 216. *See also Maroon* communities
Palmares, Palenque of, 28, 44
Panama, xiv, xix, 21, 44, 93, 203
Panama, present-day, xix
papal bull in Kongolese politics, 6, 8, 13, 13n, 19
Pardo/Parda, 71, 79, 91, 95, 97, 99n, 101
patriarchy, 180
Pernambuco (Brazil), xvii, 170–72, 175–78
Peru, xiv, xvii, xviii, 21, 44, 55, 68, 72, 77, 80, 93–99, 101, 192, 218; Afro-Latino women litigants in, 180–91; women's legal testaments in, 68–80; census numbers, 68; Lima, xvii, xviii, xxxvi, 55, 68–80, 93, 101, 140n, 169, 171, 180–91
petitions, xiii, xxiv, 1, 23–25, 35–42, 58, 83, 85–86, 89–90, 105, 155, 158–59, 167, 182, 184–91, 195, 197n, 203–4, 206–7. *See also memorial*
petty commerce, 36, 101
Phelan, John Leddy, 21
pirates, 44, 115, 126
plantation workers, xiii, xvi, xvii, xviii, 21, 27, 36, 82
plazas, town, 16, 18, 93, 108, 111, 180n, 192, 216
Polín, Palenque of, 48, 49
politics: in Africa, 1, 9, 10, 18, 20; in Ibero-American colonies, 56, 58, 81–82, 84, 85, 170, 192, 200; in *Maroon* communities, 18, 24, 43; and treason, 1, 9, 10, 18

pombeiro, 32, 34, 216

Pope, 8, 14, 29, 31n

population of Afro-Latinos, xviii, 56, 68–69, 101–2, 115–16, 127, 170, 193, 201

porters, xvii

Portugal; Afro-Iberians in, 1, 35–36, 101; conflict with Dutch, xvi, 27, 170; empire and colony building of, xiii, xvi, 170; establishing presence in Africa, xvi, 1, 3, 7, 26–27, 127; Lagos, xvi, 36; Lisbon, 36, 170–79; relations with Spain, 26, 30n, 36, 69, 126–27, 171; São Tomé, xvi, 2, 4, 6–7, 127

Portugal and African peoples; alliances with, 3n, 7n, 26; as ambassadors to, 28; attitudes toward, 7, 7n; diplomacy of, xvi, 28–29; inquests into affairs of, 8; negotiations with, 3, 26, 29; relations with, 2, 3, 4, 7, 8, 26–27; trading with, xvi, 29; treaties with, 26, 28–29; wars, 3, 26–27

priests, 91, 129, 145n, 151, 171–72, 176; behaving immorally, 3, 72, 104; as biographers, 137, 140–41; and confraternities, 56, 104, 106, 164; in Kongo, 3, 13n, 28; in Ndongo, 29; mentioned in wills, 72, 73, 74, 76, 78, 97, 98; as scribes, xxii, 28; teaching the gospel, 24, 28; as witness in petition, 37

privateering, 126, 131n, 201, 216

Protector de Naturales (legal defender of Indians), 181

Protestants, 27, 115, 126, 140

pueblos, 55, 81–92, 216

Puerto Rican militia, 203

Puerto Rico, xiv, xviii, 116, 120, 200–203

punishment, 123, 124, 125, 169, 180, 181n, 187n, 192–99; of abusive spouses, 180, 184–85, 188; of confraternity members, 107, 160, 165, 167; by the Inquisition, 115, 117, 122, 172, 173, 173n, 176–79; of *palenque* residents, 43, 48. *See also* slaves

Puritans, 115, 126–36

purity of blood. See *limpieza de sangre*

quilombo, xix, 31, 32, 44, 216

Quisama (ethnonym), 49, 53, 216. *See also* Quissama

Quissama, 32, 32n, 33. See also *Quisama*

Quito (Ecuador; *Audiencia* of Quito), xvii, 21–23, 25, 180

race: labeling, 57 (See also *cuarterón, mestizo, mulato, negro,* and *zambo*); relations, 140–43; and religion, 115, 117, 138, 140–43; as social construction, xxi; and social subordination, 117, 138, 140–43; stereotypes, 87, 115, 141, 184

racial miscegenation, xvii, xxi, 22, 36, 102n, 153, 203, 216

ranch overseers, 44, 127. See also *estancias*

Real Audiencia, 21, 24, 25, 180, 182, 209, 216

real cédula, 38, 42, 146, 193, 216

rebellion, xix, 21, 46, 203, 45–46, 52–54, 180n. See also *Maroon* communities

religious records and literature, 72, 92, 95–96, 117–18, 137, 139, 154–56; forms and discourses of, xxiii, 55, 56–60, 68, 70, 72, 73–80, 97–100, 139, 143, 154; as means of knowing history of African peoples, xiii, 30, 55, 70, 72, 117–18, 154–56. *See also* hagiographies; Teresa of Avila, Saint; wills and testaments

rendas (rent-bearing property in the Kingdom of Kongo), 4–6, 12, 13, 16, 18, 216

resistance, 141, 84, 181; to abuse, 50, 181, 182, 184–85, 187–88, 192–99; to cultural erasure, 35; to enslavement, xviii, 28, 142, 203; to European governments, 21, 28, 203; to sale of family member, 181, 183, 189–91. See also *Maroon* communities

Restall, Mathew, xxii, 20

rhetorical autonomy, 173

Ribadeneyra, Rodrigo de, 22–24

rights, legal, 1, 35, 169, 187; accessed by women, 35, 36, 38, 39–42, 169, 181–82, 185, 186, 187; of slaves, xiii, 82–83, 181–82, 186

Rio de Janeiro (Brazil), xvii, xx, 115, 153–68

Río de la Plata, Viceroyalty of (Argentina), xiv, xxxviii, 101, 102, 102n, 192; Buenos Aires, 82, 101–13, 194–95; Afro-Latino population in, 101–2; confraternities in, 55, 101–13; economic growth of, 101, 194–95; as major slave port, xvii; slave population in, xx

rituals, xx, 26, 45, 45n, 55, 68, 95, 96, 105, 107, 117, 145, 149

Rous, Lieutenant William (Captain Rus), 129, 132, 135
royal slaves, 55, 81–92, 127, 216
rural areas, xviii, xix, 43–54, 94, 127, 185–86

sailors, 1, 35, 36, 37, 38, 127, 128, 131, 134, 200, 213
saints: confraternities dedicated to, 103–4, 106, 153, 154, 164; local patron, 82; requirements for sainthood, 140; stories of, 137, 139. *See also* hagiographies
sankofa (Akan: "go back and take"), 142, 217
scribes, xxi–xxiv, 2, 46, 83, 87, 95, 173–74, 177n, 194, 203. *See also* textual mediation
self-governance, xiv, xviii, 81; in Africa, 1, 26–29, 32n,144; in confraternities, 102, 106–7; in *Maroon* communities, 20, 23, 44–47; in *pueblos,* 81, 84, 81–84
sertão (hinterlands in Brazil), 171, 217
settlements, 90, 110; mining, 81, 84; *palenques*, xxxiv, 24, 44; in Pernambuco, 171; of Puritans, 132, 135; Spanish in Maroon areas, 20, 22, 24
Seville (Spain), 22, 127, 147; *Casa de Contratación*, 39, 40, 42, 210; Napoleon invades, 201, 203, 204, 206; petitions to Spanish royal court, 35, 36, 37, 38, 41
Sierra Leone, 56–58; *Zape in* 219
slave narratives, 46, 62–63, 63–64, 64–65, 89, 119–20, 122–25, 131–33, 133–34, 134–36, 137, 144–52, 173–74, 175–79, 184–85, 187–88, 188–91, 194–95, 196–97, 197, 198, 198–99
slave ports, xvi, xvii, 127, 153, 158n; Cartagena de Indias as, 1, 43, 48, 127; Luanda as, 27, 93, 127, 153; Mina Coast, xl
slavery, xv, xvi, 43, 45, 115, 116, 195, 200; in Central Africa, 5, 5n, 15n, 19; and colonial demand for slaves, xvi, xvii; in colonial society, xviii, 44, 126, 128, 130, 137; in Europe, xvi, 36, 82, 154–55, 155n, 181; justification for, 141, 142; in *Maroon* communities, 20, 43, 44; and numbers of slaves, 101, 127; and Queen Njinga, 28–34; and royal slaves, 55, 81, 85; and slave social status, xxi, 156
slaves, 22, 58; abuse of, xvii, xviii, 36, 52, 142, 160, 169, 172, 176, 182, 183, 192, 193, 194, 196–99; escape from slavery, xviii, xix, 20, 43, 90; families, xviii, 36, 87, 181, 183, 184; laws related to, 182, 183, 193; legal access to freedom, xviii,, 23, 35, 36, 86, 181, 182 (see also *papel de venta*); legal recourse against abuse, xviii, 181, 194; matrilineal transmission of bondage, 69, 99; ownership of by Afro-Latinos, xvii, 44, 55, 68, 72, 85, 94, 184; personal property of, 68, 182, 182n, 183; punishment of, 123, 169, 184, 192–99; relationships with owners, xviii, 69, 71, 85, 95, 116, 123, 139; resistance by, xix, xx, 21, 28, 44, 81, 180, 203; using colonial courts, 83, 85, 169,180–86, 184n, 192, 195; as wage earners, xviii, 70, 194
slave ships, 48, 56, 57, 58, 127, 142
slave trade, xxi, 3, 34, 36, 38n, 128, 200; in Africa, xvi, xvii, xx, 1, 3, 27, 30, 34n, 45, 57; monopoly on, 36; origins of, xvi, xx; and raids, 27, 36; in Spanish America, 93, 101, 128, 158n; trans-atlantic, 44n, 95, 126, 170. See also *pombeiro*
social status, xvii, xxi, 1, 7, 55, 86, 88, 94, 94n, 138, 143, 180, 184, 191, 193
sodomy, 169, 170, 171, 172, 172n, 173, 173n, 176
soldiers: Afro-Latino, 1, 35, 36, 37, 38, 45, 86, 108, 111, 200, 204; colonial, 1, 3, 22, 32, 43, 130, 202, 205
Spain; Afro-Iberians in, xvi, xvii, 1, 34n, 35, 36, 56, 203, 204, 205; *Casa de Contratación,* 38–42; Catholicism, 56, 115; convents in, 137, 138, 140,143; Council of State, 142, 148n; empire and colony building of, xiii, xvii, 1, 3, 20, 44, 55, 81, 88, 127, 192; laws of, xviii, 69, 71, 172, 181, 181n, 182, 185; Napoleon invades, 201, 203, 204; petitions to Spanish royal court, 35, 36, 37, 38; relations with Portugal, 26, 30n, 36, 126; shipping, 101, 126, 127; and slave trade, xvi, xvii, 36, 69, 142; Spanish Main, the, 126, 126n; Supreme Junta, 203, 204, 204, 206; unification, 26, 30n, 69, 170, 171
Spanish armed forces, 202
Spanish Inquisition. *See* Inquisition

spirituality of African descent peoples, xiii, xx, 1, 115, 140, 141, 200; in Africa, xvii, 1, 3, 7, 8, 10, 26, 27, 31–32, 45, 144n; African-based religions, 26, 45, 94, 95, 96, 102, 105, 142, 153, 154; in the Americas, 1, 45, 46n, 58, 72, 95, 96, 154; in the Americas as Catholics, 24, 35, 36, 70, 86, 120, 137, 138, 139, 140, 141, 142, 143, 164, 169 (*see also* Teresa of Avila, Saint); and beliefs, 70, 72, 106, 117, 142; blended religion, xvii, 1, 28, 56, 95, 102, 105, 115, 154; Catholic observances required of slaves, 138, 181n; in Europe, 35, 36, 38; and identity, xxi, 58, 105–07, 137, 153, 163–64; kept secret, 105, 118; paganism, xvi, 26, 46n, 115, 141, 153; practices, xxi, 82, 96, 103, 105–7, 118, 121, 122, 153, 163–65, 181n; rituals, 26, 45, 45n, 55, 95, 105, 107, 117, 144–45, 160; seen as heresy by Catholic Church, 117, 118, 121, 122, 144–45, 172, 181; transculturated notion of Catholicism, 1, 115, 117, 118. See also *candombes;* confraternities; confraternity of . . .; *sankofa*
subjectivity, 173
Suriname, xix, 44

Teresa of Avila, Saint, 137, 141, 143
Terranova (ethnonym), 71
testimonies, xxiv; in civil cases, 56, 62–67, 106, 109–13, 126, 128–30, 131–36, 187–89, 194, 195, 196–99; in civil trials, 43–47, 48–54, 118; in inquests, 1, 4, 10–19; in Inquisition trials 117–18, 119–25, 173, 175–77; in petitions, 35, 38, 39–42
textual mediation, 46n,70–71, 72, 81, 86, 96, 118, 195; scribe's role in, xxiv, xxi, 46, 71, 83, 87, 173
Thornton, John, 44, 154n
town council. See *cabildo*
towns. See *villas* and *pueblos*
traders, xvi, xvii, 72
transculturation of African peoples, xiv, xxii, xxiii, 1, 3, 7, 22, 28, 29, 115, 117, 118
travel and movement, 21, 22, 26, 35, 36, 37, 38, 38n, 40, 50–52, 132–33, 135–36, 200

treaties, 44, 203. *See also* Ndongo; Portugal and African peoples

Vatican. *See* Pope
vendors, xviii, 93, 127
Venezuela, xvii, xviii
viceroys, 193, 216, 218; of Brazil, 155, 165, 166n, 167; of New Spain, 138, 214; of Peru, 21, 69; of Río de la Plata, 105, 106, 108, 113
viceroyalty, of New Spain, 56; of Peru, xvii, 68; of Río de la Plata, xxxviii, 102n, 192
villas, 84n, 88, 92
violence, 43, 44, 45, 87, 90–91, 105, 142, 169, 184, 196. *See also* abuse; Cuba; women, Afro-Latino
voice, xxi–xxiv, 6n, 29, 46, 81, 83, 85, 142; of Afro-Iberian women in litigation, 35, 180, 184–86; in criminal defense, 118, 173–74; delivered through wills and testaments, 72; and rhetorical autonomy, 173; strategies for conveying, 139, 143

wars: African prisoners of war sold into slavery, xvi, 1, 3, 57; in Esmeraldas, 21; in Kongo, 3, 6, 12, 13, 17, 28; in Ndongo, 26–29, 30–34, 45; of the Protestant Revolution, 27; waged by *Maroon* communities, 28
West Africa, xvi, xx, 36, 55, 94, 115, 128, 154n
wills and testaments, xiii, xxiii, 55–58, 62, 68–72, 93–96, 97–100; documents, 59–60, 73–80, 97–100; inheritance of property, 35, 39–40, 66, 70, 96, 97n, 138; inventory/*inventario,* 39, 76, 77n, 79, 80, 213; as privately confessional, 96
witchcraft, 115, 116–18, 172, 209, 217
witches, 121–22, 125
women, Afro-Latino: and agency, 118, 142, 156, 180; as business owners, 55, 69; in confraternities, 58, 90–91, 154, 155, 156; economic success of, 70, 72; engaging literary practices, 55, 70, 71, 139, 139,143; and identity, 55, 93, 94, 95, 96, 142, 115; inheritance of property, 60, 98; letters of diplomacy, 28–29, 30–34; in litigation, 35, 36, 38, 169, 180, 182–86, 187–91; manumission of, 69; occupations of, 69, 70, 72, 93, 95, 118;

poetry, 151–52; as rulers/leaders, 26–34, 44, 45, 51, 53–54, 96, 153–68; sexual honor of, 140, 187; as slave owners, 55, 68, 72, 74, 78–79, 93, 94, 95, 98, 115; views of, 165; and violence, 44, 45, 53–54, 141, 142; wills and testaments, 62, 68, 70, 71, 72, 73–80, 96, 97–100. *See also* gender; gender differences

Yoruba, 93, 94, 94n, 95, 96

zambos/zambas, xxi, 22, 71, 185, 188–91, 216
Zanaguare, Palenque of, 45, 48
Zape (ethnonym), 56, 56n, 57, 58